BINGO COMES BACK
DOWN AGAIN

A Life on the Periphery of Sport

Mike Fatkin

For Seanna and Hannah

To Mum, with apologies for being so late… xx

And, of course, to Glamorgan County Cricket Club, *sine qua nihil*

Ambition and love wearing boxing gloves
And singing hearts and flowers

Oh yeah we're killing time
Just to keep you clocking on
These are the best years of your life
Now they're here and gone

Printed by Amazon

© Mike Fatkin 2021

ISBN 9798506948391

Part of the proceeds of the sale of this book will be donated to The Tom Maynard Trust, the charity set up in 2012 in memory of Tom Maynard with the object of supporting aspiring young sportspeople.

BINGO COMES BACK DOWN AGAIN

A Life on the Periphery of Sport

CARDIFF IN THE SUN
AN INTRODUCTION

"I may not have gone where I intended to go but I think I have ended up where I needed to be."
DOUGLAS ADAMS

I've never really been a fan of autobiographies. Yes, I know. Not exactly an auspicious start, that, is it? If I'm not a fan then what on earth am I doing writing one? You might well ask. But come on, be honest. They're often such bland, insipid things; packed with drab recollections which no one outside of a very small close circle could possibly find interesting; riddled with self-serving justifications and rampant name-dropping; or pockmarked with publisher-egged sensational revelations (which, more often than not, aren't the remotest bit sensational and are probably wholly unoriginal too, having been trotted out and rehashed time and again). Likely all three. Many contain a lengthy section about 'my formative years', a period of the subjects' lives that it's even more difficult to have any empathy with than the bits you actually know something about. The heart sinks at the very prospect of having to plough through it.

It seems that every Autumn we're trampled underfoot by the rush of sportspeople (I'm looking firmly at you here, Premier League footballers) and young me-me-me D-list 'personalities' fighting each other to get onto *The One Show* or scrambling to make a signing at any Waterstone's store that will accommodate them, in order that they and the poor ghost writers who have had to transcribe their illiterate ramblings can make a few bob extra from their tomes in time for Christmas. You just know their publications are going to be remaindered long before the year is out, discounted to 50p and destined to join all the old Dan Browns and celebrity self-help claptrap in our ever-growing number of high street charity shops. Here I am, I nearly won a cup once, look at my famous friends, here's me with a flash car, I'm only 24 but please buy my life story.... step forward the King of Drivel: Ashley Cole and *My Defence*. Literary tripe embellished with crayon. David Goldblatt, the football historian, once asked of the footballer's autobiography, "Is there a more debased currency?" Excellent question. No, David. There isn't.

There are exceptions, of course. There is a wealth of excellent biography out there, along with some outstanding sporting books, but in terms of sporting *auto*biographies, well, not too many have tickled my fancy, I'm afraid. There are a few I've read because I knew the subject or because theirs sounded like a good tale, but I can't say that too many have really grabbed me. In the main I find them poorly written, superficial, factually dominated accounts of what the rest of us probably already knew anyway, more often than not released to cash in on the nation's habit of only appearing to be interested in buying books in the final two months of the year.

So, here goes. Time to play the ultimate hypocrite. Not only is this an attempt at an autobiography but it's also filled with 'drab recollections which no one outside of a very small close circle could possibly find interesting' and 'self-serving justifications and rampant name-dropping' (well, the name-dropping is limited to some county cricketers and a couple of royal encounters, if I'm really honest, so don't get your hopes up too much on that score). It will also quite probably come across as poorly written. I have my own style, one for which I have been taken to task over the years by parents, teachers, lecturers, work bosses and readers alike. It's rambling; tangential; verbose; grammatically improper; full of Olympic-length sentences; and riddled with misplaced and unnecessary semi-colons. A few like it; many others don't.

One thing the story will most assuredly *not* be, however, is 'pockmarked with sensational revelations': my life hasn't been anything like interesting enough for that to be the case. Would that it had been. Much of it will be narrow in subject, self-absorbed, and will likely read as a series of lame anecdotes and opinionated rubbish. But it's *my* rubbish. Written for *my* close circle. It's not being put out there to make money. Ha! The very notion that it could ever have been envisaged as a profitable enterprise is as ridiculous as that of Ashley Cole actually *writing* a book, as opposed simply to colouring one in.

It does, being true to the genre, contain a 'formative years' section. I know. But don't judge me too hastily. I'll make you a deal: if you want to read on, I shan't discourage you. You may even find it interesting, who knows? But for those of you who are not family or close friends, or quick readers, or who have happened on this only because it suggests a series of potentially interesting cricket yarns, you may prefer to skip chapters two and three. Nothing to see there but very personal reminiscences, family myth and lore, mullet hairstyles, formative tastes in music and other such nonsense. I wouldn't blame you if you chose to ignore those bits.

I'm not well known. Oh sure, if you stick my name into *Google* you'll find a few old references to cricket, perhaps netball, but my path in life cannot be said to have resulted in me reasonably being described as 'famous'. This book isn't going to sell thousands, probably not even hundreds. It contains few revelations. It has a very niche target audience. And its prose won't win any literary prizes: it doesn't half ramble – why use three words when you can use ten? Doubtless some of my journalist friends will be shaking their heads at the writing style as they struggle through it. But do you know what? I don't care. It's been fun. I've thoroughly enjoyed the cathartic process of taking everything that exists in my head and attempting to compile some sort of sequential record of it. It's set out, more or less, in chronological order. There is a degree of jumping around but hopefully it flows and it makes sense.

It was my old pal John Haigh's initial encouragement, offered over a wee-small-hours beer on one of our old school reunion golfing weekends in Spain – while the other lads were destroying *Sweet Caroline* on the karaoke, if memory serves me correctly. I was only half serious (as well as being half cut) and the idea was barely even embryonic, but he told me to go for it. A few saddos close to me – the whole Maynard family and another old mate Andy Tomlinson in particular – have continued to cajole me to get it all written up, only then to complain that I was taking far too long to finish it. Well, excuse *me*. This isn't something you can just knock out in a couple of days, boys and girls. This is high literature we're talking about.

If nothing else it will exist as a record for my two lovely daughters, Seanna and Hannah, as an account of their dad's life. Well, some of the printable and more interesting parts of it anyway. And as neither is too interested in cricket, it could be the literary equivalent for them of wading through treacle. Sorry, girls. I wish I'd listened to the naggers more. That way my dear old Mum would have lived to see it, to have read it, doubtless to have challenged elements of it (both factual and grammatical) but, above all, I hope, to have enjoyed it. I regret being so slow to finish it for that one reason. Sorry, Mum.

The title is a loose reference to Mr Maynard, he of Glamorgan and England cricket fame. Our close friend, the former

Glamorgan and England Physio Dean Conway, once claimed that the only book Matt had ever read was a children's story called *Bingo Goes Up The Hill* (no, don't bother Googling it – it doesn't exist). A bit harsh, too, to be honest, as Matt probably reads more than Dean. But as with many of Mr Conway's claims, the gag has stuck within our small Friday evening pint-after-work gang and has since developed an extravagant life of its own. After having started as the merest of jocular half-truths, it now comes embellished with references to large print, pictures, crayons, colour-by-numbers, join the dots and such like. The hyperbole even pulled me in to the extent that I sent him Enid Blyton's *The Folk in the Faraway Tree* in the post for a birthday when he was coaching at Somerset. Anyway, *Bingo Comes Back Down Again* is a small homage to that daft pair.

As to the supplementary reference – being on the periphery of sport – well that's what my life has felt like. I've always loved sport, something I hope will shine through loud and clear. But I've never been front and centre. Nor have I ever been especially good at it. Certainly nowhere near as good as many of the characters I describe in the pages that follow. At school I swam to a reasonable standard, enjoyed cricket, jousted with Andy Tomlinson in marathon tennis nine setters and, as a footballer, had always fancied myself as a ball-playing centre half until I went back to five-a-side in my 40s and realised I wasn't so much ball-playing as good only for opponent-blocking. And even then I more often than not arrived too late to the tackle to be able to make contact with anything other than a shadow. On the very few occasions when I did end up with the ball, I was astute enough to appreciate there were four team-mates who were far better players than me and that it'd help us all if I just passed the ball to one of them instead of trying anything fancy myself. Pace, vision and skill are attributes that exist only in other folks' lockers. Oh sure, I talk the talk. But I'm incapable, sadly, of walking the walk.

And when it came to cricket, I wasn't as good as I thought I was at that, either. During a rain break in a Glamorgan match at Neath in the late 1980s there wasn't a lot going on so I announced to a couple of office colleagues that I fancied having a bit of a net in the adjoining indoor cricket school. I'd seen our own players, and many of their opponents too. How difficult could it be? My colleague Tony Dilloway and one of the players who was on twelfth man duties, Michael Cann, said they'd bowl me a few deliveries. Within five minutes some of the Glamorgan lads had emerged, bored, from the adjoining changing room, and in addition to there now being a small gallery of players forming at the end of the lane I was batting in, a couple of them decided to take turns to bowl to me. Ian Smith and Greg Thomas. Quick bowlers. Gradually ramping up the pace. I was perfectly OK cover driving one of Tony's loopy efforts, or executing a perfect forward defensive to one of 'Canny's' slower off-breaks. The session ended abruptly, however, as Ian Smith decided to bounce me and I flounced off in a huff, muttering obscenities to myself about him trying to kill me, while all he could do was smirk. John Holder was umpiring the game and as I walked past him, tail firmly between my legs, he smiled that knowing smile of his and said, consolingly, "Don't worry, Mike. We all serve where we can. Those two wouldn't be able to do your job either." It turns out batting was rather more difficult than I'd imagined. And no, I wasn't up to much. I looked good against the slower bowlers, or at least when they chose not to turn the ball, but to paraphrase Corporal Jones in *Dad's Army*, I didn't like it up me. And I didn't know how on earth to play it. The perfectly timed pull shot to a 50 mile-an-hour straight one was one thing. But dealing with an 85 mile-an-hour bouncer aimed at my head only resulted in me thrashing about the crease with a flailing bat like a drunken octopus trying to pop half a dozen balloons simultaneously. Having a less than average talent for cricket hasn't diminished my love of the game, however. I've spent my whole life following it, for much of that time at quarters as close as you can get without actually being a direct participant on the field. Cricket has given me so much.

In terms of the tale itself I hope it comes across as honest. There are times I know I've over-egged the melodrama and the self-pity. A wee bit of that is intentional, though. After all, why write about events or times when things haven't gone wholly your way without at least trying to elicit some measure of sympathy? And it's my account, after all. The opening chapter, which details my departure from Glamorgan, much of which has been in the public domain for years, and is a little more self-centred, and Chapter 18, a lot of which is very personal, are less light in tone than the rest. But most of the time I have tried to tell the story exactly as I like to think I come across in real life: affable, easy-going, loyal, empathetic; someone whose default setting is instinctively cynical and sarcastic, borderline grumpy, but someone who definitely knows how to take the piss out of himself. I hope I'm sufficiently self-aware to have been able to realise when it's me who has screwed things up, rather than someone else, and to have said so. Above all, I've tried my very hardest to be authentic. What you will read in the pages that follow is 100% me.

I would never set out to upset people unnecessarily and if I've offended anyone here (other, of course, than the one or two people it may have been my absolute avowed *intention* to offend), my apologies in advance. Be mindful, too, that embellishment is a privilege of authorship. As Winston Churchill once said, "History will be kind to me, for I intend to write it." Some stories will have had more than a sprinkling of hype added to them along the way. Go with it. Don't take everything too literally. Embrace the exaggeration.

Anyway, here it is. Make of it what you will. If you've gone to the trouble of acquiring a hard copy version, feel free to use it as a prop for a particularly stubborn door. I shan't be offended. At least that way it will enjoy a lasting practical use – what folk drone on interminably about as a 'legacy': everything must have a legacy (though little ever does). I'm not too fussed about how it's received either (though if you do review it, please be as kind as you can); I've written it to be able to say that I'm a published author, not with the aim of winning any literary plaudits. And note that this is none of your ghosted nonsense either (though do please bear in mind that it's been produced entirely by (the clumsy forefingers of) my own two hands, index and all – I wouldn't have dreamed of boring someone senseless by asking them to transcribe it or ghost it, and I'm not arrogant enough to have even contemplated it). Two-finger typing, 'tis true, but at a decent lick, to be fair. (And apologies for all the brackets.)

I would love to be able to write as poetically as Michael Henderson, as readably at Matthew Engel, as caustically as Marina Hyde, or as wittily as Harry Pearson – four of my favourites – but I can't, so I haven't tried to. And even if I could, there's precious little to be gained by seeking to mimic someone else's style. It wouldn't be authentic. Any clichés, rambling sentences, poor grammar: all are entirely down to me, as are what are likely to be any number of factual inaccuracies. Oh, and if you do come across any typos, which despite my best efforts I reckon you're bound to, I'd be ever so grateful if you'd keep them to yourselves. I'm not sure I could bear the shame.

Cardiff, July 2021

1   PLEASE STAND UP

'Getting fired is what happens to a manager sooner or later.'
JOE TORRE

Losing your job in any circumstances is tough. After you've been in post for more than 20 years, when you thought you were doing OK, without a ghost of a clue it's coming, and it's especially tough. When it's being played out in the public eye too, that's one heck of a combination. This opening salvo tells the tale of how it happened to me and how the man who chose to fire the bullet unaccountably opted to hand the pistol to someone else to do it for him.

I'm not sure I was ever cut out to be a Chief Executive. It wasn't my calling. I'm not sufficiently thick-skinned. I'm not particularly hard-nosed, either. Nor am I very commercially savvy. As for ruthlessness, well, let's just say that although I could play the tough guy when required to do so, it generally meant crossing several comfort zones in order to be able to clamber into the appropriate character. I'd worry far too much about hurting others' feelings. I'd dither.

Before you start wondering, I should say that the balance sheet isn't entirely loaded with negatives. I do have <u>some</u> skills, otherwise one would be entitled to question the sanity and competence of those who appointed me. No, I was perfectly capable of doing a Chief Executive's job – I'm bright, I have good ideas, I'm good with people, persuasive, well organized, and I'm as hard a worker as any ant, any shire horse or any Trojan you could find to set before me, but in terms of being in charge, the one out front, I always preferred someone else to be in the limelight taking both the rap and the crap. I know I make a wonderful number two: supportive, loyal, diligent, protective and all that. Unfortunately, it took me well over two decades as a Chief Executive, after mistakes aplenty and an unfeasibly large library of reflective wisdom acquired along the way, to fully appreciate all this.

By the time 10th September 2008 had come around I'd somehow been CEO at a county cricket club for nearly 14 years. By my own modest admission, I reckon I'd done OK. I'd had some triumphs, done some positive things, always fronted up, had the backing of my staff, and I enjoyed a very healthy professional reputation. But deep down I knew I was never really cut out to be top dog. It never came naturally, put it that way. But if one is to be defined by one's last moments in post then my exit from the position of CEO at Glamorgan County Cricket Club that September day was textbook boss-exits-organization: indeed, it could have been lifted from the 'Perfect Departure' chapter of the definitive '*How To Be A Chief Executive*' instruction manual. It was a classic dismissal of its kind. Brutally efficient. And very un-county cricket-like. Given the way it played out, much of the detail has been in the public domain for a long time. Just because the specifics weren't leaked to a journalist as the basis for an exclusive (not that it's *that* exclusive, you understand, or even that interesting) didn't mean that people wouldn't find out, and almost everyone whom I came across in the years following knew something of the circumstances, even though I'd dutifully kept my mouth shut. There are few secrets in sport, it seems. What follows here is therefore more clarification than revelation.

It was all over inside five minutes. In less time than it takes to put the bins out, my near 25-year career with the organization was brought to something of a juddering halt. Imagine Usain Bolt sprinting on a treadmill just as someone pulls the plug out from the wall behind him. Mentally, that's pretty much what it felt like. Five days after Cardiff's redeveloped Swalec Stadium (as it was known at the time) had hosted its first full England international – a damp, soulless affair, of which more later – I was meandering through what I had imagined would be a pretty routine day in the office, the tail end of which had me down to attend a meeting with Barry O'Brien, the lawyer Paul Russell had brought in to help with the Club's incorporation as an Industrial and Provident Society, and the Glamorgan President, David East, before presenting on the next phase of our ground redevelopment plans – timescales, costs, tendering, all that palaver – to the club's General Committee later in the evening. Or at least that's what I was *expecting*. Even bumping into East in the gents a minute or two before our five o'clock meeting was due to start and catching his mumbled throwaway phrase "this isn't going to be easy" didn't hint at anything particularly unusual. It certainly didn't sound any alarm bells or anything. "It's about incorporation, David," I replied. "Subject's a bit dry, I grant you, but it's not exactly quantum physics. Barry's the expert. He's briefing us." Five minutes later I'd been dismissed. Or, as the terminology has it, Glamorgan and

I had 'mutually agreed to part company.' I hadn't mutually agreed anything. But the deed was done. I was no longer part of the company.

If you happen upon a copy of the 2009 Glamorgan County Cricket Club Yearbook (there must be hundreds still lying around – we always used to print way too many) you will find as many mentions in there of Barney the purple dinosaur giving Brad Pitt a piggy-back as you will of me. There isn't one. Not a sausage. Nothing. Nil. Rien. Niente. Nada. Zilch. The Chairman manages to contribute a detailed written review of the year, including specific individual references to incoming and outgoing staff, but there is ne'er a mention of his erstwhile Chief Executive Officer. It was as if I hadn't been there at all. Airbrushed out. Close the door behind you, son, there's a good lad. Now when my turn came to leave I wouldn't have been so egocentric as to have expected a glossy tribute magazine with a special pull-out colour supplement choc-full of 'This Is Your Life'-style anecdotes and tributes or anything, but to leave a place you have been associated with, largely successfully, for the thick end of a quarter of a century without so much as a single mention – even one tiny throwaway, under duress, oh-go-on-then-if-I-really-must acknowledgement – still rankles, years on. When I was editing the Club's Yearbook, which I enjoyed doing for many years, I made certain that anyone leaving Glamorgan having worked for or been associated with the club was given at least some sort of name-check – player, employee, committee member, volunteer, prominent supporter: they'd be singled out for at least a brief mention. The irony of me now as the one being erased from the club's official records wasn't lost on me. Sure, there was the standard off-the-shelf legal go-to line that the Club couldn't make any public comment for legal reasons but I don't buy that, frankly. 'Tis but a bollocks excuse, as Shakespeare might have put it.

It took several more years for anyone in the hierarchy officially to acknowledge that I'd been part of the furniture, the irony being that it was Barry O'Brien, by then Chairman himself, who ended up putting that right by offering me life membership of the Club. Given the way that honour (and it is an honour) had been doled out by the committee for pretty much anything over the years I was around – and there were some seriously spurious and undeserving cases – I was more than a bit miffed that the organization into which I had thrown myself so wholeheartedly for such a long time had effectively stuck two fingers up at me with one hand as it waved me off hurriedly with the other. As if being shown the door like that wasn't enough, it meant tiptoeing around the ground for the next season or two like some reluctantly-tolerated neighbourhood pest. It was pretty undignified and it felt mighty uncomfortable. On the few occasions I did feel sufficiently emboldened to want to go along to watch some cricket it needed a call in advance to one of the staff from my time still working there (Russell had got rid of quite a few on his watch, so the number of contacts I had was dwindling rapidly) to come and sneak me past ~~border control~~ the stewards. I even paid on the gate on one occasion just to avoid any embarrassment. I felt I deserved better than that. I am incredibly proud to be an Honorary Life Member of Glamorgan, and I really appreciated Barry pushing for it. But I'm afraid the manner of my exit, and the way it was handled in the immediate aftermath, will forever stick in my throat.

It turned out that the meeting that day with East and O'Brien never had anything to do with incorporation at all. *('No shit, Michael' – Ed)*. That had simply been a ruse to lure me into a private situation, in a hospitality suite well away from everyone else, its late afternoon scheduling such that when the meeting had finished most employees would already be out of the buildings and on their way home. And even though I had prided myself that my political antennae were generally primed and ready, I really hadn't seen this one coming at all. It seemed that East, a former policeman who had ingratiated himself into Russell's inner circle so successfully that he had been parachuted into the President's office ahead of (in my view and that of many others) a whole host of far worthier candidates, had been sent in as a henchman to get rid of me. I still don't know why they chose that way to carry out the job, or why he was chosen to pull the trigger.

"You're being invited to resign," he began our meeting by saying, stiffly, as if having memorized a script. "If you choose not to do so, you will be dismissed. You are instructed not to attend the General Committee meeting this evening," he went on. "You will not be welcome. The Committee are to be told that your services are no longer required, and you are instructed to sign this," he added, pushing an A4 envelope across the table towards me. It seemed that in keeping with his standard default position, Russell was assuming money would be the answer to the problem. And before I go on, it doesn't need a spoiler alert to tell you that I didn't like Paul Russell

16

and that he didn't like me. We may have recognized strengths in one another but we were pretty much diametrically opposed as personalities. He was a clever man, in some ways quite brilliant, but as a person he was everything I hoped I would never be. I'm afraid I never really took to him.

The whole thing seemed so surreal. I'm not a particularly loquacious soul but I've rarely been at such a complete loss for words as I was at that moment. I had nothing to offer in return, nothing at all, my mouth bobbing open and closed, like a goldfish just force-fed methamphetamine, as my brain tried to process exactly what he was saying. Even as someone rarely short of a rapid sarcastic one-liner, I honestly didn't have a clue what to come back with. It was proper suspension-of-belief stuff. I picked up the envelope he'd slid across the table to me. Having been 'instructed' to sign it, this was of course the last thing I was going to do. For some reason the address on it was wrong, which I pointed out, much to East's befuddlement. It had 'draft' written on it as well, and I later discovered there were two references to 'Ms Fatkin.' But the upshot was that Russell was proposing to buy me off. I told East I would not be signing anything in a hurry, correct address and gender or not, and would need time to think about it, to which he didn't seem to know how to react, turning to Barry, who simply nodded calmly. But I knew there could be no Lazarus-like comeback from here. There was no metaphorical Ian Wright or Thierry Henry I could summon off the bench to turn the situation around. It was over. It was a question of trying to think and act rationally and with as much dignity as I could muster. Which in the circumstances probably wasn't all that much.

Finally, in the style of some Old Bailey high court judge in an old black and white film who has just donned his black handkerchief and was offering a condemned man the opportunity of a few final words, East asked me if there was anything I wished to say. There was an uncomfortable pause before I found myself leaning forward ever so slightly, East craning his neck to make sure he heard me properly, and asking, quietly, with a gentle nod in Barry's general direction as I did, "Does your friend talk?" before getting to my feet. I really don't know why. Rational thought had long since left the building.

East explained that I was to clear my desk and leave the premises immediately, stressing every last syllable of his words in the style of a 1950s BBC continuity announcer. I was told I could continue to have use of the club car 'for the time being.' All very high-flying-big-City-firm. Which, given Paul Russell's background, and the way he'd clearly insisted on Barry being in the room, was no surprise. I imagine it was exactly how Andersen Consulting, where Russell had worked for many years, would carry out this sort of exercise. I have never attached any blame at all to O'Brien, incidentally. I may be wrong, but I always thought he was asked to be there purely as a legal expert on a 'just in case' basis.

As I wandered back upstairs to my office, David East man-marking me more tightly than an Italian central defender in a late 1960s *Serie A* game, never once straying more than two feet from me, I wondered why, if this was the decision he had arrived at, Russell hadn't had the guts to come along and fire the bullet himself. It was unlike him. And why ask East? And then I just asked myself.... why? Why, after such a lengthy period working at the club, man and boy, was this happening? What had I done wrong? Who had actually taken the decision? And with that, my mind spiralled into a free-for-all of chaotic conflicting conspiracy theories, hurtling into one another, making me feel as though my head was going to explode.

By the time I'd made it to my office there was already a security guard posted on the door, sentry-like. Perhaps they thought I would try something reckless, like smash up my desk or attempt to steal an honours board. It was his duty, he explained, to escort me from the premises when I was done. Like some common criminal, I thought. He followed this by proceeding to apologize continually, alternating that with thanking me for giving him the opportunity to work for Glamorgan in the first place. It was bizarre. I couldn't even send a quick email to anyone explaining the circumstances: in the brief period I'd been downstairs with East and O'Brien the settings on my computer had been changed and I was now locked out and barred from accessing it. All very cloak and dagger. I was given two cardboard boxes, into which I put my bits and pieces, including my photographs from the walls. They wouldn't all fit, so my apologetic security shadow commandeered a plastic pedal bin from the home dressing room down the corridor. As I was leaving East assured me that there was no rush to get the pedal bin back. Such generosity. It had, of course, been the only concern in my mind. Most people receive a gold watch or a carriage clock when they leave a company after such a lengthy period of service. My 'gift' was a grey plastic rubbish bin. And I had to commandeer it. Yet it was somehow befitting of the situation. If it wasn't so serious it would have been laughable. *Carry On Escorted Off the Premises.*

Interestingly, having subsequently visited that same room on a number of occasions in its different guises as an office for the club's cricket management and as the third umpire's room on televised match days, for several years the nails for my pictures remained in the walls exactly where they had been when I'd left them. No one touched them. No other photos replaced mine. It was only when the room was redecorated half a dozen years later that they were taken out.

And then it was out to the car, stuffing the boxes and my grey plastic leaving present in the boot and out of the gates I drove, my Glamorgan career over. Basically, I had been fired. I was unemployed. It was weird. I wasn't able to think straight. My head was spinning. I pulled the car over at the top of nearby Cathedral Road and rang Dean Conway, our old 'Glammy' physio, by then no longer working full-time for England and so back home in Cardiff. I'm not sure why he was the first person I thought to call, but he was. Maybe because he lived closest.

"I've just been sacked," I said.

"Oh piss off, you dozy bugger," came the predictably pithy reply.

"No, Deano, really. They've just fired me."

"Why?"

Long pause.

"I don't know."

"What reason did they give? They must have said something to you."

"Nope. Nothing."

"Didn't you ask?" At which point it dawned on me that I had been so shocked I hadn't even thought to question them as to a reason.

"How can they do that?" he asked, echoing what was on my mind, before I explained that I was on my way home. "Alright, butt. Does Ollie know? Give him a bell. We'll meet up at his place."

'Ollie' was, of course, Matthew Maynard, then our Cricket Manager, so I rang Matt, explained what had happened and headed up to his house on the outskirts of Cardiff for some tea and sympathy. Well, OK, a can of cider and sympathy. I realised I hadn't yet told my wife Carol. I guess I wanted to talk to people who understood the cast of characters and the background first. When I did get back home a while later and explained to her what had happened, she was as dumbfounded as Dean and Matt had been. After all, there had been no sign of it, and there was no explanation any of us could offer other than Russell just wanting me out. Carol and I had been going through a difficult patch in the months leading up – we were a year away from divorcing – but she was very understanding and supportive. As well as upset and angry. My own primary emotion was probably more confused that night than anything else. I think I was still in shock.

The following morning David East rang me at home in a bit of a flap. Apparently, people at the Club had noticed that I wasn't there. And several journalists had latched on to the fact that there might be a bit of a story brewing. Which somehow came as a huge shock to him. Clearly not all policemen are possessed of the deductive reasoning of a Sherlock Holmes. The clues were all there, Mr Plod. Let's go over them and see what you were missing.

Number One: It being a match day, our dressing room attendant Roger Skyrme would have popped his head around the door first thing (I generally arrived in the office first on match days, with Roger never too far behind me) and offered to make me a cup of coffee. That particular morning he would have been greeted by a desk and chair and a load of nails in the walls, stripped bare as they would have been of all of their photographs, all other sign of any personal occupancy also having vanished.

Number Two: Joan Pockett on reception would have been able to see that there was nothing in the central diary to explain my absence, which, as I was a stickler for making sure that my movements were known to all of the other staff, would also have been hugely out of character. If I'd have been due to be off site the diary would have recorded it.

Number Three: One of the groundstaff had seen me leaving the previous evening carting boxes and pulling a full grey plastic bin behind me with a security guard in tow. Again, tongues would have been wagging. It didn't take a genius, officer. But it was still a surprise to some, it seemed.

"The staff know you're not around," offered our razor-sharp Dixon of Dock Green, by way of an opener, "and they seem to know what has happened."

"Well, I'm not around, am I?" I observed, "and in any event it's not really my problem, is it? I was told not to say anything to any of the staff or anyone else and I haven't."

"So what am I supposed to tell them? There are journalists here asking questions as well. They say they know what happened too. They're going to report something."

"Use your imagination," I said, and put the phone down.

Not content with firing me, blocking access to my computer and escorting me humiliatingly off the premises, he was now asking me for advice on how to deal with the fallout from my own sacking. The only surprise was that he hadn't taken the opportunity to ask when I'd be returning the plastic bin.

He seemed genuinely to imagine that no one would notice. That someone who had been working – in the eyes of anyone who knew Glamorgan – as passionately and as enthusiastically as ever for the same organization for such a long time, the CEO no less, would just disappear in a glorious puff of smoke, like some latter-day Mr Benn (ask your parents, kids), not a trace of his movements anywhere to be found, and that everyone would just carry on regardless, with no questions asked and not so much as a peep of curiosity emanating from anyone. 'Naïve' doesn't come close.

There was also the fact that the manner of the dismissal would be left just a little open to interpretation. If it hadn't crossed their minds, it had certainly crossed mine. Surely you only get marched off the premises if you've been caught playing around with a secretary or with your fingers in the till. How was this going to look? That was something I needed some advice on. If you're whisked out of a company via the back door then reputationally everything is up for grabs. And I wasn't going to let Russell control what people were saying. I didn't want him in charge of the narrative.

As far as a settlement was concerned Matt had put me on to Richard Bevan, previously CEO of the Professional Cricketers' Association but by then CEO at the League Managers' Association. He recommended a lawyer friend of his, Paul Daniels (yes, I know, but not that one) from a firm of London solicitors. Daniels told me it was now a game of blink: I was to say nothing, sign nothing, be patient, and make no commitments or concessions of any kind to anyone connected to the club. He assured me I had a good case for a significantly improved settlement to the one East had passed across the table but it's something I couldn't discuss with anyone. Which I didn't. And haven't to this day. Obviously, I was keen to avoid having to go to any employment tribunal. Not because I wouldn't have been successful – both of us were very confident that I would – but because I wasn't sure I had the energy to go through a protracted process like that, and I loved Glamorgan too much to see the Club's reputation being dragged through the mud. In the end, if I was going to have to go, I was at least able to do so with a decent settlement, so both parties exited the process with honour, if, in my own case, not necessarily dignity, intact; though it saddened me to think there were folk who believed loyalty and reputation were just commodities that could be bought at 'the right price.' Easy come, easy go. I'd never had a written contract with the Club, which I'd imagined might be a concern. But Daniels wasn't worried about that. He asked me to check certain information with my CEO colleagues at other counties, which they were only too happy to share, before taking their average pay, benefits and notice period as 'industry standard,' and going from there.

By then the phone calls had started. The mobile was in use all day every day for the next month which, for someone with nigh-on phone phobia like me (I much prefer to text or email) was unusual too. It was heartening that so many people were in touch: Glamorgan and other players going back 20-odd years; umpires; county chief executives, past and present (Durham's CEO, David Harker, left a message simply shouting, loudly, "BIG ISSUE!" before hanging up, which made me chuckle); members and supporters; journalists; other county chairmen; ECB and MCC staff; friends. It was nice to know I was being thought of and it felt good to have such overwhelming backing. There were some surprising people who came to the fore in terms of offering support, meeting up for a coffee or a beer or suggesting a round of golf; people I'd always got along with well but whom I wouldn't necessarily have counted as close friends, or even friends at all. Conversely there were also some from whom I perhaps expected to hear more but who seemed, whether consciously or subconsciously, to melt away into the background. When people say you find out who your friends are when the going gets tough, they are absolutely right. Loyalty is a value I've always prized very highly. I discovered in the ensuing weeks that not everyone you're loyal to reciprocates. Some of the reactions, or more rather the lack of them, were disappointing. Cards were metaphorically marked.

I really struggled to come to terms with it all, I have to say, and I'm referring here mainly to the manner of the departure. For up to a year afterwards I couldn't really talk about it as the anger and emotion would just rush to the surface. And yes, I was bitter. Very bitter. A whole lorry-load of pure, unadulterated, viscerally concentrated bitterness. But I defy anyone to go through all that and not be bitter at least to some degree. For the life of me I just couldn't understand why. No one gave me an official reason then, nor have they since. I'd had my appraisal with Paul Russell three weeks beforehand. I still have his handwritten notes from that meeting, along with associated emails on a memory stick (I always backed up from my computer every evening, so being locked out wasn't the inconvenience it might have been). All of that information would have been very useful had we been unable to settle before reaching a tribunal. The broad thrust of that review was very positive. Yes, it had thrown up a couple of areas I needed to work on, but that's what appraisals do: nobody goes through a cycle of performance reviews without some element of criticism or a requirement to focus on areas where more effort was needed. Russell's notes indicated as much. But formal indications that my arse was for the jack boot? Nope. Nothing, guv. Had there been an employment tribunal – and knowing what I do now having subsequently completed a Masters in HR Management and worked in the HR profession – I'm confident that had we not reached an agreement, we would have had an exceptionally strong case for unfair dismissal.

Perhaps I had been at the Club too long, whatever that means. How long is 'too long' in a role anyway? Anyway, that's what a few people said, though generally those with little real knowledge of the personalities involved. I didn't feel it was the case here. The role I'd performed had changed in focus every three or four years and I'd just headed up a team that had delivered a major new international Test match venue to Cardiff, on time, and to (a very tight) budget. There was some talk that the Head Groundsman Len Smith (who, remarkably coincidentally, took early retirement just a couple of days after my own departure) and I were made scapegoats for what had been a disappointing One-Day International five days previously but I don't buy that either. The weather was awful, both in the lead up to the game and on the day itself. Len and his team battled like mad to get some cricket on and the fact that there was any cricket played at

23

all was amazing. But I heard talk that Paul Russell and a couple of his acolytes had been blaming us for the fact that there was so little play. However even if that were true – and it was probably just talk – I will continue to say it's a load of old rubbish. If so, it would presumably have followed that had the day of the England game been dry the pair of us would have remained in gainful employment. No, it was premeditated. And I know now that there had been whispers all summer of people going, with Russell talking quite openly about people he had doubts about. Plenty of others followed Len and me. It felt to me like a bit of an old school cleansing; Russell doing away with the people he didn't like, didn't rate, felt didn't support him enough, or those from whom he felt he'd got everything he needed. His call as Chairman, but there are ways of doing these things.

I don't know to this day whether any of the committee knew about it beforehand. East's comment about them being informed at the meeting suggested not. Nigel Roberts, a co-opted member of the committee at the time, later to become Deputy Chairman (in which capacity he would experience his own personal ups and downs with Russell), and someone with whom I have maintained a relationship throughout the period since, insists that they didn't. He certainly didn't. But it wouldn't have surprised me if a few had been primed. However, I doubt it would have affected anything anyway. The committee's consistently supine behaviour, their collective sycophancy, their willingness blindly to do anything their Chairman demanded, suggests to me that even had they known they wouldn't have paid the slightest heed to the question of whether it was morally right, let alone done anything to resist it. Look up the words 'obsequious' and 'unctuous' in the dictionary: that appears to reflect the character of some of the people sat around the committee table at that time. They had the collective backbone of a bloom of jellyfish and a group moral compass that Jeffrey Archer and Boris Johnson could only look upon with envy.

I haven't exchanged more than a handful of words with most of them in all the years since it happened. I don't think I've missed much. They won't have either, given that I'd nothing positive to say to any of them. Their ineffectiveness had been amply demonstrated on many occasions while I was in post; rolling over now would have been a given, a default. Many of them were in awe of Russell and rarely offered so much as a single word of criticism about anything he said. I can also say, hand on heart, that whatever their faults, their obsession with process-driven protocols, not to mention, in one or two cases, their insufferable pomposity, what happened to me that September would never have been allowed to happen in the way it did back in the 1980s and '90s when the committee comprised a cast of thousands. They may have been largely ineffective as a collective body – more nineteenth century gentlemen's club decision-making than modern multi-million-pound business – but most of them at least knew what a principle was and there was at least some moral backbone within the folk sat around the committee table back then. Resistance would have been far, far stronger.

I did wonder at the time where David Morgan stood on all this. David was a previous Club Chairman. He was the man who gave me the opportunity to be a CEO in the first place (yes, it was his fault!) and he was an enormously positive influence throughout my career. He was only in the background at the time my services were dispensed with, and no longer on the club's committee, but I can't imagine he would have approved of the way everything happened and I'm pretty certain he would have done it very differently. He understood Glamorgan, he understood me, and he would have known how to handle a difficult situation in as sensitive a way as possible. He was a diplomat, a skill he became renowned for throughout the global game. As for Hugh Davies, Russell's lapdog deputy chairman, I can imagine he probably threw a party when I left the building. He never had very much time for me. That much will become obvious as we go along.

It probably just came down to the fact that the Chairman wanted to take more control, for his own individual stamp to be put on the place. And I get that. However, he was more than once heard to refer to 'the Fatkin/Maynard/Conway triumvirate,' as though we were some kind of terrorist cell plotting to blow up his chairmanship, and he made repeated reference while I was in post to my 'folksy' style (never subsequently defined or any examples given). He also talked afterwards about the Glamorgan 'family' being a dysfunctional one (as if his style and methods somehow defined the word 'functional'). With the ground redevelopment successfully delivered on time and to budget it may have simply been a case of him not needing me around any more. Were that so it would have been disappointing. Hugely. But I'm sufficiently grown up to understand that these things happen. And surely you should be man enough to have a grown-up conversation about it; I wouldn't have liked it at all, but at least afford me the privilege of being able to leave with my dignity intact, exiting head up and in full view, as opposed to skulking out with my belongings in a loaned plastic bin and without so much as an opportunity to say farewell or offer a word of explanation to a single soul. In practice, no sum of money can fully compensate for such a loss of dignity and reputation. It was only a few weeks later that I was able to have a drink with some of the staff and say goodbye properly. And even then, I felt a few of them were nervous about being seen to be doing so. Heaven only knows what they'd been told. Most of them were frightened to death of Russell.

I was more than a bit naïve. Some of the signs, with the benefit of hindsight, should have been pretty obvious, and I don't think I helped myself. As Dean put it to me one time while we were reminiscing over a beer, "Sometimes I wonder how on earth you ever became a Chief Executive." (Though he used two words instead of 'on earth,' the first of which was 'the.') He was right. I'd switched my radar off. When the Sophia Gardens development had been signed off that Spring, I'd taken the opportunity to move over to a brand new office on the top floor of the new pavilion. That had been a bit of a carrot for me throughout the hard work I'd put in on the build and even though I'd have to vacate on televised match days to allow the third umpire to come in I was really looking forward to having a spot close to all of the cricket for a change. It came with the added bonus of being a good distance away from Paul Russell, something I hadn't had the luxury of for several years. He'd insisted that we shared offices, an arrangement I loathed. I ought to have realised that a move like this would isolate me. It doesn't exactly need a detective with the vision of a Poirot or a Morse (or even an East) to see that.

As we were going through the process of bidding for the Ashes Test match and working on the redevelopment plan, Russell had brought in a couple of his own people to advise him and, again using those spectacularly effective hindsight glasses, that was clearly another step closer to marginalizing me. In came Dil Thomas, a former colleague of his at Accenture, to take a greater lead on operational matters, and Dan Barnsley, who was going out at the time with Russell's daughter, was brought in to help with general ground work. Thomas knew systems, albeit having no knowledge of cricket.

Barnsley appeared to know very little about anything but he did what he was told. It meant Russell had a couple of allies on the ground. He was many things, but he certainly wasn't daft.

The landscape was changing in other ways too. In the early weeks of the 2008 season Caryl Watkin, my PA of many years and by then our Operations Director, had walked out. No fan of Russell either, the last straw had been him criticizing her in front of other members of staff, and although it was for something relatively trivial it was what finally tipped her over the edge. Caryl just grabbed her stuff and walked out of the place for good. I was devastated by that. She was a fantastic operator and a truly loyal colleague, friend and ally. I also felt very guilty. It was me who had pushed hard for her to take on the role of Operations Director, a position that, with the benefit of being able to look back, she probably didn't want, especially with outsiders like Thomas and Barnsley querying her pitch and cluttering up her opportunities to take and implement her own decisions.

Caryl had recruited a couple of people in support of her new role. Dan Cherry, not long retired as a player, came in to look after the growing number of stadium issues, and he has gone on to carve out a fine career at the Club, taking in Ashes Test matches, the Hundred and the small matter of a Covid-19 pandemic. Sarah Bell was also brought in as 'the new Caryl,' someone to come in and look after the cricket administration while she stepped up and took on wider responsibilities. It was a pathway I was only too familiar with as I'd done the same in the mid-'90s when stepping up to the CEO role, Caryl picking up much of the cricket work I'd done previously. I left the recruitment process to her, though she passed the CVs for the candidates she was interested in on to me to have a look through. I remember her telling me she'd appointed Sarah. 'Wasn't that the lady who sent in the six-page letter of application?' I asked. Indeed it had been. Sarah (now Sarah Hamilton after marrying former Yorkshire and England all-rounder Gavin Hamilton) went on to work for the ECB. We still joke about that long-winded letter to this day. But, as she continues to point out, the tactic obviously worked.

Part of me was disappointed that Caryl ended up leaving without any kind of pay-off, though a huge part of me admired the style with which she did it, the whole sticking two fingers up, accompanied by an I'm-not-having-that-I'm-off. But the place certainly changed for the worse with her departure. Caryl would also have ensured that my radar remained primed: she knew me inside out and would have made certain I was more aware of what was going on. She read me like no one else, knew where my weaknesses were, and always had my back. For me, it was where the rot set in.

In truth I had become so disillusioned with the idea of working with the Chairman that I took every opportunity to avoid having to do so in any way other than directly and by the book. I was probably playing into his hands. My real love – the cricket – had had to take a back seat and the team on the field now was, to put if frankly, very ordinary. The job wasn't anything like as enjoyable any more, though I knew I was still performing it well. The drive and energy I'd always enjoyed were missing. I had to drag myself out of bed some mornings. I felt a bit stale, a bit flat. I was exhausted after all the why-is-the-Ashes-going-to-Wales hoo-ha and the financial constraints and it was as if, having completed the redevelopment project, there was nothing else to do now but to shuffle on and wait for the punches. My mental health, never rock solidly robust at the best of times, wasn't exactly flourishing either. Looking back, I can see the tell-tale signs of the start of a potential breakdown. I was fair game for anyone coming after me.

As well as moving offices with more haste than was probably decent I was avoiding Russell socially wherever I could too. In each of the previous few years, when Glamorgan were enjoying their annual North Wales festival cricket week up in Colwyn Bay, he'd book his usual apartment in Llandudno and invite the Glamorgan management team around one evening for a meal. Very generous man with his hospitality, Paul Russell, no argument there, but it just wasn't fun; it wasn't me. I hated the small talk, dreaded the prospect of being expected to impress his friends, and listen to his interminable stories. I'd use any excuse at all to avoid having to visit his house in Warwickshire (he divided his time between there and an apartment he had bought in Cardiff): a beautiful house, with sprawling gardens, a summer house, tennis courts, high ceilings, portraits and photographs (many of him, naturally) and expensive furniture, fittings and ornaments. I'd been there a few times for work purposes but to do so socially was another matter altogether. I managed to dodge his invitation for me and Carol to visit when he knew we were going to be in nearby Stratford (we were taking our daughters to see a play) but having made up an excuse for not coming around for an evening meal I couldn't really avoid the invitation to pop in for a coffee on the way back home (with hindsight I don't know why I opened my mouth to mention the visit in the first place). We just wanted to get in and get out as quickly as possible without any fuss and without either of the girls saying anything they shouldn't or, heaven forbid, accidentally breaking something.

Paul invited Alan Hamer, whom the Club had brought in as Finance Director, and me to a Premier League game between Birmingham City and Arsenal in February that year. I had no issue with Alan, who knew and liked his football, being a Cardiff City season ticket holder, but I dreaded the thought of spending my own free time sitting with Paul all afternoon, all blazered up in a corporate hospitality area of St Andrews, listening as he tried to impress with his football knowledge, when all I really wanted was to don a replica shirt and go and sit in the away end and yell my head off supporting the team. I have to be myself at football matches; I don't want to be having to chit-chat my way through a game. With anyone. He was a master of many subjects, Russell, but football wasn't one of them (he called it 'soccer,' always a giveaway). I told him I was committed. And then went to the match anyway. If Arsenal's title challenge was going to implode there – which it did, spectacularly – I was buggered if I was going to watch that implosion whilst having to smile my way falsely through his inexpert match analysis in the corporate bubble of posh nibbles, house Shiraz and men in suits. I'd lost the stomach. In truth, I was fed up with his Matchbox and Dinky car collections, his classic cars, his rugby refereeing, his *Wisden*s, his Glamorgan yearbook collection, his vanity, his ego, and, most of all, his never-ending catalogue of bloody stories.

Glamorgan was no longer the club that I'd first joined. It wasn't even the club of five years previously. It had changed beyond recognition. The focus now was almost exclusively on making money. There was hardly any attention being paid to the cricket, which had become a bit of a sideshow, and to Russell something of a personal embarrassment. I was a cricket and operations man, and very much a people person. I will readily admit to being much weaker commercially and not in his league. Not that I believe any Chief Executive automatically has to be expert in everything but the focus after the redevelopment would, inevitably, be on generating

29

commercial revenue streams and on debt management. Not running cricket matches. A more commercially minded beast would be required. My days would probably have been numbered anyway. But in my view that still didn't justify the manner of the exit.

I recall a meeting towards the end of the 2006 season when Paul and I had gone over to the Glamorgan dressing room in the old pavilion at Sophia Gardens to try to dispel some concerns coming from the players. At that stage I was very much with him that we had little choice but to go down the ground redevelopment pathway but, again, looking back I'm surprised I didn't see that it was at this precise point that the rules of the game were altering for good and that there could be no going back: a 'paradigm shift' (© R P Russell) indeed. There was talk of no overseas players; signings only if existing players made way; of sticking with youth, of relying on our own players. Effectively we were telling the players that they wouldn't be winning anything any time soon. One quote sticks in my mind. In answer to a question from our opening batsman Gareth Rees he turned to him and told him that what we were doing was ensuring that 'the light at the end of the tunnel is no longer that of an oncoming train.'

I'm not quite sure why the finances went so awry. The debt when I left Glamorgan was £9.2 million, with an Ashes Test match in the bag and a financial plan supported by stakeholders agreed and in place. It rose to a rather more alarming £17 million before Hugh Morris and Barry O'Brien managed to negotiate it down to a more manageable level with the local authority, the bank and with Paul Russell himself. They did a terrific job too. But although I sided with Paul about the need to generate more commercial income, and on the plan to try to attract an Ashes Test match, it always felt as though he wouldn't want to stop there. The plan was either way too ambitious or it can't have been followed properly because the debt all but doubled inside three years. Whichever (and it could have been both), at that point, in September 2006, I should have seen the writing on the wall. My relationship with the Chairman, such as it was, went downhill from that moment on and it was probably just a case of how it was going to end. I should have gone before I was pushed.

What happened in the years after I left Glamorgan is something I was no longer close enough to comment on with any authority. Ten months later I attended the first four days of the 2009 Cardiff Ashes Test match and, like so many others, I was blown away by just how good a show the Club put on. I was also incredibly proud to think that I'd been one of just a handful of people who persuaded the powers-that-be to allocate one of the UK's blue riband sporting events to a venue I had probably played a bigger part than anyone in developing. More significantly perhaps, after puffing out my chest I could simply adjourn to the nearest bar, drink cider and watch cricket without a care in the world. But seriously, looking back, how much better would it have been had I been watching England and Australia in a newly built Cardiff ground having managed to depart with my head held high? The lady who crooned '*Je ne regrette rien*' was wrong.

Looking round during the Test match I had been surprised to see how much extra money must have been spent in the intervening months. We'd always planned the new drainage system but the corporate facilities in the indoor school building had been completely revamped, for example, and it looked as though the work on the River Taff end of the ground had been much more extensive than we'd first anticipated. There seemed to be way more stewards than we'd originally planned for as well and there were other alterations too. I didn't believe any of these was absolutely necessary. An extra floodlight pylon went in the following winter. None of these additional costs was going to deliver any additional revenue either. Inevitably they would have put enormous pressure on what was already the tightest of budget models. We were pushing it.

The lack of cricketing success in my last four years at Glamorgan hurt. I want them to win every time they take the field and at that point we were struggling even to compete. I had been delighted when Matt had agreed to come back in a Cricket Manager role in 2007 – Russell dismissing any idea of Duncan Fletcher becoming involved again by referring to him, somewhat dismissively, as 'yesterday's man' (he went on to coach India for four years, so he was presumably 'tomorrow's man' as well). I was even more delighted when Matt followed through by persuading the likes of Jamie Dalrymple, Matt Wood, Jason Gillespie and Adam Shantry to join us, all within the budget we'd set him. He also recruited well after I'd gone, with Jim Allenby and Graham Wagg coming in, and it seemed to those of us looking in from outside that there were the makings of a really decent side there, with some good characters in the dressing room. But it began to unravel almost as soon as it had started. After winning seven

Championship matches in 2010 – and Glamorgan don't win seven in a season very often, I assure you – they were pipped to promotion on the final day of the season after Worcestershire and Sussex contrived a declaration and the former chased down a fabricated target to pinch the second promotion spot ahead of us. The result was a very public airing of the Club's dirty washing as Russell used the excuse of under-performance in one-day cricket to announce a detailed review into cricket operations. To conduct it he chose a former player, Colin Metson, by now a serving member of the committee and certainly no pal of Matt's. Metson's recommendation was to appoint a new Managing Director of Cricket, with Matt reverting from Director of Cricket back to a coaching role. Russell launched an extensive 'global search,' that search ultimately stretching all of two hundred yards with the appointment of Metson himself, fresh from a paper-pushing administrative role at Sport Wales in the building next door to the ground at Sophia Gardens. It seemed extraordinarily convenient.

Matt had already gone on record as saying he wanted Dalrymple to continue as captain, with Mark Cosgrove as overseas player. "If Jamie's not captain, then I shan't be Director of Cricket," appeared to be the gist. Then Metson and Russell, along with Alan Hamer, very recently confirmed as Chief Executive after a two-year period where Russell had effectively filled the role himself, were seen in Dubai in November watching Alviro Petersen playing for South Africa against Pakistan. Petersen was subsequently confirmed as captain, Jamie duly resigned, Matt's job became untenable, and his son Tom's ongoing place on the playing staff became almost impossible as result. All for what? No longer my watch, but goodness me, as dog's dinners go this was a seven-course banquet. Not subsequently helped by the fact that Petersen appeared to have been a hopeless Glamorgan captain. I can see why some changes might have been necessary (and I personally maintain that Matt is far too good a coach and man manager to want to constrain him by giving him a load of administrative clutter to waste his time on) but I wouldn't have pushed for the changes at that time, certainly not after seven wins and being pipped on the final afternoon. However, if you want a textbook step-by-step guide of how not to handle them, this would have been close. Russell and Metson, with an understandably acquiescent and malleable Hamer fresh in as CEO, working with the Machiavellian Hugh Davies, who at some stage or another had it in for every single captain and coach he ever worked with, loitering traitorously in the background like some Iago-type character lurking on the outer fringes of a Caravaggio painting. Hamer did at least have some empathetic qualities but the other three were about as well equipped to motivate and encourage a squad of professional cricketers as a trio of mute Pontllanfraith cub scout leaders supervising an Under-11s overnight camping badge expedition group up the North face of the Eiger. They didn't realise just how little respect the players and coaches had for them.

Glamorgan finally seemed to be trying to recapture some of the soul they had lost over the previous decade when they appointed Hugh Morris as Chief Executive in 2013, Russell having vacated the chairman post a couple of years earlier and been replaced by Barry O'Brien. Hugh faced enormous challenges, especially financially (some of them bequeathed to him through decisions I was a party to – sorry, 'Banners'), but he is a good man, very personable and determined, a Glamorgan legend as a player, and he would have learned a lot from his time with the England and Wales Cricket Board. He is also a friend. Privately I queried the occasional decision but it was his watch now and whether I agreed or disagreed with his recruitment, appointments, retention, strategy or whatever, I had the upmost respect for the integrity of his decision-making. I know how difficult that role is.

I only talked to Paul Russell twice following his issuing of my red card. The first was at the funeral of Geoff Holmes, the former Glamorgan all-rounder, then Cricket Wales's lead administrator, the following Spring, 2009. There was a huge turnout at Thornhill Crematorium on the day, as one would have expected for such a popular and special character. I had been asked, along with Matt and Tom Maynard and John Derrick, to be a pall bearer, which I was very proud to agree to do. I was outside waiting to go in when across marched Russell, right arm outstretched, offering to shake hands, knowing that many of the eyes of what was essentially the wider Glamorgan clan past and present coming together would be trained on the pair of us. Neither the time, nor the place, Paul, I thought. But to refuse to do so in the circumstances would have been churlish. So I didn't. We both knew it was forced. So did everyone else.

The other occasion was at Colwyn Bay later that summer when Glamorgan were playing there. I was chatting with a friend in the main car park next to the pavilion and Russell strolled over, shook hands and attempted to make small talk, saying how nice it was to see me. I told him very firmly, but very politely, that there was no use us pretending there could ever be any kind of relationship between us. He accepted that, though he sounded disappointed. I'm sure he assumed I'd view what happened as simply part of the rough and tumble of business, that there had been a business transaction between us and that we'd moved on, but if that were the case he didn't know me properly. I have pride and I have integrity. I couldn't just let bygones be bygones. I didn't have any communication with him from that day until his death in January 2018. I had nothing to say to him. I doubt he had anything to say to me either, frankly. He had no place in my life, nor I in his.

I saw David East at the Cardiff Test match in 2009 when my old school pal Stefan Cockerill and I were wandering round the ground (taking a break from our non-stop drinking at the bar underneath the stands, if the truth be told). Having popped into the main pavilion reception to see my former colleagues Joan Pockett and Dan Cherry, I was there, right hand in my pocket, the left clutching a pint of cider (in a plastic glass, naturally), when up steps East, head at a jaunty how-are-you-my-old-mate angle, arm outstretched, wearing a sickeningly false conciliatory smile. He practically forced my hand out of my pocket in order to shake it. I hope he felt better knowing that I was so 'willing' to do so. I haven't seen him since, either. And nor do I want to.

And just to complete my subsequent encounters with my personal unholy trinity, I was with my then boss at Welsh Netball, Stephanie Hazlehurst, in the Autumn of 2009, having lunch in the *Mochyn Du*, the pub close to Glamorgan's Sophia Gardens ground, prior to a meeting with Sport Wales when I spotted Hugh Davies between us and the gents, a destination I needed rather urgently to visit. Steph's advice was that I should just march up to him, bold as brass, ask after his health and that of his family and shake him forcefully by the hand, not giving him a chance to say anything. So I did. And she was right. It felt magnificent. He wasn't expecting such a non-confrontational encounter. He didn't know what to say.

Paul and Hugh passed away within a few weeks of one another as 2017 turned into 2018. Death diminishes us all, of course, and in their own ways they both did much for Glamorgan, but I can't be overly hypocritical here. The former managed to reduce my self-esteem to a shell of what it had been previously. I was at a low ebb anyway, what with a divorce, the stress of the Ashes scrutiny and the pressure of the ground redevelopment, not to mention the internal wranglings about the team, and what Russell and his inner circle did – or more specifically the way that they did it – completely shredded my confidence. It took years for me to piece it back together. I had been turfed out of an organization I loved, and a job I adored, one which, despite my initial misgivings and any tittle tattle that Russell and his cronies may have tried to peddle at the time, I knew I was very good at, and been humiliated very publicly in the process. No amount of money could ever adequately compensate for that as far as I was concerned. Partings happen in business, something I absolutely acknowledge, and I recognize that change may well have been something the Club needed. But this wasn't the City of London and this wasn't the way to handle it. It just wasn't the Glamorgan way of doing things. I could never forgive him for that.

Although this story may have begun with something of a dark and very personal episode, I need to put it into some kind of context. My career at Glamorgan was an overwhelmingly positive experience. It was fun. A *lot* of fun. Indeed, despite working hard to cultivate an increasingly curmudgeonly demeanour, my whole life has been positive, full of wonderful people and fantastic memories. And it is Glamorgan Cricket that has given me so much of that. My argument with the tiny minority of people (it doesn't even constitute a handful) who were responsible for me leaving was exactly that – an argument with *them* – and what grudges there may have been (though I'm not much of a grudge person anyway: life's too short) would have been confined to those people alone.

What happened to me that day wasn't carried out by the Glamorgan I had come to love, and it didn't bear the imprint of the Glamorgan that exists now. I consider it to have been some kind of production line quality control aberration, albeit one that I became nastily tangled up in, which chewed me and several others up and spat us back out. Much like experiencing a bout of violent turbulence on a long-haul flight, it passes, and the flight continues. I have certainly never had any grouse with the organization. I love Glamorgan, and I always have. Even as I looked on during the period after I'd left, I wanted the team to win every game, and the Club to succeed in everything it did, and no one was more delighted than I was of the way they ran the Ashes Test matches of 2009 and 2013. I am as passionate about Glamorgan as anyone. And I am tremendously proud to have been invited by Barry O'Brien to be an Honorary Life Member.

If you're looking to place this particular episode chronologically it probably belongs somewhere between Chapters 16 and 17. It appears here at the beginning because it's an obvious reference point for me and even though I'm aware that much about the events of that day in September 2008 is fairly common knowledge, I also know there are people interested in my version of the events that took place. I refuse to allow one bad day at the office, orchestrated by one person working to his own personal agenda, to cast a shadow over the other 8,000-odd I enjoyed at the Club. How it ended for me at Glamorgan is just one moment in time. That incident does not define my career, nor does it start to tell anything like the whole story of my life. To begin to do that, we have to go back almost six decades right to the very beginning.

2 AT HOME HE'S A TOURIST

'What would I forfeit to have the days of my childhood restored?'
CHARLES DICKENS (Pickwick Papers)

There can't be too many things linking Derbyshire, Cheshire, Milan and West Yorkshire, but such was the path of my own childhood. OK, so this chapter is a bit self-indulgent, but it's my story and I don't care. For family reasons it stays in. I envy anyone who says they had anything other than a wonderful childhood. I look back on mine with nothing but fondness. Keep an eye out for the early football references and a completely out of context royal anecdote.

I had a wonderful upbringing. It seems more than a trifle uncool these days to admit it, but it's true. Yes, there does exist the occasional northern twentieth century childhood that didn't involve children being horsewhipped half to death every week, forced to sleep eight to a room, or that didn't consist of paupers' meals of potato peelings and gruel served up in a communal matchbox every third Sunday. I exaggerate for effect, obviously. But the truth is that I can't regale you with any hyperbolic, *Monty-Python*-Four-Yorkshiremen-sketch tales involving outside loos, fortnightly tin baths in front rooms or drunken parental punch-ups. If I tried to, I'd be lying through my teeth. No, whenever I reflect on my formative years it's always with a smile. Sure, there were the kind of standard irrational anxieties, overblown adolescent crises, family tiffs and typical teenage dramas that exist in many households but from my earliest memories, of the Fatkins as a family on Grammar School Road in Lymm, near Manchester, through a handful of wonderfully evocative years living in northern Italy, back to Yorkshire and boarding school from the age of eight, all the way to leaving home permanently at the age of 21, I'm not sure I would have changed very much. I really do feel sorry for folk whose memories of childhood are painful. Mine were anything but.

I am the middle of three siblings. My sister Catherine was born a couple of years before me and, around sixteen months after me, my younger brother Duncan came along. All three of us were born in the Peak District, while my dad was working as a mining engineer in Derbyshire and my mum teaching at a school in Sheffield; Catherine in Chesterfield and Duncan and I in a place called Darley

Dale. The house in Grindleford where Mum and Dad lived isn't one I can remember, but I do have memories of Lymm, where we moved shortly after Duncan was born. On only my second day at the primary school I managed to break a bird's egg which one of my classmates had brought in for a 'show and tell' lesson. Not surprisingly I was severely told off (though a few years down the line the boy's dad would probably have been the one to be told off – by being prosecuted for nicking the egg in the first place). I can remember the half mile walk to and from school. And spending the occasional afternoon at a friend's house – another Michael – who owned the most spectacular collection of Dinky and Matchbox cars you could wish to see. Hundreds of the things. All gleaming. All still in their boxes. They'd be worth an absolute fortune these days. Maybe he eventually sold them to Paul Russell, who knows? I was at school in Lymm for barely a term, though, but I can at least lay claim to having been in the same year group there as the former Lancashire and England cricketer Neil Fairbrother, something I only found out many years later.

I'm told that when I was little I contracted double pneumonia and endured a lengthy spell in hospital. And that I managed to crack my head open falling off a table at one of my own birthday parties. I don't recall either of these (rather dramatic) events, or indeed what I would have been doing perched on a table in the first place. I do recall my Grandma and Grandad (my father's parents) visiting from Leeds and at least once (it probably *was* only once even though the three of us seem to make out that it happened frequently) playing traffic cops with us in the garden. I also have a few hazy recollections of other random incidents, such as the time Catherine and I met Father Christmas* for the first time at Dad's works Christmas party. (*The real one, obviously – a visit to a mining company's works canteen just outside Warrington every first week in December remains a highlight of Santa's annual global itinerary to this day.)

Memories of the next few years in Milan are much more powerful. We moved there when I was five, in late 1969. My father, Gordon, was a mining engineer and he'd taken up a job for a company which had offices in Milan city centre. My mother, Shirley, ended up teaching at the senior International School in Milan. She also became fluent in Italian, no real surprise as she was the one who had to shepherd the three children around, do the shopping and generally keep the family in order. I saw how much Italian she must have absorbed when she came on holiday with me, Carol and our daughters, Seanna and Hannah, to Sicily in 2001 and she struck up conversations with the waiters, bar staff and random locals. None of your makeshift, poorly-accented Italian, either. She was told she spoke in an authentic Milanese dialect. Her face was the very picture of pride.

School for us was also the International School of Milan – or 'Scuola Internazionale di Milano', to give it its proper moniker – at the junior school site, located on a street called Via Osoppo, around three kilometres from home. Home was a first-floor apartment on Viale Caprilli, a Sandro Mazzola free kick away from the Giuseppe Meazza Stadium – the San Siro as it's more commonly known – where Internazionale ('Inter') and AC Milan (pronounced Mee-lan by the locals) shared a home. And that, my friends, explains a great deal, of which much more later…

It being an international school, there was a real mix of nationalities in the classroom but we were taught in English. From what I can gather the curriculum was loosely based on the American educational system. There were plenty of Italian students to go with the Americans, Japanese, Dutch, Australians, Russians and Brits. The inside of my copy of Rudyard Kipling's *Just So Stories*, a present from the time, is inscribed – no, let's be honest, I did it: it's more defaced in thick crayon – with some of the names: Ivo Van Loon, Timmy Wilkins, Ricky Di Giacomo, Kaoro Umino, Andrea Benetti, Glenn Harding; I occasionally wonder where they all ended up.

There were Italian lessons, naturally, and I still shudder at the sound of the word 'dettato' (trans: dictation) as uttered by the old battle-axe of an Italian teacher, whose name I have mercifully managed to forget. Catherine and I were placed in with the Italian students of our respective years, such were the teachers' complimentary impressions of our linguistic ability and potential. Duncan, on the other hand, in the year below me, was in with the international non-Italian also-rans, waifs and strays. I like to think it was because he wasn't considered star material, though undoubtedly this wasn't the reason. But perhaps it's what spurred him on to a place at Oxford University a decade or so later. Strange as it may seem to some, including Duncan, I was considered a model pupil back then, someone to whom others in the class looked up, some of them even bringing their work to me for checking or for comment before then handing it in to the teacher. I'm not quite where it all went so hopelessly wrong but it was a decent start, to be fair. I devoured the work. I loved school. It was only much later that I became a bit blasé and lazy and that both Catherine and Duncan were able to demonstrate their far greater application.

Milan was a cool place to live. We were based out in the suburbs, off the beaten tourist track for pretty much everything other than football, but we would often venture into the heart of the city. I've heard Milan described by many people as industrial, grey, lacking in character; as being, well, boring, but I just didn't see that. Not then, and not now either. And in any event, any city will have its eyesores, its estates, its factories, its grim facades. The Duomo, the Castello Sforzesco, the Last Supper, La Scala, the trams, Galleria Vittorio Emmanuele II…. I thought it was a wonderful place. Even though we were right at the very end of the Metro line, close to Lotto station, on Sundays we'd jump into Dad's car and he'd brave the psychotic deathwish-laden Milanese motorists to make the trip across town towards the Stazione Centrale, to a shop near the Pirelli HQ building which sold that day's English language Sunday papers. For us, it also meant we might be allowed a couple of American comics, a real treat. Other Sundays we'd sometimes lunch out at the Hotel Continentale, just down the road from La Scala. This invariably meant a visit to the English language bookshop nearby, where Mum would buy her Erle Stanley Gardners, John Creaseys and other thrillers. When we moved back to the UK there seemed to be millions of them in the house. When Mum and Dad split up and Mum moved to Harrogate in the early '90s, they were all thrown out. I've since started collecting the Perry Masons myself, picking up a couple every time Seanna, Hannah and I venture up to Hay-On-Wye for one of our regular bookish outings.

I can reel off what I would order from the Hotel Continentale menu as it never changed: consommé, followed by steak and chips, followed by meringues and ice cream – *meringa con panna* to the locals. Adventurous palate back then, clearly. After lunch we'd end up making a nuisance of ourselves in the cavernous main lobby, which was choc-full of all sorts of different types of covered armchair, playing cowboys and Indians with some of the waiters, including our favourite, the drinks waiter, a Russ Abbott lookalike (it seemed to me, with the benefit of some cloudy, long range hindsight) who became known as the 'Poom Poom Man' because of his habit of shouting 'poom poom' when firing his imaginary gun at us.

The boss of the company Dad worked for owned a flat on Lake Como, around an hour's drive north of Milan, and we'd spend regular weekends up there. It was in a place called Faggeto Lario, situated midway between Como and Bellagio. Those weekends meant the three of us children sharing a room – a rarity, for obvious reasons – and in addition to still having the rugs from that apartment in my own flat in Cardiff, Mum still had all of the bedding at the time of her death in 2017. Not that she was a hoarder or anything. Lake Como was a beautiful place. If you haven't visited the Italian Lakes, do go. Those weekends, including several spent with visiting grandparents, added to a blissful upbringing and some lasting memories. It was a real treat to be spending regular times there. I loved the place.

As young children, the adjustment to Italian television took a bit of doing. We'd be able to receive very occasional American cartoons but much of the English language content was dubbed – often hilariously badly – and non-Italian children's programmes were scarce. Of the local fare we all enjoyed watching *Canzonissima*, a singing contest with all the Italian stars of the day – Mina, Patty Pravo, Mino Reitano, Gigliola Cinquetti and Mum's favourite, Massimo Ranieri. *Erba Di Casa Mia* ('Grass of My Home' to thee and me) was the 1972 competition winner and Mum played the LP to death around the flat. In the end the three of us became experts, singing along to *La Tua Innocenza*, *Vent 'anni* and *L'Infinito*. It took some digging around but much later I found a CD version and gave it to Mum as a birthday present. Doubtless she'd have been blissfully unaware of annoying all the neighbours in the apartment block in Harrogate where she lived.

We'd egg on the Italians and the Brits in the annual Eurovision Song Contest. Ranieri had come fifth in 1971 and represented Italy again in 1973. Big Ranieri fans, us, now, but we would be disappointed. Just a fortnight before starting our big adventure as boarders at Brontë House School back in the UK, Duncan and I watched Ranieri stumble to 13th place. No doubt Duncan cried. He cried whenever the Italians or the Brits were beaten. Even in *It's a Knockout*. In fact, he cried at anything. He made the lachrymose Gwyneth Paltrow seem callously stony-faced and emotionless.

41

Another Italian classic on the main channel, RAI Uno, was *Rischiatutto*, a quiz show hosted by a fellow called Mike Buongiorno (literal translation: 'Mike good morning') which ran from 1970 to 1974. I can't pretend to have had a clue about what was going on. Lots of questions, and contestants who appeared to be winning telephone numbers worth of money. I didn't understand the concept of currency. This was Italy, where a hundred Lire was worth around a quarter of a broken button. Mum often boasted that her monthly pay cheque made her a millionaire. But Signor Buongiorno had some magnificent clichés. He used to trot out the Italian equivalents of um, like, sort of, kind of, erm, you know, let's see: dunque, allora, adesso, vediamo un po', commune. He used them all. Often in the one sentence.

A little more suited to our age bracket, the three of us used to watch the *Zecchino D'Oro*, a singing contest for Italian children. The 1971 Final went down in Fatkin family folklore as it featured such classics as *Annibale, Cannibale, Terribile; Il Sorpasista;* and *Partiam Si Partiam*. I recalled those three songs very fondly until I googled them recently and watched them on You Tube. None of them won. And it's not hard to see or hear why: they're bloody terrible. Though the expressions on the kids' faces are fantastic. The lad singing *Partiam* was particularly aggressive, giving it all barrels as he belted it out in front of the cameras. To us it was great television. And back then it was quite probably up there with the best entertainment Italian TV had to offer. To save her having to look it up I was able to tell Mum that the winner was something called *Il Caffe Della Peppina*. Peppa's coffee. No. Me neither, Mum.

Our Milan apartment was quite something. When we first moved, we were billeted in rooms in an hotel, the Monte Rosa, before occupying a flat on Via Corregio, in the same block as Dad's office. My only memory of that place – bar the one Christmas we spent there – was the noise in the streets on the night of 17th June 1970. I can place it that accurately because it was the evening Italy beat West Germany 4-3 to reach the 1970 World Cup Final, their first in 32 years. Everyone took to the streets and the noise from the horns was deafening. It went on for hours. Shame they were thumped by the great Pele-inspired Brazil side in the Final. At the time I had no idea at all what was going on, just that the whole city appeared to have gone bananas and it was keeping me awake.

Milan was where I picked up my interest in – some might say obsession for – football. You couldn't help it, really; it was all around you. As I have mentioned we were a two-minute walk from the San Siro and on match days I'd lean over the balcony and watch the supporters traipsing down Viale Caprilli from Lotto Metro station half a mile away. Internazionale – Inter Milan – quickly became 'my' team. They'd won the European Cup in 1964 and 1965, reached the final in 1967, and would do so again in 1972. A dour, defensively-fixated team, their star players were Sandro Mazzola, Giacinto Facchetti and Roberto Boninsegna. And those colours! Blue and black vertical stripes. What was not to like? I recalled the 1972/73 Italian season fondly as a riot of colour, goals and edge-of-the-seat excitement. The reality was somewhat more mundane. The football magazine *When Saturday Comes*, in a feature in February 2016, described that season as 'the nadir of catenaccio', pointing out that Napoli, who finished ninth, scored just 18 goals in 30 matches, and just one in their 15 away games combined. Not as exciting as my eight-year-old mind had tricked me into believing, it would appear.

With me having bagged Inter the field was open for Duncan to adopt the red and black of their city rivals, AC Milan. For some unfathomable reason, however, Duncan opted instead to support Juventus. Of Turin. I'm not too sure why. Maybe he just wanted to be a bit contrary. Or perhaps it was just a reaction to being consistently fobbed off as a family afterthought. I was chosen to join Dad, my Grandpa (Mum's dad) and Dad's boss – who was an Inter director – and his sons at the Milan derby in late November 1971, with Duncan earmarked for the girls' team who were going to do a bit of shopping and watch the trotting across the road with Mum, my Granny, Dad's boss's wife and Catherine. He was considered too young to be taken to a football match. Not that he reacted. Oh no. And it hardly ever* comes up in conversation when we meet (*usually).

That derby game was a life-defining experience for me. Not only was it a free-scoring 3-2 (sadly to Milan, not Inter), rare in those highly defensively orientated days, but the whole occasion captivated me. The walk to the stadium, past all the street vendors; the colour, the noise, the flares. It was magnificent. To quote the great Bobby Robson, "It's a small boy clambering up the stadium steps for the very first time, gripping his father's hand, gawping at the hallowed stretch of turf beneath him and, without being able to do a thing about it, falling in love." That's exactly how it grabbed me, too. I remember asking why people were playing golf at half time. It turns out it was the groundstaff replacing divots. And the more I went on about it, the more increasingly pissed off Duncan became. So the more I went on about it. Repeat to fade...

My Grandpa fuelled my burgeoning interest. I was given a 1972 Letts pocket football diary that Christmas, a diary which listed domestic Championship and Cup winners, league tables, home international results and caps and all sorts of other statistical paraphernalia. Most of it, of course, utterly useless information. Grandpa would test me. At meal-times he'd pick the diary up and fire questions at me. I'd get one lira for each one I got right. As I've acknowledged, awareness of currency worth wasn't exactly target subject market for me back then and I wasn't to know that one lira was the about as valuable as half a leaf off your average sprout. Even answering a hundred questions in one go didn't begin to dent the bank. But for me it was all about the challenge. I studied that information so hard. Had I brought the same measure of application and commitment to studying for 'O' Levels and 'A' Levels a decade or so later I'd have flown into Oxford myself. I can still trot out FA Cup winners back to the 1930s. (The fact that there have been occasions when I've ended up in the supermarket and forgotten the one item I set out to pick up is slightly more disturbing.) Grandpa didn't know it at the time but he was fanning the flames of what was a rapidly burning passion. I even got taken to a second live game: Inter's 1-1 draw with Bologna in March '72. Thankfully Duncan was allowed along this time too. To compound the perceived favouritism of that first derby game, a colleague teacher of Mum's came back from a trip home to the UK a few months later with a Leeds United mug for me (Leeds were our family team in those days) and a copy of *Shoot!* magazine for Duncan. He gets a magazine and I'm given a commemorative FA Cup winners' mug. Scarred? You betcha. Mum had to ask my Grandma to scramble around in the Keighley shops for the same mug for him so that he wouldn't feel even more left out.

Grandpa did the same with my swimming. I hated the swimming pool. All that chlorine wrecking your eyes – pre-goggles days, these, remember. I particularly hated putting my head under the water. So what does he do? He offers me a couple of lire every time I did it. Again, it worked. This time, though, it was so successful a halt had to be called. Otherwise I would have drained his bank account. Gullible? Not this time. He was a fine man, my Grandpa, and an enormous influence on me throughout my childhood. I have many happy memories of spending time with him and my Granny in Adel, on the outskirts of Leeds, where he lived and was working as a university lecturer after having moved the family (including Mum) down from Scotland in the 1940s. The drive over the top of the moors from Keighley, where we settled, to Leeds, via Leeds/Bradford Airport is one I make regularly whenever I'm back in Yorkshire. I remember every hill, every corner, every bump and dip in the road. Grandpa's mannerisms, stories and gentle chiding and ribbing have stayed with me all my life and we used to enjoy spending New Year's Day every year at their house, with all their Scottish traditions and rituals. They would have come to us in Keighley on Christmas Day, with Dad having to drive all the way to get them and then take them back in the evening as neither Grandpa or Granny could drive. It was only years later I learned that the only reason they didn't stay over was because they thought that our house was too cold! I was devastated when Grandpa died in 1981 and I still remember the evening Mum and Dad came to the school to tell us. His photo – complete with trademark pipe – features proudly on a wall at home.

Although I sometimes can't remember what I did yesterday it is true that I can remember many obscure facts and events from years gone by. Indeed I surprised myself with my recall of events when pottering around this particular period as part of my research. For example, my recollection of one particular Saturday afternoon in the flat on Lake Como can be traced back to 1st April 1972. Leeds United were playing Derby County and, as was customary, Dad had BBC World Service on for the Saturday afternoon sport. I can remember doing some school homework while listening to Peter Jones and Bryon Butler describing the second half commentary on a 2-0 away win for Derby, who were on their way to winning the tightest of First Division title races. Just three weeks later and Duncan and I were allowed to stay up in Milan to watch England's European Nations Cup quarter-final home leg against West Germany. They lost, 3-1. But the grainy black and white pictures from Wembley, the Italian commentary and Gunter Netzer's control of the game are still vivid. What I hadn't appreciated was how close together those two matches actually were.

My method for recalling events is a bit Nick Hornby-esque (if you haven't yet read *Fever Pitch*, shame on you; it's brilliant). When trying to place the exact date of her eldest sister Sandra's wedding (there was a middle sister Sue as well – both lovely) I remember piping up to Carol that it was late January 1990. How on earth did I know that? We drew 0-0 with QPR in an FA Cup fourth round game, much of the second half of which I listened to on the car radio while the photos were being taken before the reception. I went and looked it up. It was January 27th 1990. See, it does occasionally come in useful. And no, I don't think it's anything to be especially proud about. Let's move on.

By Spring 1973, with Catherine now away at boarding school on the North Yorkshire coast, Duncan and I joined Mum and Dad in a small town called Villars, in Switzerland, where Dad had been sent to recuperate after suffering a mild heart attack (he would have a second in February 1976). I remember us going on a newsagent hunt to try to find out the football scores – discovering the scores in the papers, those were the days. Leeds were on their way to the European Cup Winners Cup Final (which they eventually lost, shamefully, to AC Milan in what was subsequently proved to have been a game where the referee had been 'bought'). I also recall drawing in small crowds of waiters with my daily evening order in the hotel restaurant of 'spaghetti senza niente': spaghetti on its own. No sauce. No salt. No pepper. Very occasionally a little butter. They couldn't believe someone could be so cretinously unadventurous. Yep. Me. Pretty much every evening meal for two weeks solid.

It was while we were in Villars that I fell irretrievably in love with football. The foundations had already been laid but this is where it really took off. The hotel had a games room in the basement, where Duncan and I spent a lot of time. Next to it was an indoor pool, and in another room overlooking the pool was a large black and white TV. On 7th March 1973, on that black and white TV, I watched Ajax take Bayern Munich apart 4-0, Johan Cruyff and company dismantling a Bayern team that would take over as European Champions from them the following year; a team containing Sepp Maier, Franz Beckenbauer and Gerd Muller. I didn't move for the full ninety minutes. I was mesmerized by Cruyff. His death in March 2016 hasn't diminished that affection. To me, he defined how football should be played. He remains my ultimate sporting idol. Everything he did as a player exuded cool.

I have a photo at home of the Italy team before the 1974 World Cup game against Argentina: Zoff; Spinosi, Morini, Burgnich, Facchetti; Benetti; Mazzola, Rivera, Capello; Riva, Anastasi. Put Sabadini in for Spinosi and that was the same eleven we watched in qualifying, a 5-0 hammering of Luxemburg (Gigi Riva bagged four), on TV at a restaurant in a village way up in the hills above Faggeto Lario in March 1973, just a few weeks before Duncan and I started at school back in the UK. Throw in a Causio, a Chinaglia and a Boninsegna and that was the first bunch of players I really supported.

I couldn't get enough of the game. I had a pretty decent collection of Matchbox cars (no boxes, though; they went in the bin straight away) but I often ignored the Hot Wheels track games they were designed for and found what I thought was a much more interesting use for them. I used to split them into teams, mark out a section of the carpet and, using a small marble as a ball, play games of football with the cars as the players. Ajax/Bayern, Inter/Milan, Leeds/Juventus (a repeat of the 1971 Fairs Cup Final (a forerunner of the Europa League), which Leeds won on away goals), England/Italy... you name it, I played it. I even commentated. Occasionally in Italian. With a shameful emphasis when I was using the names of British players, Brem-*ner* in an exaggerated, dodgy Italian accent was a particular favourite. Mum thought I was bonkers. She wasn't wrong.

Those games could occasionally get a little out of hand. Entry from the lift to our apartment on Viale Caprilli was through an ornate wrought iron door, opening out onto a long corridor which ran the length of the main lounge. Beyond was a door and then another corridor, with a bathroom right at the end. I'm not too proud to say that on occasion our visitors would be greeted with the sight of hundreds of cars in the foreground, randomly scattered across the carpet, with a young lad in the distance, sat on the loo reading a football magazine, taking a break from the big match, but without having bothered to close the door. Although that was hardly a sight visitors would have been too pleased to see, the more dangerous occasions were those when you couldn't get into the place without risking treading on one of the players (sorry, one of the *cars*). It could be anything up to fifty-a-side.

I used to play those games solo. I really didn't like anyone else joining in. Which, when you have a kid brother, a mustard-keen, desperate-to-join-in kid brother with a proper tantrum-chucking temper tucked away in his locker, is probably not good. Mum was always pleading with me to let him join in. On one occasion, after a standard bout of crying, Duncan's anger could be contained no longer and he picked up one of the cars and hurled it out of our first-floor window. It was a key player, too. A blue Pontiac. Left sided midfielder, No.11, tricky dribbler. Needless to say, I went all the way down to the communal gardens to get it while Duncan got a rocket up his backside from Mum. Which would have led to more tears and more tantrums. It was like living with a schoolboy Paul Gascoigne. On another occasion, again having gone through the crying and shrieking stage, he just stamped on one of my two Mini Coopers (the red one played left back, the maroon one played right back and skippered the side). The maroon Mini managed to withstand this career-threatening injury to go on and play many thousands more matches, depressed front passenger-side wheel and all. I still have it today. Senza box, naturalmente.

Duncan and I used to have regular run-ins. I was considered to be a bright, well-behaved, butter-wouldn't-melt young lad and Duncan was a short-tempered, angry cry baby. And I'm not exaggerating, I assure you. The fact that I could play him like a violin and wind him up to order wouldn't have helped. But there was one incident where I tried to shift the blame for something on to him and was unable to get away with it. Mum discovered the word 'Michael' written, in crayon, on one of the walls of the apartment. (Actually, strictly speaking it was 'Micheal', but as one of life's spelling fascists, best not open up the can of worms marked "Couldn't Even Spell His Own Name Correctly.") I immediately did the innocent young lad equivalent of fluttering my eyelashes but for some reason this standard technique didn't work on this occasion. Firstly, I was asked, why on earth would Duncan write 'Michael' (or 'Micheal') on the wall? Fair point, I suppose. Secondly, and the killer blow: Duncan hadn't yet learned to write. Rumbled. Even I couldn't charm my way out of that situation.

Generally, these were typical fraternal jousts and no more. We got on most of the time. The only occasion it really escalated came after Milan, in Keighley four or five years later. A game of cricket on the lawn descended into an argument. I probably nicked one and didn't own up to it. He threw a bat at me. And missed. I threw a stump at him. And missed. Mum and Dad were not at all amused. We could have killed each other, they said. Relax. Not with our throwing arms, folks. More chance of Stevie Wonder hitting three consecutive 180s at darts. But it did have the potential to get a bit messy, that one.

Stories of Duncan and I are regularly trotted out routinely at family gatherings. But there's one mystery that I can't solve and am going on the record to confirm it to the family in writing. I did the eulogy at Mum's funeral – one of the hardest things I have ever had to do in my life – and I confirmed it then too. One night in Milan, our bedroom door – a very heavy door, it must be said – came away from its hinges and crashed back into the room that we shared. We were both in bed, so there were no injuries but to her dying day Mum always used to ask us 'what really happened?' OK, for one last time, Mum, wherever you are, let's analyse this. Two young boys, aged, what? Around seven and six respectively? Lifting a particularly heavy oak door off its hinges in the middle of the night, setting it to fall inwards to order – and ensure that it avoided hitting either of us – and yet somehow still safely tucked up in bed within seconds. First of all, how could we? Secondly, why would we? Sorry, Mum. Can't help you. It was either mechanical or it was a ghost. But it categorically wasn't us.

Milan for me is a collage of interwoven happy memories. From the AC Milan-supporting milkman to the cleaner, Signora Bose; from every member of the family baiting Mum's Spurs-supporting teaching colleague, Mr Tye, the Monday after Leeds put them out of the FA Cup in 1972 to munching focaccia or eating gelati on the walk home from school on a sunny afternoon; from the flying back and forth (including being sick on the plane after an obstructive passenger had refused to move to allow us all to sit together) to parties Mum and Dad held in the flat; from kicking footballs off the balcony and trudging down in the lift to fetch them to security alerts after a shooting incident in a neighbouring flat. And all those Panini sticker albums. Every subject under the sun: football; wild animals; birds; famous battles. We were sticker mad. So many vivid recollections.

Then, in mid-April 1973, it was off to school in England as Mum and Dad wanted us to be educated back in the UK. Specifically, to a prep school called Brontë House, in a place called Apperley Bridge, more or less smack in between Bradford and Leeds. Down the road was the 'big school' – Woodhouse Grove – but before we could be accepted there, we had to get our heads down and get through the old 11+ exam. I was eight, turning nine the month after I arrived there; Duncan was just seven. I hated the first few weeks, I'll be honest, quite literally clutching my teddy bear in the dormitory at night and crying myself to sleep. That eventually wore off but I do know that when my own two daughters reached seven or eight there is no way I would have been able to pack them off to a boarding school, even had I been able to afford it. I personally don't believe in a two-tiered education system but when you're eight years old I guess you don't get the chance to raise any political objections, even assuming you had any at such an early age. It did me a lot of good: it made me independent, toughened me up, made me think and fend for myself. But it felt like a really cold-hearted way for parents to see their children brought up.

While I was blubbing myself to sleep Duncan, conversely, seemed to take to it like a duck to water. I've always been the sensitive one, clearly, despite his pantomime tears. For seven terms Brontë was my home, though as Mum and Dad had bought a house in Keighley, a dozen or so miles away, just before we moved to Italy, it was to there that we returned for holidays and not back to Milan. Catherine was already in situ at a school near Filey on the North Yorkshire coast. Our Italian adventure was over.

At Brontë we were allowed 'tuck' once a week. Basically, you put a load of sweets and other treats into a plastic container three months in advance and on occasional Sunday evenings a teacher would let you have one, maybe two items, as a special treat. So we had to stockpile chocolate and sweets to last several months. Long before the days of 'best before' or 'use by' labels. Little wonder that I was pinching Club biscuits and Blue Ribands from the kitchens in my final year, something which later saw me stripped of my responsibilities as a prefect. Nothing stands in the way of my hunger, not even a public shaming.

School plays were a highlight. For others, if not for me. I seemed to end up playing female roles. In one, I was cast as the Wicked Queen in a version of *Snow White*, with full-on regal dress, tiara and wig, and a more exaggerated facial decoration than an over-

50

painted Ronald MacDonald. The make-up was applied by pupils from the main school. Quite why, I don't know. It's not as though they had any kind of training or qualifications. But being sat there while someone liberally daubed rouge all over my face, listening to the theme from *Van der Valk* played on a loop as parents congregated outside, is another memory that refuses to go away. I was told I looked a bit like Catherine. Which is either flattering to me and my make-up artistes or one of the gravest possible insults to her, not sure which.

Academically I was still doing fine, generally in the top handful for most subjects. I won public speaking competitions and prizes for Music and History – inscribed prize books which I still have. One of them is about Music, which I get. The other is about insects. Which I don't. I can't ever remember being the remotest bit interested in insects. Or what they really have to do with History. I also won a couple of House prizes, one of which earned me a book about dinosaurs. Nope. Never had any interest in them either, nor can I remember studying them. Though we were taught by a few (insert canned laughter here). My reports were good. I was told I had a really good singing voice and when the Christmas carol service of 1974 came around, an event the school put on fabulously well, it must be said, it was me who was chosen to open it with the solo from *Once In Royal David's City*. As I said, butter wouldn't melt. Though if you heard me singing away in the car these days I doubt whether the phrase 'good voice' would be used. Other, perhaps, than to preface it with the words 'he hasn't got a particularly.'

I enjoyed my sport. I made the First XI at cricket and even won a couple of batting prizes. For the Glammy boys reading this, I could play once, lads. And there's no need for those raised eyebrows, either. You used to be given a cricket ball if you made 25 runs or more (a better quality one for passing 35), a pair of pads for 50 and a new bat if you made a century. The latter were rare. I managed a couple of the better cricket balls, one of which I still have, for a particularly hard-fought unbeaten 49 to earn us a draw at Giggleswick School. I was especially proud of myself for not seeking the glory of that extra run and blocking out the final over as we were eight down. Especially as I could have done with the pads. Team man, see. In my final summer term, 1975, our weekly cricket nets were attended by Don Wilson, the Yorkshire all-rounder. At senior school we subsequently had a winter's coaching from Geoff Cope, the Yorkshire off-spinner.

I came to know Geoff later in life when he was looking after day-to-day operations at Yorkshire and I was at Glamorgan and I was flabbergasted he couldn't recall my textbook pull shot. I remain convinced that I played a part in his subsequent selection for England.

Boarding life was all very alien at first. Well it would be, wouldn't it? Suddenly there's no family around you, just a load of boys your sort of age, many of whom were good lads but, inevitably, a handful of whom were complete wankers (a few years before the practical application of that word would come into operation – and I'm also conscious that I probably shouldn't have used the word 'handful' when referring to wankers). Meals, when they were actually edible, which wasn't often, were predictably stodgy. Treats, as we've seen, were rarer than gloves on an ostrich, though the school did bake you a cake on your birthday, which was a nice touch, even if all you ended up with yourself was the one slice. But it was all so very different to what I'd been used to. The whole dormitory thing, being attached to houses, being regimented as to what you could do and when, 'prep' periods in the evening, cold baths (yep, they existed), camping out, gruelly porridge – all a far cry from Milan. It's no wonder we had to toughen up.

Access to television was an extremely rare privilege. And the teachers had a bizarre idea of what it was we ought to be watching. Princess Anne's wedding in November 1973, for example. All classes stop and let's watch that. Great. I'd rather have been in the lesson, thank you very much. I can't say I've ever been a fan of the royals. Sure, I understand the income they generate from tourism via the whole pomp and pageantry thing but it's always seemed invidious to me that people born into wealth and privilege should be propped up by the rest of us, their pampered lifestyles paid for by the general public, especially the hangers-on around the fringes. The whole royal-wedding-royal-baby thing just leaves me cold. Maybe some deep-rooted psychosomatic trigger was flicked on that November day of Anne's wedding, who knows? *Vive la république.*

By way of an early tangent, I did actually meet Princess Anne in 2005. Our old coach at Glamorgan, Duncan Fletcher, then England Coach, had been named Coach of the Year by UK Sport and as he was at home in South Africa he rang and asked me if I'd pick the award up on his behalf at a swanky lunch at the Grosvenor House Hotel in London. I didn't really want to but I was in London that week anyway and he was pretty insistent, telling me it would mean a lot to him. Anyway, it should be said that I really don't do posh. Sartorially I'm far closer to Worzel Gummidge than a Savile Row dandy, and I come over all irascible at the merest sight of anything monied. But I went along because it was him who was asking. Gordon Lord of the England and Wales Cricket Board was also picking up an award so I shared a taxi from Lord's with him and Hugh Morris, Glamorgan's former opening batsman, by then Technical Director of the ECB. They were on a different table and all the main table plan said against my name was 'Table 1 x 10'. No one else's names or anything. So, we went our separate ways and I moseyed over to Table 1 and awaited the arrival of my mystery dining companions.

First in was Steve Rider, the TV presenter (much shorter than I imagined him to be), who was compèring; then it was Mike Ruddock, Wales's rugby union coach, who had won an award as well; he was followed by Adrian Moorhouse, who I tried – unsuccessfully – to get to recall swimming against me for Bradford Grammar School in the Northern School relay finals of 1982 but, like Geoff Cope, I'd failed to leave any impression on him either. Then in came the unctuous Lord Coe, or 'Seb' as he insisted on being called (though seemingly wincing every time we proceeded to do so) and someone I remember being rather badly disposed towards as I was very firmly in his running rival Steve Ovett's camp when they were at the height of their famous running rivalry. Next up was Bobby Robson, who was receiving the lifetime achievement award. Lovely man. Just wanted to talk about cricket and, when he found out my football leanings, about 'The Arsenal'. Then in comes Steve Redgrave. Smiling a lot and talking very little. I'm getting a bit blasé at this point, sorry. Last but one was Sue Campbell, Chair of UK Sport. Eventually there was only one spot left, between me and my new best mate, Bobby Robson. In comes Princess Anne, and all eyes are following her as she enters the room, meandering her way through the various tables until she comes towards ours. And stops. Taking the chair next to me. Talk about being out of your depth. Fathoms deep. She was charming, though. And thankfully for most of the lunch she was busy fielding a range of horrendously sycophantic questions from my mate Lord ("call me/don't call me Seb") Coe on the other side of the table. So that's how you reach the heights of being a Lord, I thought. But Anne and I didn't hit it off so well that my reactionary and republican leanings could realistically be weaved into the conversation, or even any chit-chat about her wedding 32 years previously. Even I'm not that tactless. And yes, I'm aware that if you look carefully, I've only counted nine people. I really can't remember the tenth. He must have been even less famous than me.

Anyway, I digress (and not for the last time, be warned). Back at Brontë I remember TV snippets from the two 1974 General Elections but what little television we were allowed to watch was overwhelmingly sport-based. We were able to catch some of the group games in the 1974 World Cup, so I was able to get my Johan Cruyff fix. And we were always allowed to watch the FA Cup Finals. Leeds losing to Sunderland in '73 I remember very well. 95% of the occupants of the room were in floods of tears when the Sunderland manager Bob Stokoe raced on to the pitch to hug his goalkeeper Jim Montgomery at the end. But within a matter of a twelvemonth many of the same group were dyed-in-the-wool Liverpool fans, worshipping at the altar of Kevin Keegan. Kids, eh. Fickle, or what?

The 1975 European Cup Final (Champions League for you whippersnappers who can't remember a time when the actual champions of each country were the only teams allowed to enter) was a major event because Leeds United, down the road, were in it. We were allowed into the Headmaster's study to watch it, a gang of around 30 of us. Leeds lost 2-0, complete with controversial dodgy penalty decisions and disallowed goals. My mate Mike 'Crow' Bedford still spits bile and feathers every time I mention Franz Beckenbauer's name. So easy to wind up. Crow, that is, not Franz. And how wonderfully ironic to see they're going to be linked together in perpetuity, cosied up to one another alphabetically in the index.

But other than that, and the odd glimpse of Glam Rock or Terry Jacks and *Seasons In The Sun* on *Top Of The Pops* in the Spring of 1974, there was little TV for us to enjoy. It was a period of inedible food, lessons, house points, book reviews, speech competitions, dormitory life, playing outside, table tennis and chess matches, sprinkled with events such as an elaborate Bonfire Night, inter-house games, or a trip to the pictures, including when we were all taken to see *The Man With The Golden Gun* in January 1975 after we'd sat and passed our 11+. And, in September of that year, it was off with the grey shorts and on with the (seriously flared) grey trousers as we headed to big school. Now that would be an experience.

54

3   UNCERTAIN SMILE

'The only place I considered home was the boarding school, in Yorkshire, my parents sent me to.'
JOE STRUMMER

Boarding school. Conjures up all sorts of images for those who have never experienced it. And those of us who have will probably confirm them all too. Tough upbringing, but it sets you up to be independent and respectful if not, in my own case, on a particular path to scholarship, and the bonds of some of the friendships formed have been amazing. Trent Poly was essentially boarding school without rules: three years of freedom after ten years of confinement.

In the early 1970s one of the popular programmes on television was a drama series called *Colditz*. Featuring life in one of the most formidable World War II prisoner-of-war camps in Germany, its imposing dark-bricked and dimly lit castle silhouette still reminds me of that first approach to Woodhouse Grove School as a pupil in September 1975. And when the car drove away, this time I was on my own as Duncan was still a year behind back at Brontë. Intimidating isn't the word.

I was at least lucky enough to have a number of friends coming up from Brontë with me, including my oldest pal Andy Tomlinson, who had started with me there on the same day in April '73, and Greg Marchbank among others. The year one boarders were billeted in two dormitories – Old North and Price – and divided up alphabetically. Andy ended up in Price, I was in Old North, as was Greg. That first day introduced another couple of characters who have gone on to be friends to this day: Stefan Cockerill and Steve Burnhill. From our late 30s those two, Andy and I have met up at least once a year for a couple of rounds of golf, dinner, bed and breakfast, more recently with others – Greg, Andrew North, John Haigh, Tony Walker, Tony Hope, Mark Hammes – and basically just reminisce with the same old stories and some merciless piss-taking. The bond already established with Andy and Greg was formed with Stef and Steve in those early years, and with others over the coming months and years. Boarding schools had a pretty poor reputation for their harsh regimes, and that was especially true back in the '70s, but one thing they did manage to throw up was tight, longstanding friendships. During the Coronavirus lockdown in 2020, for example, Andy organized for the ten of us to come together every week on Zoom to keep each other going. I really valued that contact. The fact that the bonds are still strong getting on for 50 years later says a lot.

Boarding life was tough and your general state of happiness could basically just amount to who you were lucky enough – or, in many cases *un*lucky enough – to have as your dormitory prefects. I had some absolute shockers down the years. Complete sadists. They weren't so bad in year one, but it got progressively worse. In the second year our dormitories were divided into the houses we were all in. There were three boarding houses: Findlay, Southerns and Vinter. Andy, Stef and Greg were in Findlay; Steve, along with John, Andrew and Mark, were in Vinter; I was in Southerns, which is where I later became friends with the two Tonys. So I ended up in a completely different part of the school. On the first day of our second year, I was the first into the new dorm – rather originally called 'West' – and came across our two prefects. Practising lacrosse. With a hedgehog.

In the second year we were subjected to some of the worst bullying I can remember, much of it at the hands of a guy called Keith Secker. Doing something wrong led to the dreaded words, 'stand at the end of your bed', and, from there, any punishment was possible. Often you didn't actually have to have done anything wrong. If they wanted to bully you, then they would just bully you. Secker wasn't even in charge of the dorm I was in but he seemed to go around looking for youngsters to pick on. He once forced me to drink several litres of water quickly and then, when I wasn't watching, punched me as hard as he could in my stomach. Bear in mind he was nearly 18, I was only 12. I always vowed that if I ever saw him after I'd left school, I'd hammer the crap out of him. I've never come across him since. But imagine my delight when we met up for our lads' golfing weekend thirty-odd years later and I learned from Andy and Steve that they'd met up with Tony Walker recently and he had a Keith Secker revenge story to tell. Tony had been playing rugby a few years after leaving school and came across Secker in the opposition side. After asking him to confirm that he was indeed the Keith Secker who had gone to Woodhouse Grove School, Tony proceeded, in front of his team-mates, to go over and knock him to the ground, telling him it was something he'd also promised himself he'd do after all the bullying he'd been subjected to by him. And then when Secker had got back to his feet, he punched him again. Tony – or 'Denis' as we knew him back then – wasn't too proud of having done that, but I loved to hear it. Apparently, Secker accepted he'd behaved like a sadistic prick back then.

Prefects ran the roost and set the bar on discipline. Some enjoyed casual bullying, much of it verbal, others just using youngsters for errands a la *Tom Brown's Schooldays* – the back end of Victorian 'fagging' I guess – but quite a few preferred to dole out physical punishment just for the hell of it: bacon slicers (metal coat hangers sliced down your backside, which hurt like hell), rats' tails (wet towels flicked at you, the point of which left a hell of a mark if it caught you), trials by ordeal, or just basic fisticuffs. Others were a little more subtle. The issuing of quirkily-titled essays was a common throwaway punishment – 500 words on 'Trout Fishing in the Sahara Desert Without Using the Letter T', or 750 words on 'Life Inside a Table Tennis Ball'. It seemed funny back then, even when you were on the receiving end. Now, at a half century's distance away, it all seems rather puerile. Mind you, it was better than having your head kicked in, which was a very real alternative depending on the depraved mindset of the prefect you had managed to upset. Some welcomed the authority that had been bestowed on them and learned how to use it properly; but many others just assumed they now had a licence to behave like some Marquis de Sade, Irma Grese and Lord Voldemort hybrid breeding experiment gone wrong.

Secker was just typical of the time. A small-minded, insecure young man struggling to work out how to use his newly-conferred authority. Come across such people in the real world and you probably wouldn't even notice them, such is their insignificance. Tiny fish in an ocean. And Stef, Steve, Andy and the others in our circle all had tales of the equivalents in their own houses and dorms. But it was the mid-1970s, hardly the most PC of times. You just got on with it. I vowed I would never behave like Secker and I was true to my word when my turn came to be a dorm prefect to others. By the time we reached our final year we were sharing study bedrooms, two to a room. Nowadays there are very few boarders and those who do board are pampered as though they were a President undergoing a state visit to a foreign country.

I was still pretty musical back then and decided to take up the flute. Mum and Dad shelled out and bought one for me (Santa

Spoiler Alert!) for Christmas 1975 and I was playing it all the time. I became quite proficient, rattling through the various exams, along with exams in piano and theory of music and, annoyingly for those within earshot, I had a crack at the violin too. I say 'annoyingly' because I produced the most awful screeching noise. It sounded like I was strangling a howling banshee. I soon gave that one up. My elder daughter Seanna has the flute now. And, like me, she blitzed it, passed a number of exams, and then it ended up in a drawer somewhere. It'll be my granddaughter's turn next. That Christmas I'd repeated the previous year's feat of singing the solo to open the carol Service. But being in a choir would soon be seen as something completely uncool, and as the hair grew longer and the voice broke, singing in a choir too was ditched.

We had some unbelievably bad teachers at Woodhouse Grove and I have to say that we were astonishingly poorly behaved towards many of them. Mr Noble – I think his Christian name was John – taught us Maths. Badly. Really badly. How the hell I got through the 'O' Level I'll never know (kids – ask your parents what an 'O' Level is; they will tell you, and they will also confirm that they were indeed significantly harder than the easy-peasy GCSEs of today). By now I was more interested in playing up and acting the fool than in calculating cosines and tangents and working on simultaneous equations. Noble had a nervous cough, which we mimicked and took turns repeating loudly behind his back. Every ten seconds. We kept that up for three years. Childish, I know. But then in our defence I suppose we were children.

Our French teacher, Mr Roddick, was another terrible teacher whose life we made hell. He was hopelessly short-sighted and sported a pair of glasses the lenses of which were thicker than a medieval castle wall. We could swap desks, get up and move around, even occasionally leave the classroom. The poor bloke just didn't notice. Again, a miracle that the 'O' Level was passed.

Perhaps the textbook boarding school teacher would have been a fellow called Nicholas Briggs, who taught us Latin. 'Bomber,' as he was known, moved at such a pace up and down the classroom aisles that his black gown trailed high behind him like Batman's cape, and with his slicked back hair and moustache he sported something of the look of Terry Thomas trying out as a porn star. He was another bully. Chuck textbooks at you, smack you over the head, slam the desk on your fingers, hurl the blackboard rubber at you – everything. On the first night at the school Stef and I had been given the hairbrush by Bomber. Yep, exactly as it sounds; you have to bend over and get smacked hard on your backside with an enormous hairbrush (not, despite this being a public school, a euphemism). I can't remember what we were alleged to have done wrong but he loved it (Bomber, that is, not Stef). If ever there was a candidate for auto-erotic sadism, there he was (again, Bomber, not Stef, though come to think of it…). I failed Latin. Twice. Maybe in my own masochistic way I enjoyed the clips round the ear. Duncan, on the other hand, sailed through with an A at 'O' Level, this despite Bomber actually writing a formal letter to my Mum and Dad complaining about Duncan's "strange behaviour in class". This from a bloke who serially yelled, shouted, belted and threw things at you in formal lesson time and whacked you with a hairbrush after dark. But that wasn't considered strange behaviour apparently.

Probably the worst teacher we had, though, was the Reverend Clarke. He had been appointed as the school chaplain and part of the deal was that he had to teach Religious Education to a few of the year groups. Unfortunately, he just wasn't cut out for it. He had no control. And I mean none whatsoever. The man was incapable of controlling a legless spider trapped in a jam jar. After all, he wasn't a teacher. He was a chaplain. We teased him mercilessly, we paid little formal attention to him, we shouted him down – once, famously, as the Headmaster David Miller stood in the doorway, the noise dying down row by row until there was just one lad at the front shouting on his own. We threw textbooks out of the window. We were nothing but an unruly mob. Even the quiet and studious lads like Pat Rawnsley seemed to lose their inhibitions. I don't know how but every single member of that class passed the R.E. 'O' Level a year early. Best grades ever. And I can't tell you how guilty we all felt after he'd left his post. Our behaviour was inexcusable.

One of my favourites was Mr Peel, who took us for German. He recognized that a handful of us weren't interested and he did a deal with us: those who didn't want to learn could sit at the back and do whatever the hell we liked, provided we were quiet and didn't interrupt or put off the handful of hardy souls who wanted to get on. I eventually came round to his way of thinking, joined the learners at the front of the class and even came away with an 'O' Level. I loved

Peel's cynicism and his sarcasm. He looked and sounded as though he really didn't want to be there. But he was actually fun, and very fair.

We all had Housemasters and the head of Southerns was a guy called John Bryant, or 'Fash' as he was known (as in 'fascist'). He had an apartment by the main dormitory, South (yep, yet more hopelessly unoriginal geographical thinking) and you really didn't want to cross him. As his nickname suggested, he had a reputation as a fierce disciplinarian. However, in his case it wasn't gratuitous; punishment was generally only meted out when merited. I managed, somehow, to stay out of his way for seven years, bar the very occasional low-level run-in. In the Upper Sixth, the Southerns contingent of four or five would be invited over from our study bedrooms on a Friday evening to his rooms to have something to eat, generally chew the fat, watch a film. His personality in such situations was a far cry from the character walking the floors during daytime. He treated us like adults. And came across as a really good bloke.

Not that I was a complete rebel but I made life more difficult for myself than I should have. I struggled to be engaged. If there were teachers who weren't able to grab my attention, I found it difficult to focus. And when my concentration went, I wasn't a great influence in that I'd try to pull others in with me. The determined, hardworking youngster from the International School of Milan had become a bit of a disaffected teenager who didn't really want to use his brain. As the years went on I began to resent the whole routine: the daily hour's evening prep; being forced to don a suit and go to church every Sunday; the regimented meal times; the Saturday morning lessons; everything. But I loved the camaraderie and my friends.

At the end of the second year a few of us were asked to sit a series of exams, the leading pupil being awarded what was known as the Henry Price scholarship, which helped towards paying boarding fees. By now Mum and Dad had moved back to the U.K. permanently and although Dad was still spending long periods working overseas, Four Oaks, in Keighley, eleven miles or so from Bradford, was now the family home. Catherine had a scholarship at her school, so did Duncan at ours, so costs were kept within manageable limits, even though I know Mum and Dad made enormous financial sacrifices for the three of us. They gave us the option of giving up the boarding if we wanted to and probably deep down, they would have preferred us to do so as it would save a bit more money. But when I surprised everyone, myself included, by being awarded a share of the scholarship – coincidentally Steve Burnhill was the other recipient – even though the sum was relatively modest, I felt it justified my preference to stay. I knew I'd have to work harder but the truth was that despite the initial forebodings, the bullying and the somewhat Edwardian environment, this was now home. I was settled, acclimatized, independent, tougher, and actually enjoying it.

The best teacher I came across at that time was a man called Ian Cleland, who taught us History. I thought he was brilliant. He treated us like grown-ups all the time, seemed genuinely interested in our opinions and was constantly challenging us, debating with us. He reminded me of the Robin Williams character in the film *Dead Poet's Society*. You were encouraged to disagree provided you could back up your disagreement with at least some line of argument. He liked people to challenge the natural order. He used to take me to one side and offer me advice. Good advice. Often nothing to do with History and more about growing up. I was devastated when he left after we'd completed our 'O' Levels. I'd opted to go on and study History at 'A' Level largely because of him. The two teachers we ended up with – John 'Spotty' Clay and David Wilberforce – just weren't in his league. Cleland taught me a lot more than just History. If anyone asks me now about who my favourite teacher was, he wins, hands down. It's no accident that I have retained a love of History throughout my life.

Sport continued to provide a great 'out'. I enjoyed my cricket and I became more than decent at swimming. But I'd try anything. My first game of rugby union came for the Woodhouse Grove Under-12s against a school called Drax, based out near the Drax power stations on the road to York. We won 10-0 and my first steps as a loose head prop were, I felt, more than likely the early steps towards what was quite clearly going to turn out to be a glittering rugby career. I was a dreamer even then. We thought we were toast after that win. Our next outing, against Pocklington, another York school, finished 60-0. To them. And that, pretty much, was my rugby career right there. A few annual house games for Southerns apart, I don't think I played another game after that year. Certainly not 15-a-side. Steve was the rugby star, going on to be selected for England's tour to South Africa in 1984 and playing for Leicester, Sale, the Barbarians and

Yorkshire. (Though Stef's try as a winger for the Old Grovians against the school First XV in September 1982 has the edge in terms of rugby legend. I didn't see it. But having heard tell of it at every gathering since then I feel as though I was there.)

In cricket, I played for all of the age group sides right through to the First XI. A non-ball-turning off-spinner and middle order batsman, a demon spell of 6 for 6 for the Colts (Under-16s) against Trent College was the school career highlight. And I made 55 in the same game. Although I did make the First XI I was largely a peripheral figure, to be honest, bar the very occasional contribution. From that side Simon Kippax, his brother Chris, and Bruce Percy each went on to play Minor County cricket. But Stef was the leading light in our year group. A left arm seam bowler who was also possessed of the heaviest bat known to humankind – 'the log' as it was christened – he was quite sharp. In one Colts game against Bradford Grammar School he took umbrage at Ashley Metcalfe, later to play for Yorkshire, coming out to bat in a helmet. 'F***ing poser, he'll need it now. I'll show 'im,' he chuntered, before proceeding to bounce Metcalfe out and give him the full 'Get Out' send off in his follow through, helpfully pointing out where the pavilion was with a digit-led physical demonstration. And he was still playing club cricket in York – mainly for his average, it has to be said – well into his 50s.

Swimming was where I really found myself, however, and I eventually won school colours and plenty of races and medals, mainly in backstroke and butterfly. I've already made mention of coming up against Adrian Moorhouse in the Northern Schools' relays. We'd reached the semi-finals, held at Bootham School in York, and we really fancied our chances, with the fastest two teams going through to the national finals. I always started on backstroke, followed by Rich Penniall on breaststroke, Bruce Tomlinson (Andy's younger brother) on butterfly, with David Privett bringing us home. After the backstroke leg I was neck and neck with the Bradford Grammar swimmer. Rich dived in alongside Moorhouse. And emerged ten metres behind. Over the two lengths, he came in over two thirds of a length behind. We didn't qualify. As with the early rugby union, we were nowhere near as good as we'd imagined.

Meal times were much like the inmates' dining experience in the BBC comedy series *Porridge*: hold out your tray, someone would slop something onto your plate, you'd ask what it was, the kitchen staff would shrug their shoulders, and then you'd pull a face as you headed towards the benches you shared with your house mates. As you progressed through the years, you'd move closer toward the top of the main hall (I refuse to call it a refectory), but the food didn't get any better. Plum tomatoes on toast were about the only meal you could eat in the full knowledge of what the ingredients actually were. I can picture the eggs now. Like those Haribo jelly eggs, only bigger and even more rubbery looking. Stick a fork into the yolk and instead of watching the yolk ooze out you were more likely to have ended up breaking the prongs on your fork. And they tasted like rubber too.

My stint as a dorm prefect (I never reached the giddy heights of being a school prefect like Andy, Steve, John, Andrew and Denis, which is perhaps why me and Stef have always roomed together on our golf trips) was a total contrast to when I was the twelve-year-old on the other end. We had a laugh. Disciplined, yes, but always fairly. We also tried to introduce a few new traditions for the generations to follow, such as the 'Chippy Run.' Every other Friday after lights out we'd send a couple of the lads down the West fire escape, out of the school grounds and up the road half a mile or so to the chip shop. 15 orders for fish, chips, fish cakes, pasties, whatever. How the smell in the dorm afterwards never gave us away I'll never know. It probably did. I can't believe that John Bryant wouldn't have been fully aware of exactly what was going on.

I never had myself down as a thespian – Andy was the one who demonstrated acting tendencies, later going on to play a policeman in both *Coronation Street* and *The New Statesman*, as well as taking the key (and largely made up by me) extras role of Man Behind Man With Line in Series 3, Episode 5 of *All Creatures Great and Small* – but for some reason I was asked to play a part in Robert Bolt's *A Man For All Seasons* in my lower sixth year. I didn't think I'd shown any acting potential up to then so I'm unsure what the talent-spotters (aka Alec Andrews and Phil Silk, our English teachers) had seen in me. But my one showstopping scene as Cardinal Wolsey must have been an absolute belter because I was picked out and asked to play Iago in Shakespeare's *Othello* the following year. "Sure," I said, having been asked if I would be interested, thinking "how hard can that be?" Really bloody hard, actually. At 1,097 lines, Iago speaks more lines in the play than Othello himself, and more than any other non-title character in Shakespeare's entire back catalogue (amazing tool, Wikipedia, isn't it?). My highlight was a cock-up though. A missed cue in the dress rehearsal resulted in Tony Walker (Rodrigo) standing idly for a minute or so at the front of the stage when he should have been dead. Amateurs, eh. I improvised. As soon as I realized he should be dead, I just reached over and 'stabbed' him. Seamless. I thought I was rather good. And Denis fell to the ground spectacularly theatrically too. I still wonder at how I remembered all those lines. I guess a memory trained on all those Scottish League Second Division Champions back to 1910 probably helped.

For our first few years at Woodhouse Grove it was just us lads together. All 550-odd of us. The only women on site were a handful of teaching and clerical staff. When we were in the fourth year there was an intake of half a dozen girls in the upper sixth form, with a similar number coming along in each year thereafter. Of course, the whole place is completely mixed now but back in the late 1970s the appearance of girls in an all-boys school was a real novelty. When we reached sixth form a few years later it still was. I must admit to a couple of dalliances myself, but I'll spare the girls the shame of being identified in what is so obviously going to be a major bestseller for fear the embarrassment and public shame could tip them over the edge. I wouldn't wish the paparazzi on anyone.

Stef was our somewhat unlikely champion in this field. Steve, Andrew, John, Tony and I tested the waters, as most young men of our age probably would. Andy was keen to dabble but by his own admission was probably a bit too neurotic in that final year to get too far. But Stef, the very embodiment of the direct Yorkshireman, succeeded by presumably just getting straight to the point. The names of the conquests of our very own Pool Bank Lothario are legendary within our circle and we toast them on every golfing trip. School discos were hilarious events. Once a term our sixth form would host the sixth form of a nearby girls' school, with hilarious consequences. All of our lot believed they possessed the looks of a Richard Gere and the moves of a John Travolta. The girls were probably just squirming in horrified anticipation of the cringeworthy chat-up lines they were about to be subjected to. Suffice to say the chat-up action was generally muted, the lowlights of those discos generally involving a couple of lads throwing up, a fight between a few more (often started innocently by Chris Schofield, who was a particularly aggressive mover on the dance floor and loved nothing more than showcasing

64

his breakdancing skills to any record – Boney M, Captain Sensible, Abba, whatever, it didn't matter – though he was astute enough to have long disappeared when any fighting actually became serious). The field was generally then clear for someone – often Stef – to nip in and see what's what. We never really learned etiquette or what approach might prove successful with the ladies. We were so wet behind the ears we may as well have been fully submerged in water. And we were more often than not too pissed to make too much headway anyway.

We had started our boozing, as was obligatory back then, with Woodpecker cider, moving on, for some reason, straight to Carlsberg Special Brew. From 3.9% ABV to 8%. Like you do. It was like learning to drive in a clapped-out Renault Clio and then test-driving a Bugatti Veyron. Having graduated from occasional trips to the local off licences on Saturday evenings, drinking our ill-gotten gains in the fields a couple of miles away from the school grounds, we became a bit more emboldened and moved on to expeditions to pubs in the local Rawdon area. These were, in truth, rather pathetic. We carried the borrowed driving licences of other, older lads with us as proof of identity. I mean, who would instantly produce a paper driving licence in 1978 as proof of ID? We would have given ourselves away with the rounds we ordered anyway – the odd pint of Tetleys mixed with a pernod and blackcurrant or a vodka and lime – so it was far more than likely we were being tolerated and indulged by sympathetic landlords who welcomed the cash.

Mum, when she found out that I smoked, used to bring in cigarettes on the odd Sunday when she came to the school church service on an occasional Sunday. Not that this legitimized my habit, you understand. She hated the fact that I had taken it up but it was difficult for her, as a smoker herself, to be too judgmental. She also hated it when I suggested she was actually smuggling contraband into school. Sadly, having started on the fags in late 1980 it took me until the end of September 2007 to give them up. Still off them, though.

Opposite West dorm was a building called the Sixth Form Centre. When we reached the lower sixth, we used to hang out there as a group, playing vinyl records (there weren't any other kind in those days) and idling away our free time. Andrew North and I were regulars, listening to music and enjoying the odd illicit beer and cigarette. One night we in West (I was one of the dorm prefects at that point) were awoken to the sight of the Sixth Form Centre building on fire. The fire drills we all hated having to undertake at other times were re-enacted for the only time I can remember when there was an actual genuine emergency taking place. We'll never know for sure how the fire started but the smart money was on an unextinguished cigarette and as there were only a few of us who used to smoke in there, we were target market in terms of school gossip and folklore. Thankfully, though, we weren't target market in the eyes of the fire service or the police. I suppose it might have been us but who knows? Andrew, along with another of our pals Jim Dale, and a couple of others were part of the 'Fire Squad' that represented the school's first line of defence against any outbreak of fire. Not that they would do anything but point a hose in the general direction of the flames but they were subsequently pictured in the local paper the following week doing exactly that and looking suitably moody and heroic, Andrew in the role of possible-poacher-turned-gamekeeper.

School holidays were idyllic. When not on family breaks in locations as diverse as Corsica, Skye, Anglesey, Norfolk, Mid-Wales and Provence, Four Oaks was perfect. The garden was big enough for us to have our own games of cricket, often involving a line-up of Duncan's and my soft toys playing against a team of flowers or some such in our own made-up Test matches. One of those soft toys didn't actually possess any arms but was down on the scorecard as a quick bowler. Impressive skills. There was a large field above the house where we'd repair with Dad's golf clubs, trying to avoid hitting the cows that were grazing there. We'd also cycle for miles around Utley, Braithwaite and Laycock without coming across any real traffic, and there was even room enough for penalty shoot outs at the front of the house, albeit resulting in the occasional broken window. In the cellar rooms we set up an impromptu table tennis table on a concrete slab, with a dart board in a room next door. Non-stop activity. The holidays flew by.

My memories of Four Oaks are of fantastic Christmases and basically playing out all day every day on what seemed to be perennially sunny Spring and Summer holidays. I'm sure that wasn't the case, but it certainly felt like it. Apart from the persistent racket made by the crows, a minor annoyance, it was perfect, and the slightest trigger can take me back there: from *Morecambe and Wise* to Saturday tea in front of *Doctor Who*; children's TV programmes in the holidays to watching Test matches next door on my Grandad's black and white TV; Labour politics and strikes and the rise of Thatcherism to Christmas *Top Of The Pops*; *M*A*S*H* and *High Chaparral* on BBC2 to blu-tacked *Shoot!* posters and league ladders on the wall. As with Milan, it was a happy place. Bloody cold, but happy. In later holidays, when I was older, I'd spend long periods of time with Andrew North at his house in Ilkley. Or with another close pal Dave Tillotson, pootling around between Keighley and Skipton in his Citroen 2CV.

By now music was beginning to take an increasing hold on me. I had an old radiogram and used to spend hours listening to records, or to David Jensen and John Peel on the radio of an evening. Music-wise, Jim Dale was always one step ahead of the rest of us and it was he who introduced me to the likes of Joy Division, Killing Joke, Bauhaus and The Cure. In my first term at Trent Polytechnic in Nottingham he sent me a tape with all sorts of new stuff on it. I still have it. Sadly, I no longer have a cassette player on which to play it. But I have it as a playlist on the computer. Dave T, too, was a keen music follower. We shared a love of, amongst others, The The and Prefab Sprout. I bumped into Dave again after 15 years of no contact – he'd been living in Hong Kong – and was pleasantly surprised that the new bands we were listening to were very similar. Not a lot had changed.

As we hurtled towards our 'A' Level exams one or two of us chose that moment to switch off academically. I really wish I'd worked harder. I felt something of a hypocrite in later years telling Seanna and Hannah about the importance of them working hard at school. Mainly because I didn't. I was unfocused and lazy. I did manage to achieve the grades I needed to go on and study Media & Communications at Trent Polytechnic (now Nottingham Trent University) but it was a close-run thing. And it needed an 'A' Level in General Studies, which was just a glorified general knowledge test, to (Sky Sports cliché coming up, folks) get me over the line. It was the end of an era. Andy and Steve were going to Loughborough, John to Leeds, Andrew to Liverpool, Greg had left before sixth form, and Stef had decided against going to University and had already joined the Inland Revenue in Shipley. The rumour that this had something to do with the fact that he and his room-mate Mark Hammes had been caught on the last night with two of the kitchen staff in their study bedroom, one of them in the process of being shoved into a cupboard as a teacher walked in, was never substantiated. It was a pity, anyway. If ever there was University form, there it was. Stef was a huge loss to higher education.

Stef was a passionate York City supporter and even managed to get himself gated (confined to barracks) for a whole term after being caught 'nipping out' from school in Bradford to watch them in a cup game. At Nottingham Forest. Years later Arsenal were drawn at York in the FA Cup fourth round. I was in Nottingham myself by now but we agreed we had to go to the game, though I wanted to stand with the away fans at the Bootham End, Stef and his dad taking up their normal season ticket seats in the main stand. It didn't end well. For me, anyway. Steve Williams gave away a penalty in the last minute of a game that may as well have been played on a skating rink it was so snowy and slippery. Keith Houchen scored and York pulled off one of the competition's biggest-ever shocks. Stef's grin was wider than the mouth of the Amazon. But it was never a penalty in a million years. I was sneakily delighted when Liverpool thumped them 7-0 in the next round.

The summer of '82 – or at least the weeks immediately before receiving my 'A' Level results – I recall with a smile. We had a couple of weeks in a place called Aix-Les-Bains (Ayks Lez Baynes, as pronounced phonetically by my Leodensian (i.e. from Leeds) Grandad, who once later tried to pass off Viv Richards as 'that Cliff Richard what plays cricket for your Welsh lot'). I even took a load of vinyl singles as we were driving there and there was a record player on the farm we were staying at. The holiday was fondly remembered as much for one of Mum's many memorable statements as for anything else. On a rainy Sunday afternoon post lunch Dad, Duncan and I were watching a Grand Prix on the TV and Catherine was reading a book. Other than the commentary to the formula one we had the relatively rare situation in the Fatkin household of relative calm and silence. Normally there were at least four voices, carrying out four completely separate conversations. Ears were a family luxury. Without looking up from her knitting, Mum announced: "There are some dominos in the cupboard, you know." We assume she had interpreted silence as boredom. We still use the phrase occasionally.

Trent Poly was an eye opener. All of the things I'd been prevented from doing at Woodhouse Grove – drinking, smoking, missing lessons, mixing with girls, staying out stupidly late – were on the agenda at Trent as soon as we arrived on campus. It was here that I learned – *really* learned – about the opposite sex; and here that I started to understand and appreciate alcohol, what I liked and what I didn't. I used to be a bitter drinker (a drinker of bitter, not someone who sits hunched over his beer glass and chunters away endlessly about the world being against him (though I am doing that more and more frequently as I get older)), but the taste, the wind, the bloating and the thick heads put me off over the next few years. Since then I've never had a hangover. The less said about the wind, the better.

We were based at the satellite campus in Clifton, a few miles South West of Nottingham, in a couple of dozen 'blocks' of accommodation. I was billeted in F Block (sensationally creative nomenclature, I'm sure you'd agree; it seems to have been following me around) and among the characters I came across were Paul White, Pete Davies, Andrew Keighley and Ian Curryer. Ian went on to be Chief Executive of Nottingham City Council, something I would never have had him down to when he was watching *Will O' The* Wisp and listening to Huang Chung whilst lovingly preparing what could be termed 'interesting smoking material' during his training as a primary school teacher. The first year was just a blast. I don't remember doing too much work – which led to me having to resit two of my exams – but I do remember the gigs, the trips into town, student nights at Rock City, the football (both Nottingham Forest and Notts County were in the top flight at that time), the girls and the drinking.

Rock City was an amazing venue. My music tastes had moved on and I was in my existentialist phase, by now heavily into new wave and post punk. I must have spent much of my first-year grant on attending gigs – Bauhaus, The Cure, Simple Minds, Billy Bragg, the Psychedelic Furs, Prefab Sprout, Killing Joke, the Sisters of Mercy, A Flock of Seagulls, New Order, Squeeze…. I was at a gig every week. On Thursdays, designated student night, a whole gang of us would pile into Rock City after having been on the pop in town for several hours. It was a huge place, with a massive dance floor, obviously there to accommodate a sizeable standing audience for the concerts. On one occasion my pal John Lloyd dared me – the princely temptation of one pint – that I wouldn't last out in the middle on my own for a complete song. During the early part of the evening, up to around 10.30, there were very few people venturing out onto the floor even though the venue was pretty full. "You're on," I said. He'd chosen Aztec Camera's *Walk Out To Winter*. Not so bad, I thought. But it soon dawned on me that he'd gone for the 12" version, all eight minutes of it, the intro on its own lasting well over four minutes. But I'd do anything for a pint. Challenge accepted. And reward earned. I got a substantial round of applause when I came off. Such was the shortage of money we'd spend much of the evening looking out for groups who had left half-drunk pints to go and dance, and then just hoover up what they left behind. I also now have, courtesy of my sister Catherine, a piece of that same dance floor, sold off when they replaced it. I like to think my size tens have featured on that very piece of wood.

My time at Trent Poly shaped my politics. Towards the end of our second year the miners went out on strike, and the strike lasted well into our third. Nottinghamshire was right at the heart of the strike and it's fair to say that of all of the coal regions it was the most divided. It meant miners and the many others who supported them focused much of their attention on the county. It was bitter and nasty, frequently violent. I still have one of the 'Coal not Dole' button badges but even though I now understand much more about the whole thing – the economic arguments and the refusal to ballot in particular – it fuelled my political beliefs. I'm sure I wasn't the only one who couldn't bring himself to shed a tear when Margaret Thatcher eventually died in 2013. Whatever the rights and wrongs of her ideological argument, and economically she was often right, she essentially ploughed on, displaying little compassion or empathy, not giving two hoots about the destruction of entire communities and the livelihoods of thousands of working people.

I look back on some of the old photos from this period and to say that I was an '80s stereotype wouldn't be at all unkind. Towards the end of year one I was wandering around Clifton campus with suede boots on, sporting a mullet that would have turned Chris Waddle shamrock green with envy. I compounded these fashion faux pas by attempting to grow a moustache early in year three. Not my finest decision. If you imagine the negative of a photo of Adolf Hitler's moustache, that was what it looked like: gap at the centre, with two bum-fluff-riddled wings. That it lasted several weeks is all the more remarkable. It was pathetic. Why Carol – my future wife, whom I'd met at the end of year one and started going out with at the beginning of year two – didn't immediately run a mile in the opposite direction is even more remarkable. A suave, debonair Errol Flynn I most certainly was not.

In the first year, and this may come as something of a surprise to those who've only known me in my dotage, I was quite a catch. I was half the weight I am now, for starters. But I was genuinely more interested in beer, music and football than in girls. I still am, if the truth be told. There were a few dalliances, of course, as you might expect, especially in a city reputed to have a ratio of women to men of 4:1, but just as at Woodhouse Grove, the names of the innocent will be protected. Most of them. I was stalked in the first two terms by a girl called Virginia, or 'Gin' as she insisted on being known. And I mean stalked. She popped up everywhere. She even managed to write something in one of the books I kept in my room in F Block while I was away watching Arsenal lose spectacularly 0-3 at the City Ground (The Arsenal sporting a shocking green and navy away kit, as I recall). The room was locked. I still have no idea how she got in. Glenn Close had nothing on her. Lovely looking girl, pleasant enough, but I thought she was more than a little unhinged.

My first year at Trent didn't end in a fanfare. The exams shouldn't have been too taxing to anyone who had turned up to the lectures and done a bit of reading but I was too casual and I hadn't paid any attention to the need to get my head down and revise. A familiar tale. I was out every night in Nottingham enjoying myself, dipping into Mum and Dad's emergency money, having long since spent the grant that we used to enjoy back in those days (before it was abolished in England). The fact that I was enjoying myself wasn't being replicated up and down the country, was it? Students wouldn't do that in large numbers, surely. I managed to correct things in years two and three, revision consisting of endless lists of mnemonics memorized whilst knocking back whisky and coke to the accompaniment of loud music. Not exactly textbook academic study but it managed to see me through to a safe but unspectacular 2:2 degree.

The summer of 1983 was special. Having re-sat my first year exams, Dave T and I and a couple of pals headed up in his 2CV to the Lake District for a week's holiday. I still tell Seanna, who of my two daughters is probably the more interested in my general taste in music, that it was one of the finest years for music, though it has been

71

ridiculed by one or two so-called musical experts. A whole chunk of my favourite songs hail from that year and the journeys around the towns of Cumbria were accompanied by classics from the Lotus Eaters, The The, the B-52's (misplaced apostrophe and all), Aztec Camera, The Smiths, New Order, Altered Images…. hazy, happy days. We drove up to see two of my friends from Trent Poly, Sue Coughlan and Lorraine Pater, in deepest Cumbria. They promised us a night out in Whitehaven. Wow. And I thought Keighley was a ghost town. In comparison to Whitehaven it was Vegas Plus. We ended up at a disco in a rugby club in the middle of nowhere, and this time I managed to dance on my own to a segued mix of *Baby Jane* by Rod Stewart and *Give It Up* by KC and the Sunshine Band. Ok, so maybe 1983 <u>wasn't</u> that great a music year. And I acknowledge that there are now alarming signs of a trend as far as drinking too much and then venturing out for some solo dancing. That trend was upheld, spectacularly, as late as 2014, on my 50th birthday. But I take comfort that whilst everyone around me would have been embarrassed I was far too far gone to be giving a monkey's.

The summer of 1983 also saw me venture to Trent Bridge, but not to watch Nottinghamshire play cricket, even though, for the final two years at Poly, we lived on the Musters Road just behind the ground, but to watch a World Cup match between Australia and Zimbabwe. The former were massive favourites but somehow, led by some bloke called Duncan Fletcher, Zimbabwe pulled off one of the great World Cup shocks, Fletcher scoring 69 not out and taking 4-42. 14 years later and we were working together. But I'm sorry, Fletch; I don't remember that much about it. I was probably pissed again.

Right next to the Trent Bridge ground is a pub called the Trent Bridge Inn, or 'TBI' as it's known. We enjoyed many an evening in there partaking of happy hour (as students do) before heading into the city for a night out. The early evening of my 21st birthday was spent there as a whole gang of us sampled the pub's cocktail menu. Being the stubborn northerner that I was, I eschewed any notion of a fruity cocktail. I wasn't having any of those poncy daiquiris or umbrellas ruining my reputation as a beer drinker. Oh no. So I settled for something that sounded a little more manly: a Rusty Nail. Double whisky, double Drambuie, and a twist of lemon. As if the lemon would somehow make any substantial difference to its potency. I was wolfing them back to the extent that when, the following day, Carol said it was nice to have seen Jane and Neil (two other Poly friends) out in The Bell with us I had to confess that I didn't remember them being there. Apparently, I'd been talking to them for an hour. Carol also had to follow me off the last bus back to West Bridgford just as we'd taken our seats and as I disappeared into the underground toilets in Market Square in the centre of Nottingham she was left to hang around and wait for me. I could have been hours, bless her. Mum and Dad were due down the following day to take us out for Sunday lunch. I eventually spent the night on the bathroom floor. The only reason Carol knew I was still alive was the fact that I was snoring.

I tried really hard to get Carol into football but she just wasn't interested. Not a jot. She still isn't. She preferred the theatre or the cinema. The former I've enjoyed from time to time but I've never really been a cinemagoer. Other than with kids in tow the last film I saw at the cinema was *Ghostbusters*, in Keighley back in the Summer of 1984. But she did get dragged to one game: Nottingham Forest against Everton on a wet midweek Tuesday in March 1984. A positively dreadful 1-0 home win (Steve Hodge in the last minute). She couldn't see anything, it was wet, and it was freezing. Not surprisingly, she never showed any interest in attending another. Probably the only other football crowd encounter she had would have experienced would be when Celtic were in Nottingham for a UEFA Cup tie in late November 1983. We nipped round the corner from our digs for fish and chips only to find, at just before six o'clock, the place wasn't open, so we decided to pop across the road for a quiet one in the Test Match pub. Did I say 'quiet one'? As we opened the doors we were greeted by a sea of green and white, bodies everywhere, fans jumping over the counter to help themselves to drinks. Not sure that would have helped me in selling football to her. "It's just a few lads in high spirits before the game, love." Seanna showed some interest in later years, travelling with me a dozen or so times up to Highbury and once, with Hannah, to the Emirates. Hannah's only other game was a 4-0 thrashing of Charlton at Highbury, but it included a back-heeled Thierry Henry goal that's still one of my all-time favourites. So the ladies in my life didn't have much of an appetite for football. You can't win them all, I guess, though I still retain hopes that their respective other halves can win them over. In the meantime I am working on my granddaughter, Willow...

For year two I was supposed to be sharing a house in the Meadows area with Andrew Keighley and three other girls. I think I must have spent the sum total of five nights there over the course of the whole academic year. By now Carol and I were very much a couple and I was far more interested in being with her over the other side of the River Trent in West Bridgford, where she shared a house with her friends Sue Fitzsimons and Helen Cocker and a couple of others. In year three we shared a house with half a dozen friends on the Musters Road, not very far away. I somehow muddled through my final year. Andrew, who was on the same course as me, scraped a 3rd. But we fared better than another of our mates, Steve Gilder, who decided with just six weeks of his three-year course to go, to drop out. He was last heard of driving a truck over in the United States.

Somehow, despite any excuse to bunk off lectures and play pool or darts while hogging the jukebox in the Embankment on the Trent, university was complete, and it was on to the summer of '85: a summer of *Live Aid*, Dave's 2CV, local pubs, Gower's Ashes and visits to see Duncan, by now established at Oxford University, demonstrating that a bright-spark-and-hard-work combination did actually work. But as the weeks went by it dawned on me that my lazy days were over. I'd only worked once in my life – an eight-week spell at a factory manufacturing cotton and wool in Howarth the previous year – and I now had to get my arse into gear and start looking. A sobering thought.

Carol opted to stay in Nottingham for a year after we'd both graduated. Sue and Helen had spent a year out in France as part of their course and they wouldn't graduate until the following summer, so Carol shared a house with them while I set out to find work back in the People's Republic of West Yorkshire, with fortnightly trips down to Nottingham, alternating with Carol coming up to Keighley, or to Halifax, where her family lived. By now we were engaged, following a predictably unromantic proposal which essentially involved me just offering up a ring and hoping for a positive reaction. I was now a responsible young adult, with a lame degree in an off-piste topic, and with a fiancée. Dad said it was high time to grow up, on one of the rare occasions he was around and showing an interest.

Finding work didn't prove that easy. I applied for over 200 jobs between August 1985 and March 1986. I had interviews for management training courses with Virgin Megastores, Mars and

Deloittes; I was offered unpaid work experience on the Keighley News; and I attended a couple of other interviews, but it's safe to say that my CV wasn't a world-beater, even in an era when having a degree was relatively uncommon. I was making no headway. I recall Duncan and a couple of his mates being home in late March 1986 and after a few too many drinks I broke down, bawling my eyes out wondering where on earth I was going. I'd continued to apply for all sorts of jobs, the overwhelming majority of which I knew in my heart of hearts that I'd either be totally unsuited for or would hate, but nothing was happening. I was getting nowhere. My career hadn't so much stalled as been left at the starting gate.

By now, as well as a passion for football I'd developed a real love of cricket and this set me thinking. My interest had started by watching passages of England's Test matches in the summer of 1971 and the Ashes in 1972 with my Grandad when we were over on holiday from Italy. He and my Grandma had moved to Keighley from Leeds after Mum and Dad bought Four Oaks. The Lodge next door came as part of the purchase, and they had moved in there. Grandad was very patient with me, explaining what was going on and highlighting the tactics and some of the laws of the game (never rules, as I later learned to my cost by mentioning it in front of Reg Simpson, the Nottinghamshire President at the time, and getting a real verbal hammering about not knowing better). I ended up going next door as my Dad couldn't watch the BBC coverage without moaning about one of the commentators, Jim Laker, and specifically his habit of dropping Gs – 'innin's', 'winnin', 'beginnin' – it drove Dad mad to the extent where he'd want to turn the sound down or worse, switch the TV off completely. Grandad was a little more tolerant, mainly because, like Laker, he wasn't scared of dropping a G either. Alan Knott was an early favourite of mine. Half a dozen years on and David Gower was the player I watched religiously. He'd captained England to a 3-1 Ashes series win in 1985, hitting three easy-on-the-eye hundreds in the process, so I picked out his county boss, a man called Mike Turner, who was Secretary of Leicestershire County Cricket Club, Gower's county, and wrote to him offering to work for nothing for six months. I'm not quite sure what I was expecting to happen but Mike actually wrote back, which was not only very kind, but which by today's standards would have represented something of a miracle. He couldn't offer me anything but he generously provided addresses for the other sixteen counties, with the names of the Secretary at each club. I wrote to all of them, enclosing my content-light and Tippex-pockmarked CV. By the time of that Easter weekend with Duncan, one or two had started to come back but although they each offered encouraging words (and it's interesting that several of those who did respond subsequently became county cricket colleagues and friends – Steve Coverdale, Chris Hassell, Tim Lamb, Mike Vockins), none of them felt able to give me a go. I was running out of ideas and at a real loss as to what I was going to do next.

And then the phone rang.

4 LIVING IN ANOTHER WORLD

'I like to think if I'd stuck with cricket I could have been a Welsh Ian Botham.'
NICKY WIRE

My early days at Glamorgan were pretty responsibility-free too. Given the chance to shine in county cricket, the inhabitants of the world into which I'd been catapulted came from across the spectrum: from 'Smudger' and 'Nobby' to some well-meaning but generally hopeless septuagenarian stewards. This section contains a few early lessons as well as my first brush with stardom, involving a spectacular (but deserved) put-down from one of the game's legends.

"Hello, could I speak to Michael?"

It was with that simple question that my long association with Glamorgan County Cricket Club began. It was a Monday morning in early April 1986 and the voice on the other end of the phone belonged to Philip Carling, Glamorgan's Secretary. (I always thought it was a bit of a demeaning word – 'Secretary' – for someone who was *de facto* running the organization, but what mattered here was that Philip was the decision-maker.) This was probably more than just a chat and a few encouraging words, I thought to myself, otherwise why bother ringing?

"I received your letter," he went on. "There might be some work here. I just wondered if you'd like to pop in for a chat some time over the next few days." My heart sank. A chat. A different way (and with the cost of the train journey, a far more expensive way) of convincing me that they'd end up hanging on to my (tippex-riddled) CV in case something turned up, but that if I kept working hard, well, you never know, blah blah. Yeah, righto. And he must surely know that the edge of the Yorkshire Dales down to Cardiff is more than just a hop. He probably assumes I can drive as well. But then only one of us was desperate for any kind of opportunity.

"Of course," I said, the words coming out of my mouth in almost antithetical proportion to what I was actually thinking. Not as though I had too many other competing commitments, was it? "When would suit you?" I asked, expecting him perhaps to suggest a day the following week. When I'd put the phone down, I'd just committed to being in Cardiff three days hence. It might have been even sooner, but the following day I was due to travel all the way down to deepest Cornwall for an interview for a place on a national radio journalism course. The course itself was run in London but for some inexplicable reason the interviews were being held in Falmouth, nearer to Cork than to London. Or so it seemed. And now I would have to get myself up to Cardiff for a first-thing-in-the-morning meeting with Glamorgan, having stayed the second night miles away in Oxford with Duncan. Without a car. Yeah, good one Mike.

Having made my way from Oxford to Cardiff on the milk train there I was, in my – ahem – fashionable navy blue Arsenal tank top, student greatcoat and Duran-Duran mulleted hair, strolling through Sophia Gardens for 'a chat'. Glamorgan's cricket ground, when I eventually located it, having initially wandered off in completely the wrong direction, didn't exactly knock me for six, to use that well-worn cricketing cliché. A portacabin, which housed their admin function, a tiny scoreboard, some rickety seats and a pavilion that wouldn't have looked out of place architecturally in 1950s East Berlin and, well, that was about it. Panoramic it most certainly was not. It turned out the club had actually been operating out of offices in the centre of Cardiff until just a few months previously. They'd fought tooth and nail to persuade Cardiff Athletic Club, their landlords, to let them to put up some sort of temporary structure to allow them to run a county cricket club from an actual county cricket ground, instead of from the top floor of some rented offices on St Mary Street half a mile away in the centre of the city. Looking back, that was quite a step they'd taken right there. And here I was sneeringly taking in the view and drawing all sorts of condescending conclusions. I certainly wasn't envisaging myself in that environment.

Being honest, I don't remember anything at all about the chat with Philip. I was probably half asleep. But either I impressed him or he was more desperate than I thought because two weeks later I was back down in Cardiff, officially working for a county cricket club. I even had a title: I was the rather glamorously billed 'Administrative Assistant'. Philip was kind enough to keep his thoughts about my appearance to himself for a respectable few months before telling me what his initial reaction to my tank top/greatcoat/mullet combo had been. But by then I had my feet under the table and he seemed to be pleased with the contribution I was making, even if it took me a while to realise that my faux George Michael-cum-Charlie Nicholas look wasn't going to prove a winner with the average septuagenarian Glamorgan Member.

The interview in Falmouth had also gone well because they too had made me an offer of a place on the course. But even though Glamorgan weren't proposing to pay me anything – just a bit of pocket money and use of a former player's flat – I was by now smitten with the idea of working in professional sport. Peripheral I may have been, at the very bottom of the corporate food chain, but a door had opened and I was through it. Mind you, for someone who later on in his administrative career prided himself on his contract negotiating skills that first 'chat' hadn't exactly gone according to plan. I'd walked in with ideas of seriously half-decent salaries in my head, maybe even a car – to hell with the fact that I couldn't even drive – only to discover, on being told that the deal was six months in return for nothing but a roof over my head and a few quid to cover basic food, that I was as acquiescent as an overly trusting Labrador puppy rolling over to have its tummy tickled. To be fair, Philip would teach me a lot about negotiating. He was very good at it. He would have haggled for sofa space with his Nan. And wouldn't have cared how upset his Nan was when he won.

And so I found myself back in Cardiff a fortnight later, with what I had convinced myself would be a career. I'm not sure Mum and Dad believed it would actually amount to anything other than six months-worth of unpaid experience, but I didn't really give a fig. I had wanted to find a way into sport and here was a way. The fact that I knew very little about county cricket, Glamorgan or indeed Wales was largely irrelevant. I could learn. All I'd wanted was some kind of opportunity.

My office colleagues were a motley collection, and we didn't exactly amount to much in terms of number, either. Other than Philip there was his secretary – the Secretary has a secretary, but this person wasn't at that stage an Assistant Secretary, which I will (try to) explain – Sue Wood; the pipe-smoking book-keeper, Mostyn Stacey, who despite conveying the outward appearance of someone who had lived two full lives and was now the merest of gentle pushes away from a retirement home I was astonished to find he had yet to reach 50 years of age; two receptionists/typists, one of whom, although perfectly pleasant, appeared to possess the intellectual capacity of a Savoy cabbage; and then there was the Marketing Assistant, one Tony Dilloway.

Tony and I had nothing in common. And I mean absolutely nothing. I was a smoking beer-drinker from Yorkshire, he was a non-smoking wine connoisseur from Essex; he was arty, I wasn't; I loved football, he had only a passing interest in it; I 'got' cricket, he didn't pretend to; he would happily schmooze all day, I loathed the very thought. I guess I was 'a Northern lad', and he was what I would previously have termed 'a Southerner'. OK, so I know I'm really pigeonholing and stereotyping for effect here, but it's my tale, so that's how it is. However, despite those apparent personality contradictions, our relationship somehow just clicked. After the first time we went to a meeting together and he politely suggested that I bring his bag, receiving in return the sort of withering look I normally reserved for people who asked me why I didn't like Manchester United, we got on handsomely. Sure, we would have our issues and disagreements, more often than not to do with his lamentable driving or his illiterate handwriting (imagine dipping an inebriated spider in ink and then charting its course as it scuttled across the page, and you have it) but Tony was to be a key part of my working life for fully fifteen years.

A small, but perfectly formed crew, I liked to think. Sort of. Sue and I would run all of the match day stuff, with Tony dropping in and out depending on any meetings he may have arranged, though he would always be around for the one-day games; Philip picking and choosing any outground appearances based on the weather and state of the game, which I guess was his right as the boss. When there, he focused on the big conversations – with committee, with the journalists (of which there were a goodly number present every match day back then in an era when people actually bought and read newspapers and listened to the radio), and with the players. In short, Philip had all the important-but-fun stuff. All of the match day dirge, all of the dealing with the ever-present grouses from the membership, was down to Sue and me, occasionally Tony.

We had a ragtag collection of stewards to help us. I say 'stewards' but they were a far cry from the army-style, fully-trained stewards of the post-Hillsborough era – all hi-vis bibs, über-efficiency and CVs choc-full of NVQs (though often possessed of all the charm and grace of a lobotomized glove puppet). No, these were generally longstanding pensioners who had a bit of time on their hands. They loved a chat. And I mean *loved* a chat. They couldn't balance the smallest of takings on the gate at the end of a day and they wouldn't have been remotely effective in the event of even the mildest of spats breaking out between spectators or corporate guests, but there they stood, white-coated and generally moving at all the wrong times when the bowling was from their end, or nonchalantly allowing an army of admission-dodging schoolchildren in while their backs were turned chatting to old pals. One of them was so fixated with his meagre 20p-per-scorecard takings he completely missed the fact that on every match day dozens of potentially paying spectators were pouring into the ground behind him while he counted his £3.80. Or, more likely, as he couldn't actually get anything right, £3.37.

Part of my match day role was to pinpoint where we were going to deploy these geriatric ninjas so as to see them at their most effective, as if they were hardened SAS agents operating on their own specialist missions: "We'll put Les on the sight screens, Ronnie can cover the vice presidents, Des on the main gate, I think, and we need Hamlyn up on the pavilion bar steps; two non-members got in last week." As if Hamlyn was some kind of crack ex-paratrooper when, in fact, he was a 77-year-old ex-inland revenue tax collector from Ystradgynlais with a gammy knee and an intermittently-functioning hearing aid. As early as my second one-day game down at Swansea, I recognized what we were up against. Sent across after the tea interval to open the main gate at the end of the Grandstand to allow a vehicle in (it was years before the Council began to allow even the players to park inside the perimeter of the ground), one of our mighty matchday Dad's Army had only gone and left the gate open all day. Small wonder the gate takings were a little down on normal.

But, and not for the first time, I know, I digress. (I promised myself I'd run the words 'but' and 'and' together at least once somewhere in this tome, just for the record, so here we are. Just managed it twice. And I've now managed two consecutive 'ands' too. Bonus stuff. Go me.) The place that would become my working home for the next quarter century, and the diverse group of people I was thrown in among, was all very alien. I was leagues out of my comfort zone and until Carol joined me a few weeks later it was also a lonely existence as I tried to get to know everyone and a new city. We were billeted in a flat in Canton, half a mile away from the ground. It was owned by a former Glamorgan player, John Solanky, who had moved to Northern Ireland to coach and relied on the club to rent it out in the summer, normally to a player. Philip guaranteed the rent in my case and Carol and I spent our first summer there. Although it was against the rental conditions, we went out and got two kittens for company for Carol while she looked for work. Hawkeye and Radar, they were called. Yep, fans of M*A*S*H, a programme I remember watching with Mum back in the late '70s and not having a clue what she was laughing about, so subtle were some of the jokes. Theirs was a partnership that lasted until 2000, when first Hawkeye had to be put down and then, a few years of blindness and infirmity later, Radar followed. But in Solanky's flat we had one psychotic male kitten chasing reflections up and down walls and his hyperactive female counterpart climbing up and down, and badly scragging, curtains. Not surprisingly there was a deposit issue with Solanky when we moved out at the end of the summer to our new place at the top of Cathedral Road. The Bonnie and Clyde of the feline world had left their youthful marks. Or pawprints. Clawmarks. Whatever.

That summer is one I will always look back upon very fondly. It was the excitement of starting out on a career, the Mexico football World Cup forming a backdrop for the forging of some friendships which have lasted well over thirty years. Among the first people I got close to was Ian Smith, a big strapping Geordie all-rounder, just a couple of years younger than me but a lad for whom the sages at the club were predicting great things, possibly even the makings of a future international player. I didn't know much about his cricket but I was in awe of his drinking skills. He was a phenomenon when it came to downing pints. It doesn't take a detective of Maigret's deductive skills to conclude that this may just have had something to do with the fact that 'Smudger' (the first of many dozens of wonderfully unoriginal Glamorgan dressing room nicknames) didn't reach the heights for which many felt he was destined. But he was great company and we got on famously. I mentioned in the introduction that he bowled a couple of bouncers at me in the Neath Indoor School during a rain break once. I reckon that was revenge for me bowling him once in the nets at Oxford University. He had been left out of the side for a three-day game at The Parks and I was at the game to meet up with my brother, who was at St Anne's College at the time, and Smudger asked me to give him a few throw-downs. After a few, I tried to bowl him one of my legendary (in my own mind, at least) tortoise-pace off-cutters. And promptly bowled him. I think I must have over-celebrated, though, as the next one was hit back over my head and ended up somewhere in neighbouring Buckinghamshire. "Fetch that, you cocky tw*t," came the pithy Geordie riposte.

Back then we all used to wear the same blazers on home match days, players and staff alike. The full bloom daffodil badge was for capped players, and for Philip as our off-field boss, with the remainder of the contracted players and the other full-time admin staff having a daffodil bud embroidered on the jacket pocket. That's until Hugh Davies, a former player who was elected to the Committee, came along years later and lobbied to have it changed it because he didn't like the fact that staff had the same jacket badges as players. So we ended up having a completely differently designed daffodil on our blazers as a result. It wasn't the only thing he meddled in, either, but more of that later. I have always been 'of a size', though in the '80s I wasn't anything like the size I am as I type these words. After a day's play, everyone used to congregate in the Members' Bar in the pavilion at Sophia Gardens – players, staff, umpires, groundstaff, members – have a beer or two and generally chew the cud. On one occasion Smudge had had a difficult day, being dismissed cheaply and then going for a few when it had been his turn to bowl. We were chatting together before he nipped to the loo and I was approached by a Glamorgan member clearly a little the worse for drink. "Are you Ian Smith?" he asked, or at least I translated from something more akin to, "Aroooeeansmiffbutt?" Seizing my moment and puffing out my chest I replied, in mock lilting Geordie, "Aye, that's me". Might as well play along, I thought. There was a pause as I anticipated the withdrawal of pen and autograph book or scorecard, ready for my signature. Instead, he looked me squarely in the eye and grunted, "Lose some f***ing weight." Or "loosumfikkinway". Before turning on his heels and wandering off. Cue the door opening, Smudge returning and inquiring, with raised eyebrow, "Another?"

I went to stay with him once in Winlaton, just outside Newcastle, a few years later after he had left Glamorgan to join Durham. Carol and I were on our way to Edinburgh with my mum for a short break, and Smudge's parents, Jim and Mary, with whom I'd always got on really well, had offered to put us up for the night to help us break up the journey. Smudge himself suggested he and I enjoy 'a few quiet pints' down at his local working mens' club. I should have known better, staggering in in the early hours much the worse for wear. We had plenty of nights like that, the pair of us. Far easier back then, when the accent was on skills and not the fixation with weights and strength and conditioning that the game seems to have veered towards, and in an era when camera phones were still something for BBC's *Tomorrow's World* on a Thursday evening. The players could have a few beers and generally run them off the following morning. It sounds unprofessional by today's exacting standards but in the '80s it was par for the course. We lost touch, as you do, but I know Smudger ended up in Johannesburg because the Glamorgan lads caught up with him on a pre-season tour years later. He'll be my size now, I reckon. And I bet he can still drink.

Another close buddy was Phil North, the team's diminutive, moustachioed left arm spinner from Newport. He was a fabulous character, possessed of a rapier-like wit and who told some of the funniest stories I've ever heard. I had no idea if he could actually bowl but I do know he dined out on the fact that he had been at the other end – on 0 – while Matthew Maynard had gone to a debut first class century with three consecutive sixes at the end of the previous 1985 season. "Without me, he'd be back in the seconds," he would say. "He'd be nothing." Phil became my closest pal in those early years. I was Best Man at his wedding and we also went on (a riotously funny) holiday with partners to Morocco in 1989. His marriage to Natalie didn't last, though she is my elder daughter Seanna's godmother and despite now living in Sydney she is in regular contact with her. Phil is my younger daughter Hannah's godfather. He is not quite as communicative. Sorry, Han. *inserts rueful emoji face*

After Phil had finished playing first class cricket in the early '90s we actually went on to share a couple of memorable moments on the cricket field, playing for Chartered Trust in division four of the Cardiff Midweek League. You didn't need to work for Chartered Trust, obviously. I'm not actually sure if more than a couple of our team members actually did at that time, but that's by the by. We all wore the shirt with pride. Or would have done, had there actually been team shirts. This was parks cricket in the '80s, after all. The old pitches in Pontcanna, Llandaff and Blackweir weren't exactly renowned for their horticultural beauty and you'd frequently encounter glass, socks, condoms, dog turds, discarded needles – often all in one chase of the ball. But on one occasion, I can proudly boast that Phil and I put on 75 in one partnership. That might not sound a lot to you but when you're as untalented as I am, it's something to get the bunting out over. The fact that I only faced two balls, one of which I completely missed and the other which knocked my stumps halfway back towards the city centre, is academic. A mere detail. On another occasion, this time using a Slazenger bat the great Isaac Vivian Alexander Richards had given to me, I also only managed to face two balls in partnership with Phil. But on this occasion the first was struck with such power, right out of the sweet spot, that it went miles, almost sailing into a neighbouring county. "YEEEES! Two!" I cried, and started running. "Why?" asked Phil, unmoved, still leaning on his bat at the non-striker's end, with a bemused expression on his face. It was as clear a six as you could ever wish to see. Feeling unbelievably proud of myself, and now with added delusions of grandeur, I tried to repeat the shot next ball and my stumps were again sent cartwheeling.

In 1990 we reached the Final of the Cardiff Midweek League Fourth and Fifth Division Cup. A big deal, let me tell you, before you start rolling those eyes of yours. We couldn't lose. We had Phil. A humble Chartered Trust worker, of course, but a handy ex-professional cricketer, and we were probably breaking every rule in the book by keeping quiet about his background, though his career as a pro had obviously flown by under the radar as none of our opponents ever said anything. Another close pal, Richard Jones, was our captain. He was the nicest skipper the game of cricket has ever known, allowing everyone to bat, bowl and field pretty much where and when they liked. Potential chaos, of course, but as an example of genuine Marxist socialist captaincy I was inordinately proud of him. Until he started taking wickets with his off spin, bowling the kind of delivery that was so slow he could have jogged after it if he didn't like it and recovered the ball before it had reached the batsman at the other end.

I'm not sure if he played in that Final but we were always a better side for the presence of the pugnacious Rob John. In addition to our handsome partnership in the annual 'tour match' at Llanfapli (the word 'tour' is used advisedly in this context as Llanfapli is all of 30 miles from Cardiff, near Abergavenny, and we travelled up, played the game and came home all in one day, so it can hardly be described as such) one topic still comes up in conversation: the occasion when Rob almost came to blows with the entire Clwb Rwgbi team out on Blackweir 1. One of their fielders had chased and picked the ball up before it had come to rest and hurled it back in to the 'keeper thereby trying to save, as Rob thought, two runs. Incensed, he claimed the ball had crossed the (virtual) boundary 'line.' The boundary consisted of various items of cricket kit drawn from the two teams' kit bags, set out at thirty-yard intervals, and in that section of the playing area, between a battered old wicket-keeping glove and a used and cracked box (abdominal protector) – Rob was adamant it had been four runs and that the Clwb Rwgbi fielder had been cheating. In a seemingly instantaneous *Incredible Hulk* transformation he moved from the laid-back team-mate we had got used to playing alongside into some kind of Gray Nicolls bat-wielding Mike Tyson as he led the subsequent shouting and joshing in what could only be termed 'an incident.' We'll always have Llanfapli, though, eh Rob? But back to that Final. 'Jonesy' won the toss, opted to bat, and out strode Phil to take first strike. Hardly any of us remaining batsmen would have padded up, such would have been the confidence and faith we had in our 'pro.' First ball, Phil tw*ts it round the corner. Straight into the hands of square leg. We were all out for 45. No way back from there. Bloody professional cricketers. They always let you down.

Back in the late '80s Glamorgan was something of a peripatetic club. The lease at the Sophia Gardens ground only allowed the team to play there on four weekends during the course of a six-month season. First class matches were then three days in length and we played 24 of them, meaning that Glamorgan, like every county, had to have its fair share of home weekend cricket in April and September. That, in turn, meant the outgrounds generally received many of the plum high summer matches and slots, Cardiff having to host early and late season because the outgrounds almost all shared rugby or football pitches, meaning they were off limits early and late summer. I think that's what's known as 'a bum deal'. But until we took the bull by the horns and bought the head lease from the Athletic Club some years later, that was just how it was. We didn't know any different.

It meant we were on the road a heck of a lot. In 1988 Glamorgan played sixteen Sunday League matches on sixteen different grounds, for example, with eight different home venues. Wales was our back garden. For some years the travelling one-day circus hit Cardiff, Swansea, Newport, Merthyr Tydfil, Neath, Llanelli, Ebbw Vale, Aberystwyth and Pontypridd. We also played Championship matches at Abergavenny and shortly afterwards started playing in Colwyn Bay again. We even dropped in on Pentyrch, of which more elsewhere. We were nomads. The players were constantly moaning about how it negated home advantage and it was very difficult to argue with them even if fifth place in 1988 was the club's highest ever finish up to that point. But for us in the office it was great fun. Tony would be the advance party, having set up whatever sponsorship deals he could, generally agreements with local authorities, with me bringing up the rear in terms of fetching along all of the match day paraphernalia, then setting up and running the matches themselves on the day. They were really long days and our office was anything from a gardening shed to a local CB radio broadcaster's broom cupboard. But I loved it.

I came late to driving, so was not much help to my colleagues until 1988, when I belatedly took lessons and passed my test. Philip's promise that I could use a pool car if there was one floating around focused my attention and I managed to pass first time. There were indeed sometimes cars 'floating around' and I managed a succession of Montegos and Mondeos in those early years. When my Granny passed away in 1990 Philip let me borrow his Saab Turbo to travel to her funeral up in Cheshire. I quickly learned the reason I had been lumbered with the Montegos. What a car. I remember getting back into one of the old pool cars when back in Cardiff and pulling out to overtake on a dual carriageway. Where the Saab turbo had kicked in and accelerated me rapidly past the car in front, this time there was nothing there. Back into your lane, Fatkin, and look sheepish about it. The only vehicle that came close to the Saab in those early years was an Alfa Romeo 33, which, looking back on it, was a ridiculous deal to have done for county cricketers, even though it was only for our overseas players: you could barely get two people inside, let alone a load of cricket kit. I've never been one for cars, or indeed other 'boys' toys,' like watches. Car bores drive me nuts. People have a go at me for rabbiting on about football but then seem to find it totally acceptable to be sending an audience to sleep as they go on and on about cars. For me, so long as a car is reliable and comfortable, that's sufficient. I've never understood the need to drone on about torque or brake horsepower or whatever litre engine the thing has got, and I don't get the need to change your car every few months. I remember bringing a lovely BMW 3 Series home in the late '90s (as CEO I had access to a more upmarket vehicle as a piggy-back to any deal done for the players) and feeling immensely proud, dragging my daughters out to have a look at it, only for Hannah to come running back into the house exclaiming, "Daddy's got a blue car!" Not for her the model, engine capacity, fuel economy or 0-60 speed. Like father, like daughter.

My first experience of cricket at Swansea was also my first working experience of the then Glamorgan Chairman, Gwyn Craven, a rather self-important little bank manager. When we played at Swansea's St. Helen's ground back then the Glamorgan offices were right behind the bowler's arm overlooking a bank of seats, just above the top of the sight screens. Up a short spiral staircase from us was where the committee members of the two counties were housed to watch the game. The combination of sight screens and committee members proved a potent one. We couldn't go two overs without one of the dull sods wandering around right in the batsman's eyeline, necessitating the umpire to wave frantically and ask the miscreant to sit down. On one occasion the skipper, Rodney Ontong, who was batting, actually yelled out at the top of his voice, "PLAY DEAD, YOU DINOSAUR C***S!" Thankfully the watching committee members couldn't make out his words. A few seasons later we moved them. We put the press there instead, which made far more sense anyway. It was the perfect view, right behind the bowler's arm. And at least they understood the game and its etiquette.

My Swansea match day debut had come at a Benson and Hedges Cup group stage match against Sussex, and with Jim Parks, the former England wicket-keeper, visiting as part of the Sussex contingent, Craven was at his obsequious best, fawning all over him. On the basis that they couldn't get to their viewing area by not walking past me and just ignoring me, he introduced me to Jim on the way downstairs as they all headed off out to lunch, which they enjoyed elsewhere on the ground ('enjoyed' being a very loose description, if the food they had was anything like the stuff we had to put up with). Inevitably the introduction came as part of a wider anecdote, which was Gwyn's way, this one concerning his recommendation to Ontong before a key game against Hampshire that the captain and players should set a run out trap for Gordon Greenidge, who always seemed to score a double century against us: drop mid-off back ten yards deeper, bowl a fuller length just outside off stump and Gordon would [inevitably] drive it to mid-off, run and, well, Bob's Your Uncle. He'd be run out. QED. This coming from someone whose very highest playing achievement was representing Swansea Civil Service in South Wales Cricket Association league division five. He had all the tactical astuteness of General Haig, only without any of the knowledge. Anyway, the story, such as it was, ended with mention of Peter May, whereupon Gwyn turned to me and asked, "Do you know Peter May?" Yes, of course I know Pete, I felt like saying. Been pals for aeons. Close friend of the family and all that. I'd been in cricket for quite literally a matter of days and you expect me to know a former England captain and the then Chairman of Selectors? And it wasn't the last time I heard the Greenidge anecdote, either. I doubt Rodney would have given it any house room, let's just say that. I'd love to have been there when he'd first broached it with Rodney, though. Rodney's face would have been a picture.

When I was Chief Executive many years later and Gwyn was one of the club's four trustees, an honorary position with no executive status, I was having a private conversation in a rain break on a match day with our Scorer, Byron Denning, in my office in Cardiff. In came Gwyn, following a barely discernible knock on the door (he did most things extremely furtively and quietly). It didn't matter that Byron and I were both just looking at him; he wasn't going anywhere. "Sorry, Gwyn," said Byron, who knew him well having served on the committee with him for many years, "we're having a private chat. Could you just give us five minutes?" "Of course," said Gwyn, and proceeded to close the door. Whilst still in the room. It took all of Byron's diplomacy to usher Gwyn outside but not after he'd explained his (obviously vital) purpose for interrupting: a message from Reg Simpson, then Nottinghamshire's President, wishing Glamorgan well in a forthcoming game. Like many, Gwyn treated me throughout my career as the 21-year-old lad who first came into the club. In many ways there was nothing I could have done to change that perception. Even as we were winning Championships, one-day trophies and staging international matches I was still a boy to him, a young lad on the first rung of the employment ladder. In the end I gave up trying to change that perception and just let him run with it.

I realize now that back in those first few weeks in the job I occasionally behaved rather naively when around the more famous cricketers. Being honest, I hadn't really heard too much about any of the Glamorgan players so it wasn't an issue with them, and in any event they were so down to earth and welcoming – in the main – that even if it had been, it wouldn't have lingered. Greg Thomas was the one player I *had* heard of. He'd been picked as England's latest Great White Fast Bowling Hope™ for their tour to the West Indies that winter and he arrived back a little late for pre-season as a result. It hadn't gone too well for England. Alright, yes. They lost five-nil. But Greg had done OK. And as one of only a handful of Glamorgan players to have gone on to play international cricket for England, he was something of a sporting superstar back in Wales. And a smashing bloke too. I overstepped the mark a couple of years later, around the time Greg was considering leaving Glamorgan in search of the quicker pitches which he felt would help him regain his place in the England team (he eventually joined Northamptonshire), when I wrote an article in the Glamorgan Yearbook, an article I had intended to be both affectionate and congratulatory. But I used a phrase 'in between fibular and cerebral strains' which implied he was injury prone and had potentially missed matches when he'd merely *felt* he wasn't fit. It was meant in jest but it was naïve of me to commit it to print without someone checking it. I was trying to be clever with words and it backfired. Of course he wasn't missing games for any other reason than he wasn't fit to play. Philip took the flak for having allowed it to go to print and he rightfully gave me a bollocking for writing it. I had to make a formal apology in the following year's edition and also, much harder for me, to Greg directly. But rightly so. It was a stupid thing to have written. The moment passed but it was one of my many early cock-ups.

Having met an England international in Greg, a few weeks later came the appearance of two genuine box office superstars as Somerset rolled into town at the end of May, still less than a month after I'd started. Although I loved watching David Gower bat, two other heroes from my teenage years were undoubtedly Ian Botham and Viv Richards, as they were for many. Back in those days England players always turned out for their counties – none of this resting them from key games only for the players to use their time off popping up at Ascot or Wimbledon on jollies, or as pundits on the TV – and overseas players were out of the very top drawer. They littered the teams in my early seasons in county cricket: Hadlee, Rice, Zaheer, Imran, Lloyd, Greenidge, Barry Richards, Turner, Roberts, Daniel… there was top quality in every side. But two of the biggest box office names in the game were Botham and Richards. Botham's exploits in the 1981 Ashes are the stuff of legend (I've already referred to my own memories of that summer revolving around lazy days spent watching the series on TV with Andrew North in Ilkley) and you couldn't help but get caught up in all the Botham hype. He was a proper Falstaffian sporting hero. And the hype around him was even greater as, following a confession in a newspaper column about having once smoked cannabis, the with-it blazer brigade at the Test and County Cricket Board (the forerunner of today's England and Wales Cricket Board) decided to ban him from first class cricket for two months, and that ban was about to start. As for Viv, he too was a proper legend, fresh off the back of that 5-0 thrashing of England – including our own Mr Thomas – and a 56-ball century on his home ground in Antigua. I'd always enjoyed watching him play and the memories of West Indian summers of 1976 (Tony Grieg's 'we intend to make them grovel' series), 1980 and 1984 (including an utterly wonderful exhibition of power hitting by Viv in a One-Day International at Old Trafford) are fresh still now. He was a magnificent player.

Whenever there were decent players in town it was the fashion to try to get them to sign some bats, be it for beneficiaries, charities, sponsors, or just for the club to keep as a memento, and it was obvious that the signatures of a Somerset side containing Richards and Botham, not to mention Viv's West Indian team-mate Joel Garner, and Vic Marks, another England international, who took 8-100 in Glamorgan's second innings in this particular match, would be sought after. I was duly dispatched to the Somerset dressing room to drop said bats off and, on day three, at Phil Carling's prompting, I marched back over purposefully to pick them up again. Richards had made 136 in the first innings before being run out (presumably having fallen for one of Gwyn Craven's carefully-laid run out traps) but managed only 15 in the second innings and had just arrived back in the visitors' dressing room when in I sauntered, full of youthful innocence, to ask for the bats. To compound the fact that I'd entered hallowed territory without permission it turned out that Richards hadn't signed the bats, so I just turned to him nonchalantly and asked him if he wouldn't mind doing so, then I'd be on my way. "Why don't you take your f***ing bats, man, and shove them deep where the sun don't shine, and then f** right outta my space, man." And in case you were wondering how that might have been said, there was a very heavy emphasis on the Es in the word 'deep'. He was right, of course. I hadn't yet understood proper dressing room etiquette and cocky young whippersnappers like me weren't exactly on the approved guest list, especially when appearing uninvited.

Botham's impending ban meant he was even more of a media magnet than normal, which is saying something. Everyone in the press was after him for a comment: news reporters as well as the traditional cricket writers. In the end he sought refuge in Philip's office in our portacabin. I decided to nip in and see if he was OK, ask him if he wanted anything. So in I barge, trying to make casual conversation about this and that. For some reason he was reluctant to engage in conversation. I mean, I was in the county cricket 'gang' now, so surely it followed that we'd be able to pass the time of day chatting about cigars, Elton John's music, mullets, Glenfiddich, fly fishing – whatever he fancied discussing. I seem to recall I even tried a gag about the fact that between us we had 354 Test wickets (Botham was just two short of breaking Dennis Lillee's Test record, which he eventually did later in the summer). Nothing. It took Philip giving me the metaphorical equivalent of the old off-stage shepherd's crook to pull me out of his hair. Botham must have thought I was a right knob. I know Philip did. I'm fairly sure he let me talk away to Botham just to make a point. And I got it. Eventually I learned to rationalize, the stars in my eyes gradually faded away and, for all but a handful of cases, disappeared. This was a job. The people I dealt with were well-known compared to most jobs, in some cases household names, but it was a job nonetheless.

There was no real danger of me being starstruck with the inhabitants of the Glamorgan dressing room. Other than Greg, it was a collection of journeymen, the odd player no other county wanted and a sprinkling of youngsters we had down as rising stars. In my first summer, this motley group was led by Rodney Ontong, who always treated me respectfully and of whom I grew to be very fond, even if he was, by reputation, ever so slightly bonkers. Others such as John Hopkins, Alan Lewis Jones, John Derrick, Steve Barwick, Geoff Holmes and Terry Davies I came to know well, 'JD' and 'Holmesy' in particular. They were a very honest, hardworking and likeable bunch. Just not, as a county side, a particularly threatening one. Midway through the summer, without a Championship win as August approached, Rodney resigned. His replacement was a 22-year-old gap-toothed rugby-playing ex-public schoolboy, Hugh Morris. At the time I didn't think his age made that much of a big difference but looking back it does seem astonishing that the club imagined someone so young and inexperienced could turn around the fortunes of a team steeped in a tradition of over-underachievement. Hugh was my age. He was to get a second crack at it later on – with some talent around him he achieved some success, too – but with hindsight it surely can't have been too much of a surprise when his first spell in charge ended in failure.

Hugh had tremendous character and is one of the gutsiest cricketers I have seen. His approach to life is no different, as evidenced by a personal battle with cancer and the fact that he took on and succeeded in such challenging roles as the ECB's Technical Director, then its Managing Director looking after the England teams, before taking on the poisoned chalice that is the role of Chief Executive of Glamorgan. Tough nut to crack, that one. But back in 1986 the environment just wasn't equipped to support a 22-year-old trying to lead a distinctly ordinary county side. Philip tried hard, asking John Steele to stand down from playing in order to look after the cricket operations. I think his title was Assistant Secretary (Cricket). Working alongside three other Assistant Secretaries in Sue (Admin), Mostyn (Finance) and Tony (Marketing). (I did say that I would explain the whole 'Secretary' thing but I reckon I was the only one in the office that summer who *wasn't* a Secretary or an Assistant Secretary. I was just an assistant) Despite John being earmarked to provide direct cricket support for Hugh, our cricket was still being run by a cumbersome 30-strong committee, we had no home ground, no money and, if truth be told, little ambition and no real plan. We seemed happy just to plod along. We finished that season with two wins in 24 games, almost three dozen points adrift at the bottom of the table.

We had the odd sniff of success in those early seasons but it was fleeting. In 1988 Glamorgan enjoyed a good run in the Benson and Hedges Cup, a competition which comprised some early season zonal matches in regional groups before quarter-finals, semi-finals and the first of the summer's two major domestic Finals at Lord's. We made it out of the group stage (for Glamorgan a considerable feat) and proceeded to beat Nottinghamshire in Cardiff in the quarter-final, Matthew Maynard making his second century in the competition that summer, setting us up for a home semi-final against Derbyshire at Swansea. That, in itself, glosses over a major challenge the club faced at that time. We had no control over the preparation of pitches at St. Helen's. We had minimal input back at Sophia Gardens, if truth be told, but at Swansea we were in the hands of Richard Stevens who, although a lovely man and a great support to the club over a long period of time and an expert on the health and safety intricacies of the ground, wasn't the greatest when it came to producing a decent 22-yard cut strip out in the middle. We would turn up for matches with absolutely no idea at all of what we would get. If we wanted a slow, turning pitch, we might come across a green seamer, and vice versa. There were often good contests between bat and ball but when you're rocking up on an outground for your biggest game in over a decade you would probably prefer to have had some element of control over the surface you're going to be playing on. Anyway, after all that, let's just say it didn't end gloriously. We bowled well and were chasing a modest 218 to win in 55 overs but after a solid start our star man Maynard, in the act of hitting a boundary off Michael Holding, saw his helmet fall off and clatter back into the stumps. He still has a series of photos depicting the incident up on the wall of his study at home. Shastri, Ontong, Holmes and Thomas saw us past 200 but we fell short. It would be five years before our next semi-final. Tony Dilloway and I could console ourselves as we strolled down to the local branch of the HSBC (then Midland) Bank with the tens of thousands of pounds in takings in a briefcase, the counting of which we had been helped with by no less a name than Micky Stewart, not long since appointed as England's first Head Coach. He was in town to watch Matt play but had needed to find safe refuge in our office in order to escape the media and to make phone calls, that being the very day the names of the England captain Mike Gatting and a Nottingham barmaid became inextricably linked in the saucier sections of the press. Gatting would lose the captaincy the following day. First Botham, then Stewart. For an unfashionable and pretty average county we were proving very adept at providing a safe haven for high profile escapees trying to flee media attention.

For Matt it was a mixed summer. He was in superb form early on and there was talk of an England call-up. That call eventually came, for the final Test match against the West Indies at The Oval. Knocks of 3 and 10 later, and he was back out of the side, replaced by Derbyshire's Kim Barnett, selected for the one-off Test against the marginally less threatening Sri Lankan bowling attack, who made 66, and promptly went on the winter tour. It wouldn't happen in the modern game. He'd have been picked when in form and then given a few matches in which to make his mark, not dropped after one appearance. For Matt, it was a frustrating time and I watched him wrestle with it. Towards the end of the 1989 season it was announced that he was in a rebel squad to tour South Africa the following February, led by Gatting. I must confess to being disappointed. I had to respect his right to make whatever choices he wanted to, and I of course totally understood the way he'd been treated by England and the fact that this tour would give him significant financial security. But I struggled to reconcile in my mind the fact that a good pal of mine was choosing to go to a place that openly practised racial segregation. I then looked on along with everyone else as the political situation deteriorated, leading to the eventual release – while the tour was still taking place – of Nelson Mandela the following February. It was a naïve venture, and one could only conclude that the players had been let down in terms of the promises that had been made to them, but the upshot was that the participants were banned from international cricket for three years. The second tour, scheduled for the following winter, was cancelled. Matt and I have never really spoken about it. I understand the choices he was faced with. And I respect the decision he took. But although I fundamentally disagreed with it, it wasn't me in his shoes so any discussion would have been hugely hypothetical. I'm so glad it didn't wreck his chances of playing again for England. It certainly didn't harm his Glamorgan career.

The players coming through in the late '80s were mates. Not only Matt, who remains one of my very closest friends, but JD and Holmesy – bless them, who both died well before their time – Hugh,

Ian Smith, Phil North, Steve James and a number of others, such as Steve Monkhouse, Simon Dennis and Michael Cann. Philip Carling used to tell me that as an administrator you had to be careful to keep a distance from the players, something which Tony Lewis, when he returned to the fold first as Cricket Committee Chairman and then, in 1988, as Chairman of the Club, reiterated. Tony, or 'AR' as he was known to us, did qualify that by telling me it was impossible to go anywhere as a club without taking the players with us but stressed that it was down to me to get the balance right between them being friends and fellow employees. He didn't impose. He let me work it out for myself. I did struggle to make the distinction sometimes and I'm not sure at that stage of my fledgling career that I was particularly good at compartmentalizing. I was the same age as many of these lads after all and had much in common with a number of them. I spent a lot of time helping and supporting them, often defending them. But as Philip moved on in 1990 – perhaps *was* moved on might have been more accurate – and Gwyn Stone came in as his replacement, I had some growing up to do.

5 RUBICON

'I wish you luck with a capital F.'
ELVIS COSTELLO

The characters around the county game were legion. We all had them. This is a tale of junior players, outgrounds, scorers, umpires and cantankerous members who were never happier than when they were able to corral you into a quiet corner and moan away about something so trivial it wouldn't even make a list of the top billion and one things to complain about. They'd paid their subs: as far as they were concerned that gave them licence to whinge. About everything.

In my defence there had been *some* growing up. Carol and I had married in 1988, for a start, and after a couple more years of scraping by and living in a rented top floor flat in Cardiff, we'd bought our first house just outside Pontypridd. I was punching several divisions above my weight too: she was petite; warm; bright; wonderfully feisty; and gorgeous. She was also a Yorkie. I couldn't believe my luck. By now I'd even started driving, albeit at the rather advanced age these days of 24. It remains the only test my brother and I have both sat in which I've managed to do better than him (a minor, yet somehow important, victory to set against the glaring truth that he was not only academically brighter than I was but clearly worked harder as well).

Those early years at Glamorgan continued in much the same manner as the first one. Little cash, little control, no facilities, and yet, for all that, it was a happy club. By now my responsibilities had extended to running all match day operations, which sounds incredibly grand but in reality meant little more than arriving at whichever ground we were playing at at the crack of dawn, deploying our army of pensioner stewards, reacting to the petty whims of home and away committee, wandering around listening to the interminable whinges and complaints from members, journalists and occasionally players too, before attempting to balance the takings, paying anyone who needed paying and closing everything down until the following day. Put like that, it sounds like a series of chores but I always enjoyed a match day, especially the period before players, staff or spectators arrived. I miss the days of being able to sit outside just after the sun has come up, the field of play spread out in front of you, puffing away contentedly on a cigarette and sipping a black coffee, just enjoying the calm before the storm. The bigger the game, the more exciting the feeling.

Philip Carling had given me responsibility very early on for editing the Glamorgan Yearbook, an annual publication (as the title may perhaps have given away) which contained a summary of the previous year's efforts on the field, with an attempt to dress up our almost constant under-performance with some sign of promise or other – an emerging star player, for example – and a brief look forward to the next. I had nothing to go on really. He just threw me a copy of the 1986 edition and asked, "Think you could improve on that?" I chatted briefly to Lawrence Hourahane, who had done a similar job to mine up to 1985 before leaving to join BBC Radio Sport in London. Really good man, Lawrence, and I stayed in touch with him through the years after he'd returned to Cardiff to a broadcasting role with BBC Wales. We also share a love of baseball, for what that's worth to you. Probably not much. Anyway, he was really helpful and encouraging. Just pointed me in the direction of a few people who might be able to help and bid me crack on. I've already alluded to the fact that I had managed to upset Greg Thomas with something I wrote in one of my early efforts. I also managed to upset the doyen of Glamorgan former players, Don Shepherd, when I penned a brief tribute in one of the editions to Norman Hever, a 1948 Glamorgan Championship-winning veteran. I described him as a left arm seamer when he was, in fact, the very opposite, something 'Shep' took little time in having a go at me about after a few glasses of red wine at some function or other. And, like Greg, he was right. He said it was about the detail. But I'd got the more than the detail wrong. Quite why I didn't ask someone who'd actually known Norman Hever to write it, or even just check it, I'm not quite sure.

But Philip let me carry on putting the book together and I was grateful to him for that show of faith. I continued to edit it until the early 2000s, when – probably long after I ought to have done – I handed it over. My workload was very heavy by now and there were far weightier issues for me to be fretting over than the number of no balls bowled by some unknown Leicestershire Second XI cricketer in a rain-affected one-day match at Hinckley. Editing it also gave me the opportunity to write, which I love. Whether I was considered any good at it was immaterial to me. I was editor and that meant I was going to contribute to each edition and that was that. I also edited the

Sunday League match programmes for donkey's years, giving that up for the same reasons at around the same time. These had become examples of 'old Glamorgan', many of which had to be binned after the role had moved me into the realms of international match staging, strategic planning and elite player performance. Necessary, but a shame nonetheless. I was relinquishing a lot of the very tasks that I enjoyed.

To be fair to Philip Carling he took a number of risks on me which, looking back, he really needn't have done. I shall always be grateful to him for that. He was far braver than I think I would have been in his position. He had quickly identified my strengths and helped me to play to them. He had recognized that my original role at the club, that of helping with the sales and marketing and supporting some of the membership administration, wasn't one for which I was really cut out, and so when Sue Wood left the Club in 1987 he gave me all of the match days to run on my own and allowed me to start working on a few players' contracts. He kept all of the important ones, understandably. Who on earth would trust a 23-year-old novice with key player negotiations? I was left to cut my teeth on the younger summer contract players, taking advice from Alan Jones, our Senior Coach. 'Uncle Al' taught me a lot about how you should deal with young cricketers and their parents. I worked closely with Alan on all cricket matters up to his retirement in 1998. He is a bona fide Glamorgan legend and one of the nicest people you could ever wish to meet.

County cricket in the late 1980s was a world away from twenty-first century sport, not least in terms of the money on offer. Back in 1986, for example, Glamorgan's overall annual club turnover was just £448,500. The salaries for the entire professional playing staff totalled just £163,348, probably not that much more than some players earn in a year nowadays, and there would have been 20+ pros on the books at the time too. Glamorgan's sponsorship deals down the years have occasionally piqued the envy of the other counties, with lucrative and innovative deals negotiated with a string of high-profile partners including ASW, Brains and Swalec. In 1984 Glamorgan had been the first county to put the logo of a sponsor on its players' shirts, the playing regulations having only just been updated to allow it. Peter Llewellyn, a photocopier company based in Swansea, were the first headline sponsors of the club, and they paved the way. I think the agreement with them in 1987 was for a sponsorship of £15,000. For the year. It was a very different world. People used to ask us what we did in the Winter and were surprised to hear that we worked full time, rather than it being purely a summer occupation. But until the mid-'90s, there was only enough work to keep a handful of us going through a full calendar year. The players were only around from April to September. Pre-season was a run on the Afan Lido sands, a net at the Neath Indoor Cricket School and a three-day friendly against Oxford or Cambridge University if the fixture list had been kind to you If not, it was a grass net if the sun was out, and straight into the competitive stuff. Simpler days.

The summer of 1987 saw a special event at Sophia Gardens as Glamorgan played host to Gloucestershire in a one-day match in July. Nothing outstanding about that, you're probably thinking, except to say it was arranged to mark the beginning of Glamorgan's centenary year and what made it extra special was the fact that the Patrons of the two counties were going to be attending. Yes, folks, we were to host the Prince and Princess of Wales. We've already established that I'm not exactly the nation's most rabid monarchist but even I knew that this was quite a big deal. The security was astonishingly tight and it didn't take me long to realise that formal planning meetings with Special Branch were not occasions at which to be wheeling out my standard flippant sarcasm. I was invited to consider leaving the room during one meeting after mumbling something about Charles needing to use one of the guest vouchers in his complimentary Glamorgan membership card in order for his wife to be given access to the ground. Yeah. I know. Though a couple of them did laugh, to be fair.

We off-field employees were way too far down the food chain to warrant getting within a hundred yards of old Charles and Diana. Or so we thought. The two of them had photo opportunities with each of the two teams and then there we were, being asked to line up in the offices to meet them just before they left. I remember Mostyn frantically putting his pipe out in a plant in the reception window. I also remember Diana being stunningly beautiful. I know it's a hoary old cliché but it was true. A few months later we were trying to find the contact sheet which had all of the photos from the day on it. Tony Dilloway searched high and low and then asked me if I would as well. We looked everywhere in the files but we had to give up. We'd lost them. Only for our YTS trainee (one of the government's employment training schemes of the time) to pipe up sheepishly that she knew where they were as she'd filed them. Under 'S'. "'S'?" I remember Tony asking, incredulously, "Why would you file them under 'S'?" We'd looked under 'R' for Royals, 'G' for Gloucestershire, 'C' for Centenary, 'P' for Patrons…. just about everywhere. "'S' for Sixth of July," came the reply. Of course. How daft of us.

By centenary year our off-field team had expanded. Philip and Tony's commercial work, and my sideways move into cricket and operations, had led to the recruitment of new staff, among them Jane John, wife of the notoriously pugilistic Rob, of Blackweir 3's let's-take-on-everyone-in-the-Clwb-Rwgbi-team 'Boundarygate' fame; Jan Herbert; Diane Parker; Freddie Wraight; and Vicky Snook, who outlasted all the others and remained with the Club until 1999. I'm not sure the work justified having four ladies working in the marketing department, even if it included membership, but hey. That wasn't my business. Philip and Tony seemed to be keeping them busy with work. We all put in some very long hours but they were fun times. They were lovely people too. I often wonder if the staff working in county cricket nowadays enjoy their jobs as much as we did then. Well, no, that's not strictly true. I hadn't actually wondered about that until just now, to be honest. But we did have a lot of fun. I hope they do these days too. I'm sure they do. There are far worse ways of making a living.

The team's support staff consisted of the Senior Coach, Uncle Al, at most home games anyway, our Scorer, Byron Denning and, well, that was it. No Physio unless you counted Tudor Jones, the Welsh rugby team's trainer, who was around for some of the home matches. We didn't get a proper physiotherapist until 1989 when we brought in Dean Conway. Tudor's regime had generally consisted of asking the lads to do a pre-season run from the ground up to Western Avenue and then a loop back down Cathedral Road, along with using an ultrasound machine on them where necessary, together with administering various pills and gels. From what I could see it didn't appear to be at the cutting edge of the sports science revolution. Lovely man, Tudor, but prone to the odd verbal gaffe. Phil North tells the story of Tudor once asking for some Tippex, only struggling to describe it having failed to remember the name for it. "You know, that white stuff which blacks things out," he'd then rather helpfully proceeded to explain. He'd also announced at one of the lads' pre-season training sessions at the Afan Lido in Port Talbot that there would be 'three Pacific exercises', compounding the misuse of the word 'specific' by holding up four fingers instead of three. Dean was to be with the team at home games but not away matches, something he couldn't quite understand and which, in due course, we would all come to acknowledge had been a perfectly legitimate concern on his part. How pointless is it to be taking on a physio with the express aim of professionalizing the medical provision and then restricting the First XI players' match day access to him by 50%? Not only was he an absolutely outstanding physiotherapist and sports scientist, with an unrivalled network of specialists and clinical experts, in my opinion Dean was – is – the absolute master of taking disparate factions of dressing rooms and knitting them together to improve the team dynamic. He was the ultimate alchemist: he understood the chemistry of a good team and what goes into producing a high-quality team spirit better than anyone I have come across before or since.

Generally, twelve players would travel to away games in their own cars with no one other than the captain to keep a tin lid on their behaviour over the days they were away. And when your captain is barely out of his teens it isn't exactly a recipe for clean living and consciously professional behaviour. The absence of any off-field management also led to some horrendous travelling cock-ups. Lawrence Hourahane once told me of the day – pre-fax or email – when the players had turned up at an hotel in Eastbourne after a late Bank Holiday finish somewhere equally obscure and miles away, say Scarborough, only to find that the hotel had closed down some weeks previously. Presumably this was the day confirming rooming lists the day before matches became *de rigueur*. The travelling then was ridiculous. Nothing was thought of a trip on a Friday evening from Swansea to Colwyn Bay, as happened in 1990, for a Championship game starting the following morning. That same season Glamorgan played Derbyshire in a three-day game starting on a Friday, travelling to Manchester for a one-day match on the Sunday, before returning to Chesterfield for the final day of the original game. When they were in Liverpool for the Championship match against Lancashire later in the summer, they split the three-day game up with a one-day game in Leeds; and when they were at Headingley playing Yorkshire, that three-day match was broken up with a one-day game against, you've guessed it, Derbyshire. Bonkers.

It was little wonder that there were occasional accidents. In fact it's a miracle no one was killed. In August 1988 our players were travelling from Colchester, after a three-day game against Essex which, thanks to a rare five-wicket haul from Geoff Holmes, had gone right down to the last ball, to Wellingborough School for the start of another three-day game against Northamptonshire the following day. Steve Barwick and Rodney Ontong were in the same car together and on their way up the M11 'Baz', who was driving, had to swerve to avoid a lorry which had pulled out in front of him. He ploughed into the central reservation and basically wrote the car off. Both players were fine, thankfully, but the injury Rodney sustained to his knee meant that despite a few aborted comeback attempts in 1989, his Benefit Year, he was forced to retire from cricket. He did make an effort to come back in South Africa a couple of years later (something which alerted the insurance company that had forked out on a career-ending injury payment) but he was finished. It seems quite remarkable that we all just viewed such careering up and down the motorways of England and Wales as the norm. That incident saw our highly talented but not overly popular wicket-keeper, Colin Metson, who had been signed from Middlesex at the start of the 1987 season to replace Terry Davies, who had decided to retire and emigrate to Australia, get himself into a ruck with John Derrick. Metson had apparently had some wine in the boot of Rodney's car and when the call came in to the hotel alerting the team to news of the accident, he wondered aloud if his wine had managed to survive the accident. JD – 'Meataxe' as Dean christened him after another, still rare, temper-losing moment involving him and Barwick on a pre-season tour in the early '90s – took umbrage at Metson's perceived insensitivity and promptly picked him up and shoved him against the wall. Possibly not the last one he shared a dressing room with who felt compelled to do that, either. Colin was very different to your average valley boy.

It wasn't all travel purgatory for the boys. In 1990, we had picked up on the fact that a four-hour schlep from Swansea on a Friday evening to Colwyn Bay for a Saturday morning start was arguably a bit much to expect them to be undertaking by car, and through a local sponsor contact the team ended up flying from Fairwood, the airport near Swansea, in two small private chartered planes, up to Hawarden in North Wales. Philip even split the team up on a just-in-case basis, half the batsmen in one plane, half in the other, and so on through the team, which went down well with Steve Barwick, The World's Worst Flyer™, when the reasons were explained to him. So, on this occasion they were travelling in style. We just had to get the players' kit up there, along with all the groundsman's paraphernalia – nets, sheets, mini-mops and the like – as it was technically still a home game for us. And guess who was commandeered to drive the kit van? Yeah, old muggins here. We eventually arrived at 2am after Tom Oldknow, the man assigned to Glamorgan to provide the new county cricket telephone commentary service, Rapid Cricketline, had offered to accompany me, and taken me to parts of Wales – and indeed England – that I never knew existed. Dean Conway decided to blag a lift with us as the boys were leaving the ground at Worcester (they'd flown from Hawarden to Birmingham as they had a Benson & Hedges Cup quarter final immediately after the game at Colwyn Bay – I did tell you the scheduling was mad!) and were likely to be a while. He reasoned that jumping in with us would be quicker. Our fuel was a little low as we skirted Ross-on-Wye but after checking the fuel gauge Tom proclaimed, in that voice which those of us who knew and loved him can recall even as they read the words, "I can personally guarantee you that this will get you to Hong Kong and back." (Every S was pronounced with a SH, for those of you wondering, in a Sean Connery-esque home counties baritone.) 60 miles later as Dean and I were pushing said van up a slip road off the A48 a couple of miles outside Cardiff, Dean ran alongside Tom, got him to wind the window down and asked him, ever so politely, if he might 'take the f***ing handbrake off you stupid f***ing clown'. We loved Tom. We used to keep our fingers crossed that, even if it happened only once, one of the teams would get to 66-6 just so we could ring the service and hear Tom confirming that Glamorgan (not that it couldn't have been the opposition, of course) were "Shixty Shix for Shix."

Daftness wasn't just confined to the support cast. One incident involved two players, Martin Roberts and Robert Pook. Pretty certain it was those two, anyway. Martin, a lovely lad, was our reserve wicket-keeper. Although arguably at best average with the gloves, he could bat. Metson was pretty inept with the bat but because he set such supremely high standards with the keepers' gloves on

Martin rarely got a look-in other than the odd one-day cup match or when Metson was injured, and was thus consigned to a life largely on the road with the Second XI. Pook had joined us in 1990 from Essex recommended by Keith Fletcher, the Essex and future England coach (though it can't have been that much of a recommendation as he'd presumably still have been at Essex had he been that good). He only played one first class game for Glamorgan against Oxford University (scoring 0 and 0 not out) so he and Martin were pretty much driving companions with 'the stiffs' throughout that summer. On one occasion I took a call from Martin, who was ringing to ask where the team hotel was. On being informed that it was the Grand Hotel, Martin proceeded to ask where exactly that was. He and Robert were calling from a payphone at Leicester Forest Services on the M1. They weren't best pleased to learn that they were actually playing Kent Second XI, in Folkestone. They'd read the wrong line in the fixture list and were a week early. The same summer – and I know it was the same summer because Pook only played for Glamorgan in that one year – our hapless twosome rang from Aust Services, just by the old (then only) Severn Bridge on the M4, now the M48. They didn't have the requisite 50p to get them over the bridge. Quite what they expected me to do about it I don't know.

On another occasion in the late '80s our Second XI, with Uncle Al in charge, was playing a one-day match at Croesyceiliog Cricket Club, near Cwmbran, in the South East corner of Wales. The start time came and went and there was no sign of our opening bowling attack of Simon Base and Steve Monkhouse. Just after 11 o'clock the phone rang. It was Base from a payphone (remember this was 1987, long before mobile phones became commonplace).

"Where's the ground, Alan?" asked Base.

"Just past Asda, there's a fire station. Take a left just after that and it's a mile or so up there, just before you get to the housing estate," said Alan. "There's a sign for the cricket club."

There was a lengthy pause at the other end of the line.

"We didn't see an Asda or a fire station. There are only some fields here. Come to think of it, we haven't seen any shops for a few miles now."

"Where exactly *are* you, Simon? What was the last place you drove through?" inquired our increasingly exasperated Coach.

Some mumbling in the background.

"We hung a left just after Carmarthen," said Base.

"CARMARTHEN?" yelled Al. "What the hell are you doing in Carmarthen?"

It turns out there are two Croesyceiliogs. Whatever the chances of that, the odds on a couple of our players duly going to the wrong one were probably very short. SatNav was invented for professional cricketers.

This sort of club cricket approach was mirrored elsewhere at Glamorgan, especially when it came to our staging of matches on outgrounds. Players judged grounds by the pitch, or the dressing rooms, or the quality of the meals; I used to judge them on the quality of the facility we were given for an office. These ranged from a gardeners' shed at Pontypridd (and onto which a tree fell one year while I was inside, counting the day's takings) to the bowls' club changing rooms at Ebbw Vale; from a CB Radio ham's broom cupboard at the Hoover ground in Merthyr Tydfil to a converted horse show bus at Abergavenny. Very few of them provided an unrestricted view of play. Our first year back in North Wales for 16 years, for example, when we took a three-day and a one-day match to Colwyn Bay, we were located in a small portacabin in the car park behind the pavilion, sharing space with a couple of players from either side – I remember Matt being one of ours, Mike Atherton one of Lancashire's – as the main team dressing rooms were so small you could barely swing a dwarf spider round without hitting the walls. On the Sunday I didn't emerge from that hole all day. Tony was back and forth to the two main gates swapping the ballot boxes we had been given to use to hold the notes people were handing over as they were coming in. I'd barely finished counting the contents of one box before another one would arrive. There were £10 and £20 notes everywhere. On that occasion we knew when a wicket had fallen by the roar of the crowd – and that first year the crowd was at least 95% Lancastrian, too. Negated home advantage be damned; we took bundles of cash to the night safe that evening.

Often my only escape from these dingy burrows would be nipping out for a cigarette. I was quite a heavy smoker back then, a habit I managed to break when the team was on a Lord's Taverners post-season jaunt to Guernsey at the end of the 2007 season. John Stern, one-time Editor of *The Cricketer* magazine but now Editor-at-Large for the *Wisden* group, once began an article on Glamorgan by describing me as 'the affable, chain-smoking Glamorgan Chief Executive'. I guess it's just 'affable' now. Or at least I hope it is. I've been described as much worse. I did try to give up the smoking many times. The least convincing occasion was on the night of 26th May 1989. The day after my birthday, so an easily memorable date, but it also happened to be the night that Arsenal went to Anfield needing to beat Liverpool in their own back yard by two clear goals to win their first Championship title in 18 years. 1-0 up as the game went into added time, I announced to Carol I would give up smoking if they managed to nick a winner. They did. I celebrated ten minutes later with a fag.

Nipping out of whatever passed for our office for the day generally brought you into contact with the punters and whilst that was something you had to do, especially, I believed, when the team was struggling, you were something of an easy target for the many whinges and complaints. My good friend Tom Richardson, who was Gloucestershire's Chief Executive for a decade towards the end of my time at Glamorgan, used to say that the folk on his side of the Bridge would sidle up to him on a match day and utter, in a West Country drawl which I couldn't begin to mimic accurately, "Oi! I wanna word wi' you." In my case I would be in the middle of a lap of the ground, often accompanied by one of the players (Hugh Morris and Robert Croft were inveterate 'lappers', as were the media duo of Edward Bevan and Richard Thomas) and I'd be stopped a good couple of dozen times. On occasions I may as well have held an al fresco members' surgery, such were the numbers I was being asked to respond to. The worst types – and I couldn't possibly name them here – were the ones I termed 'The Apologists'; the sort who began every complaint with a 'sorry to bother you' or a 'you know I'm not the type to complain' (when it was clear the reason for their very existence as a member of the human race was to drone on more than a hyperactive bluebottle overdosing on Haribos). You'd think you'd got away with it as you passed them, having gazed through their eyes into the internal workings of their minds, watching the cogs slowly wheeling round as they racked their brains to try to come up with something about which to complain, only for them to thrust out an outstretched arm at the very last moment, stopping you in your tracks. They had you. Most of the time their 'complaint' turned out to be something nonsensically trivial, such as a broken lock on one of the toilet cubicles, the price of chips, or one of the umpires' accents. And no, that last one is not made up. I genuinely received a letter from a member complaining that they were talking to Ian 'Gunner' Gould, one of the ICC's elite panel in his later years, but they couldn't understand his accent. And just what was I supposed to do with that one? Send Gunner to elocution lessons? Teach him Welsh?

Some of the letters we used to receive from members were wonderful. Most were routine – autograph requests, membership queries, ticket applications and such like. Some were about selection policy and were both well intentioned and informed, such as those I used to receive from a fellow called David Hay, who lived up in Cheshire, or the regular emails I used to get from Paul Mokler, from Hereford. We did occasionally receive a nasty one. In 1990 there was a real poisoned pen letter aimed at Viv Richards. It was so threatening and racist we called in the police. We also had a regular correspondent during the 1997 season who in every letter attacked the captain at the time, Matthew Maynard, for his decision to continue omitting Colin Metson and pick Adrian Shaw on the grounds of the latter being a better batsman (and, for the cricket management, an infinitely more team-focused personality, which was another important factor but about which for obvious reasons we weren't going to be yelling from the rooftops). This went on for much of the summer. Even one after the County Championship title had been secured. Always derogatory about Shaw, never anything but fulsome in praising Metson; never a hint of the author's identity or location. The final one proclaimed rather loftily that the Championship title would have been won even sooner had Shaw not been playing. At one point one of the staff wondered whether it might have been from Metson himself…

Our Scorer, Byron Denning, or 'Dasher', as he was known, eventually took over the role of regular matchday PA announcer. In my early years we had used a collection of committee members who'd volunteered (or more likely been volunteered) for the role of 'Match Manager', though the title was something of a misnomer. They managed nothing. Just spoke into the PA when prompted. One of them confused Steve Bastien with Mark Frost throughout the game. Easy mistake to make? Well, one was black and the other white, for a start. And whereas Bastien was indeed in the field for the game, Mark Frost wasn't even playing. Cue more letters and complaints. Byron brought a real sense of order to proceedings. As Scorer he was in the best position to know when announcements were needed and exactly when to make them, and it was a move which most of the other counties had already made by then so he knew it was coming. He also brought his mischievous sense of humour to the role. Traditionally we played a three-day (later four-day) Championship game at Abergavenny, with a one-day Sunday League match at Ebbw Vale sandwiched in between. On one occasion in the mid-'90s, against Gloucestershire, Andrew Symonds had smashed our bowlers to all parts of Abergavenny, hitting 16 sixes, in the process exhausting my stock of spare red balls and necessitating someone driving to where the Second XI were playing to grab hold of some more. At the end of the Gloucestershire innings, in which Symonds had hammered 234, Byron came on to the microphone and announced, "Ladies and gentlemen, for those of you with small children in tow, I suggest that you cover up their ears... because here come the Glamorgan bowling figures." The very next day, at Ebbw Vale, Symonds proceeded to drain me of my white spares, hitting another seven sixes, losing five balls in the process. During the search for one, Byron's voice sounded over the airwaves, aiming his comments at a group of high-spirited (oh, OK then, drunken) youths who weren't paying any attention to the cricket, preferring instead to entertain themselves by sliding down the steep grassy bank on one side of the ground. "For those lads who seem determined to ignore the match and play around on the bank, why not pay a visit to the Glamorgan shop, where official cushions are on sale at a bargain £4.95? It'll be much kinder to your behinds. Either that, or maybe just pack it in."

On another occasion, at Pontypridd, Glamorgan had just been drubbed by Hampshire early on the third morning of a four-day game. I was sat in the office (a small loft at the top of the old pavilion, accessed by means of a vertiginous climb up a ladder designed to hold the bearing weight of Kate Moss after a particularly virulent bout of anorexia. "Ladies and gentlemen, for those of you who are disappointed to see Glamorgan lose so early today and were looking forward to a full day's cricket, it may be possible for you to get your money back by going to the Glamorgan office in the pavilion..." I think 'ashen-faced' best described me at that point, as I envisaged a horde of opportunistic pensioners congregating at the foot of that ladder screaming for a minuscule proportion of their annual membership fee, but there then came a classically Denning-esque qualification. "…and addressing your complaints to a Mr Malcolm Marshall, care of Hampshire County Cricket Club." Marshall had taken eleven wickets in the match. Thanks, Dasher. He was a one-off. I'm not sure you'd get that sort of joshing from the 2021 version of the Glammy scorer-cum-announcer, Andrew Hignell, let's just say that. Away from all the T20 yelling and house music (I sound like my Dad, I know), it's all very much by the book these days.

One of my favourites came during one of our rare forays up to Merthyr Tydfil. It was in the middle of our itinerant gypsy days of the late '80s and we had employed Len Smith – previously an assistant groundsman at Sophia Gardens but subsequently recruited by Somerset as their Head Groundsman for a year – to come back to Wales and liaise with all of the hordes of amateur groundsmen who were preparing pitches for the annual grand occasion when Glamorgan brought the first-class cricket circus into town. Hugh Morris tells a story of the first occasion we were in Merthyr, playing Kent at the Hoovers sports ground in 1988, when he walked out for the toss to find the local groundsman, beaming widely at him. "Best track we've ever 'ad by 'yere, Hugh, butt," he said, "Solid as a rock, it is." As he put his thumb to the pitch, it all but disappeared. But Hugh, ever the gentleman, just smiled back. Not the quickest, the pitches at Hoovers.

In that 1988 match David Constant, not everyone's cup of tea as an umpire but someone with whom I enjoyed a tremendous relationship, decided a bit of mischief was in order and proceeded to issue his signals to the scorers slightly differently from the way he normally would. Instead of an outstretched right arm for a no ball, he'd offer a barely discernible sideways 'point' with his right forefinger. Leg byes would be communicated with the faintest flick of the thigh. And so on. There was even a 'one short' that afternoon. You could barely make them out they were so idiosyncratic. Byron quickly cottoned on, though, and the pair of them had fun throughout the day in their own little world. No one else seemed to be in the least bit interested or at all bothered and it didn't have any bearing on the game or anything.

A week or so later, at another home game, Dasher nabbed me over a coffee and produced a letter from his pocket. "This'll tickle you," he said. I read the letter, which was from a disgruntled Kent supporter who had travelled all the way from Broadstairs to the game the previous week and was complaining in no uncertain terms about Constant's signalling. Words to the effect of 'ruining the enjoyment of the game for hundreds of people', or maybe even 'the end of civilisation as we know it'. I gave it back to Byron and asked him whether he needed me to draft some sort of response. "No need, boy," he said, looking at me with a twinkle in his eye, "I've written back to him already. I told him 'Connie' was signalling in Welsh."

Our Gwent weekends always threw something up. At Ebbw Vale one year the umpire Don Oslear – never knowingly unofficious – determined half an hour before the scheduled start that one of the trees outside the ground had overhanging branches that encroached onto the playing area, indicating that the offending branches would need to be cut back before play could start. Yeah, that was always going to happen. We'll just nip back to the pavilion, check the tree-felling licence we carry with us at all times and grab the tree saw we always pack with the admission tickets and the spare balls, Don. And there was the time Monte Lynch, presumably hand-picked from within a Surrey dressing room for his reliability and sent to pick their (scarily quick) fast bowler Sylvester Clarke up from Newport station and drive him up to the ground at Ebbw Vale (Clarke wasn't playing in the concurrent Championship game in Swansea). He managed to collect him easily enough but ended up meandering through the Gwent valleys into Ebbw Vale and then circling the ground for over half an hour without being able to locate the entrance, arriving just as the toss had been completed. Lynch couldn't play. Nor could Clarke. Our lads were distraught.

At Abergavenny there was a very small tent sited adjacent to the pavilion for use by the press, just a few yards from our office, which for games at the ground consisted of a bus used for judges of equestrian events No need for anything lavish for the media back in those days, just a phone line in and a few desks and chairs. We had a good travelling contingent for home games throughout the '90s – Richard Thomas of the South Wales Evening Post; Phil Blanche or Simon Thomas from the Western Mail or Echo; Paul Rees covering the odd game for the *Guardian*; as well as a few from the nationals – many of whom actively sought out the likes of Colwyn Bay, Pontypridd and Neath because they were off the beaten track, and Abergavenny was a real favourite for many. On one occasion, just before tea on the first day of a game against Worcestershire one of our members, Bill Anderson, came and sat down in front of the press pack, proceeding to unfold his own portable desk and set out an array of coloured pens and pencils before starting to score the game. Byron, as official scorer, was located elsewhere on the ground. Knowing glances were exchanged when I joined Messrs Rees and Thomas (R) at the back of the tent a short time before lunch, for a breather away from the members (and quite probably a fag), at the very moment that David Leatherdale, later the Chief Executive of both Worcestershire and the Professional Cricketers' Association, reached his fifty.

"Watch this," said Reesy, nudging me and winking at Richard, before raising his voice and addressing Bill. "How many balls for Leatherdale's fifty, Bill?"

Pause. Then the reply: "98, Paul. Five fours."

There was another pause before, at the end of the over, Byron's voice came on to the public address to announce: "And David Leatherdale's half century came up in 123 balls, containing one six and eight fours." The polite applause round the ground couldn't drown out Bill's protestations that the official scorers had got it wrong. He must have been watching a different game, claimed our Frindall-lite chalker. The two journos next to me were crying with laughter. This was the same Bill who would set up in front of the Vice Presidents' enclosure at Sophia Gardens with his array of coloured pencils, scoring all day. Well, much of it. Nipping off for a cup of tea and a trip to the loo for ten minutes mid-session didn't get in the way. He'd simply carry on where he'd left off. Even if there'd been a hat-trick in the intervening period. Or a nuclear holocaust.

We saw it all on the outgrounds in those days. Nine separate streakers during a single one-day game in Pontypridd (the last of which was actually a rather half-hearted invasion by two drunks dressed as, respectively, a nun and a monk (one of our committee members, David Irving actually asked what convinced me they weren't genuinely holy people: perhaps the fags in their mouths and the cans of Carlsberg Special Brew they were holding being insufficient by way of convincers); play being stopped because the pitch at Abergavenny had been being incorrectly marked, Steve Watkin being pulled up for no-balling and complaining to the umpire, Graham Burgess, that something wasn't quite right (and he was proved right after the pitch was remeasured); the truly inedible food at Swansea in the early '90s; Viv Richards being prevented from entering Ynysangharad Park in Pontypridd because he didn't have the correct accreditation; coffees at Swansea with 'the Doc' – Ritabrata Bose; committee members at Neath queuing up for lunches intended for the players before the players themselves; our self-designated head steward, Des Williams, a Walter Mitty-like character if ever there was one, telling us all about his latest business trip fixing IBM's computer mainframe in New York state only to be totally flummoxed half an hour later by the breakdown of a simple three line electronic scoreboard at Newport; the legendary Ronnie Thomas, another of our crack octogenarian stewards, selling scorecards with a drawled "Get your scorecards: only fifty pence, two for a pound," or him coming into the dressing room at Swansea to inform Colin Metson that he had a flat tyre, adding that it wasn't all bad – it was only flat on the bottom half; there was the daily challenge of balancing takings which whoever was on the gate had almost certainly managed to muck up; our resident Statler and Waldorf, Gordon Eccles and Alun Jones, being pathologically incapable of getting the score on the main Sophia Gardens scoreboard right – even at 0 for 0 after one ball, there would be a mistake somewhere; mad dashes to provincial bank night safes with Tony, often with tens of thousands of pounds in a briefcase; and trying to find a qualified medic to administer first aid to a clearly-not-properly-qualified official first aider at Llanelli. I recall all of the venues with some degree of fondness. Except Christ College in Brecon, where we played a one-day friendly against Zimbabwe towards the end of the 1993 season. Nothing against the venue. We had 21 contracted players that season and other than Alun Evans and Hugh Morris every single one of them had a contract which expired at the end of that season. I spent all day negotiating (or 'in talks' as the press so laughably term the process nowadays) so I didn't see a ball bowled, never emerged from the room I was in, and therefore have no recollection whatsoever of either the match or the location.

The county game changed forever, though, when the bidding process for Test matches changed in the early 2000s. The England and Wales Cricket Board (known by the official, W-less acronym ECB) was determined to keep the counties firmly in their place and they used the issues of building up reserves and changing the old-style 'distribution' (or 'hand-out' as used by disparagingly snooty national journalists who didn't seem to understand that when someone in those days went on to play for England it was generally because one of the counties had developed them using part of that same 'hand-out') as their choice of weapon for the fight. Counties had to cut back. This meant in all but a minority of established cases the outground became a thing of the past, a distinctive relic of a sport which didn't take itself too seriously and wasn't completely obsessed with money. The four-day game became even more marginalized, played in empty concrete county HQ bowls at the two scrag end extremities of the season and largely ignored by the governing body. Then again, the old Test and County Cricket Board (TCCB) weren't always that on the ball either. When I returned from our week in Colwyn Bay in 1992 in among my post was a letter from Tony Brown, the TCCB's Administration Manager, marked for the attention of Barrie Leadbeater, one of the umpires (a lovely fellow) and a note asking me to pass it on to him. It was postmarked the day before the game, meaning it would arrive, at best, on day one when we'd already long since decamped for North Wales. Obviously 'Browny' didn't have a clue about the geography of Wales. I duly sent it back, with a compliment's slip of my own, enclosing a map of Wales, with a marker pen arrow highlighting the distance from Cardiff to Colwyn Bay, adding the words 'Four Hours' Drive'.

Success on the field still eluded us. Hugh Morris's first captaincy stint was clearly a difficult one and he made a pretty decent fist of what must have been a bit of a hopelessly bad job, always retaining his sense of humour even if his memory wasn't always the best back in those days. He once managed to sit through an entire Cricket Committee meeting in the offices at Sophia Gardens before walking out of the front door, stepping over his cricket coffin, climbing into his car and driving all the way back home to Cowbridge. The kit had remained on the doorstep throughout the meeting and he'd managed to ignore it on his way out.

In the winter of 1986 Glamorgan had signed Alan Butcher, who although having been released by Surrey was still only 32. Philip Carling was convinced he had a few miles left in the tank and so it proved. He would go on to have a significant influence in shaping the future for the club. He would also prove to be one of the most engaging of lunchtime drinking companions for Dean and me. Around the time Gwyn Stone took over as Secretary in 1991, the year Butch picked up the injury which subsequently forced him to retire, the three of us used to spend at least one lunchtime a week in one of the pubs around the corner from the ground – the *Beverley* or the *Lodge* (later the *Mochyn Du*, or *The Brewhouse and Kitchen* as it is now) – quaffing a few beers and enjoying one another's company. In those days cricketers were only engaged on contracts from April to September (year-round contracts were still a decade or more away) but Alan had been employed in the Glamorgan office for a couple of winters by that point. Nicknamed 'Morse' by Dean (a far better effort in my view than the rather lame and predictable 'Butch'), for his cerebrality (and yes, I understand the context now), his appreciation of beer and his ability to knock off the Telegraph crossword, very similar to the wonderful detective creation of Colin Dexter, the televising of whose books had begun just before that time. Those were happy winters, and the lunchtimes more often than not extended well into the afternoon. And please, don't judge too harshly. They were very different times.

When Hugh resigned the captaincy in 1989 Butch took over, working closely with Tony Lewis. When 'AR' had become involved again he'd decided we should stop signing players deemed to be on their way out at other counties and start shaping our own destiny by bringing our own young players through. Easy words, I know, and a difficult path which the Club would try to repeat in the 2000s only for those in charge then to lose patience. After Philip Carling had left the Club in 1990 I was the one AR and the committee turned to to mop up after them and implement their cricketing decisions. Looking back, I'm still not sure that people fully appreciate the enormous part that Alan Butcher played in laying the foundations for what was to become one of the great Glamorgan teams. His stint as captain was vital because it was on his watch that the likes of Adrian Dale, Steve Watkin, Tony Cottey, Robert Croft and Steve James were developed, and Matthew Maynard and Hugh Morris – now back in the runs without the shackles of leadership – began to flourish, and it was also Butch under whom Viv Richards played his first season. A half decent side was really beginning to take shape.

6   UP THE JUNCTION

'A committee is the only known form of life with a hundred bellies and no brain.'
ROBERT HEINLEIN

Committees. What does that word conjure up in your imagination? At Glamorgan, committees ran everything. And we had committees for everything too. The simplest decision was complicated by first wrapping it in a bundle of unnecessary complexity and then tying it with yards of red tape. They weren't bad people; most had hearts of gold. But when they came together, they could suffocate the life out of even the best of proposals.

Before we can get back to the cricketing thread which, after all, I'm not stupid enough to think that anyone reading this is not keen to pick up on, I did promise myself that if I ever came to write any kind of memoir, I would take the opportunity to spin a few yarns about committees and specifically about those glorious characters we worked with and some of the (often bonkers) decisions they took. As with the 'early days' stuff, feel free to plough on ahead to Chapter Seven if it's more cricket you want. I shan't be upset, honest. Oh, and this chapter darts about a bit chronologically, so be warned.

The comedian Milton Berle described a committee as a group that keeps minutes but loses hours. I can vouch for that. The minutes were certainly kept, I know that. I used to keep them. I take issue with the final bit though. We didn't lose hours. We lost days. So many committees. So many meetings. So many voices. So much wasted time. So many decisions taken that could have been taken without the need to waste everyone's time. Digging a bit deeper philosophically, the American author Mark Twain was once asked what he thought about committees. "A committee," he said, "is a group of the unwilling, picked from the unfit, to do the unnecessary." That's often how it felt in the 1980s and 1990s at Glamorgan.

Around 1987 one David Irving was first elected to the Glamorgan committee. A former Woolwich Building Society branch manager living in Swansea, he came to personify everything that, in my view, was both good and bad about being a committee member around that time. He served for around 15 years. In terms of good, he was loyal; boy, was he loyal. If you gave your time to him and his various opinions and enterprises, he was fiercely loyal. I'm pretty sure had he been around in 2008 when I left the Club he would have been a heck of a lot more vocal than the bunch who were sat around the committee table then. He wouldn't have stood for it. He was also thorough. Goodness me, he was thorough.

In terms of bad, I don't think I've ever met anyone so procedural, so meticulous, so painstakingly fastidious in his outlook. And that's coming from someone who prides himself on being reasonably ordered, punctual and organized. The phone would ring on the button at 8:46am (our office hours started officially at 8:45am) with some request or other, invariably related to his books and the library collection he'd helped to put together for Glamorgan back in the late '80s. And woe betide you if you never rang back (I still remember his number – 01792-404041). But never between 2pm and 4pm, when he would take the phone off the hook so that his wife Margaret could have an afternoon nap. Presumably the only time she could be guaranteed to get away from him. And if you hadn't called back, he'd be back on to you at 4:01pm precisely. There was no getting away. Best just do what he asked and get him off your back.

David looked after the hosting on home match days and organized the rota. Glamorgan committee members were expected to host visiting committee members on home match days and it was David's job to ensure there was always someone available, that they filled in their forms appropriately and that all chargeable items (they dined free of charge, paying – supposedly – for everything else). He had to round up the recalcitrants and remedials, the 'good eggs' who were rarely available owing to the cardinal sin of actually having to work for a living, the likes of Roger Morris, Stuart Harrison, Robin Williams and Ricky Needham, a partner in a Cardiff firm of solicitors who became a very good friend. Naughty schoolboys, the lot of them, with David behaving very much like the headmaster, admonishing them and trying to pull them all into line. Every club needs one, I guess, and without David the hosting probably would have gone to pot. He carried on helping out even after he'd stood down officially as a committee member, first with the hosting (surprisingly no one fancied taking that on initially) and then with the fundraising for the Wilfred Wooller Gates. And always, always with his beloved library.

Wine served with lunch at home matches wasn't chargeable. It didn't take too long for some of the parsimonious and more acquisitive committee members to cotton on to the fact that if they ordered a couple of bottles just as dessert was arriving they could happily quaff the rest of the wine through the afternoon and not be billed for any more drinks. And one of the other rules in the early days was that although lunch would need to be paid for, tea was free. Perhaps the only way of graphically illustrating the difference between the two was to suggest that between 1:15pm and 1:55pm the committee room resembled the Marie Celeste, only to transform into Waterloo Station concourse in the evening rush hour between 4:10pm and 4:30pm. My God, they loved a freebie. There were more people in that room than on the Shibuya Crossing in Tokyo.

Away games were freebies. Committee members had complimentary tickets for themselves and a guest, drinks all day on the opposition, with free lunch and tea thrown in as well. One Swansea-based committee member went on every single away trip for three seasons in a row, enjoying hospitality on every single match day. We had a sweep on which match he'd finally be unable to travel to. No one came close. It was seasons later. He was even known to stock up with sandwiches at tea so that he could also enjoy his evening meal on the host county back at the hotel. Inevitably all this meant pressure of numbers. Pity the poor sod who was deputed to be in contact with the home county in the lead up to a game as the committee members all came out of hiding. I used to have to do that job and it was such a hot potato that I was forever trying to offload it to someone else. And bear in mind at one point there were 24 elected members, a President, a couple of honorary positions, three Officers, four Trustees and a couple of co-opted members too. (Quite why you need co-opted members when you already have a cast of thousands is probably a question for another time; let's just say it hints at an election system that favoured quantity over quality.) Even though they were told to confirm arrangements at least 48 hours beforehand so that we could liaise with the host county, none of the buggers ever did. Lord's, The Oval and Worcester were the three most popular destinations. The other counties didn't know what had hit them. It was like a pensioners' coach party on an all-you-can-eat-and-drink day out to the coast.

And for big games the woodwork would be crumbling so much it was in imminent danger of collapse. Out they came with their requests and demands, often for more free tickets for friends. We only made one Lord's Final in my time at the Club – the 2000 Benson and Hedges Cup Final against Gloucestershire – but organizing the ticketing for the committee must have been very like organizing the ins and outs of the D-Day landings. We had 24 elected committee members, each of whom it was decided (by them) had the right to bring their partners. Having first won the battle to charge them for the privilege (I never responded to the point some of them made along the lines of 'after all I do for this club' because the only honest response was 'you don't actually do anything') we then had to shoehorn all 24, plus guests, officers, President, Trustees and Co. into one hospitality box, which we were of course paying for. And there was only one interval and therefore only one occasion for a formal sit-down meal. In the end we had to sort them into two groups and pay for two separate sittings. Bloody ridiculous. Some of them seemed to be incapable of actually sitting in a normal seat in a stand and watching the cricket, such was the over-inflated sense of their own importance. A few didn't bother. I remember watching much of the game with Ricky Needham and Roger Morris from a bar in Q Stand. Neither could be bothered with the whole committee hospitality circus. They preferred to watch the game with a pint. And no, I didn't get a lunch.

I only sat with the committee for lunch on a home match day once in a blue moon. And for away match days, probably on but half a dozen occasions in 23 seasons, one of which – at Trent Bridge – was to experience one of the most excruciatingly embarrassing hours of my professional life as I listened to David Davies and Philip James demonstrating pristine cricketing ignorance and behaving with fawning obsequiousness in the company of 'Dickie' Bird, Tim Lamb, Brian Bolus and Chris Broad. One of them – I'll spare their blushes as to which – even collared me before we sat down to ask me how to address Tim Lamb, then the ECB's Chief Executive. When I suggested that calling him 'Tim' might be a good idea, he pointed out that he was the second son of the Earl of Rochester and was surprised when I said 'yep, still Tim.' I should have said 'your beatification' or something similar. He wouldn't have batted an eyelid in using it to open a conversation. Tim would have enjoyed that too. He'd have known it to have been a put-up job.

Those sorts of away day jollies were just SO not for me. Firstly, I couldn't stand the embarrassment. Secondly, I was generally there either to meet my counterpart, in which case we'd eat elsewhere, or there in my own time, in which case I could sit and mind my own business, earphones in with a book or a crossword, and a catch-up meal with the captain and the coach in the evening. I'd rather sink a 500-year-old rusty arrowhead slowly into one of my eyeballs than openly choose to dine with the committee.

I have already mentioned my first encounter with our then Chairman, Gwyn Craven. He made some truly epic recommendations during his time in the chair. He once proposed in a meeting that the Club should buy a racehorse and run it in Centenary Year in Glamorgan colours. He also suggested we try to acquire the bridge of the HMS Glamorgan and somehow convert it into an office or a hospitality area for one of the two main grounds. Is it any wonder we weren't winning anything on the field? There was also the famous 'Vice Presidents Enclosure (St. Helen's) White Fence Working Party' too. This was a small working group set up by Gwyn to look at how to tart up the small enclosure of around 40 seats at Swansea so that the surroundings would be commensurate with the premium VPs were paying over and above the ordinary members. What it amounted to was a choice of what colour to paint the fence around it. And the clue was in the working party's title anyway. There weren't any other decisions to make. Yet it met three times. Three times! There were official minutes and everything.

One of my favourite committee members back then was Bill Cawdron, the Treasurer, a senior figure within the NatWest bank. Let me declare a bit of personal bias: he was the one who agreed to take me on after my initial six-month stint working for nothing because he was the one who had to sign off the cost. Not that it amounted to very much, but even so. Bill was a really good man, commercially knowledgeable but with a real empathy, and long after he retired, around the time I had taken over as Chief Executive, he would seek me out for a chat, not just a reminiscence of 'the old days' but to discuss specific cricket issues. He had a genuine interest in and knowledge of the team. His was a steady hand on the financial tiller in the days when county clubs used book-keepers, long before the Finance Director became commonplace. He was also probably the only one who could read Mostyn's writing.

Back in those days we had committees for absolutely everything: Cricket; Coaching; Marketing; Membership; Finance;

Investments; East Grounds; West Grounds; House & Ground; Selection; Management, comprising the chairmen of each one; and finally a full Executive Committee of 24 elected (12 from the East and 12 from the West), Chairman, Vice Chairman, Treasurer, Honorary Secretary (I never quite understood what he actually did – probably as much as the others I suppose), Honorary Solicitor, Trustees (three or four of them), President, co-opted members (30-odd people and they were finding that there would still be a shortage of skills, so they'd have to bring in specialists on top). And that was without the need for the appropriate staff to attend. So we had between 35 and 40 people sat around a table genuinely trying to run all aspects of the club's business. In detail. We needed a room the size of the Albert Hall just to cram them all in. In one meeting I remember two people having to stand as there weren't enough chairs. I loved the ironic use of the word 'Executive'. Yes, they executed decisions but blimey did it take them forever to make them. They all came along with their own specific questions. Wynne Walters would always want to know where we were in relation to signing particular types of cricketer, his pet topic being the ongoing need for a slow left arm bowler; Norman Thorne would be asking about picking up members by working with church groups; John Williams would be constantly plugging cricket in Swansea, which he kept going almost single-handedly for years; and David Irving, well, he was ten items of 'Any Other Business' and an extra hour on the end of meetings just on his own. And none of this includes the working parties and other small sub-groups, of which there were dozens. It was death by red tape suffocation.

Despite the numbers there were barely any former cricketers around the table. In 1986, my first year, there was David Lewis, who played a few games for Glamorgan back in the late '60s, and Ricky Needham, who played one match against Cambridge University in 1975. That was it. All those people available and we had one person who had any experience of competitive county cricket. Tony Lewis came back into the fold the following year as a co-opted committee member, and it was no coincidence that his stint as Chairman between 1988 and 1993 saw us focus on a youth policy, sign quality overseas players such as Ravi Shastri and Viv Richards and a decent side begin to emerge. Three more former players – Roger Davis, Hugh Davies and Stuart Harrison – were elected shortly afterwards. But it was pretty poor, to be honest. Even recognizing players – our own players – was, shall we say, hit and miss. On one occasion, when discussing a pre-season social for players, staff and committee, one committee member, Gareth Daniel, suggested the players wore name badges so that the committee would recognize them. The other way around, surely? I can remember Ricky, who was sat next to me at the meeting in which this was being discussed, turning to me and offering the priceless observation, "the players will be the ones in the Glamorgan blazers." Quite.

I used to play a game with Ricky and a few (select) others on the Cricket Committee. They had to spot the rude word that appeared in the minutes, which I had to get past Hugh Davies as Cricket Chairman first as he would naturally want to review them before they were circulated. First one won a pint. I became rather good at it. So good that no one managed to spot the fact that in one set of minutes the ending of one paragraph, about the soon-to-be-installed floodlights, had finished with the word "electric," the new one starting with the words "Until the lights…" When rolled together, they revealed the naughtiest of naughty words. I knew I couldn't top that one so I announced that I was officially retiring the game.

Unsurprisingly the quality of debate wasn't always good, especially when they were offering views about professional cricket. In the late '90s, when the England and Wales Cricket Board was debating a move towards a two-division County Championship, a massive step for the county game after 120-odd years with the same all-play-all structure, the captain, Matthew Maynard, was invited to the meeting to offer his opinion. For once everyone was singing from the same hymn sheet in being opposed to the move (Matthew Engel, the Editor of *Wisden*, said in the following year's edition that the whole country had been united in opposition to the new structure; but unfortunately that country was Wales) but although the debate received a whopping 25 minutes of the committee's time, it was still only the second longest debate of the evening behind the proposal to increase the price of committee lunches. Matt was rightly confused as to the role of a committee in the running of a modern county cricket club. And he wasn't the only one.

Matt was at the centre of another fascinating cricket debate, this time in Cricket Committee at the end of the 1992 season. Alan Butcher had been forced to retire through injury and having previously nominated Matt as his Vice Captain (I remember telling Butch I thought he was completely off his head with that one – shows what I know), Matt had led the side for much of the year. And led it well. An older and wiser Hugh Morris was also a candidate. Both would have brought different qualities but the majority of those with a cricket pedigree – Tony Lewis, Alan Jones, Alan Butcher, David Lewis, Ricky Needham, Peter Walker, Jack Bannister (the latter two co-opted) – all wanted Matt. Roger Davis was a little more ambivalent. Hugh Davies was vehemently opposed. He clearly disliked Matt. Davies was a thorn in plenty of sides over the course of the next 15 years and knifed plenty of people in the back, including me. But the non-cricketers all voted for Hugh Morris and despite it being a marginal call it was Hugh's name which was proposed to the Executive Committee. Hugh's face fitted, Matt's didn't. Not then, anyway. Even though most of those with any knowledge of the game had voted for him. And, memorably, in the main committee meeting later that evening, Brian Shackleton managed to vote for Matt, where in the previous Cricket Committee meeting he'd voted for Hugh. He said he'd been persuaded by the arguments, not realising that if he'd been 'persuaded by the arguments,' the same arguments in fact, a couple of hours earlier in the evening, it would have been Matt who would have been nominated. Presumably in that case he would have been persuaded to vote for Hugh instead. It was a shambles of a system.

Hugh Davies had some real set-tos with a number of the players, staff and committee members over the years. His son Adam had been on a development contract but when contracts were up at the end of the 2001 season the coaches didn't believe he had done enough to merit another one. As Second XI Coach John Derrick was the one who would have seen most of him, and his recommendation not to make an offer was supported by both Alan Jones and Graham Reynolds (Graham was our schools liaison officer and watched a heck of a lot of cricket at that level; outstanding man, too). But whereas Stuart Harrison would duck out of a meeting if either of his sons, David or Adam, were being discussed, and Alan Jones never participated in a debate when his son Andrew was being talked about, Hugh insisted on staying in the room throughout the debate about Adam, thus placing John in particular in a really invidious position. And he wasn't just observing. He kept trotting out statistics to support his argument. Adam wasn't a bad player. Far from it. But there would be no change of heart and he wasn't offered another contract. There is absolutely no doubt in my mind that Hugh never forgot that and that he never forgave John. As an afterthought I remember Graham taking Adam for a walk around the ground the following day (there was a Second XI match taking place). Graham had a voice which, shall we say, carried considerably, and I could hear every word as he told Adam, "Listen, son, there's one reason why you've not been given another contract and no matter what anyone tells you, you need to remember what it is. Sorry for being blunt but… you're not f***ing good enough, son." Go on, Graham. Sugar coat it for the lad.

Statistics would always be thrown on the table during Hugh's tenure as Cricket Committee Chairman. They were useful as a guide, of course, but they were relied on far too much, primarily because so few committee members ever watched sufficient cricket to be able to form a proper opinion. And many who did wouldn't have known one end of a bat from the other. Those who actually were capable of judging a cricketer were generally working full time and therefore accused by the others of not seeing enough cricket. What became of the idea that you trusted the Coaches, the Captain and the Chief Executive and supported their decisions I really don't know. Of the regular Cricket Committee members a few did. Ricky was never anything other than supportive, as were David Morgan (the Club Chairman from 1993 to 1998), Roger Morris and Stuart Harrison. Wynne Walters would ask a few awkward questions, which he was perfectly entitled to do, of course, as would Roger Davis, who was direct though never anything other than fair, but they too would more often than not end up supportive. Harry Lazarus's contribution came more outside of meetings, engaging in protracted letter-writing and often ringing me the day after a meeting to say he'd had a change of heart. Other than challenging some minor detail in the minutes at meetings he was normally quiet; if he did have a bee in his bonnet over something he would 'get at' Hugh beforehand and the two of them would nag away on particular *betes noires* of theirs. But generally speaking they were a decent bunch. Unfortunately, with Hugh I thought it all became a bit personal. He didn't like people disagreeing with him.

Ricky disproved the whole reliance on statistics debate in one meeting. The averages were there on the table for everyone as normal, and for the non-regular fringe players the Second XI averages were often vital. It seemed every year we were giving a young lad called James Williams a contract on the basis that he'd made a century in a Second XI game on the day of the relevant meeting. Jim was a good batsman, but that shouldn't happen. Either a player is proving his worth, or the coaches are going with a hunch, or he's out. Some of the committee were too easily swayed. At this one meeting Hugh pointed to Gary Butcher's numbers and explained that as he'd only scored 600 runs he wasn't showing consistency, and that he'd only taken 20 wickets. Ricky accepted the argument but pointed to the fact that two of Gary's scores had been unbeaten 150s, which showed the ability to make big hundreds, and that he'd taken his wickets at a low strike rate of 35. Powerful arguments against. The reality is that both were right. And they prove the folly of basing any decision on statistics alone.

I recall the debate about the introduction of Twenty20 cricket in 2003. Our various committees had looked at the pros and cons at sub-committee level and there was a coming together of the main committee to determine which side of the fence Glamorgan should climb down on. At that time it wasn't at all clear whether there would be sufficient support across the game for it to be brought in. It was a decent debate, ending in support for its introduction. Gerard Elias, the Chairman, had almighty challenges balancing his high-profile work as a barrister with attending all of the meetings required of the post and the ECB meeting which was to debate and determine the future of Twenty20 was one he couldn't attend, so Hugh Davies would be deputizing and attending the meeting with me. On the day there was another lengthy debate before the counties eventually came to a vote. Despite having a clear mandate from his committee, he cast Glamorgan's vote against, citing Shackleton's words of 'being persuaded by the argument' on the day. In other words, I have an opinion on this and I don't particularly care what anyone else thinks. Thankfully, the old-fashioned anti-T20 view was defeated.

I'll admit to not dealing very effectively with committees in the early days. It used to frustrate me that people who knew so little about the game felt qualified to take decisions which affected the players' livelihoods. Things changed under David Morgan and I also learned to play the game, to understand the political side of the job and to respect the processes we had to work within. David was a really good man, someone who took time to listen, and although he often had strong opinions – he was one of the few who watched a lot of cricket and understood the game – he would ensure that everyone had the opportunity to say what they wanted to, ensuring compromise where a firm decision wasn't possible. He came into every meeting with a pretty solid idea of how each individual would be thinking on each of the main topics under discussion. When I asked him how, he told me he spent time between meetings talking to the key protagonists individually, either in person or on the phone. He could therefore see the way a discussion was likely to go and would draw in people to support or oppose an argument as appropriate. He was a very skilful political operator, just what we needed in the chair.

David also had the trust of the players, including a succession of captains. Throughout my time at Glamorgan he was a constant reassuring presence, a person you respected for what he did as much as what he said, and for whom work wasn't everything: he always asked after your family, for example. He'd occasionally offer personal advice. I can't dress to look smart – I have never been able to – but David would throw in comments about the importance of me dressing smarter. Much as though you were chucking Ralph Lauren clothing on a scarecrow, it would never work, and he had the grace to give up eventually. But he was doing it to help me, to try to make me realise the importance of appearing and behaving seriously before others could learn to treat me as an established county employee, as a Chief Executive, as a face of Glamorgan. He also kept on about wine, a subject about which he knew almost everything and I knew pretty much nothing. I really don't like the stuff. I also dislike all the pretentious nonsense surrounding bouquets, vintages, traces of this and that…. load of old bollocks, as far as I am concerned. But he was a really important person in my development at Glamorgan and he taught me an enormous amount. It was also under him that we recognized the need to professionalize as an organization and to streamline. David and I lost the frequency of contact we had once enjoyed after I left the club in 2008 and his association with the Paul Russell chairmanship when he came back as President had me pondering a little on perhaps just how political he was prepared to be, but I will never forget how kind and helpful he was to me. I learned an awful lot from him.

127

David it was who pushed me to look beyond Glamorgan. He had been an elected member of the TCCB's Marketing Committee and suggested being on a Board committee would be an effective way for me to become a bit more noticed. His work in advising the Board and the counties on the merger of the TCCB and the National Cricket Association with the foundation of the England and Wales Cricket Board in 1997 led him to being elected first Deputy Chairman under Sir Ian MacLaurin and then, when he stood down, as Chairman, eventually becoming head of the International Cricket Council and then President of MCC. Quite a CV for a steelworker from Tredegar and testament not only to his knowledge and ability but to his diplomacy and political nous. There was never any danger of me following anything like the same path. For a start, it's not for me. Any of it. Secondly, I'm not cut out for it and would be no good at it whatsoever. But his point was that standing for one of the TCCB's committees would help me by mixing with different people, drag me out of the Glamorgan bubble and help with the whole 'office boy to senior exec' "journey" (© X-Factor). So I was put forward for election to the Second XI Committee, chaired by the Reverend Michael Vockins, Secretary of Worcestershire. To my surprise I was elected, and joined Mike, Steve Coverdale (Northamptonshire), Tim Lamb (TCCB) – three of the people who'd been kind enough to reply to my written 'gizza job' pleas in the Spring of 1986 – along with other established cricketing noteworthies. They were all fantastically kind and not in the least patronizing, despite my comparative lack of knowledge and experience. I went on to serve on a number of groups, including the ECB's Registration and Contracts committee for donkey's years.

Back then we used to organize Second XI fixtures on the basis of first-come-first-served and those of us based in an office (Mike, Steve and me, for example) had the advantage over the likes of our committee colleagues Peter Robinson, Don Bennett, Alan Hill and Mick Newell, who were coaching Second XIs out in the sticks somewhere in the days before mobile phones. I remember 'Robbo' ringing me once from a payphone just outside the cricket ground in Shepton Mallett. He had a stack of 10p pieces and I was the fourth on his list after Derbyshire, Durham and Essex. "F***ing nightmare, this, Mike. I bet Alan Jones doesn't have to put up with this crap. Coaching a team and then nipping halfway down the road to the....

128

BEEP BEEP..... sorry, another 10p. Yeah, I bet Alan doesn't have this in his job description. Bloody Somerset, on the other hand. Anderson can't be arsed.... BEEP BEEP.... Gets me to do it. It's not as though Sally or one of the others hasn't got the ability, but oh no, Robbo you can do it because.... BEEP" And so on went the tirade, my contribution simply being the odd "yep" or "mmm". We were at least a quid in before we started mentioning dates. I reckon by the time he got to Yorkshire, with the odd failed connection or call back he'd have been there three weeks and down £500. Happy days.

Gerard Elias, conversely, was much more difficult to deal with. Not as a person. He was always direct and honest and wanted to be supportive and I liked him and thought we worked very well together. No, the challenge with Gerard was that he was rarely around. He was always busy, even in the early days, when he chaired the Club's Centenary Appeal, but through the '90s and early 2000s he was involved in such high-profile work as the North Wales Child Abuse and Bloody Sunday inquiries and even getting hold of him on the phone could be a challenge. At that stage we were undertaking the first phase of the redevelopment at Sophia Gardens and I know that Tony Dilloway, who was doing the spadework on that project, found it hard getting some decisions. But Gerard, like Tony Lewis and David Morgan before him, was always good to me. I don't think I ever quite fitted his ideal CEO model of someone who networked, attended business events and focused on the corporate side – a role he and his Treasurer Richard Weston were constantly trying to get me to conform to – but he is an easy man to get on with and many was the time we'd end up debating club issues over a pint in Llandaff, where he lived, often with Ricky, one of his great buddies.

The combination which didn't work too well was Gerard and Hugh. David could handle Hugh, recognize his issues and grievances (many of them seemingly personal) and ensure he had the appropriate platform without rocking the boat. Hugh having become Deputy Chairman when Gerard acceded to the top job, I felt that as Gerard became busier and away far more often he demurred to Hugh too much on cricket matters and that created problems, not just for me, but for coaches and captains and other members of staff. Every contract I negotiated Hugh insisted on knowing what the terms were and if I'd made any concessions, why I'd made those concessions. He didn't appreciate that he was undermining my authority.

One example of his interfering came at the end of the 1998 season when Tony Cottey left to join Sussex. We'd offered him a two-year contract but he wanted three years. He was Matt's Vice-Captain at the time and had been an important player for the club for a decade. I felt that two years was fair but when I met Tony, he really wanted us to consider three and asked me to go back and ask for him, which I did. There was also the question of a Benefit. He, Steve James and Adrian Dale had all been capped on the same day and with the three of them coming up to ten years as capped players there would be the question at some stage of who might go first in terms of being awarded a Benefit. That wasn't something we really wanted to consider as part of a contract negotiation but it wasn't an unreasonable query on his part. In the end we reached an impasse. Hugh and the Cricket Committee weren't going to budge. Matt and I weren't really minded to either, it must be said, though we were still willing to talk to see if there might be some kind of compromise. But 'Cotts' was a stubborn little bugger and he wanted the security of a three-year deal. The need to keep referring back to Hugh ground me down and in the end the player lost his patience. Hugh had even gone back to Cotts while I was on holiday at the end of the season and offered him a two-year deal but with the promise of a third year on the coaching staff if his on-field performances weren't good, hardly a ringing endorsement. The first I heard of that was when Cotts rang me up in Cornwall to ask what sort of role they had in mind, who would be judging whether he got a third playing year or not, and when. I didn't know what he was talking about. It was a fudge. Gerard's distance and Hugh's conviction that when it came to cricket matters he should be the club's primary voice meant the whole matter dragged on and Cotts decided to leave and take up the offer of a five-year contract with Sussex. He could have been our captain and had a benefit. Had it been left to me, I'd have backed myself to have worked something out but others had become involved and it wasn't to be. To Cotts, it must have sounded as though Sussex wanted him far more than we did. It was good to see him enjoy further playing success at Hove, where he has remained long after his playing days came to an end.

I never felt I had full authority on contracts when Hugh was around. If our opinions differed he would make a huge play in trying to ensure that his view prevailed, and if that meant dragging others in to support his argument, he would have no qualms about doing that.

The disputes between Hugh and Matt in our successful 1997 Championship season became the stuff of internal legend. He and others on the committee wanted Metson to be keeping wicket as he was the better 'keeper. Matt and Duncan Fletcher didn't, and they picked Adrian Shaw, the better bat and in their view the better team man. The hours wasted debating that in meetings could have filled a year on Saturn. He didn't get it. Even when we'd won the bloody thing. When Duncan came back for his second season with us, in 1999, the squad had just returned from a pre-season trip to Cape Town and were really fired up, but there had been a couple of injuries. Owen Parkin was expecting to play as he felt he was the next seam bowler in line but Matt and Fletch had been impressed with a young lad called David Harrison in practice and they selected him ahead of Owen for the opening match of the season at Derby. Owen must have complained to Hugh Davies because the next thing I knew, Hugh and Gerard were in Derby meeting Matt and Fletch to discuss it. It had Hugh's imprint all over it. He wanted control over selection but didn't want anyone to think he was overruling the professionals. Perish the thought! All I could think of was that the last four-day game this captain and coach combination had selected a team for had won us the County Championship trophy. In later years he pushed for the introduction of a Cricket Monitoring Group, where he and Roger Davis could meet with the Captain and Coach every couple of weeks and discuss form and selection. I was included but told I wouldn't be able to vote. I don't remember there ever being a vote but had there been a 2-2 split, I can assume he would have claimed some kind of Cricket Chairman or Deputy Chairman privilege. It was just another layer of bureaucracy designed to show that the committee wasn't picking the team but which give him a greater say on cricket matters. Such different times.

Woe betide us if we wanted to do something for someone against whom Hugh held a grudge. By the time our paths diverged he'd fallen out with dozens of people including, if I'm not mistaken, every single captain and coach. Even Uncle Al was struggling with him, and Uncle Al is – along with Roger Skyrme, long time dressing room attendant – one of the nicest men in the game. There was always a crisis, always some cricketing issue that he wanted to magnify in terms of its importance and then play a hand in resolving. His way. As dear old Morrissey put it, "He bears more grudges than lonely high court judges." If you fall out with someone once it might be their fault. But if you keep falling out with people repeatedly surely it is incumbent on you to be looking in a mirror instead of blaming a succession of other people. He never did. If there was a disagreement – and there were many over the years – it was always the other person who was wrong.

There was one rather irritating committee member at the time, a fellow called David Davies, an insolvency practitioner from Penarth. I've previously mentioned his sycophantic performance in the Trent Bridge committee room. He didn't seem to have much of a clue about cricket. He is also one of the rudest men I have ever met, one of those people who insist on referring to others by their surname, and not in an affectionate way either. He often referred to staff and players as 'paid servants' of the club. He was one of the most shameless social climbers I think I've encountered in cricket too, one of his ambitions clearly being to become a member of the MCC. Obviously, the whole status thing appealed to him. All the gear and no idea, that sort of thing. Which is absolutely fine. Whatever floats your boat and all that. It's not my bag, I have to confess, though I love Lord's and the likes of Ricky Needham, Roger Morris and a number of players I count as friends are members of MCC and are very proud to be so. We had an inkling he had successfully paid to jump the queue on the waiting list when he turned up at a committee meeting in the late '90s with MCC tie on, shirt with MCC monogrammed logo on the pocket, MCC cufflinks and MCC socks on. Had he been strip-searched, he may have been found to be sporting MCC-embossed y-fronts too. Prior to a meeting in the summer of 2000, Ricky said he was thinking of a harmless competition among a handful of us, awarding one point for a nod of the head, two points for a 'hear hear' and a six-points-and-out for a slapping of the table, and inviting us to place bets as to the number of points the main runners and riders would score by the end of the meeting. Before the meeting proper had even started Gerard Elias said he wanted to congratulate the players on reaching their first Lord's Final in 23 years. As David Davies nodded, his repeated cries of 'hear hear' and his table banging acclamation were only interrupted by Needham's, "well if he's going to play like that" cry of disgust as he threw down his pen.

Davies had long been a proponent of a club benefit year, believing such a fundraiser would clear the club's significant debts (significant at the time, though nothing compared to what they ended up being). I was all for giving it a try but he didn't seem to understand me when I cautioned that the public's support of an individual would be much more forthcoming than for a professional organization as a whole, and not to expect a club testimonial to be the financial panacea he believed it could be. When we did eventually decide to go down that route, with Gareth Williams chairing '*A Test For Wales*' in 2004, he was about as much use as an ashtray on a motorbike. I don't recall him doing anything. I was at the Club for something like 15 years while Davies was on the committee. Other than whingeing about the presentation of accounts and partaking of as much hospitality as the rest of them, I don't recall a single constructive thing he did other than sitting as a member of the Finance Committee. They made him a life member, obviously. Presumably for services to hanging around.

When we were building the ground one of the basic decisions we had to take was what colour the seats should be. Not that this was a committee decision or anything but the subject came up in one meeting and one of our women committee members, Sue Eilbeck (we had three in my time – Pat Hughes, Mari Thomas and Sue, with Fran Bevan following just after I'd left) suggested that they should be red for Wales (as opposed to the blue we'd picked, that being one of the club's official colours). I think it was Ricky who pointed out sarcastically that it might be difficult for the fielders to pick the ball up from such a background. It was well-intentioned, but we stayed as we were. We also had a debate about music. Some of the committee members hated music being played over the public address at any time; and they absolutely loathed the idea that teams were being asked to choose which song they wanted to come out to bat to. I think they truly believed they ought to have an influence. My (heavily ironic) suggestion of the second movement allegretto from Shostakovich's fifth symphony appeared at one point to be a genuine runner.

Perhaps my favourite committee tale came on a trip to Dublin in 1998. Gerard Elias was by now chairman, with Hugh Davies elected as his number two. Both of them were keen to follow the team across the Irish Sea for Glamorgan's Benson and Hedges Cup zonal group game against Ireland. And who wouldn't? I even persuaded myself that it would be in the club's very best interests for me to be on the plane too. Ahem. Yes. Vitally important trip, that one. It was the first year in which the reserve day had been abolished for

133

zonal matches. Normally if there was a bit of dodgy weather about on the allotted day, you'd all come back the following day and finish the game off. Not now. There was just the one day allowed for group games, with the number of overs reduced until, if you couldn't get the specified minimum in (sometimes 25-a-side, sometimes 20, occasionally 10, depending on the competition and the year), you called a halt and both sides picked up a point. It's standard stuff nowadays. So we knew we'd be flying in, staying one night, playing the game, staying a second night and then flying home. That second night looked like it had the names of a few of us written all over it.

So having flown in to Dublin the players were taking it easy. Gerard, Hugh and I, on the other hand, had an official function (get me – like a government minister or something) at a local golf club. We were picked up around six in the evening by the President of the Irish Cricket Union, Enda McDermott, a garrulous, engaging man redolent of Henry Kelly, who proceeded to take us on a meandering guided tour of Dublin and suburbs, during which we either passed 25 golf clubs or we passed the same golf club 25 times, I'm not sure which. Eventually we arrived at Leinster Golf Club, where there was a dinner being held in honour of the Leinster Cricket Club. My table companion? One Peter Walker, by then Secretary of the Cricket Board of Wales, who was based two offices down from me back at HQ and with whom I'd spent four hours that morning planning the next CBW three-year strategic plan. He was speaking. And I'd heard all his stories before. Many times. On finishing the dinner, Enda arranged a taxi for us back to our hotel in Malahide. He accompanied us, of course, and we spent several further hours back in the hotel bar. Gerard was on magnificent form, challenging McDermott on why, if as Glamorgan Chairman, he could conduct committee meetings at Glamorgan in Welsh (he couldn't, and didn't), the Irish couldn't do the same for their own meetings in Gaelic. And he reeled off what was supposed to be a plausible Welsh sentence designed to show off his knowledge of Welsh. I did pick up from his occasional quotes, though (gwasanaethau, toiled, bwrw [services, toilet, to rain]) that we weren't in the realms of fluency. The irony was that Hugh was, of course, a fluent Welsh speaker. And he played along superbly.

It was a bit of a dusty threesome who were picked up at eight the following morning. As we arrived at the ground in Clontarf, Enda having taken us past the same 25 golf clubs as the previous evening, we were swept into the pavilion and made the one offer I doubt any of the three of us had either wanted or expected to hear.

"You'll be having a drink, of course," said Mr Irish Cricket Union President, with an emerald gleam in his eye.

"We wouldn't want to put you to any trouble, Enda," replied Gerard, politely, amid a measure of relief as he pointed to the shutters which indicated the bar was closed and, it seemed, unmanned. "Anyway, it looks like it's closed."

"Not for much longer," said Enda, as he proceeded to produce a weighty bunch of keys from his pocket and strode purposefully toward the bar.

So as the team arrived at the ground they file past the Chairman, Deputy Chairman and Chief Executive of the Club, all drinking Guinness at nine o'clock on the morning of a match day. Great example to set, that. And they dutifully followed it that evening having won the game. As did I. Well it would have been rude not to.

Despite the odd committee member who tried my patience, they were in a minority. As I was learning about cricket and about business, I worked with three chairmen – Lewis, Morgan and Elias – and a substantial number of committee members, a number of whom remain close friends, and all of whom had a profound influence on me and my development. I learned from each and every one of them, both good and bad. One thing I am absolutely certain of is that when I eventually left the organization via the tradesmen's exit door, had some of the late '80s committee members been around there is no way I would have been treated the way I was. People like Wynne Walters, Byron Denning, Bill Cawdron, Gordon Lewis, Neville Francis, David Herbert and David Irving may have had their faults but they had integrity; sitting back and allowing something like that just wouldn't have happened in the way it did. The 2008 vintage didn't have that integrity. Or the balls.

And so, as one of the first committee members on my watch – Oswyn "I've been on this committee for [insert appropriate number of] years" Davies – would say at this juncture, 'a vote of thanks to the chair' (pretty much all he ever said at meetings, in fact, though he was very fond of telling me every time he saw me that he'd 'been on this committee for [however many] years' [it was at the time]) and let's get back to the narrative.

7 SURGING OUT OF CONVALESCENCE

'First is first. Second is nowhere.'
BILL SHANKLY

Viv. No surname required. What it must be like to be known by everyone just by your Christian name. I'd say he is probably the cricketer I am most asked about. We only got to see him at the tail end of his career but if that was him winding down then he must have been absolutely astonishing in his pomp. He taught everyone at Glamorgan what winning looked like. He was fiercely loyal and determined. He was also an absolute joy to deal with.

So. Where were we? Ah yes. The end of the 1992 season. On the cusp of a year in which Glamorgan would win its first trophy in 24 years (if you exclude winning the four-team Tilcon Trophy at Harrogate in 1987, which many disappointingly appear to do); the magnificent, brooding presence of one Isaac Vivian Alexander Richards; and some burgundy blazers. Oh yes. Burgundy.

There is a photograph somewhere in one of the rooms or corridors at Glamorgan's headquarters ground of a Glamorgan Colts XI side, taken in 1987 (or at least there always used to be – and if not, it should be dug out immediately and put back up). Included in that photo, alongside Jim Pressdee and Alan Jones, the two coaches, are Steve James, Adrian Dale, Tony Cottey and Steve Watkin, all four of whom played an enormous part in Glamorgan's successes through the '90s and into the early 2000s. Also there is Phil North. In the next year or two they were joined by Robert Croft, David Hemp and Michael Cann. It was quite a nucleus. Tony Lewis, when he became involved again with the Club in 1987, had asked us to focus on the development of Welsh talent rather than signing supposed cast-offs from other counties. No disrespect to the likes of Duncan Pauline and Paul Todd but Glamorgan were not only failing as a side in the late '80s but failing with a group of players the Welsh public wouldn't really have been able to identify with. Butcher and Metson, yes, absolutely. They were high class players and were always going to go straight into the side. And others, such as Simon Dennis and Mark Frost, did a good job. But all too often the easy option was to dip into the market rather than have the patience to give our own a crack and nurture them. And when I say 'market,' I ought to point out that Glamorgan would have been toward the back of the buying queue; other counties were far more attractive prospects. That's why the whole ASW sponsorship (Allied Steel and Wire as they were at the time) – *ASW and Glamorgan: Nurturing the Grass Roots of Welsh Talen*t and all that – was such a good fit. What it required was a Chairman who understood what was needed, and who was prepared to be patient, both in private but especially in public.

The Colts had been started in 1986 as a vehicle to help pull the best young players together and control their development. I say 'control' not in a negative way, but Jim and Alan were able to ensure that the players batted and bowled at the right times, testing them in different situations, with proper practice in the nets at the newly-acquired ground at BP Llandarcy, just outside Neath, taking place on the morning of home matches. The other clubs hated it. That was understandable. Not only were we taking their best young talent from them we were then lining them up against them as the season went on. It had a shelf life, of course. These things generally do. But the principle was a sound one and the coaches – John Steele was also involved further down the line – were able to work closely with a core of talented Welsh kids as they grew up in cricketing terms. It was used as an example in the 2010s of how Glamorgan's fortunes would be improved if the Club returned to the same principle. That may be the case but I wouldn't suggest it was in any way axiomatic. There were no guarantees it would work again. It depends on so many other factors – coaching, venue, league standard etc. – and the professional sporting environment has moved on an awful lot in the last thirty years, as has society. Maybe in the late 1980s we just happen to have been blessed with a particularly talented core of cricketers. Either way, it was perfect for Glamorgan. And the lads coming through were indeed a particularly talented group. Under Lewis's guidance off the field and Butcher's on it they were given the opportunity to learn and develop.

At the start of that summer of '93, the Times's then cricket correspondent, Alan Lee, wrote: "At this time of year, the mighty have no monopoly on hope. Even Glamorgan, bless them, are harbouring that springtime illusion, beloved of chancellors, that this will be the year to end the slump. Sucker though I am for the romantic story, it really isn't feasible." That sort of patronizing comment – 'even Glamorgan, bless them' – may have put a dampener on the approach of any Glamorgan side of the mid- to late '80s, but not this one. There were genuinely optimistic vibes around; not that we were necessarily going to smash allcomers to smithereens and pick up four domestic trophies or anything, but there was a quiet confidence. We had some decent players in our squad and could really compete. Hugh Morris was back as Captain, with Matt Maynard as his number two. And we had Viv.

I remember Philip Carling calling me into his office early in 1989 to tell me that we had signed Viv Richards. Viv Richards! Coming to Glamorgan! I couldn't believe it. He was originally recruited to play in the 1989 and 1990 seasons, the first one alongside Ravi Shastri, but unfortunately he developed a medical condition which prevented him fulfilling the first of those two summers. I know it's painful because it's a condition I've had, involving ingrowing hairs, bottoms and potential abscesses. Let's leave it there, eh? Other than to say that when it was my turn – in the Spring of 1991 – I required an operation. I was picked up from hospital by Ian Smith in the Club's battered old Mini Metro, which Smudger proceeded to drive like Colin McRae, without any consideration of the fact that for every bump he went over at speed my arse was screaming blue murder at the car's failed suspension. And the first song on the radio was James, with '*Sit Down*'. Ha sodding ha. The West Indies were touring in 1991 and as Captain that would be Viv's international swansong, so at that time it was a straight two-year contract for 1989 and 1990 which the Club eventually extended in 1990 to cover seasons 1992 and 1993. But although he couldn't play, Viv did come over to Wales to do some publicity for us. I didn't get to meet him at that point. It was during the three-day tour match against the Aussies at Neath. I had rather expected him to make an immediate beeline to our ~~windowless shed in the car park~~ office to apologize on bended knee for the shameful way he'd treated me back in May 1986. He didn't bother though. So rude.

Instead, he arrived in Cardiff in April 1990, already aged 38, written off by the national journalists, and without having played county cricket since leaving Somerset under an Armageddon-delivering cloud in 1987. No county would touch him in 1987 so he ended up playing league cricket for Rishton in Lancashire. And no one thought he'd amount to anything with lowly old Glamorgan. We were wasting our money, apparently. Crucially, though, he had a real point to prove. And if there's one thing better than Viv Richards, it's a determined Viv Richards, a Viv Richards who has been written off as 'past it.' Tony Lewis had told him he wanted him to just 'be Viv', to swagger to the crease (still helmetless of course), always after a suitably appropriate delay following the disappearance into the pavilion of the outgoing batsman, chewing gum and swirling his bat; to be a growling presence in the field. Essentially the runs were a given, though quite what we were all expecting I don't know. Was he really past it? After Chris Lewis had bowled him on his Championship debut against Leicestershire at Sophia Gardens I went for a wander around the ground and there were one or two sceptics who weren't shy in proffering phrases such as 'over the hill' and 'waste of money'. But he then proceeded to make 119 in the second innings. It was tempting to grab the PA and shriek "Ladeeeeeez n Genamun, we have ourselves a proper suuuuperstar!!" I resisted. The sceptics kept quiet from then on.

Off the field, Viv was an absolute dream to work with. He had a special relationship with Tony Dilloway, to whom he would turn if there was anything wrong with his car, his flat, anything. He was set up in a luxury apartment a mile from the centre of Cardiff, one that had a particular keypad and key combination on the front door which meant that if you didn't have your wits about you, you could end up locking yourself out of your own home after three unsuccessful attempts. On one occasion he rang 'Dillers' to say he'd done just that and would Tony come up with the spare key and the landlord's instructions and bail him out. But this was beyond even Tony. An hour later I joined Viv, Tony, Alan Butcher, John Steele and Alan Jones in the corridor outside Viv's flat, all of us looking awkwardly at one another and mumbling something inane about modern technology. Viv was especially apologetic. I'm not too sure why, but it was only then that the landlord was contacted, provided us with brief system by-pass instructions and in we went.

For Viv, the Glamorgan contract was a big deal. He not only wanted to prove people wrong through his performances but also in how he left his mark. I never once saw or heard of him shirking a public appearance or request. There was never a cross word, or not to us anyway. People might want to hear the muck being raked but I can only speak as I found. By 1992 I was running the cricket operations at Glamorgan, Philip having departed in 1990, and, short of the occasional timekeeping slip, Viv was just a pleasure to deal with. If only a few of the prima donnas we subsequently had over the years, players unfit to lace his boots in terms of comparative ability, had dealt with their responsibilities in the way that he did. There were times when I worried myself sick that the anti-doping people who turned up occasionally at matches would pick Viv's name out for testing after the boys had had a couple of days off, but there was never anything wrong with him that a quick kip in the dressing room couldn't put right. I was probably trading on his reputation. I do confess, though, to producing different versions of the scorecard, which the testers used to draw the names of those required to provide a sample, with Viv's name in different batting positions to try to make sure we didn't trouble the great man with a drugs test. And it was generally Adrian Dale who was the floater, the player lined up to step in and take the fall. Sorry 'Arthur.' But it never happened. And when he was tested at away games, there was, of course, never any problem. Just me worrying again. I loved the man. And the pride in our voices when we talked about Viv as one of ours couldn't be hidden. It was like having your prize-winning boxer elder brother with you in the school playground. You felt you couldn't lose, that you had the *Top Trumps* king card in your hand.

Viv taught some of the Glamorgan players about attitude, about confidence and about winning. OK, so that sounds a little simplistic, and I'm sure there were one or two for whom the take of the Viv years would maybe be told very differently, but that's certainly how it looked from where I was watching. With Butcher in charge in 1990, the likes of James, Morris, Dale, Maynard, Cottey, Croft, Metson, Watkin and Barwick started to look like a really solid group. When Viv was back in 1992 after West Indies duties the previous summer, Matt was leading the side in Butch's enforced absence, but the same principle wore true. By the time 1993 came round, with Viv now 41 years old but still as fit as a flea, we had added one final ingredient: a chipper, likeable, highly opinionated Dutchman by the name of Roland Lefebvre, who joined us from Somerset. He proved the cherry on the cake. The team was now set. James and Morris giving us a start, with Dale's resilience and useful bowling, Maynard's flair and aggression, Richards's magnetism,

Cottey's rugged adaptability, Croft's all-round ability, Metson's mercurial talent behind the stumps, Roland's superbly disciplined seam bowling, Watkin's ability with the new ball, and Barwick's miserliness: provided they could stay injury-free we felt we had an eleven to compete. And they did stay injury-free. We only used fifteen players in going on to win the Sunday League for the first time. David Hemp, along with Steve Bastien, Mark Frost and a one-match cameo from Andrew Jones, were the only other players we used. Dean Conway must have been using all his powers to keep them on the field throughout a long and debilitating season, one which also saw a third-place finish in the Championship (with no fewer than nine wins) and a run to the semi-finals of the one-day knock-out NatWest Trophy where Sussex were arguably fortunate to come out on top after a clear run out wasn't given, the year before run out cameras became the norm.

The permutation in the field was very formulaic, but no less effective for the fact that everyone in the county game knew what was coming. Watkin would bowl the bulk of his overs straight off, opening up with Lefebvre, who would have a few overs kept back for the death. On would come Barwick and Croft, backed up by tigerish fielding, including a particularly aggressive mid-wicket in Richards, with Dale and Richards mixing it up between them to get through the overs of the fifth bowler, before Barwick and Lefebvre came back at the end. It all sounds wonderfully simple now, and for an eleven-match winning streak from the first week in June until the penultimate match, at home against Essex when it rained and rained, Glamorgan were just unbeatable in fifty over cricket. But it didn't start in the grand manner. Beaten by Derbyshire and then by Northamptonshire at Pentyrch in our first home game, by the time the rain had washed out the game at Taunton against Somerset at the end of May, Glamorgan were second bottom. Played 3, Won 0.

That Northamptonshire game was memorable for being the only time a competitive county match has been played at Pentyrch Cricket Club. Alright for Maynard, who could throw a ball from his front garden and hit the pavilion roof, but a bit of a pain for the rest of us. No trains. No bus route. Not the most accessible place to be staging a game of professional sport. But needs must. It had all started the previous year with a match against Derbyshire which, ultimately, had to be abandoned owing to persistent rain. The match was sponsored by Taff Ely Council (as was, in the days before the local authority merger with the Rhondda and Cynon valleys) but the ground in Pontypridd, in the beautiful setting of Ynysangharad Park, was owned by the Pontypridd Town Council. The Town Council was always agitating to stop any vehicles from coming into the park, which was fair enough, but for one day a year we didn't think it wholly unreasonable, given the profile of the event, for the players of both sides, the umpires, scorers, groundsman and a few officials to get to park somewhere near the pavilion so we successfully applied for special permission to do so. Unfortunately, on this particular day in July 1992 the security people on the gate – from the Town Council, not Taff Ely – decided to make their point, turning away first the groundsman, Len Smith, and then sundry others, including one Viv Richards. The first they justified on the basis that Len's van was okay, but he didn't have a pass for the trailer (which contained sheets and mini water hogs and the like). Viv was apparently the last player in and as someone who wasn't in the squad had seemingly already blagged their way in, they refused Viv on the basis that they weren't authorized to allow in more than a set number of cars. We eventually sorted it all out but if that was going to be the Town Council's approach it would be difficult for us to continue playing in Pontypridd. So, what to do? Tony Dilloway was naturally keen to keep working with Taff Ely, who were generous and supportive sponsors, but where on earth could we play if not in Ponty? He went on a bit of a recce and a couple of months later he announced that he'd found the perfect spot. I thought we were calling in for a coffee at the Maynards' until he took a turn off their road and into the rugby club instead. One dilapidated old building and a field. 'Ta dah,' proclaimed Tony, proudly. I didn't see it. But as always he, with the support of John Moore, the Pentyrch club and the Council, came up trumps. On the day there were stands, marquees, scoreboards, all of the home comforts. All was well. Even when Byron announced the opening over – "From the Sea End, Curtly Ambrose." Folk were so busy sharing looks of bemusement and craning their collective necks, the ground being at least fifteen miles inland, that they probably failed to notice that Ambrose's first delivery to Steve James had almost bounced twice as it went past him. Pentyrch was a fun diversion for a year, but we were back in Pontypridd the following year, our point having been made.

At Middlesbrough the following week, it all clicked into place and, to coin a hoary old cliché, the team never looked back. Their Sunday form was transferred to both the County Championship and the NatWest Trophy in what was probably Glamorgan's most successful ever all-round season. I secretly hoped Alan Lee was choking on his Corn Flakes every morning as he followed our progress. I followed much of it through Ceefax, the old BBC TV text service, which would in those pre-internet days update every five minutes or so (down from the half hour of a few years before), or by listening to away games via Edward Bevan and Co. on Radio Wales. That Summer I think I would have got through twice as many fags just hoping the team could stay in contention from game to game.

One of Viv's finest innings for Glamorgan was played out on Ceefax. Yes, I followed the whole thing on those old-school blue lines on black background, waiting for the periodic updates. No commentary on this one as it was a Championship match, one which took place in Viv's first year with us, in 1990, at the old Northlands Road ground in Southampton against Hampshire. And it was a belter. After a couple of engineered declarations Hampshire had set us 364 to win in just over a hundred overs but we'd slipped to 139 for 5 and with overs running out a Glamorgan win looked highly unlikely. Viv Richards was still there, though, and, supported by Nigel Cowley and Colin Metson, he took off. The last over must have been special to watch. Metson scrambled a single off Viv's West Indian team-mate Malcolm Marshall's first ball before the field was put back to allow Richards a run to get Metson back off strike. Instead, Viv stepped up and smashed 4, 6 and 4 to see us home with a couple of deliveries to spare, finishing with 164 not out. I imagine it may have been even more special for those who were actually there to see it.

Despite winning eleven in a row that 1993 summer it had proved impossible to shake Kent off our tails. The two of us had gone toe to toe right through the summer. After the penultimate game, against Essex in Cardiff, had been rained off with the visitors 7 for 2 we were left with what amounted to a final in all but name: Kent against Glamorgan at Canterbury, winner take all. The sponsors loved it. We couldn't be separated on points so in the event of a rained-off game, Kent would take the title as they the better overall run rate.

I remember that Essex game for one of my favourite photographs throughout all my time at the Club. Tony Dilloway had ordered thousands of temporary seats for the match to cater for what would – given a fair forecast – have been a huge crowd. In those days for knock-out matches we used to be able to order additional seats and offset the cost after discussions with the TCCB and our opponents, but that was only for knock-out games, where both sides picked up a share of the proceeds. It didn't apply in the Sunday League, or the AXA Equity & Law League to give its then proper title. So when the rain came, it washed all of the seat costs down the drain with it. On the Monday after that Essex non-event, play in the fourth day of the concurrent Championship match between the sides was possible. As some declaration bowling set up an Essex run chase (Steve Bastien's six wickets eventually delivering a home win), Tony was spotted at the back of the massive bank of temporary seats occasionally attempting to start his own one-man Mexican wave. He later said he'd been determined to extract some modicum of value for money from his not insignificant investment.

1993 proved the maxim that if a team delivered then its individual stars would get a look in in terms of international recognition. 'Watty' was outstanding, ending the summer as the Professional Cricketers' Association's Players' Player of the Year, and both he and Matt – after a hundred against the Australians at Neath – were selected for England squads in that summer's Ashes series (Watty had played a few games in 1991 against the West Indies but Matt hadn't been picked since his rather chastising 1988 debut). At the end of the season the pair were duly picked for England's winter tour to the Caribbean, Hugh was appointed Captain of an England A squad also containing Robert Croft and Adrian Dale (like Watty, Hugh had been picked for the England side against the West Indies on Viv's swansong tour in 1991), and both Gary Butcher and Darren Thomas were chosen for the England Under-19s. For Colin Metson the writing must have been on the wall. He had been outstanding all summer behind the stumps but was overlooked.

The NatWest Trophy campaign ended in disappointment. After wins over Oxfordshire and Durham, Richards and Maynard dominating in the respective matches, it was a home quarter-final against Worcestershire at Swansea. Rain sent the match into a second day, by which time a magnificently miserly bowling performance had reduced the visitors to 40 for 2 in fully 23 overs, chasing 280, which they never got close to. The draw then sent Glamorgan to Hove for a semi-final against Sussex. We had them on the ropes but they got away. Chasing 221, first at 44-3 from 27 overs, then 110-6 after 44, our bowlers were on top, but Alan Wells made an excellent hundred and Sussex got home with four balls to spare in front of a large but disappointed Welsh contingent. Tony had spent days working with committee member Neville Francis in chartering a train to get supporters down to Hove – the 'Daffodil Express' as it was christened – but he, like me, had chosen not to attend the match. I'm a really poor watcher of cricket, or I was back then, something that will come out much more when we look at future Glamorgan triumphs, and the pair of us were following the game on television in Gwyn Stone's office. We were, to use the sporting vernacular, absolutely gutted.

I was superstitious about making contingency plans before knowing the outcome of a semi-final but Tony's pragmatism rightly superseded that timidity. What used to happen back then – it may still do, I don't know – was that the TCCB delivered the ticket allocation for the Final, the actual physical tickets, to the county hosting each semi-final. That suddenly made the whole thing very real, and with so little time between semi-finals and final (though there is laughably sometimes only a matter of days now) it was of course important to be planning and especially, as would prove to be the case, when you had a committee as self-centred and acquisitive as we had. It was the professional, sensible thing to do. I just hated the fact that we were jumping the gun and tempting fate. And it wasn't the last time we'd lose out in a semi.

The *Independent*'s match report the following day made a great play of the fact that Viv would be missing out in his final season of professional cricket, Martin Johnson writing: "Richards, whose last two Lord's finals were both in 1983 (for Somerset in this competition, and the West Indies in the World Cup) was on a flight home to Antigua today to attend his father's funeral, and although he will be back, it will not be for the emotional farewell he had promised himself at the start of the season." Maybe not emotional at Lord's on September 4th, but there would be plenty of emotion – and a fairytale exit from the stage for Viv – fifteen days later at Canterbury.

A few elements of that day are still crystal clear, others have become more blurred. I do know that being the terrible watcher that I was, I hadn't originally planned to go. The Club had arranged for the staff to have complimentary tickets and access to a small hospitality marquee, something they didn't ordinarily do but which Gwyn Stone had arranged via his Kent counterpart Stuart Anderson. So, they were all going to be there, and rightly so. But the night before I just thought to myself, this is madness: Glamorgan are on the verge of winning a first ever one-day trophy, a first major pot for nearly a quarter of a century. What are you going to do? Watch it on the telly? Really? I'd worked my nuts off for those players for eight seasons and was going to forgo the experience. I know. It sounds pathetic. That's because it is pathetic. So I rang Phil North, asked him what he was doing the next day, quickly arranged a couple of extra tickets, set aside my burgundy blazer (our agreed uniform for the day) and we set off the following morning at the crack of dawn. We passed loads of supporters along the way, bumping into familiar groups at motorway services. It was clear we'd have a decent presence at Canterbury, something confirmed as we approached the ground. It was heaving. Traffic was almost at a standstill. This was indeed 'a big deal'.

I hadn't been aware of Viv's "speech" in the dressing room the evening before but was told about it afterwards. Kent had decided not to enforce the follow on in the Championship game between the counties after racking up 520 and bowling us out for 144, choosing instead to bat again. They smashed us about and then reduced us to 10 for 2. Viv was unhappy with their approach and when he came back into the dressing room, later than everyone else, it was to a shell-shocked bunch of Glamorgan players. Apparently, he was banging on the dressing room wall (the two dressing rooms were right next to one another so it was obvious the Kent players would be able to hear him) and shouting, "If you f*** with the game, the game will f*** with you." He had also ordered in a crate of beers and proceeded to go round the room reminding the Glamorgan players of their strengths, how well they had played all summer and how they deserved to finish off the job the following day by winning something. I don't know just how apocryphal that particular story really is. I'm sure it will have been embellished over the years, as these things tend to be, but knowing Viv, I can well believe it happened and I can certainly believe that it would have made a difference.

I don't remember too much about the actual game. Nothing new there. The more important the event, the more cowardly I would become, sneaking off into offices to 'meet' people, wandering out for a fag, nipping back to the car or going off for a lap around the ground, making sure the playing area was just out of sight. I do remember the ovation the crowd gave Viv Richards when he came out to bat, though. It was universal, everyone acknowledging a cricketing legend and a great career. I also recall a particularly hostile few overs from a young bowler called Duncan Spencer, including him dismissing Maynard for 2 and having Richards caught behind, only for the Welsh contingent to start cheering belatedly as they noticed the outstretched arm of David (subsequently 'Dai') Constant, signalling a no ball. *Google* it. It's on You Tube. And if there was an embodiment of Viv's karma-inducing rant at the Kent skipper Steve Marsh the previous evening, that 'catch' (taken by Marsh) was probably it.

The rest of proceedings are pretty hazy. It seemed that the next minute 'Cotts' was top edging Spencer over the 'keeper's head for four to mean we'd won. And then it all kicked off, the singing (or Robert Croft's embarrassingly out of tune rendition of *Alouette* anyway), the dressing room shenanigans. I'd kept clear of the dressing room all day. Normally, given my role and the relationship I had with the players, I'd wander in and grab a coffee, albeit generally preferring to do so when we were in the field, but today I took the view that I'd only have been getting in the way. At the end of the game, however, it was the only place I wanted to be. I was on the field in front of the pavilion with the masses when Hugh Morris lifted the trophy. Our photographer Huw John took a picture from the balcony showing Hugh, the trophy and the hordes of supporters cheering in front of him. And I'm in it. That burgundy blazer.

The dressing room was chaos. There were so many people in there, including the predictable hangers-on and committee glory hunters. I was shown the trophy by our Chairman David Morgan and a tall gentleman whom I didn't recognize. It was a very striking trophy as well, a sort of sharp twisted silver ribbon with a cricket ball on an ornate plinth, very like a Walnut Whip, for those of you who are old enough to remember those. And I'm aware that would go down as an entry in the Bumper Book of Naff Descriptions, so you can *Google* that one too. "What do you think of the trophy, Michael?" asked David, with a beaming smile, "striking, isn't it?" He got a beaming smile back, too. (And a 'got', something which will bring a smile to his face as the rest of you wonder what the hell I'm on about. Can't

148

stop. In the middle of a story.) "I don't care if it's a walnut whip with a turd on top," I replied, "it's ours." Yep. The very first sentence that came into my head included walnut whips and turds. No. Me neither. But I'm sure David forgave me in the heat of the moment. He then took the opportunity to introduce his companion, the Chief Executive of AXA Equity and Law. Not exactly a career-propelling moment, to be honest.

After a few hours of celebrating (I could have a beer, even if Phil, as the driver, had to be a little more restrained), we had to head off. Not trusting anyone else with the trophy, a feat I was to repeat when we won the Championship title in Taunton four years later, I took it upon myself to look after it and we left the players and supporters in the Bat and Ball, the pub by the main entrance to the ground at Canterbury, and headed back to the car. That meant we had to walk through the ground as the car was parked in the huge school field that acted as a spillover on Kent's major match days. And when we got to the other end of the ground, we found that the gates were locked. It was midnight, pitch black, and we were confronted by gates ten feet high. As if that wasn't bad enough there was barbed wire across the top. And one of us had been drinking. Heavily. Phil, as a recently-retired professional athlete, went first and made it to the top. I then had to throw up our new trophy, complete with its specially made wooden cased box, up to Phil as he teetered on the top of the gate trying to avoid the barbed wire catching his 'gentleman's furniture'. And when that particular manoeuvre had succeeded, which, give or take a few trial runs, it did, we needed to get an 18-stone non-athlete dressed in a burgundy blazer up and over. I don't know how long it took us, but we did eventually make it. I'd worried we may not be able to find our car. Ours was the only car left in the whole car park.

So a season which had started with Arsenal winning two cup finals within eight weeks (oh, and by the way, thank you Steve Morrow for the League Cup and Andy Linighan for the FA Cup), my daughter Seanna choosing the day of the former to walk for the first time while I was at Wembley with my brother, was to end at the Prince of Wales's home in Gloucestershire at a special reception to commemorate Glamorgan's first trophy win since 1969. And three weeks later, our second daughter Hannah was born. Quite a year.

And no. Viv never did apologize. The charlatan.

8   SLICE OF LIFE

'I never knew of a morning in Africa when I woke up that I was not happy.'
ERNEST HEMINGWAY

I only went away with the Glamorgan squad on one pre-season tour – to Zimbabwe in 1995. And yet it provided enough material for a whole chapter. Anyone who has been on any kind of team tour will recognize much of what went on. Even professional sport is not immune to the schoolboy humour, the japes and the wholesale mickey-taking. I loved it, though I was delighted to make it back home to Wales. I was never asked to manage another one.

I've always hated speaking in public. I don't know many people who genuinely enjoy it but even though I've done it for many years, rarely with anything but positive comments, I still find it uncomfortable. I'm also hopeless commercially. I don't have a particularly ruthless business streak in me. I dislike confrontation. I worry about finances, And because I hate the idea of making small talk with people I'd generally walk a mile to avoid having to speak with I can't say I'm very keen on networking either. No, I am a behind-the-scenes person. I prefer working to support others. My detailed Myers Briggs personality test is uncannily accurate and one of the characters it identifies me with is Jiminy Cricket from the Disney film *Pinocchio*: generally low key; principled; conscientious; level-headed; dependable; loyal. Yep. That's me. A million miles away from someone who craved being a leader. Which presumably was how I came to be a Chief Executive of a county cricket club.

    Successive Glamorgan chairmen tried to mould me into the Chief Executive *they* wanted, a picture they had of what a CEO should look like. First David Morgan would make suggestions about dress, and about the appropriate use of humour in formal situations; then Gerard Elias, and the then Treasurer Richard Weston, would go on about attending breakfast talks and posh lunches, getting myself 'out there'; finally Paul Russell would – thankfully unsuccessfully – try to get me to act more like him, presumably because I didn't conform to his view of how a Chief Executive should behave (good, is what I say to that). I'd listen to them all, though. I like reflection and I have always wanted to improve where I could. They each, in their own way, had good points to make. But although prepared to try things and ever willing to please, I'm also a believer in the importance of being authentic and remaining true to myself. Life isn't something you can act your way through, even if there are plenty of people I've met along the way who have been so desperate to mould themselves into what they think others want them to be that they may as well have entered this world as a chunk of playdough. But in the mid-1990s I was full of confidence. The team was winning, the Club was doing well, my personal life couldn't have been better. I was happy. And part of that happiness was a consequence of knowing that the people I was working for believed in me and that their decision to promote me and give me the top job at the age of just 31 – then the youngest on the circuit by some distance – was a result of who I was as much as how I'd gone about my job. I would later discover that there are others who couldn't care less about things like that.

In the summer of 1995, it was announced that Gwyn Stone would be retiring as Glamorgan Secretary and David Morgan asked me if I would take over. It was, without doubt, the proudest moment of my professional life. I was particularly chuffed when invited to lunch at Cardiff Golf Club by Wilf Wooller, legendary former Captain and long-time Secretary himself, at that stage President of the Club. Over a two-hour one-to-one he gave me all sorts of advice, some of it – such as there being no such thing as a Labour Party-supporting Secretary in cricket – I enjoyed hearing but was never going to pay any real attention to. But much of it was priceless and incredibly personal. I hadn't had too much to do with Wilf up to that point but he seemed to have followed my progress over the previous eight or nine years. He emphasized the need for strong personal values, citing his and Phil Clift's long service (both had, as Alan Jones would go on to do, worked for Glamorgan their entire adult lives) and the importance of Glamorgan County Cricket Club as an institution, but his main advice centred on four principles: (i) always listen to players, even if you don't always act on what they say; (ii) if you trust your captain and your coaches (not that he believed in coaches) you should ignore anything different if it comes from anywhere else, especially a committee (he had a distrust of committees); (iii) don't take any bullshit (his word) from the governing body; and (iv) stand up for yourself. Wilf passed away a couple of years later. I like to think I paid attention to what he had to say.

In January that year I had been called to a meeting with David Morgan at his offices on the outskirts of Newport, always a sign that there was something important to discuss or, more often than not, that he was about to tell me to do. It turned out that this particular meeting was about the squad's pre-season tour, which had been pencilled in for Zimbabwe in April. David had decided, after consulting his key confidantes on the committee, that in the interests of costs the travelling party should be restricted to 15. Ok, I thought, that'll be a challenge but it's doable. He then explained that we wouldn't be taking a coach and that it was going to be me, Dean Conway and 13 players. Now that would be a challenge. Not least explaining that to the players, and more pertinently, the coaches. He said it was important for my development, something I can see with the benefit of hindsight, especially if there were plans then for me to succeed Gwyn. To my protestations about the need for a coach he pointed out that there was plenty of experience across the playing group and with the amount of cricket being planned on the tour managing practice shouldn't be that big a deal. To him, perhaps. Not to me though. I immediately felt a fraud. I also felt a bit out of my depth. Although I'd worked closely with Barry Dudleston, the umpire, whose travel company had put everything together for us, managing a group of people overseas was a huge step and I instantly found around a thousand things to worry about. In the end, it proved to be three of the most manic, enjoyable and memorable weeks I think I've ever had in my life.

I have the squad photo on my study wall at home (it's on the cover of the print version of this book too, incidentally). I'm looking ridiculously serious in the front row (probably after I'd sent Darren Thomas and Gary Butcher home for the fourth time in ten days), sandwiched by the two senior pros, Morris and Maynard, with Watkin, Metson and Barwick making up the row. The back row rogues' gallery consists of Messrs. Conway, Cottey, Lefebvre, Croft, Kendrick, Hemp, Thomas, Dale and Butcher. Steve James would certainly have been with us but just before we were due to leave he had fallen down the stairs at his digs in Zimbabwe, where he was playing and where we were to link up with him, and put his leg through a plate glass door, thus ruling him out, Gary Butcher being called up instead).

Departure day dawned and I was as ready as I would ever be. Skipper Hugh Morris and I had worked closely to try to button down all of the cricketing issues and I'd had several meetings with Barry to look at the logistics and finances. An added potential complication was that we had three supporters who had paid to make the trip. Barry had argued that as there were only three it wasn't cost effective for his company to be sending someone as a 'rep' to look after them so that too was going to fall to me. He had organized their itinerary so that there shouldn't be too much for them to be bothering me about. We were all due to be billeted in the Monomatapa Hotel in Harare for the first ten days (as would Northamptonshire), moving by road down to the middle of Zimbabwe for a couple of one-day games in Kwe Kwe, before finishing off with a three-day game in Bulawayo in the South of the country. It was a complicated schedule and with us self-managing, in a country flirting with volatility and unrest, the chances of something going wrong were probably quite high. The political situation was nothing like the one it escalated to a few years later but there were plenty of rumblings and we were told to be extremely careful. Inflation was around 40% even then, for example – not the 600% it reached fewer than eight years later, but pressing enough. Mind you, even that was relatively stable. In mid-November 2008, with a rate estimated at 79,600,000,000% per month, it meant that one US Dollar equated to the staggering sum of 2,621,984,228 Zimbabwean Dollars. Between the time you'd taken your Zim Dollar out of your pocket and handed it over, it was already worth less than half the value. So whilst the cricketing arguments for a tour were pretty compelling, the political and economic situation was, well, let's just say it was somewhat dodgy. And I was responsible for shepherding our little group through the next three weeks. Great.

On the day we left I remember Steve Watkin shaking hands with Caryl Lloyd Jones, my PA, with whom he'd just started going out. Typical 'Watty' to be so bloody formal about it, we all thought, but as Ms Lloyd Jones went on to become Mrs Watkin within a few years that formal approach presumably must have paid off. Caryl, also Sue Maynard's sister (we like our relationships close and cosy at Glamorgan) had joined the club in 1994 to help with administering membership and promoting the £15 membership drive which we'd just undertaken, but she found her niche working on the cricket administration in the areas I used to deal with, player contracts excepted, combining that role with keeping me organized, which, let me tell you, took some doing. She was by some distance the best worker I ever saw at Glamorgan; a perfect combination of initiative, intelligence, humour, flair, energy, charm and diligence…. she had it all. She got on with everyone, knew exactly which buttons to press. She was a brilliant operator.

My touring naivete kicked in right from the off, when offered the choice of smoking or non-smoking seats (yes, kids, you used to be able to puff away on your fags in a confined space up at 35,000 feet – I often wondered about the 'invisible wall' which separated smokers from non-smokers at the back, presumably helping the smoke and the smell from spreading further up the plane, but that's a debate for another time). I went for the former, joining Steve Barwick and Gary Butcher. It was only an hour into the long overnight flight to Harare that I realised I'd made the wrong choice when Matt drifted back from the comfy, odourless seats at the front to enjoy a fag with us before returning to his seat nearer the front of the plane. An hour in and I'd also learned that 'Baz' was petrified of flying. Not only did he knock back enough whisky to keep an average-sized distillery in business for a month but he insisted on accompanying every tiny little bump of turbulence with an audible 'Whooooooa', on the odd occasion grabbing hold of me with an expression of wide-eyed fear in his eyes. By the time the whisky had calmed him down he'd nodded off and he proceeded to snore loudly for the rest of the flight, picking up with more 'Whooooooa', 'Mike, mun' and arm-grabbing as we descended. For the record, 'Butch' and I managed exactly no sleep at all. And Matt just laughed sagaciously every time he nipped back to enjoy a cigarette with the Three Stooges.

Before flying back to the UK at the end of the three weeks we had a short internal flight from Bulawayo to Harare. Seats were allocated randomly but I happened to end up next to Baz again. There was no time for a drink on this flight. Which was a shame, as I would have joined him on the Scotch. The landing was one of the worst I have ever experienced. I swear we were close to being at right angles when we touched down in the capital, so strong were the cross winds. Baz nearly broke my fingers hanging on, and the 'Whooooooooooas' were peak decibel.

155

Baz had an amazing capacity. For coffee, which he drank in copious quantities, always the first into the office on an outground morning to put the kettle on; for cigarettes, very rarely his own; for alcohol; for lack of sleep; for regularity of small bets… he was a machine. But he was very rarely unfit to do his job on the cricket field. Old school indeed. After we'd landed in Harare on our original flight from London, Dean Conway signalled that the players should make sure their suitcases were in their rooms, take a quick shower and then reconvene in the hotel lobby 45 minutes later as they would be taking the short bus journey to the Harare Sports Club ground for a gentle fitness loosener. Twelve players had no issue obeying that instruction. Baz, on the other hand, just went straight to the bar. "No point in having a shower, mun," he'd mumble, sending his 'roomie' Adrian Dale on ahead with his bag. "I'll only be needing one in a couple of hours after training anyway." And into the hotel bar he'd lope, justifying a quick couple of lager tops on the basis that he needed to settle his nerves after such a strenuous flight. A flight which, dear reader, you'll recall he slept 90% of the way through anyway. When at the sports club, as Dean was sorting everything out, Hugh and I were getting our bearings, and the other lads were throwing a rugby ball around, Baz grabbed a cricket ball out of one of the kit bags and proceeded, with his first three deliveries, to run up and hit the one stump standing. "That's me done," he'd then add, with a flamboyant throwing out of the arms. And, do you know, I believe him. I reckon he would have been able to bowl a spell of 30 overs unbroken the following day, probably with figures of something like one for 50, no problem. He often used to say to me that he wondered why he was playing the game. "Mike, mun, I don't bat; I'm not a very good fielder; I don't take masses of wickets; and I don't give runs away. Boring cricketer, me." But by crikey what an effective one he was in that side. A genuinely legendary character but a good bloke and a mighty fine player too.

Neil Fairbrother, the Lancashire and England batsman, tells the story of a Lancashire team meeting prior to a one-day match at Colwyn Bay in 1994, the entire session being spent in dealing with how to combat Baz's miserly off-cutters. In the days before maximum 5:4 split fields in one-day cricket, Baz could tie an end up beautifully, and Fairbrother was one batsman who just couldn't play him, more than once claiming to be left in a cold sweat because he just couldn't get him away. The first three overs Baz bowled the following day, though, went for 27 before he was taken off. The visitors had cracked him. Or so they thought. When he came back for his remaining five overs, he conceded just eleven more to finish with four for 38 and have the last word. John Crawley, a Lancashire team-mate of Fairbrother's, and one of Barwick's victims that day, asked him in the bar at the end of play how he did it. "John, when I get my arm here," gesturing as if he was three quarters of the way through his bowling action, "you don't know whether to charge or stay where you are in the crease. But when I get my arm here," gesturing slightly further on in his action, "I've got you." I can't think of any comparable bowlers I've seen since Baz. I'd love to have seen him play Twenty20 cricket.

After that first run-around session in the morning had been completed, I had to sort out all the financial stuff and that meant a trip to the bank to sort out some cash for subsistence allowances. I had to gather all of the passports in order to do this and Hugh and Matt said they would take a walk into downtown Harare with me. While we were sitting around waiting for our appointment we took time, as you would, glancing at the passports and laughing at some of the photos. It was at this point we discovered that Dean Conway, social bon viveur and organizer of any number of parties and birthday surprises for others over the six years he'd been involved at Glamorgan, would be turning 30 bang slap in the middle of this tour, when we were in Kwe Kwe to be precise. If I used the phrase 'knowing glances were exchanged' I think you'd know exactly how Hugh, Matt and I were feeling. We thought Christmas had come early. A plot was duly hatched.

But before we could get to Kwe Kwe there were to be any number of incidents and shenanigans in Harare. I jokingly referred earlier to having sent Darren Thomas and Gary Butcher home for the fourth time in ten days but that wasn't so far wide of the mark. Our first match, at a venue in a country club around 45 minutes' drive from the Monomatapa, had seen the first disciplining of Bill and Ted (whose 'Excellent Adventure' had appeared on the big screen a few years earlier). 'Butch' had worked so hard on the first morning he'd thrown up the evidence of the night before in some bushes just off the 11th green. Hugh was livid. And rightly so. There were only 13 players on the trip and he needed them all to be behaving professionally, especially the two youngsters, one of whom had had the luck to be called up very late. Without Steve James, and our overseas player, who that year would be Hamish Anthony as Ottis Gibson was touring the UK with the West Indies, Hugh was keen to try to use the Zimbabwe matches to test some new combinations, with Hemp, Dale and Butcher opening with him, even leaving Metson out of the final (first class) game in Bulawayo so Matt could keep. Dean, the injured Roland Lefebvre and I thanked him for that, the three of us having to spend the three days of the match on the boundary edge listening to 'Meto' wittering away to us about being omitted.

The Monomatapa is the only hotel out of the windows of which I've nearly fallen. No high jinks on this occasion (they're coming within a matter of a few paragraphs, don't worry) but, not for the last time, the story involves the love triangle of me, Adrian Dale and Arsenal Football Club. 1994/5 had been a difficult season for The Arsenal, although a run to a second successive European Cup Winners Cup had brightened things a little. George Graham's functional approach was being enacted on the field by a bunch of hopeless, talentless and uncreative midfield types bolted on to the ruthlessly well drilled back four of Dixon, Adams, Bould and Winterburn to produce what can only be described as 'a boring bag of shit'. The middle four of Morrow, Selley, Hillier and Jensen weren't exactly a dream to watch and the over-reliance on Ian Wright-Wright-Wright up front was glaringly obvious. They'd managed to lose four consecutive league matches in March to leave them flirting dangerously with relegation from the top division. No such thing as wall-to-wall television coverage in those days, especially not in downtown Harare, so me and 'Arthur' (Daley, gerrit?), a fellow Gooner, had to resort to listening to the BBC World Service on the radio. Reception was so bad that we had to take turns hanging out of the window to get the best signal. Three up in 14 minutes, we hammered Norwich 5-1. Before losing the next two. Oh I know you're interested – you don't fool me… Only after back-to-back wins over Easter – an Ian Wright hat-trick against Ipswich on Easter Saturday, which I listened to while trying to ignore Metson's complaints about being left out of the side at Bulawayo, and a 4-0 win at Villa on the Monday – could we deem ourselves safe. I can confirm that the 22nd floor of the Monomatapa Hotel in Zimbabwe wasn't the place to be to follow foot-of-the-table Premiership football in the mid-

'90s. How I didn't plummet to an unseemly and somewhat patio-splattered end is amazing.

Arthur and I would be reunited just over six years later when we watched the 2001 FA Cup Final at the Millennium Stadium in Cardiff. Arsenal battered Liverpool and led through a Freddie Ljungberg goal which we both celebrated with a fervour and passion which ignored the fact that we were deep in Liverpool fan territory. We'd had a blatant penalty turned down as well but looked as though we would go on to win when Michael Owen struck twice in the final few minutes. You can imagine the stick we got from the Liverpool fans around us. I remember wandering back to Pontcanna to meet Dean and Duncan Fletcher, who had managed to blag tickets for the game (probably thinking it was a rugby match) and telling Arthur that whilst I could just about cope with one of them telling me that Patrick Vieira had been outstanding and didn't deserve to end up on the losing side, if either of them, both occasional Liverpool followers, so much as hinted about it being 'just a game' I'd give them a good clip around the ear before disappearing out of the door faster than Usain Bolt in a souped-up Ferrari. As they walked into the pub, some time after us because we'd rather sourly refused to stay and watch Liverpool lift the trophy, Fletch mumbled something about Vieira's quality only for his wife Marina to tell me to cheer up as it was only a game. The script hadn't included me giving Marina a clip.

And so to the high jinks back in Harare. 'And not before time,' I hear you cry. It started on the 18th floor of the hotel, in Dean Conway's room. However, on this occasion Dean Conway was an innocent party. It was a day in between matches so his bedroom was being used as a treatment room for dealing with the players' sundry aches and pains. Dean was busy administering to one of the lads when a bored Steve Barwick decided to start filling up condoms obtained from a machine down the corridor with water and use a sunbathing Tony Cottey and Robert Croft down by the pool, 18 floors below, as target practice. This might have been mildly amusing were it not for the fact that it was also downright bloody dangerous. Even with Baz's famed accuracy. The hotel staff weren't amused at what was going on – nor were 'Cotts' and 'Crofty' – but they couldn't pinpoint where the missiles were emanating from.

As if that wasn't enough, the final evening before the Glamorgan and Northamptonshire players went their separate ways, us to Kwe Kwe and they to Mutare, developed into a now-famous 'Cops and Robbers' battle between the squads. Let me first of all explain that for once I had gone early to bed. I was completely oblivious to what subsequently went on. It turned out that a group from either side – I'll spare personal blushes by not naming names – had decided to re-enact a famous mid-American state 1930s bank heist using the foyer, the lift and a couple of the landings on the floors above as their backdrop and, before anyone starts worrying, using their fingers as guns. One of the lifts was broken because a load of lobby furniture had been piled into it. Plants were strewn across several floors. Some minor damage was done. It wasn't exactly the rockstar crime of the century but the following morning, before I'd even had a chance to grab a coffee at breakfast, I was swept away to see the hotel manager. I proceeded to receive the kind of dressing down a repeat offender in a primary school class would have received from his teacher. And we were asked to pay several hundred pounds to cover the damages. I couldn't discuss this with anyone from Northamptonshire. They'd set off for Mutare at the crack of dawn. So I had to cough up. When I did return to the UK my efforts at exacting at least a contribution from the Northants club drew a blank with the most beautifully dismissive letter from Steve Coverdale, their Secretary, who more or less said that his lads were angelic paragons of perfection who wouldn't so much as whisper 'boo' to a passing goose. It couldn't have been them, he insisted. That was proved to be a hopeless distortion of the truth when, in the winter of 1998/99, we tried to sign Jeremy Snape from Northamptonshire and invited him for lunch to discuss it. Having sat down in an Italian restaurant in Canton, close to Sophia Gardens, Dean Conway, who was on my left, leant across to Jeremy, who was on my right and asked, innocently enough, "Cop?" Jeremy shook his head and just said, "No. Robber." Dean then leaned forward a little more, put his finger to his lips and said, pointing at me, "Shhhh. Chief of Police."

One of the robbers on that night, though as Northamptonshire Captain at the time he may well have managed to avoid being implicated, was Allan Lamb, the England batsman, for whom 1995 would be his last season playing. 'Lamby' (we weren't the only team with a lack of imagination when it came to nicknames) had been an idol of mine in my late teenage years and I met him for the very first time on this trip to Zimbabwe. Matt Maynard will

160

probably not remember this but after tagging along with him and a couple of others who were meeting Lamb for a drink in another hotel, Allan obviously knew the handful of Glamorgan lads in our group but wasn't sure about me, turning to Matt and, pointing at me, inquiring politely, "and tell me, who the f*** is this, Matty?" Matt could have laughed it off, or told him my position at Glamorgan, but instead he replied by saying, "This is Mike Fatkin, a good pal of mine." I really liked that. And it did the trick. I was immediately accepted, and for two hours Lamb was wonderful company. My role came up, but only later, and it didn't matter by then.

After the Cops and Robbers shenanigans, as we all squeezed into the minibus that was to take us across country from Harare to Kwe Kwe, Hugh and I decided to make a point about the behaviour of the previous day by announcing to the team that it had been all over Radio Harare that members of a visiting professional cricket team had been involved in endangering tourists sitting around an hotel swimming pool and causing thousands of pounds of damage to hotel property. Baz was genuinely worried, I think, and we managed to keep our well-hatched lie up all the way to Kwe Kwe (a journey interrupted by a vehicle breakdown, which even the mechanically proficient Steve Watkin was unable to rectify and which led to the squad having an impromptu game of football in the middle of Zimbabwe's equivalent of the M1 motorway as we waited for the breakdown to be attended to).

Once we got to Kwe Kwe, Hugh and I told the squad we would be going around the chalets (players were billeted in chalets in pairs) by way of a formal investigation into the previous day's behaviour. Heads would be rolling, Hugh said. For the fifth time, I said to myself, in Darren and Butch's case. As we'd driven into Kwe Kwe, remembering that this was Dean's 30th birthday, a party had been lined up at Kwe Kwe Sports Club which, according to locals, would be really well-attended, it being a rarity to see a touring professional cricket team in these parts. Well as the minibus made its way into town you could almost see the tumbleweed blowing across the main street such was the lack of life there. There wasn't a soul about. Typical, we thought. We had a great plan but it would only work if there were plenty of people to see it. Dean was going to get away with it, the lucky sod.

Hugh and I duly visited each chalet in turn, emphasizing the concerns and trying to draw out of the players exactly what had taken place. We were greeted with wall after wall of silence and it was clear we would be getting nowhere. The boys weren't for grassing on their team-mates. When we got to Dean's chalet, the penultimate visit, we thought we were about to make a little progress. "Well," said Dean, in response to Hugh's question about what the hell had happened in the hotel foyer in the wee small hours, "I believe it had something to do with cops and robbers." And that was that. He wouldn't elaborate any more and there was no way we were going to find out who was involved from him. Hugh knew Dean hadn't been to blame for the condoms incident, so we retreated. I was only just holding it together now but there was still one more chalet to visit and one more pair to grill: Dale and Barwick.

I never understood how Arthur and Baz came to end up rooming together, let alone how they remained a permanent rooming combination. They were so different, their approaches to away matches so completely and diametrically opposed, that it should have been a partnership made in hell. But it worked. As Hugh and I walked in, he nudged me and said that this would be the clincher. Baz was bound to be at the heart of it, he reckoned. On entering the room we were greeted by Adrian lying on the bed, reading. He looked up very briefly, nodded towards a door on the other side of the room and just said, "He's in there," before re-immersing himself in his book. His timing was impeccable. As the word 'there' came out of Arthur's mouth, the toilet flushed, the door he'd nodded towards opened and out came our Briton Ferry hero, clothed only in y-fronts, half-smoked cigarette in mouth, clutching a two-day old copy of the *Sporting Life*. His hands went up in mock surrender as he said, "I know, I know, I know." I was really struggling now, and lost it completely when Baz added, between puffs on his cigarette, "You see, we were the cops... and they were the robbers." As Hugh started off with a "Now Stephen, you must realise that this sort of behaviour just isn't good enough," I was a couple of feet behind him almost wetting myself laughing. It wasn't too professional. Hugh was really doing what I should have been doing. But the whole situation just had a Marx Brothers element to it and I'm afraid I'd gone completely. Looking back now, it was a magically hilarious moment.

We agreed an amnesty with the principal suspects as we had a reception to attend back at the Kwe Kwe Sports Club. It now being common knowledge that it was Dean's 30th birthday, Messrs Cottey and Croft were deputed to make him as 'presentable' as possible. Having undertaken some important pre-event planning we had managed to commandeer some of the Kwe Kwe club president's wife's clothing – she was the best built available female, apparently – and when Dean finally emerged for the reception he was clad in a burgundy skirt and outsize bra, with full make-up on (more Coco the Clown than Coco Chanel, to be honest, after that pair had finished with him), mock ear-rings and the lipsticked slogan "$50 A Time" scrawled in large numbers and letters on his back. He was remarkably laid back about it, no doubt as a result of the fact he'd clocked that the Kwe Kwe streets had been completely deserted on our arrival. I don't think any of us were anticipating anything more than a dozen people being in attendance as the fifteen of us – fourteen in regulation Glammy polo shirt and chinos, one dressed as RuPaul – sat sipping beers waiting for the bus to take us to the club.

How wrong we were. As the minibus pulled up outside the sports club we could already hear the buzz of anticipation emanating from inside. And as we walked up the corridors towards the main bar and function room it was clear where that noise was coming from. It seems that farmers had travelled from miles around to come and greet the first county cricket side from the UK to bother turning up and play in Kwe Kwe for donkey's years. We were minor celebrities (one of our number soon to be a major celebrity for all the wrong reasons) and they genuinely wanted to show their appreciation. I'm sure Dean's expression and mood would have turned in those few seconds as the line of men laughed, catcalled and wolf whistled him into the clubhouse. Fair play to Dean, he hammed it up. They loved it. Later in the evening, which consisted of a hog roast and more crates of beer than we could possibly come close to drinking, the guest of honour was asked to take the first cut of the pig. The guest of honour was now, of course, Dean, and to this day I'm sure he believes that first cut was the pig's cock. No hiding place, either, as the few hundred people around the patio area were watching his every move. Again, he didn't flinch. He may have dished out plenty of different punishments on rugby and cricket tours in the past but he was – still is – the best man I've ever seen for fostering a good team spirit and part of the earning of that reputation is learning to take as well as give. It was never in doubt. Attention soon turned to Darren Thomas, when, in one of those awkward moments when the noise dies down just as you're about to speak, he yelled to Gary Butcher who was at the buffet helping himself to some more meat, "Cut me some more beef off that pig, Butch." Most folk might mix their tenses or their metaphors. Not 'Teds.' He was mixing up his farm animals. In full hearing. The ribbing was merciless. The evening's entertainment continued later with naked relay races, Wales against Zimbabwe. Of course it did. And when I say 'Zimbabwe' I'm talking about Andy Flower, Henry Olonga, Alistair Campbell, Grant Flower and others in the national side at the time. Kevin Pietersen may have called Andy Flower 'a mood hoover' in his 2014 autobiography but he was nothing but phenomenally good fun on this trip. I left a gang of them on their way to the Chairman's house in the early hours, where I understand our lot, led by Conway and Cottey, performed a fabulous Austin Powers-esque rendition of *Bohemian Rhapsody*, complete with Scaramouche-like bobbing up and down from behind a wall during the operatic section. Makes you proud to be associated with a team from Wales.

In amongst all this frivolity, though, the team was performing really well and it was great preparation for the season ahead. They wouldn't be allowed to get away with much, perhaps any, of their behaviour in the modern era. There are too many camera phones, not to mention too many rigidly inflexible coaches who insist on their players doing nothing but live, breathe and train cricket. I can hear Steve James now muttering on about it all being very unprofessional, and of course he has a point, but to me it isn't, not on a pre-season tour when you're pulling a bunch of players together. There was always going to be plenty of opportunity for the protein shakes, ice baths, tactics meetings, fitness supplements, soft drinks, room service and early nights when the real stuff started.

The boys had decided on that tour that they needed a USP (unique selling product) to mark them out from other counties. And so the idea of them all speaking Welsh in the field was born. I'm not sure if I'm 100% accurate but even though a few of them had some basic knowledge I think that only Robert Croft and Tony Cottey actually spoke any Welsh. Matt had been banned from driving the previous year and had used the early part of the winter to take formal lessons. I know that as I was the one picking him up from home each morning and dropping him into town. He'd subsequently bagged them though. However, apart from Gary Butcher, Neil Kendrick and Roland Lefebvre, the rest of the squad could certainly stumble into Welsh and had a few phrases that would probably be passable to most non-Welsh speakers. So we had Butch learning place names and yelling out 'Pontardulais yr Haverfordwest' from mid-wicket or wherever he was fielding; 'Kendo' learning specific phrases such as 'Hufen Ya' (ice cream) and 'Bara Menen' (bread and butter); and Roland clapping his hands encouragingly and using whatever Dutch words most sounded like Welsh. The opposition didn't really like it. Especially when Cotts came out with something shortly before lunch on the third day of the game at Bulawayo and the batsman, Mark Dekker, was almost immediately stumped by Matt off Crofty eight short of a hundred. He was gesticulating madly towards our players all the way back to the pavilion. When the lads, by now pissing themselves laughing, came in a few minutes after him, it emerged that Cotts had said, "Bet fat boy's looking forward to his lunch" in Welsh. It was only after a few moments that it was translated. Cue anger, loss of focus and resultant stumping. I'm not sure how far into the season the Welsh speaking lasted but it struck me at the time not so much that it was a bit childish, which it probably was, but that it was also potentially a highly effective way of getting under the opposition's skin.

The last squad function of the trip was the internal fines meeting, organized – was there ever going to be any other candidate for the role? – by Dean Conway. A special dress code was devised comprising boxer shorts, flip flops, burgundy tour blazers, sunglasses and, bizarrely, shower cap. One by one the players were called up and interrogated about some 'offence' or other before judgment was passed (everyone would be guilty, surprise surprise) and punishment – involving drink – levied. I was fined, though unlike Philip Carling in Trinidad in 1990 not for 'impersonating a snooker ball' (Phil was bald and so his head started white, then went, in turn, pink, brown then black); no, I was fined for making boring speeches in public, keeping a low profile and a couple of other rather lame reasons. My fine was to pay for the team meal that evening. I took my punishment with pleasure. So, a host of cheap fags later (Baz and I picking off the non-smokers in the party for their duty-free allocations) and a last night, the highlight of which was watching Maynard attempting unsuccessfully to light a succession of sambucas, and we were on our way back home. A three-week trip that I'd been dreading because I was so far out of my comfort zone, with no coach, to a country that was dangerously close to economic and political collapse, which had thrown up unforeseen Harare hotel costs and the need to change the Bulawayo Athletic Club's constitution to enable them to play for the very first time on a Good Friday after we'd learned that our flight had been changed, not to mention a string of what I look back upon as hilarious events but which at the time I worried would get me into serious trouble, was over. Every time I come across any of the players who were on that trip, they tell me that it remains one of the very best they ever took part in, so it must have been a good 'un.

Me? I was never asked to manage a tour again.

9 EVERYTHING HAS ITS SHAPE

'I am afraid that there is not much to be said in favour of either the lawyer or the journalist.'
OSCAR WILDE

I once entertained ambitions of becoming a journalist. A different door opened, however, and the chance never materialized. Whether I'd have made a decent fist of it is debatable. Even though I've always believed I could write, I don't think I would have been able to sniff out the stories or badger people for quotes, which all good journalists do as standard. I've come across some good ones, and a handful have become friends. A few are given an outing here.

Despite being bagged as far as managing future pre-season tours were concerned the mid-1990s was a fabulous time for me. David Morgan allowed me to grow into the role of Chief Executive and with Tony Dilloway on a similar internal footing with me and looking after all of the commercial issues – never a great strength of mine – it enabled me to put my own stamp on the position. I am a people person and I tried to bring that to the way I operated in the role. I went to see some of my oppos on the county circuit, the ones to whom I looked up, such as Mike Vockins, Chris Hassell and Peter Anderson, and threw some of their suggestions into the mix back at base. The county game in the mid-'90s wasn't the place it was to become – everyone chasing international matches, revolving door overseas players, non-cricket business dominating and all of us scratching around for every penny. The relationship between the TCCB and the counties was occasionally fractious but there were no signs at that stage of any direct confrontations over huge issues such as central contracts, two divisions or performance-related fee payments. We were developing cricketers and in return we knew that we would be receiving a slug of money with which to cover our playing and other costs. There were six international venues and there was no real thought given to challenging what, in truth, was a pretty straightforward and comfortable existence.

Back in the '90s the role afforded you the luxury of taking time to talk to people, rather than what it was to develop into in the

2000s, a seemingly endless round of meetings with the game lurching from one major disagreement to another. I particularly enjoyed the relationship with the press boys. This was an era when county matches received decent coverage, at both local and national levels. Contrast the 2014 season, for example, when poor old Gareth Griffiths was left to cover Western Mail, South Wales Echo, Wales On Sunday and Wales Online on his own with the 1994 season, when there was one reporter assigned to each of the three Thomson House papers ('online' was still a bit of a futuristic mirage). In Phil Carling's day it was John Billot of the Western Mail, based in Cardiff, and Ron Griffiths of the South Wales Evening Post, in Swansea. John was a gentleman and an absolute pleasure to deal with, always interested, courteous and supportive. Griffiths was, well, Griffiths was awful. He may for all I know have been a decent bloke underneath but he came across to me as grouchy, pushy, rude, and constantly looking to rubbish everything we did, especially if it meant he could bring out the old chip on the shoulder topic of Swansea playing second fiddle to Cardiff. I was quite glad when he retired, to be honest.

I can't remember where I read it but one definition of a journalist tickled me, and isn't far from the truth. It described him or her as "someone who hides in the mountains and watches the battle raging below before coming down and bayoneting the wounded." Despite originally fancying a career in journalism the truth is I don't think I'd have cut it. Oh, the writing side would have been fine, I'm sure, but the sniffing out of stories would have challenged me and depending who I'd have ended up working for I'm not sure I would have been too good at writing overly critical pieces, certainly not on a regular basis. I can't see myself as a hatchet man. The way the national hacks pile in to managers in football, for example, or indeed anyone in the public eye who puts the slightest foot wrong, is pretty unedifying. Bayoneting indeed.

But my experience was that those covering county cricket were a good bunch. In addition to Edward Bevan and his BBC radio colleagues, such as Nick Webb, we regularly saw the likes of Phil Blanche of the Western Mail (still, along with Huw Waters and Paul Sussex, one of the very few in my experience whose claims to be a Manchester United supporter are backed up with proper knowledge of and passion for the club), Richard Thomas of the South Wales Evening Post, Paul Tully from the South Wales Argus, Simon

Thomas of the South Wales Echo, and the double act from Westgate Sports, Howard Evans and Mike Gouge. They were present at most matches and on the phone most weeks out of season.

They were augmented by the occasional visit from one of their allegedly more esteemed national colleagues. Michael Henderson – an incredibly talented writer if a somewhat eccentric, pompous and opinionated individual – used to bring some very upmarket packed lunches along with him, all clarets, posh pates and whiffy cheeses. The first time I came across one of his lunchtime picnics it was accompanied by a rather aggressive Q&A with his colleagues on the subject of the best recording of Beethoven's seventh symphony. Far more Q than A, on that occasion. David Foot would tell the most wonderfully evocative tales of West Country cricketers gone by; Frank Keating was always a theatrical and linguistic hoot; and Christopher Martin-Jenkins, ever forgetful, was forever arriving late, more often than not having got lost on the way. I loved it when the *Guardian* sent someone along. As a *Guardian* reader myself, not only had I convinced myself that their representatives would of course be somehow more erudite and naturally witty than those from every other newspaper, but I knew I'd be reading their stuff the following day so I paid attention. Foot, Keating, Andy Wilson, the excellent David Hopps – a role model for me as a future Twitter grumpy old man – and, on the rare occasions Glamorgan were playing well enough to warrant a visit, the cricket correspondent himself, Mike Selvey; they were good men and very good writers but I particularly enjoyed it when we were paid a visit by Matthew Engel, one time Guardian Cricket Correspondent himself before moving on to edit *Wisden* and then work for the Financial Times (by which time his visits, rare at best, had dried up completely). Generally, he would appear on an outground, Abergavenny being a particular favourite – he liked the venue, and it happened to be a few miles down the road from where he lived. Matthew was never a fan of the whole concrete bowl stadium thing. He would probably consider it a highly dubious recommendation but, along with Henderson and, more recently, *Guardian* columnist Marina Hyde and travel and football writer Harry Pearson, I consider him to be the very best of all writers, whatever the subject (his recent books have included subjects as whimsical as trains, a travelogue on English counties and a tome on the growing influence of Americanisms on the English language); the king of prose in my eyes. He makes writing seem so easy. And he was both witty and charming company, a really lovely man. I have fond memories of travelling with Carol and the girls a couple of times to the Engel family home in Herefordshire and spending time with his wife Hilary, their son Laurie and their daughter Vika. It was a tragedy when Laurie contracted a rare form of cancer and died in 2005.

Many's the coffee I shared with the journos, and many an evening beer too on away trips, especially with Edward and Richard, the latter memorably being the target of a particularly impressive rugby tackle of mine, effected as he tried to escape after one insult too many as we were leaving a Blackpool nightclub in 1999: both arms round the thighs, took him down good and proper. Shame there were no cameras about. Or maybe not, as it was after 2am in the middle of a four-day game and I was a chief executive, after all, even if I wasn't behaving like one. The cameras would also that night have captured my first encounter with Andrew Flintoff in that same night spot. 'Fred' thought I looked like Elvis Presley for some reason (though it made a refreshing change from being 'Big' Sam Allardyce, I suppose, whom I seem to have resembled since I emerged from my mother's womb) and kept coming up to me and ruffling my (heavily-gelled) hair. If I hadn't been so pissed I'd have lost my temper. But then he's bigger than me, so I chose instead to take it out on Richard Thomas. Who isn't.

Simon Thomas has a similar taste in music as mine, something I discovered several years after I'd left Glamorgan when we bumped into each other leaving a Half Man Half Biscuit gig in Cardiff. Nick Webb's must be similarly aligned as I've seen him at Squeeze and other gigs I've been at. One of the press corps I got to know well was Paul Rees, first as a writer for the Echo, Wales On Sunday and the Mirror but for a long time now a rugby writer for The Guardian; he also ghosted Matt Maynard's autobiography in the early 2000s. Paul is a fellow Arsenal fan and many's the journey we made up to Highbury and the Emirates, the pair of generally laden with doom on the way up as we collectively anticipated – as football fans do – the various worst case scenarios involving team selection, fitness, tactics, refereeing decisions and, of course, the result. On occasions at cricket matches we'd play the 'dictionary challenge', a game Paul came up with one County Championship morning in Swansea in the early 1990s. 'Reesy' was covering the match for the

Guardian and Richard Thomas for the Evening Post. The challenge involved being asked to pick a page in the dictionary, then select the left or right column and, if there are, say, 14 words in a column, picking a number between one and 14. Whatever word is selected has then to be weaved into the newspaper reporter's copy as part of the following day's match report. On that occasion, Reesy selected the word "Finn". Not 'fin' as in 'appearing on the back of a dolphin' but as in 'native of Finland'. He managed to include it by making some spurious reference to the weather and it being too cold even for a Swede or a Finn or something. Still. It matters not how you squeeze the word in, I suppose, just that you manage to do so. Challenge successful.

They were good people and we enjoyed – I think – a very good relationship. Philip Carling had drummed into me the importance of establishing a good rapport with key journalists and I always recognized that they had a job to do. I can't remember a single occasion when any of this group broke a confidence; they were always professional. Even when they could have landed me in it, they never did. They too recognized the value of the relationship and they weren't about to jeopardize that with one quick-win story. In fact the only person who chose to behave like a true 'hack,' the way the profession is often portrayed in television dramas, was a guy called Giles Smith, then working for HTV Wales. He came down to Swansea during our annual festival there in the early part of the 1999 season ostensibly to talk about the forthcoming Cricket World Cup and our signing of Jacques Kallis for the period after it had finished. When the camera was rolling he proceeded to challenge me about the club's commitment to cricket in Swansea. I kept my wits about me and didn't answer, just staring blankly at him until his cameraman stopped recording and we started again, this time with questions on the topic I had been expecting. Hardly a major media moment but if people who are expecting to have a working relationship with you shaft you like that it's unlikely they'll have much of a price in terms of retaining your co-operation, will they? We never had that sort of treatment from anyone else. We also enjoyed decent publicity throughout the period. So it was probably just him. I never had a problem with journalists criticizing the team's performances, provided it wasn't gratuitous. I wouldn't expect them not to. It was their job. And if players were performing badly I don't think they

171

could have expected anything else either. Some were probably a bit too sensitive about it, and we had the odd incident when a player challenged a journalist because he didn't like what had been written or said about him. But the majority took the lows with the highs as part and parcel of the rough and tumble of being a professional sportsman. And if the club as a whole deserved criticism, for whatever reason, we had to suck it up.

Edward Bevan was a fixture around Glamorgan matches and he is another with whom I enjoyed a really good relationship. He was very careful to stay 'in' with people and consequently his public criticism was close to being non-existent. I don't know whether that was because he was worried there would be a comeback on his close – some might have said cosy – relationship with the Club. He stayed in the same hotels and dined out with the players throughout the season, something which used to drive Hugh Davies in particular demented, but he was very rarely critical on air. He was never anything other than helpful and co-operative. I really enjoyed his company too, particularly his rude Grumpy-and-Sweary-Old-Man persona when it popped up from time to time. I used to grab snatches of commentary on Radio Wales on a Sunday afternoon when the team was playing away to stay in touch with what was going on. He had a lovely resonant voice, perfectly suited to the radio, and he was nothing if not beautifully one-eyed in favour of his beloved Glamorgan. There was the odd on-air faux pas too. I recall one occasion when we were playing Kent at Canterbury in the late '90s there was one spell of commentary where Edward said, "And in comes Alan, sorry, Mark Ealham to bowl to Mark, erm Alan, erm sorry, Gary Butcher, who hits it carefully out to cover where it's fielded by Colin, erm Chris, sorry I mean Graham Cowdrey. No run." Classic Bevs. Two Ealhams, three Butchers and three Cowdreys all in the one delivery. And he wouldn't have batted an eyelid.

The journos were proud of the Glamorgan players and championed their cause at every opportunity, sometimes wearing their bias just a little too obviously. This enabled Dean Conway and I once to use it to our advantage to play a prank on England's Chairman of Selectors, David Graveney. It would have been in 1998, when Steve James was in the form of his life, scoring centuries for fun. 'Grav' had come over to Cardiff to watch Glamorgan for a couple of days and Steve was one of the players he had his eye on. Over coffee he told us how strongly people had been pressing his case, led by the media boys, and that whenever he came over to Wales he was greeted by a chorus of people, all entreating him to pick him for England. Dean and I cobbled a letter together about how disgraceful it was that England were championing the causes of players far worse than James and that Graveney's continued reluctance to pick him might even amount to some form of racist slur on the people of Wales. We left it on Grav's car windscreen. The following morning, he nabbed us both over a coffee, withdrew the letter from his pocket with a flourish and proceeded to read it out to us, signing off with a 'you see the kind of thing I'm up against?' Neither Dean nor I could keep a straight face. And it dawned on Grav that he'd been had. Childish? Perhaps, but Grav is a friend and we knew he would take it in the right spirit. James scored 152 that day. And played for England later that summer.

A cuppa with the working hacks would be part of my various match day laps of the ground, a practice which seems to have disappeared over the years as grounds have become more built up, not to mention stewarded by inflexible jobsworths in bright yellow tabards. These laps brought me into contact with the Glamorgan members, which might have been tortuous on occasion but was in my view vital in terms of the need to be engaging with them. No point in locking yourself away in your office all day. In the old days, Sophia Gardens was much more open, with our 1966-built pavilion at square leg to the South of the ground, with what was grandly termed the Vice Presidents enclosure to its right. That area contained the members who paid a little more by way of subscription, the premium entitling them to their own separate seating area and a bar to the rear. By 'bar' in this instance we meant 'converted portacabin'. We liked converted portacabins at Glamorgan. Some of my favourite people were VPs, principal among them a man called Geoff Lister, a Yorkshireman from Sheffield who had been working with Bass brewers in South Wales since the '70s. He famously described England as a strip of land which connects Wales with Yorkshire, and claimed to be doing vital white rose missionary work. He was a delightful man. Imagine the face of the Churchill insurance dog, complete with 'oh yas' accent, and you wouldn't be far removed from what he both looked and sounded like. I suppose because I too had come down to Wales from Yorkshire he took me under his wing and loved nothing better than to natter away about the Yorkshire players of yesteryear (he had chaired Phil Sharpe's benefit in 1971) and in the pre-two division County Championship days, when Yorkshire's visits to Wales could be anticipated, he used to organize an event every other year – generally a sports quiz – at the old Crawshay Arms pub in Cardiff (which then became part of the Brains brewery) with the proceeds shared between the Glamorgan and Yorkshire beneficiaries. Those quizzes were legendary. Everybody would turn up so there would be 12 players from each side, two umpires, a load of office staff and their friends, all packed into a private brewery with a buffet and free ale available all evening. What on earth was there not to like? And the quizzes themselves were highly competitive, as competitive, in fact, as the prizes were naff. Geoff pulled in a load of Bass and Carling freebies – key rings, fridge magnets, tee shirts, velcro-fastening canvas wallets, whatever he could lay his hands on, provided it cost less than three quid – and we'd all end up winning something or other. I recall one of the early ones, circa 1987, when the team I was in had gone into the final round of ten questions with a lead of six points. All we needed were five correct answers and we would have the pick of the riches available on the prize table. In fact we did better than that and scored eight. We'd won! Only for us to hear Geoff announce that we'd finished second, the winners being the Yorkshire Veterans team of Phil Carrick, David Bairstow, Arnie Sidebottom and Jim Love... who had been fifth going into the final round, 18 points down. The senior Yorkshire team always won, I was told. No protests or appeals considered. If not a quiz, it would be a dinner at the (Bass-owned) Mason's Arms in Whitchurch, beneficiaries in those years including Neil Hartley and Hugh Morris, and at the end of each season Geoff would insist on taking the girls from the office out for lunch at the Beverley pub, around the corner from the ground, to thank them for everything they did for the members during the year. He was a true gentleman, Geoff, and I was very upset when he died in 2003.

With the benefit of hindsight, I realise that these were wonderful days. There was the occasional irritation, of course, but there was nothing really to get in the way of just enjoying county cricket: no ground redevelopment, no international cricket, no debt, and no real governing body politics. The job changed beyond recognition between 1998 and 2008, when I left. Behind the scenes in 1996 the old Test and County Cricket Board and National Cricket

Association were being merged into one organization which would take control of both the professional and recreational games across England and Wales. The new England and Wales Cricket Board would come into being at the beginning of 1997. They may have dropped the 'W' from the acronym (and the reasons for insisting on running with 'ECB' were rather lame in my opinion) but that particular 'W' was to enjoy a successful summer. It took over eighteen months for one of the seventeen first class county 'Es' in the ECB to win its own domestic County Championship.

In 1995 we managed to reach the semi-finals of the NatWest Trophy again. Roland Lefebvre had been forced out by a career-ending groin injury, his place in the regular line up going to Hamish Anthony. David Hemp had filled Viv's spot. Other than that it was the same side which had enjoyed such a magnificent summer two years previously. But it didn't *play* like that side. We were bowled out for just 86, albeit taking fully 47 overs to get there. Warwickshire, our opponents and the eventual winners, knocked them off inside 25 overs. They were to beat us again the following summer in a Benson and Hedges Cup quarter final, though on that occasion we did at least make a fist of it and only lost by twelve runs. Not for the first time, Hugh Davies was apoplectic. There may have been wars, famines and pandemics across the planet, but hold the front page: we had our latest crisis right here. He demanded a meeting, someone's head on a plate. He loved an emergency meeting, did Hugh. And loved a scapegoat. He was Cricket Chairman at the time but, much like the modern politician, it was always someone else's fault. It wasn't unreasonable to be asking a few questions, of course, but the accompanying drama would have done justice to the BAFTAs.

But even Hugh Davies was powerless to prevent the change in captaincy that took place at the end of that 1995 season. Hugh (Morris, not Davies – do keep up at the back) had decided enough was enough and told David Morgan and I that he wanted to stand down as captain. He'd lost the enjoyment. But whereas his first spell, when he was lobbed something of a hand grenade, with a very ordinary team to lead at the ridiculously tender age of 22, had ended in him resigning three years later, this time it had been different. Not only had he used the period when Alan Butcher was captain to rediscover his form – he hit over 2,000 runs in 1990 and played for England the following year – but he'd gone on to lead the club to its first ever one-day trophy in his first season back at the helm. The team was gently knocking on the door of consistent success, with a group of fine players and strong characters, and much of that was down to Hugh. I enjoyed working with him. He was meticulous, thoughtful and good company, but it was taking its toll and he wasn't enjoying it any more. We shared a mutual antipathy of committees but we worked with them and acted together to try to get the decisions we wanted through. I will even forgive him the fact that one of his final acts was to give a county debut to the curmudgeonly Eeyore that is Andrew Davies in the final game of the 1995 season. I jest, of course. Andrew remains one of my favourite people. But moan…. by jiminy he loves a moan. There was only one candidate to replace Hugh: Matt Maynard. He had argued that he should have been appointed in 1992 after standing in for 'Butch' but he couldn't argue with subsequent events and as time wore on I think he realised that it might have come just that little too early for him at that point. I know Matt had enormous respect for Hugh as a player and he did, after all, lead Glamorgan to a title the very next summer. That respect didn't apply to the other Hugh, though, and I would soon lose count of the number of topics over which the two of them were to fall out. Suggesting that they never saw eye to eye would be something of an understatement. I can't remember the meeting at which his recommendation and candidature would have been endorsed but I suspect that whatever came out of Hugh Davies's mouth would have had to clamber through some particularly aggressively gritted teeth.

There were two further decisions taken in the second half of 1996 which were to have a profound impact on the team's subsequent on-field fortunes. The first, to be fair to him, involved Hugh Davies in undoubtedly his most positive action as a Glamorgan committee member. We had been scrambling around for a few years without a full-time, dedicated First XI Coach. Alan Jones had been helping out, and John Derrick had come back to the club to work with the Second XI, but the First XI players were more or less left to self-coach. In 1996 the swing towards us taking on a full-time figure to work with the First XI was becoming irresistible. Hugh Morris had suggested it was time for the club to take that step and Matt agreed, though obviously it would depend very much on the sort of person we were able to bring in. Some of the names mentioned didn't exactly inspire but one of them – Duncan Fletcher – was in the process of impressing on a tour of the UK with a South Africa 'A' side which included players such as Lance Klusener, Jacques Kallis, Nic Pothas and Paul Adams. They'd thrashed Glamorgan by an innings in mid-July and Duncan's work had been noticed by Hugh Davies and Roger Davis. Jack Bannister, the broadcaster, then living in Pontypridd, was a co-opted member of our Cricket Committee and he backed up their views by confirming that Fletcher was very highly thought of back home in South Africa, where he had started working with Western Province. Three weeks after he'd been at Sophia Gardens, Hugh and Roger went up to Worcester to sound him out. He was interested.

Matt was asked to speak with Duncan and he too came back to say he thought he could work with him. From there it wasn't especially complicated. I contacted the Western Province CEO, Arthur Turner, and he was able to confirm that they would be willing to release Duncan from his duties there for the duration of the 1997 UK county season. At that stage, although there were some tentative discussions about 1998, there was nothing more. Obviously, Duncan needed to see how things went and we needed to be sure we had the right man. We also had to be fair to Western Province. There was no haggling over money. We drew up a contract with a suggested salary, he signed it, and back it came. There were no frills; there was no hassle. And nor, in all the time I worked with him, would there be. He was a straightforward negotiator. But my relationship with him at that point wasn't important. Matt was the one he had to establish a good rapport with. Pre-season 1997 we decided we would remain in the UK, with just a brief stint up in Brecon by way of team bonding. Duncan wasn't one of those precious coaches who demanded all sorts of conditions; staying at home was fine with him so long as he would have plenty of opportunity to work with the players. We agreed a date when he would come over. It wouldn't be announced until November, but one key piece of the jigsaw puzzle was in place.

We needed to make a second decision. We had to find an overseas player to replace Ottis Gibson, whose contract was not being renewed. Ottis was a lovely lad and a mighty talented cricketer but it just hadn't clicked the way we'd wanted it to. He went on to have a really successful county career, winning trophies at Durham and going on to be a highly respected international coach, but we felt we needed someone different. Hugh Morris had always been a fan of pace bowling – Corrie Van Zyl had been an earlier overseas recruit during his first stint as skipper – and Matt agreed that if we could find the right player, pace was the main area of weakness. Steve Watkin was a magnificent seam bowler. What we really needed was someone to complement him.

Out of the blue I took a phone call from Tony Lewis, then working with BBC television on the England/Pakistan Test series. He told me that he'd sat next to Waqar Younis at a dinner the previous evening and Waqar had said he was interested in returning to county cricket after a couple of years out. He had been with Surrey in the early '90s and Alec Stewart was, we were told, very confident that he would go back to them. 'AR' told me it was worth a call to his agent, Jonathan Barnett, and he passed on his number. I mentioned it to Matt. He didn't hesitate. He checked with Fletch. All he said was "Now if you could get *him*…." But we all felt it was bit of a long shot.

Barnett said there was a lot of interest but he agreed to meet and suggested Matt came along too, so that he and Waqar could chat, feel one another out. It seemed we were through the door, even if we were still very much the outsiders. As with so many signings Glamorgan would make, once we'd persuaded people into our inner circle they became increasingly more comfortable and trusting, and we did make some excellent signings over the years. Our problem was that we often struggled to get players to take us seriously in the first place. Before 1993 many saw us as something of a last stop pay cheque before retirement which, although true of the club in the '70s and early '80s, was by now far from being the case. This was a decent side. Viv was 38 when we signed him and no other county even expressed an interest, for example, and we missed out on plenty of good players domestically – Jason Gallian, Paul Johnson, John Crawley, Gary Keedy, Paul Jarvis, Paul Hutchison, Mark Lathwell, Mark Ealham – loads of them, in fact, many not even giving us so much as a second glance, because they just didn't see Glamorgan as a genuine career step forward. I remember mentioning to Matt, as we were waiting to meet with Paul Johnson of Nottinghamshire during a game against them in Colwyn Bay in the late 1990s. We were catching up for a drink after play one evening in Llandudno. I mentioned the fact that we'd talked about trying to bring him in once before. "I don't remember that," said Matt, "when was that?" he asked. "When you were threatening to go in '95 he was the bloke we'd targeted to replace you", was my reply.

178

We needed to approach something like this differently. Tony Dilloway went off to talk to some sponsors, among them Ian and Richard Brice at our insurance brokers, and they eventually came up with an insurance scheme which would cover the club in the event of us having to shell out prize money, with part of that enabling us to offer Waqar some really chunky pay outs in the event of him helping Glamorgan to win a major trophy. There would be some individual incentives for taking wickets as well, of course; all players of his international stature would expect those. But we wanted to demonstrate how we could really reward a top-of-the-bill player by helping him see the role he could play in delivering a collective success for the club. I don't know if it made the difference but it was a very clever, innovative deal.

So Matt and I travelled up a few days later to a restaurant in London's West End to meet up with Waqar and Jonathan, as well as catching up with AR, who had continued to keep the player and his agent sweet in the meantime. After the pleasantries had been exchanged, Barnett suggested the two of us found somewhere to 'talk turkey,' as he put it, and we disappeared into a private bar next door. He immediately told me that six counties had all matched the salary he wanted for Waqar but that the two of them had been impressed with the way Glamorgan had gone about its business and provided we were able to confirm the headline terms, Waqar had told him he'd like to come and play for Glamorgan. I had a job holding in my excitement. Barnett and I were in the other room for a good three quarters of an hour, though we must have been actually negotiating for all of five minutes. The rest of the time he was telling me stories about some of his other clients. He would go on to manage Ashley Cole, Brian Lara and Gareth Bale, from whose transfer from Tottenham to Real Madrid it was alleged that he and his partner David Manasseh, with whom we also did business in later years, had made around ten million pounds. I like to think those 45 minutes in that West London hotel annexe were crucial to his negotiating education and taught him everything he needed to know about how to negotiate deals for those three.

Anyway, out we emerged, to be encountered by an expectant Maynard. "How'd it go, Chief?" he asked. "Well, it was hell, to be honest," I said. "Really difficult negotiator, Jonathan Barnett, but we got there," I lied, blatantly, before adding, rather weakly, "It seems that Waqar is a Welshman." It was a while before I told him just how straightforward it had really been. It turned out that Surrey had come back and offered more but for once it wasn't all about the money. Our integrity, creativity and careful approach as a club had brought its reward. We already knew he would miss the first game of the season owing to Pakistan commitments, but we didn't care. We'd bagged a worldie.

The train journey back to Cardiff was a memorable one. Matt and I have shared many a drink down the years (he says, probably rather glibly) but on this occasion it was two close friends toasting one of *the* moments in their respective, and very different, professional careers. As the beer flowed (half a dozen each, I think) we remembered we'd agreed with Barnett that to kill speculation we should put the story out that evening. I suggested Matt did the TV – local BBC and ITV news – and Radio Wales, ostensibly because he was the one they'd want to talk to and he was much better at it than me, while I went back to the office to type out the media release I'd been knocking up on the train, get it checked by Barnett, and then faxed (yes, that long ago, folks) around to all the other written journalists. He readily agreed. It was only when I later saw footage of him with Bob Humphrys on the BBC that I realised just how tiddly the pair of us must have been. He had a wide grin on his face which may partly have been because he'd just been instrumental in signing the player who could deliver him his first trophy as captain…. Or it could have been the Stella Artois. My money was firmly on the latter. He wasn't slow the following day to tell me that he'd had no say on who did what that evening. Well, if he had been objecting when it was being discussed, I didn't hear him. We'd agreed to meet up at the Beverley, around the corner from the ground, when we'd done our respective tasks and as we walked in we bumped into Steve James and Adrian Dale. "I've just signed Waqar Younis," announced Matt, so matter-of-factly he might have been telling the two of them that he was nipping to the loo. But I could tell by their reaction that this was, indeed, another Very Big Deal™. 'Jamer' was grinning like a Cheshire cat. "I reckon we could win something now," he said, excitedly, rubbing his hands.

The stage was set.

10   LUCKY YOU

'People rarely succeed unless they have fun in what they are doing.'
DALE CARNEGIE

*I can look back now and recognize that 1997 was the peak of my working career. I was
33. That's not an admission that the rest of my working life has been any kind of failure
or anything. It's just an acknowledgement that the forces will never collide in quite the
same way as they did in that year. The role I was in; the people I was working with,
and for; the players; the overseas pro; the new coach: it was the perfect package at the
perfect time.*

Over the last decade or so I've been lucky enough to get to know
Graeme Fowler, the former Lancashire, Durham and England
opening batsman, more recently a highly successful coach. He's
become a pal, too; he's considerate, interesting, loyal, and very, very
funny. 'Foxy', as he's known in the game, also does after dinner
speaking – extremely well; his Jack Simmons stories are the stuff of
legend – and one of the stories he tells is preceded with a comment
along the lines of looking back from the present and realising only
now that a certain time back in the past was, in fact, the time of your
life. Professionally, for me, that time was 1997. It was laden with
stories, bursting with vivid memories and choc-full of people I'm
proud still to call close friends. It was also a high point in terms of
achievement.

    It all started quietly. After trips to Barbados, Trinidad,
Zimbabwe and South Africa in previous years pre-season 1997 was
identified as one we'd decided to spend at home. The doom-mongers
warned of an April of rain, a freak Ice Age, probably even
Armageddon, but the opposite turned out to be the case. The weather
was glorious. Len Smith, our Head Groundsman, was ahead of the
game in terms of middle practice and net preparation and it seemed
to be a really constructive, positive few weeks. Obviously, there was
no Waqar yet and Duncan Fletcher needed to be integrated, meet the
players, assess their abilities and attitudes and start to build a working
relationship with Matt. I wasn't too worried about the latter. The two
of them had spoken regularly during the Winter, with Matt providing
a summary of each player and his strengths and weaknesses, and I

was confident from my conversations with the two of them that they would quickly find the same wavelength. Both were strong team men, both were committed to surrounding themselves with the right characters, both had solid work ethics, but both were rounded enough not to be obsessed by cricket 24/7: it would prove to be the best captain/coach combination I ever saw close up.

'Fletch' was as even tempered a man as I've ever encountered. Never high when the team was winning; never low when it was struggling. I must admit that such equanimity was beyond me back then, however hard I tried. The only occasion on which I saw Fletch lose his temper was during the Abergavenny game against Northamptonshire. Robert Croft had cut his socks so that when he put them on, they'd go up to his knees. A childish prank, regularly trotted out I'm sure, but the reaction was surprisingly unexpected. He came in to see me the day after the game to apologize if I had heard anything back from any of the players, but he felt at the time that it had been a pre-planned team prank and that it had undermined his authority. He wasn't particularly complimentary about Croft either.

Duncan's modus operandi was for the Captain to act as *de facto* Managing Director of the team, with him as a Consultant. Supporting them would be a management group which would be consulted on important issues; some cricket-related, some not. That group in 1997 comprised Matt, Tony Cottey as his Vice Captain, Steve Watkin and Hugh Morris. I thought that was a rather neat way of looking at the whole dressing room dynamic. Needless to say there was a battle over who selected the side. Fletcher and Maynard, quite naturally, felt that it should be the captain's call; Hugh Davies and one or two others felt that at the very least selection ought to be influenced by the off-field cricket committee chairman (and, by extension, sundry hangers-on). I personally followed Ricky Needham's maxim: why buy a dog and then try to bark yourself? (Or, knowing Ricky's penchant for grammatical precision, try to bark *oneself*). We'd invested a lot of time and effort into bringing Fletch over and to let him build a close relationship with Matt. Surely they ought to be allowed to pick the team unencumbered by off-field prejudices? In what way did Hugh think that his experience of the county game in the 1950s would trump their knowledge? These two would eventually go on to coach an England Ashes victory, for heaven's sake. It was important to find a harmonious compromise, though, one that enabled Hugh to feel he was being consulted, and we managed to do that, but it was another example of unnecessary process.

Rather than send someone else to do it, I always volunteered for the job of picking overseas players up from the airport and I saw no reason to change that policy with Fletch. I liked to get a flavour of the person over the few hours it took to get back to South Wales, work out what made him tick, find out if there were any concerns so that I could try to address them sooner, rather than later. So it was that one early April morning in 1997 I headed up to Heathrow on the pre-dawn run to pick Duncan and his wife Marina up. It was freezing. They took a while to clear customs, so much so that the arrivals hall was pretty much deserted when they came through. I could tell they were wondering what on earth they'd let themselves in for. However, the conversation came easily. Duncan very methodically picked my brains about the club, the staff, the players, the press, the pitches, and anything else he could think to ask about. It was, other than when we've been golfing or sharing a few beers, probably the most I've ever heard him talk. But I felt comfortable in his company. And I know he was comfortable with me. We would, as they say, 'get on'. We'd gone all out to look after him. My PA Caryl had found digs for him in a mews house just off Cathedral Road in Cardiff, five minutes' walk from the ground; the perfect spot.

He didn't say a lot during that pre-season. I remember Matt telling me that we'd 'recruited a mute'. But what he did say was powerful and recalled the old Theodore Roosevelt maxim: "Speak softly but carry a big stick." Three incidents suggested to me that he would make an impact. The first was during a routine practice session. My office in the portacabin had sliding patio doors, all the easier for me to slip outside for one of my many cigarettes every day, and they were wide open on what was a glorious April afternoon. Duncan had been doing throw downs with Mike Powell, who had been practicing pull and sweep shots. After a while the supply of balls Duncan was using had run out. Mike leaned back on his bat, probably quite innocently, but all I could hear was a Southern African drawl, "What am I, Paaarl, your lackey? You hit 'em, you go fetch 'em." Later the same week he came in and told me – with not even the hint of an apology or a negotiation – that the players needed more warm-up kit. Caryl and I had been quite proud of the fact that we'd done a really cost-effective deal with Reebok for some decent training kit for the boys but that didn't matter. They needed more kit – more tee-shirts, more sweatshirts, more shorts. "We must have more shorts," I remember him saying. Once said, up he gets and off he goes. Make your point and move on. The third illustration came in the last couple of days before our opening game of the season, against Warwickshire. Steve James and Hugh Morris were working in the nets and had the bowling machine cranked up to 90mph, somewhere close to the pace at which Allan Donald bowled. As they did so, Fletch, walking past on his way to work with another player, moved the bowling machine a couple of feet further to the left. "Donald bowls from wider on the crease, Sid" was all he said. Attention to detail. Meaningful practice. Economy of message.

He wasn't daft, Duncan. He once told me about his work devising number plates for the Zimbabwean equivalent of the DVLA. He said his brief had been to make it easier for witnesses of hit-and-run accidents to remember the number-plate. If I've remembered it correctly, they added a character to the end of the existing six-digit sequential system. Taking the letters I, O and U out, as they could be confused, that left 23 letters to play with. The computer then divided the six-digit number by 23. The "remainder" determined the letter, so a remainder of one would give you the letter A on the number plate, two would be B and so on. Fascinating. And the only two reasons for including this paragraph are (a) to show Fletch that I was listening, and (b) so that I can picture Dean Conway reading it and shaking his head at just how boring it all is. He'd add that it explains a lot...

Fletch's advice about Donald seemed to have paid off as James and Morris put on 190 for the first wicket, the latter going on to make 233 (though Donald still manage to hit him on the head with a bouncer and force him to retire hurt) but Warwickshire came away with a draw, so perhaps he had the last laugh after all. Waqar had missed that game, as planned, and when he arrived shortly afterwards it was with a stress fracture in one of his toes. I remember the feeling of deflation when I was told he was injured but Dean had a look at him, did some checks and said he was fit to play. I should imagine in this day and age there would have been a reluctance to pitch him in but we all had 100% faith in Dean's judgment. He was the best about. And generally it would be a case of 'get on with it, mun.' So away we went. His debut at Headingley resulted in another drawn game but that all changed at Canterbury as Glamorgan won their first match of the season. Waqar didn't do too much damage, just the one wicket in the first innings and three in the second, but he did cause some problems for Nigel Llong, the Kent batsman, later to become a leading umpire. After three deliveries had beaten Llong's bat in one over, a fourth was followed by Waqar sauntering calmly down the pitch [never refer to it as a 'wicket,' I was told] and remarking to Llong, "You haven't got a f***ing clue, have you?" He was already fitting in.

That April we experienced one of those little things that pulls a group of people together. The players' catering at Sophia Gardens had, down the years, proved to be less Michelin-starred and more Michelin-tyred, and Tony Dilloway had taken a few risks and decided to recommend we appoint our first in-house head of catering the previous year. Enter one Andrew Walker, who had a less than negligible knowledge of cricket but immediately turned everything around on the catering front. He asked the players what they wanted, then asked Dean what they needed, married the two, and transformed the Club's culinary reputation. In his preview of the 1997 season for some reason Simon Hughes of the *Daily Telegraph* went rambling on about the poor quality of the catering at Sophia Gardens (I think there was some side mention of Glamorgan's prospects on the field as well). He clearly hadn't been to the ground for a year or two, not that a preview of a sporting team's chances justified a rant about food. It led to a robust defence and a tongue-in-cheek letter to the paper pointing the changes out and inviting Mr Hughes down to sample the new fare. Unsurprisingly it didn't elicit a response but it was something around which players and staff rallied. No one puts Glammy in the corner. Or something like that.

That season, as with 1993, there were very few injuries. Much of that is down to luck, of course, but never underestimate the importance of having a top-quality physio, someone who is confident in his diagnoses, understands which characters need what work, and ensures players know how to get through the rigours of a tough season with the right combination of technical skills, fitness, diet and rest. Only 14 players were used in the County Championship all summer. There was the standard XI – James; Morris; Dale; Maynard; Cottey; Croft; Shaw; Thomas; Waqar; Watkin; Cosker – and this was supplemented by appearances from Gary Butcher, with some walk on parts for Mike Powell when 'Cotts' lost some form, and for Alun Evans when Hugh went over on his ankle in the warm-up at Abergavenny. No one else came close. Shaw played every Championship game while Metson, a far more accomplished 'keeper – along with Alan Knott, Jack Russell and James Foster, the best I've seen – sat through his benefit year watching from the sidelines. Brave call from Maynard and Fletcher, that, especially in the face of repeated criticism from the snipers on the committee, but it proved to be absolutely the right one.

In June the team faced its Championship season low point – and the predictable clamour for 'something to be done.' Nothing spectacular heralded it. Glamorgan made 281, and Middlesex replied with 319, a first innings lead of 38. But unbelievably that 38 proved enough for Middlesex to win by an innings. I was sat watching with one of Matt's closest pals, John Edwards, as we collapsed to an ignominious 31 all out, only Cotts making double figures. It was embarrassing to witness. And I knew it would provoke a reaction. Fletch and Matt reacted calmly. Bitterly disappointed, of course, but Fletch's line when I spoke to him was more 'bad day at the office' than 'end of the world as we know it'. The next few games demonstrated that he was right. The reaction from Davies and the committee wasn't quite so measured. Nor, in truth, had been mine.

Immediately afterwards came Lancashire at Liverpool. Day one had seen Glamorgan perform rather better, reaching 173 for 1, with Steve James 99 not out. It then proceeded to rain. And rain. In fact the next two days were complete wash-outs. The poor old St. Helen's Balconiers supporters' bus had arrived just after tea on the first day to be met by the bedraggled players trudging off the field. On the fourth morning, with rain again falling, one of the Balconiers organizers contacted the Liverpool club to be told it probably wasn't worth their while making the journey. So as Matt and his Lancashire counterpart Neil Fairbrother attempted to set up a run chase, our own travelling band of intrepid supporters were spread across the North West, visiting Anfield, the Trafford Centre and the set of *Coronation Street*. What they missed has passed into Glammy folklore. Declaration bowling took Glamorgan to 272-1 and after a couple of forfeitures, the home side needed 273 to win in 60 overs. They only used 14 of them as they were bowled out for just 51, Waqar finishing with 7 for 25, including a hat-trick. A postscript to a weekend to forget for the Balconiers ended as their supporters' bus drove into Old Trafford for the one-day match between the counties the following day to be greeted by the Glamorgan players' cars coming the other way. The square was waterlogged and the game had been called off long before the scheduled start.

Waqar continued his post-Middlesex overdrive with back-to-back world class spells at Swansea against Sussex (8 for 17, with Darren Thomas hoovering up in the second innings in a 234-run win) and then a fine Morris century saw Gloucestershire off by ten wickets. The only incident of note in the latter was the fact that Steve James finished the match with a six – by his own admission these were rare beasts – which landed on the head of a sleeping spectator, who ended up having to be hospitalized. But the reaction to the Middlesex humiliation couldn't have been more emphatic. Three in three. The team was on a roll.

In Liverpool I managed one of my periodic away day catch-ups with captain and coach. A couple of times a season I liked to travel to a four-day game, watch some cricket, meet up with my opposition counterpart, have a meal with the cricket management and stay over. I preferred picking a four-day game as it was less frenetic. I'd keep myself to myself, grab a book or my *Guardian*, immerse myself in some music and just watch the game unfold from a vantage point on the opposite side of the ground to wherever the committee were being entertained. I hated that whole committee room thing. There wasn't much chance of me being able to watch for anything other than snatched fag breaks at home matches as I'd be dragged every which way from the moment I walked through the door at the start of the day so the opportunity to sit and watch at an away ground was always very welcome. On this particular occasion I'd agreed to meet with Matt and Duncan for an Italian meal and the three of us were joined by Adrian Dale. One of my favourite pastimes, exaggerated over the years, was childishly baiting Matt about the level of subsistence the players received for away games. He constantly whined that it was too low; I, on the other hand, used to explain the cost of an average meal and how easy it ought to be to be able to survive on what we were giving them. We weren't there to subsidize their drinks and in any event it was something we had to apply for an HMRC dispensation for. I think at that time the rate was something like £14 (and writing this, over 20 years on, that would still be enough to get you most of a reasonable main course). The bill eventually arrived and, with a couple of bottles of wine, it came to around £55. My mental arithmetic is sharp; always has been. I enjoyed that split second when I was able to watch Matt's brain ticking over as he realised that the bill for the four of us had come in well within the subsistence figure we'd argued about. And that it had included the wine.

At that meal I recall the two of them striking a bet about which player, of Mike Powell and Wayne Law, would go further. They each rated both youngsters very highly but Duncan felt that it would be Wayne, a supremely talented and instinctive batsman from Llanelli who scored a wonderful hundred at Colwyn Bay against Lancashire the following year. Matt also told me he loved watching Wayne (or to refer to him by one of the more original Glamorgan dressing room nickname, 'Sods') score a painstaking 18 followed by a rapid-fire 53 against Lancashire at Blackpool in 1999, a match dominated by the mesmerizing Muttiah Muralitharan; really contrasting innings which illustrated his adaptability. However, Matt himself believed Mike would go further. He'd started the 1997 season with a succession of hundreds in the Second XI, followed by an unbeaten 200 against Oxford University and would make his Championship debut the following month. He felt that Mike had the more level-headed attitude and that this would help him go further than Wayne. They bet a tenner. Which I kept. And theoretically should still have. Wayne's county career didn't bloom in the way he or we had hoped and Mike ended up playing nearly 500 matches in all, so I guess Matt can claim it. Not that he'll ever see it, of course.

When the four of us returned to the hotel we walked straight into the middle of one of those evenings that you just know is going to be memorable. Everyone was together. Even the (boring) non-drinking ones were there. Despite being 99 not out Steve James was part of the group, and the others had kept 'Watty' up past his regular bedtime. The rain was lashing down outside and it was pretty obvious that there wouldn't be much going on at the ground the following morning. Hugh Morris, the only one who might legitimately have played a rain card as he was the only batsman out, was a bit worse for wear and was being put in a lift and sent up and down the various floors of the hotel. Waqar and Duncan were actually scrummaging at one point, the latter demonstrating front row techniques to the former.

A little over-enthusiastically. And at one point Gordon Lewis, our Scorer, who at the time was on the Glamorgan Committee (he later resigned when he went onto the payroll) was accused by Duncan of being a spy in the camp. "You've been planted here!" he yelled, planting a finger firmly into Gordon's solar plexus, though, to be fair, it was all done tongue in cheek. The following morning Duncan suggested it would probably be a good idea for me to check the weather forecast before travelling up on any future trips. Strangely enough, having enjoyed the obvious camaraderie within the squad, I thought the opposite. But I did listen. My next trip, to Chesterfield for the Derbyshire game, where I saw Adrian Dale make a battling 142 to ensure we avoided the follow on, was a far more sedate, and thankfully more sober, affair.

Some of the incidents in 1997 were just plain bizarre. Just as the game against Northamptonshire at Abergavenny in August started I did what I usually did when the players and umpires were safely out in the middle and the first ball had been bowled, and nipped into the pavilion to grab a coffee. I'd barely popped my head outside before the players were all coming off again. It turned out that the wickets weren't quite properly aligned. Len must have been on the Scotch that morning. Watty had struggled with his run up and bowled a no-ball, and on the basis that Watty *never* bowled no-balls, he pleaded with Graham Burgess, the umpire at his end, to ask the groundstaff to re-measure the pitch. Watty had been right. There was a three-inch skew.

A few weeks earlier we'd had our traditional week in North Wales with fixtures against Nottinghamshire in Colwyn Bay. In the lead-up to the game we learned that we'd have to do without our left arm spin bowler Dean Cosker as he'd been selected for the England Under-19 side for their internationals. It was a ludicrous rule, but at the time those matches took priority over first class cricket. Dean (or 'Lurker' as he's affectionately known) was playing a part in taking Glamorgan to the County Championship title, and an important part too, only to have to pack his bags and disappear off to help thrash a very weak Zimbabwe Under-19 team. Nonsensical. I remember a battle we had with the old TCCB when Hugh Morris was captain and Darren Thomas had been selected to play against South Africa's Under-19s in 1994. It was a daft rule then, too. Though strangely enough it wasn't such a daft rule a decade or so later when Hugh, in his capacity as ECB's Performance Director, was arguing with us over the same point....

Lurker's absence forced a rethink in terms of Glamorgan selection. He would be missing for three weeks and at that stage of the season a second spinner to play alongside Robert Croft was certainly desirable. Gary Butcher was the normal 'go to' reserve that Summer and did a steady job but both Matt and Duncan felt a second spinner would be a sensible option to have. There wasn't really one ready on the staff. We did have a second off-spinner on the books in Gareth Edwards but Fletch had already told me in no uncertain terms, in a meeting the day after Gareth's one and only first-class appearance at Oxford University, that he did not think Gareth was a first-class cricketer and however many wickets he took his lack of batting and his inability to field or catch (his words, not mine) meant he would never be considered. Fair enough, I suppose. As it turned out 'Legs' went on to enjoy a really successful career in television, producing the BBC's *A Question of Sport*. He was a decent cricketer too, even if he failed to meet Duncan's exacting standards. That meant we had to look elsewhere. This was in the days before you could take players on loan for short periods of time so who was the next best? It turned out to be our old friend Philip North, who had been captaining the Wales Minor Counties side that Summer and, to be fair, bowling really well and taking wickets. His registration was rushed through and he was named in the squad for the Championship match against Nottinghamshire at the end of July.

It didn't work out. Phil managed to be led astray and enjoyed a few too many beers the night before the game, promptly overslept the following morning, and when Matt came to name the side he had to name Butch in his place as Phil still hadn't arrived at the ground. He had been rooming with Hugh, who had left him asleep when he'd gone to breakfast. Whether he might have tried a bit harder to wake him is a moot point but if he'd come back to the room late, presumably a little the worse for wear and quite probably making a bit too much noise, I guess Hugh was just annoyed with him, and who could blame him? He was potentially a month away from a Championship winners medal and the last thing he needed was Phil mucking about with his sleep patterns. Either way, it led to Matt (for whose son Tom Phil was Godfather) and I (for whose daughter Hannah Phil was Godfather) having to discipline him and send him on his way back to Cardiff with his tail firmly between his legs before we gave an impromptu press conference on the dressing room fire escape steps. Duncan called Phil 'unprofessional'. I rather pedantically pointed out that that was understandable as he wasn't strictly speaking a professional anyway. And the withering look I was given back left me in little doubt that this wasn't the moment for flippancy. Another typically misplaced attempt at levity. The levity would come a few weeks later, at a barbeque for a friend of ours, (Big) Dave Evans, when Phil turned up with a massive alarm clock around his neck, saying "I wasn't going to miss this bugger." How ironic that a couple of months later, on the morning the team and staff were all due to travel to London to receive the Championship trophy from the Duke of Edinburgh at Buckingham Palace, Phil rang and asked whether I was free for a bite to eat at lunchtime. I explained why I wasn't. There was a pause as I explained. "I could have been on that bus," came the considered reply. He knew he'd screwed up.

Although the Championship was the focus that Summer, the NatWest Trophy wasn't without incident and the team won through to the semi-finals for the third time in five years. In the second round, away at Hampshire, we were chasing what was, for the era, a pretty formidable total of 303 to win in our 60 overs after being on the receiving end of a Robin Smith masterclass. But we were up with the rate, albeit having lost a few wickets, after having been given a great start with half centuries from Hugh Morris and Adrian Dale. Adrian Shaw had joined Steve James, batting lower in the order to allow Robert Croft to open (which Steve hated, and it didn't work that day as 'Crofty' was out for 0) and we were still in the hunt when Shaw was run out. I was watching on TV and it's only fair to say that 'Jamer' went bananas. He went right up to the Hampshire captain John Stephenson and had him by the throat. It turned out that Shaun Udal, the bowler, in attempting to gather the fielder's throw, had broken the stumps without having collected the ball. Eventually – possibly because of the pressure exerted by our Lydney Tyson Fury – Stephenson recalled Shaw who, thankfully, hadn't quite reached the perimeter rope. We went on to win with two balls to spare, 'Shawsy' seeing us through to the end and Jamer finishing as man of the match with a vital 69. It was inevitable that there would be some disciplinary reprisals and Jamer was fully expecting to be hit in the pocket. He wasn't fined in the end, but he was severely reprimanded. And he accepted that he had crossed a line, albeit that the rest of us all found it hilarious that such a mild-mannered and easy-going member of the side had 'lost it' in quite such a fashion.

We were drawn in the next round against Yorkshire at Sophia Gardens, the game to be played a couple of days before we were due up in Colwyn Bay. This time it was a Darren Lehmann masterclass we were on the receiving end of but the required total we would be chasing was lower. And on this occasion the pinch-hitting worked, Crofty making 55 and Jamer taking his turn to be out for 0. When Steve Watkin was out Glamorgan were 209 for 9, still requiring 28 to win as Dean Cosker joined Waqar in the middle. I was over in the pavilion by now. Sky Sports were covering the game and the customary signal for them to start making their preparations for the post-match presentations, which took place in those days on the home dressing room balcony, was the fall of the seventh wicket. So by the time 'Lurker' loped out to bat the full TV crew, led by Bob Willis, was in place in the room Dean Conway used next to our dressing room, ready for the balcony interviews and presentation. It was a long wait, too, as the pair inched towards the target, and when they got there, there was an explosive release of tension and relief. After Sky had done their bit Bob Humphrys stepped up to interview Matt and Waqar, man of the match for his batting for once, for *BBC Wales Today*. Bob's closing question was to Waqar: "It's your first season with Glamorgan. Just how good would it be to cap it with a visit to Lord's for a major final?" It was a pretty obvious question. But it didn't get an obvious reply. "It would be f***ing lovely," was what Waqar said. Cue profuse apologies from Bob, a sheepish smile from Matt and the sort of look from Waqar which suggested 'what have I said wrong?' And yes. I did receive letters.

That brought us to the semi-finals, where we were drawn to play Essex at Chelmsford. We batted first this time, and made an impressive 301 for 8, Steve James hitting a fine century. But Essex got off to a flier, Darren Robinson and Stuart Law making 150 for the opening wicket. Darren Thomas managed to unsettle Law by bowling him a beamer when he was on 44. It looked very much like an accident from what I could see but Law made a bit of a meal of it and was told to put his rattle and dummy back in his pram by one or two of our fielders. Essex were going really well when Darren trapped Ronnie Irani leg before for 51, one of four wickets for him in 19 deliveries. In his follow through Darren turned to appeal and as he was turning back he celebrated with a triumphant fist pump which caught Irani on the head. It was clearly an accident but Irani, drama queen that he was, made out it was something more and taken with the Law incident it appeared that a few seeds of bad feeling had been firmly sewn.

Essex were five runs short, with eight wickets down, and it was getting very dark indeed. There were still 46 balls remaining, with Waqar's inswinging toe-breaking yorkers to come, and the umpires, Chris Balderstone and David Constant (it always seemed to be 'Conny') decided to offer the batsmen the light. Unsurprisingly, they took it. Cue a kerfuffle between Robert Croft and Mark Ilott, close friends off the field and whose wives were actually watching the game together.

"It's not that dark, mate, come on," said Croft.

"Not too dark! I can see the bloody moon up there!" replied Ilott.

"Well how far do you need to bloody see?" quipped Croft in response.

We could have done without the pushing and shoving which accompanied all this but it was an obvious case of handbags. However, I knew it would be Another Big Deal™ when it came in as third item on *News At Ten*, ahead of a story about global aid for the victims of the Montserrat volcano disaster. The following morning that most useless of useless batsmen, Peter Such, somehow managed to hit a boundary in the second over to win the game for Essex. That elusive final would have to wait a further three years.

The fall out was another disciplinary hearing, this time with Robert Croft in the dock for his shoving match with Ilott. I attended an ECB hearing in Bristol, accompanied by Roger Morris, one of the lawyers on the Glamorgan Committee, which took its own course, but we also had to have our own internal hearing. Our own procedures entailed convening a panel of five, chaired by Ricky Needham, and one of those five was always a player representative. In this case it was Steve James. The same Steve James who had grabbed John Stephenson by the scruff of the throat two rounds ago. When it came to passing judgment, he at least had the decency to point out the irony of the situation. I think he felt a bit of a fraud.

1997 was Jamer's year. In between threatening to lamp Stephenson and sitting in judgment over one of his team-mates he was scoring a bundle of runs. He hit well over 1,700 in Championship cricket, including seven centuries, and followed in Steve Watkin's footsteps by being named as the PCA's Player of the Year. I've always liked Jamer (I didn't find out until after he'd finished playing that he doesn't particularly like being called 'Sid', after the *Carry On* actor, hence the use of an alternative here). And I would have followed his career as a journalist had he (a) not written about rugby union, and (b) not written for a long time for the *Telegraph*. I'm afraid I'm not a fan of either. His journey (word ©X-Factor) on the nationals started on the *Guardian*, though, I'm proud to confirm. I recall him asking me for my opinion on one of his early pieces, presumably as there weren't too many other *Guardian* readers he knew to ask. I had to point out that just the fourth word of his career as a national newspaper journalist – 'specious' – although of course used in the correct context, and most definitely a very good word, wouldn't necessarily go down well. Folk didn't want to be looking in dictionaries while they were simultaneously wolfing down their Corn Flakes and trying to catch up with the previous day's events. I'm delighted to see that, in the main, he manages to keep the show-off words out of his articles, which are now courtesy of *The Times*. He may not yet be Neville Cardus but he's a fine journalist. And a bloody good bloke, too. Which is much more important.

As the season galloped towards its climax Glamorgan went to The Oval to play Surrey. There were only three matches left. It was at this stage that Matt decided to demonstrate his pragmatism as a skipper. Having established a first innings lead of 234 he would have had high hopes of forcing a victory but a Graham Thorpe double hundred frustrated the visitors and Surrey were eventually bowled out for 487, leaving Glamorgan 254 to win in the 46 overs that remained. They gave it a go for a while but at 65 for 3 and overs running out, common sense took over and they batted out the remainder of the time to ensure a draw. Surrey's Coach Dave Gilbert had a right old rant to the media afterwards. "It was outrageous that they gave up the chance [of outright victory] so early," he told them. "It had all the makings of a great finish. If they are going to play like that, they can't expect too many favours when we play Kent." Strange choice of words, I thought then, and he ended up having to defend them when our local journalists, as they were always going to do, probed for some kind of explanation, especially as he'd added the rider "Kent are the best all-round side in the Championship and deserve to win." For our part we knew that wins in our remaining two games with full bonus points and we'd win the title.

Our final home game was against our friends from the NatWest semi-final, Essex. It went according to the textbook. Glamorgan made 361, bowled Essex out for 169 and enforced the follow on. I've always been wary of a follow on being enforced for a lead of fewer than 200 runs but I suppose that's why I was an administrator, not a captain. That, and a complete lack of any ability, of course. Second time around the visitors made a better fist of it, totalling 340, and we were left with 149 to win with plenty of time to get them. No problem. Hugh went for 0. A blip. Then Jamer went for 4. 13 for 2. A minor setback. And then 'Daley' was out for 12. 26 for 3. It'll be fiiiiiiine. Not for me, it wouldn't. I was a danger to anyone when we were on a nervy run chase like that. Fletch exuded confidence, which I suppose is why he is what he is: a highly respected coach. And he was proved right as Matt, with an unbeaten 75, and Cotts, who played possibly his most vital knock of what had proved a difficult summer for him personally, chipped in with 35 not out to see us home by seven wickets. I didn't see it. I was round the back of the pavilion taking it in turns to relieve the stewards and giving them a break, chain-smoking Marlboro reds for two hours solid. I know. Wimp.

And so on to the big one. Taunton. A call the day before from my great friend Peter Anderson, the Somerset CEO, put everything into context: "Don't be doing any gloating if it goes well, Fatkin. We've never won the bloody thing." Wilf Wooller was the only other Championship-winning Secretary Glamorgan had ever had. How poignant it would be if we could win the title for a third time in the year Wilf passed away. Whatever the outcome, I was definitely going to see this one live. When I announced this a couple of the journos – Richard Thomas and Paul Rees – tried to persuade me to stay away, pointing out that for the three away games I'd turned up (Liverpool, Chesterfield and Leicester) it had pissed down with rain. Kent were playing Surrey (remember them?) at Canterbury and by all accounts there was a bit of a sporty pitch prepared for that one. They suggested I went there instead.

195

Taunton was the pinnacle. Our cricket was magnificent, our support was sensational, and the outcome was, well, it was as good at it was ever going to get. By the end of the first day we'd raced to 159 for 2 in reply to Somerset's 259, and our batting on what was a first innings spread over three days was some of the most memorable I think I ever saw. Hugh hit a century, Matt hit an even better one, and Crofty and Shawsy then came in and just rubbed it in. We had a lead of 268 and provided it didn't rain, we'd surely nailed it. The home side began their second innings reasonably well but once Darren Thomas had removed both openers we just chipped away, taking regular wickets, until Ben Trott was given out leg before to Dean Cosker. We needed 12 to win. Even I couldn't try to pretend it was anything other than a formality. And then in a flash it was all over. A group of cricketers at the very peak of their collective games, all playing with unbridled confidence. How very different from those days just a decade before.

As at Canterbury in 1993, just about everyone ended up in the dressing room. I'd learned a couple of lessons from then and helped our photographer Huw John organize some photos for the team on the field with the Championship pennant and trophy. We'd not done that at Canterbury. Though even that didn't *quite* work. In some photos Watty is not present (he was doing an interview) and in others he is there, but Crofty isn't (ditto). Ah well. Maybe next time. And I was confident there would be a next time. The core of the side was too good for us to believe that this would be the end of any trophy-gathering. One of my favourite photos was taken in that dressing room: me, the Lord's Taverners County Championship Trophy and, erm, a pair of pink underpants hanging up in the background. Well it was a dressing room, I suppose. I'm grinning from ear to ear. And why not? Although I was only 33, as a moment in my professional career it just couldn't be topped. Fletch was in the Wales rugby shirt I'd brought down with me which the players wanted to present to him as a parting gift. Waqar was – and if you'd had a thousand guesses you wouldn't have come up with this – sporting a Nelson Mandela mask. The beer was flowing. And the case of champagne, which Peter Anderson had, completely unprompted, arranged to be there. Everyone who mattered was there. As at Canterbury four years before I didn't trust any of the buggers with the trophy and after a discreet period I slouched away. As I was coming down the stairs I was collared by one of our more regular members, a frequent moaner, serial complainer, and one of the band of middle-aged autograph hunters who used to line up outside the players' area at the grounds we played on, armed with books, photos and other paraphernalia that they wanted signing. I never understood quite why. It was long before E-Bay, after all. They'd claim they needed that elusive signature from a Paul Todd or a Steve Bastien. What they actually needed, I thought, was a life. For once, I reasoned, he's going to be speechless. There is nothing he can possibly say that's critical. Wrong. "It'll be bloody difficult to repeat this next year, Mike," he said. Oh do sod off, I thought. What is it with some people? They can't resist pissing on the biggest and best of parades.

Talking of parades, the next few weeks were a haze of congratulations and receptions. Tony Dilloway had arranged the very first Glamorgan Player of the Year lunch for a few days later, in a marquee on the outfield, and that was a special occasion. We enjoyed an open-top bus drive, complete with trophy, through Cardiff city centre and on to a reception at the Mansion House, which gave us the opportunity to involve 'Uncle Al', 'JD', Graham Reynolds, the office staff, caterers and groundstaff. It was such a joyous few weeks. Shakespearean salad days indeed.

One of the more formal occasions involved a return to our Patron The Prince of Wales's Highgrove home in Gloucestershire. This time David Morgan asked me to do a quick recce the day before so we wouldn't be faffing around looking for the hidden entrance, which had been the case in 1993. I dutifully did so, only to forget that we were travelling at night, meaning I didn't recognize many of the landmarks, and so we ended up faffing around anyway. One of our staff, Vicky Snook, suggested that it was pretty poor form for the entrance not to be much more clearly signposted. Of course, Vic. Presumably to make it easier for any passing protestor, journalist or terrorist! Anyway, as we pulled up, one of the security staff, along with Charles's Equerry, came on board to remind us of the royal etiquette. Three key messages: don't start the conversation, wait for HRH to do so; never, on any occasion other than in any formal introduction, touch HRH; and when you are first introduced you call him 'Your Royal Highness', and from then on, 'Sir'. I was sure that the younger lads in the squad were picking all this up. Once again, Charles was fantastically briefed, genuinely interested in the team's performances, and enthusiastic. When he came to the last group, however, the conversation had dried up a little. He'd already had the excitement of meeting our phonically-challenged Fishguardian, Alun Evans. On discovering that the Prince had recently been in Haverfordwest, Alun perplexingly asked him if he'd stayed on the caravan park. As any heir to the throne was always going to do. Before, just a few moments later, Alun bumped into a table and deposited a priceless sword onto the floor. Way to go Al. In that last group stood our beloved Physio, Dean Conway, who had played such a massive role in building team spirit and keeping all the key players fit and performing. As the awkward silence went on, Dean put his arm to the Prince's shoulder (immediately breaking rule two – security advisers ready to move in) and, failing to address him in any way other than a 'butt' at the end of the first question (rule three), asked him a direct question (completing the full house by breaking rule one and initiating a conversation). The question was about whether His Royal Highness had attended the recent *Spice World* film premiere and, if so, who his favourite was. Classic Conway. But as the bodyguards hovered, you could see that the Prince loved it. Whether or not he liked cricket didn't appear to matter. Afterwards one of his staff told me that he really enjoys such informal gatherings, and we had a lovely letter from the senior Equerry telling us that the Prince had really enjoyed the evening. Prince or pauper, the Glamorgan lads were, as ever, the very best at making anyone, whatever their social status, feel completely relaxed.

The final element of the lap of honour was the trip to Buckingham Palace in October to pick up the cup formally from the Duke of Edinburgh (Patron of the Lord's Taverners, whose trophy it was named after), along with the County Championship medals. Matt was in New Zealand with Otago and had to miss out but David Morgan agreed that we could fly Fletch back over from South Africa to be involved, Tony Cottey leading the players' delegation as Matt's Vice Captain. I only noticed in looking it up as part of the memory-jog for this particular chapter, but one of the photos shows the players all lined up with the Duke showing their individual Championship medals. All except Colin Metson, who didn't have a medal to show as he hadn't played a Championship game. As at Highgrove, the Duke did some networking, going round the room to talk to the players, their wives and some of the staff and committee. I say 'networking'.

He wasn't anything like as good as his eldest son. And he was as generally uninterested as he was dismissive. Perhaps 'perfunctory' would be the most appropriate word to describe his performance on the day. It looked like he had something else he was in a rush to get to. I was in a group with Tony Dilloway and the man from the Birmingham Mint who had made the medals (they're beautiful, too). After a quick ten-second conversation with me about my role and a quick exchange with the medal man about the medals, he turned to Tony and, pointing directly at the daffodil on his blazer, asked "what's your job, then?" Tony had barely uttered the word 'Commercial' when the Duke cried "Oh!" and just turned on his heels to move to another group. Way to go, Phil.

After the Palace the Lord's Taverners held a reception at the Hilton Hotel on Park Lane and we were all presented with our medals by Nicholas Parsons, who was the Chairman of the Taverners that year. It was another convivial gathering. On the bus on the way home Dean persuaded David Morgan – acknowledged wine buff that he is (David, not Dean, who merely likes to think he is a wine buff) – to stop at a wine merchants in Knightsbridge and we loaded the bus with reds, whites, and some beers and ciders for the plebs, of which I was of course one. Dean led the communal singing with his 'Best of the '70s' cassette including, just before David Morgan was disembarking at one of the Newport turn-offs, persuading him to lead the singing to Gary Glitter's '*Do You Wanna Be In My Gang*'. As he got off the coach, he was being heralded by the whole bus. "Leader! Leader!" A mad, happy day, to finish off a mad, happy season. The best I would ever be involved in.

11 LIFE ON MARS

'Stars don't beg the world for attention; their beauty forces us to look up.'
JORDAN HOECHLIN

Overseas players were staples of county teams back in the day. We'd sign them for all formats and there was very little movement from club to club: players became associated with particular counties. I don't envy the modern coaches and administrators flying them in and out these days, like some mercenary carrier pigeons. During my time at Glamorgan, we had some crackers. Viv and Waqar stand out but there were plenty of other good 'uns. This chapter picks a few out.

One of the privileges of my job at Glamorgan was coming into contact with so many wonderful overseas players. Not all of them were out of the top drawer, it has to be said – no names, no pack drill and all that – but it was a fantastic experience, even meeting the ones we eventually failed to sign, of which some detail will emerge as this chapter unfolds. I know. But you'll just have to contain yourselves. There were a handful of really great ones, too. 'Great' is such a ridiculously overused word in the modern sporting lexicon that it's come to be attached to what are, in truth, some pretty ordinary sportspeople. But Glamorgan have had a few genuine greats. And once I'd overcome my initial starstruck, open-eyed demeanour when around some of them, and even got to know a few of them, I began to appreciate not only their contributions but their characters and personalities.

I could do this in chronological order, and just move through the players I worked with over the years, but I'm not going to. Because I'm bound to miss someone out and on the basis that I can't be bothered to research every single player I am taking the view that it would be an awful lot easier just to mention the ones I want to. So there. We'll start at the beginning and then, in line with much of the rest of this scattergun tome, we'll just dart about to no useful purpose, like a heavily dosed-up grey squirrel dodging the traffic on the M4.

If the likes of Viv Richards and Waqar Younis were Champions League quality, let's just say that my first overseas player experiences were more BetVictor Southern League Fifth Division. As

I walked through the door at Glamorgan back in April 1986 passing me metaphorically in the opposite direction was one Javed Miandad. He'd enjoyed several successful individual seasons with the club, and the year before had scored a memorable double hundred against the Australians at Neath, but he hadn't appeared at the start of the season and no one seemed to know where he was. In the final of the Austral-Asia Cup game between Pakistan and India in Sharjah, Pakistan, with only the one wicket remaining, needed six off the final delivery to win the match. You can guess the outcome. Javed was at the crease, belted Chetan Sharma into the crowd and finished with an unbeaten 116 to be feted by all-comers. Obviously, those celebrations continued for a good while because despite being issued with deadlines by the club there was no sighting of him and in the end it seemed to be clear that he wasn't going to be coming back.

This was the era of two overseas players per county and there were some pretty dangerous looking duos out there: Imran and Le Roux at Sussex; Hadlee and Rice at Nottinghamshire; Greenidge and Marshall at Hampshire; Lloyd and Croft at Lancashire; Garner and Richards at Somerset; and that's to name just a handful. Glamorgan? We ended up with West Indian Ezra Moseley (but only on weekdays as his contract allowed him to play league cricket in Lancashire at weekends) and an Australian lad called Dennis Hickey, who had come over on a scholarship to play some Second XI cricket and found himself promoted to the First XI. Over-promoted, as it turned out, to the surprise of probably just about nobody, including Dennis, but maybe that was no bad thing as he went on to become CEO of ING Real Estate in Australia and included an advanced MBA from Harvard on his CV. Not your typical cricketer, obviously. But as all of these other overseas county partnerships – and many other 'worldies' besides – were putting the fear of God into batsmen and smashing balls all round county grounds the length and breadth of the country the fact was we were only able to respond with a part-time West Indian quickie with a dodgy back, and an Aussie rookie. Bows and arrows against the lightning. We finished the season bottom by a country mile.

In 1986 we also had a batsman on the books called Younis Ahmed. He had played two Tests for Pakistan in 1969 but no longer counted as an overseas player, though the then impenetrable TCCB registration regulations can't have been that clear as he would go on and play two more in 1987; it was a good 15 years later that the rules governing qualification became clearer to me and I needed to spend a few years as an elected member of the Board's Registration Committee as well as sitting on a group which helped re-write them in order to even begin to understand them. It would have been quicker to learn advanced Mandarin and explain how to do so, in Swahili, to a bunch of Kazakhstanis. Anyway, Younis was famed for his entrepreneurial ventures, an Islamabad Derek Trotter if you will, and his very first words to me, upon being introduced around the time of the pre-season photocall, were, "Hi. I'm Younis. Let me know if you ever need a leather jacket, mite. I can get them in four different colours, mite." Yep. Of course you can, mite. And no, that's not a typo. Nor had he misheard my name. Geoff Holmes had spotted my quizzical expression. He told me that Younis called everyone 'mite' (he said he couldn't quite get his tongue around the 'a' in the word 'mate', apparently).

Viv and Waqar notwithstanding I still maintain that the best overseas player we had at the Club in the 20-odd years I was associated with it was Michael Kasprowicz. He played for us for three seasons from 2002 to 2004 and would have played a fourth had he not been picked for the Ashes series in England in 2005. After a lot of to-ing and fro-ing between us, he subsequently pulled out of his contract for 2006 as he wanted to focus on one last shot at the Australian Test team but he left it very late to do so, notifying us less than a month before the season was due to start. However, there wasn't any residual bad feeling. This was the era when international commitments were increasingly encroaching on our county season and the days of finding top quality players who were available all season were already numbered. In any event I've mentioned a few potential candidates for the 'All Round Good Bloke' award, such as Alan Jones and Roger Skyrme, but as well as being a wonderful bowler 'Kasper' was also a major contender so it was difficult for anyone to fall out with him, whatever the circumstances – even when those circumstances involved having to react to a police incident after a game in Lincoln in 2004. He was the last person in the squad I'd have expected to see associated with trouble. Turned out he'd done nothing wrong.

His record – 151 first class wickets at 26 – doesn't tell the full story. Not that I'm a slave to individual statistics. It's about the team. Kasper took 130 of those in his first two seasons, his last being interrupted by injury and international commitments. And in 2003 the Durham lads would have been heartily sick of him as he twice took nine wickets in an innings in matches against them, once at home and once away. But it was what he brought to the organization away from his own contribution with bat and ball which impressed me. He was by some distance the best cricketer I saw with sponsors and committee; polite, engaging, interested. He was also a superb encourager of other players, particularly the young ones. A real leader. Even his put-downs were delivered with style and class. His time at Glamorgan coincided with the advent of Twenty20 cricket. In that first season of the new format, Kasper's second, many players were still finding their feet with all the hurly-burly, many not really taking it at all seriously even though it was obvious even then that it was a form of the game that was going to pull in the crowds. The umpires had their common sense heads on too, keeping matches going when there was a drop of rain around or when the evening light was fading a little (hardly any grounds had floodlights when the competition began, Sussex being the first to install permanent ones a few years earlier).We only played five matches that year and as Glamorgan had three at home, we were desperate to maximize revenue. The run chase for the visit of Somerset to Cardiff coincided with persistent drizzle but we still managed to attract around 4,000 people so naturally enough we were desperate to play. The umpires were Mike Harris and, you've probably already guessed, one David Constant. Normally 'Connie' would play things by the book but not this time. He took the teams out and probably kept them out in conditions which they shouldn't really have been playing in. If I heard 'like a bar of soap' once that night I heard it a thousand times. Anyway, Glamorgan had made 193 for 7 in our 20 overs, a decent score at Sophia Gardens, probably 30-odd above par. The run chase was, even I would admit, a little farcical. David Harrison's one over went for 18 and his new ball partner, Kasper, managed to maintain that average over three overs – 3-0-54-0 were his final figures – as Somerset cantered home with a couple of overs to spare. As the players were coming off I was standing having a cigarette by Head Groundsman Len Smith's office, which the home players passed as they went back to the dressing room. I was there to thank the umpires, to be honest, but Kasper hung back. Once I'd seen Mike and David he came forward, shook me by the hand and said, "Well, I hope you f***ing enjoyed that, Chief." Delivered with a forced smile, but still.

My other favourite Kasper tale came at the end of May 2003, just a few weeks before that Somerset Twenty20 match. We were playing Derbyshire in a C&G Trophy knock-out cup match and at the end of the game, which we lost, the boys adjourned, as they often did, to the *Mochyn Du* pub just a short hop from the main gates to the ground. Paul Russell had very recently taken over as Chairman, with a formal announcement made just six days before the game, and this was his first in situ as Gerard Elias's successor. The mood was subdued, as one would have expected. Russell came over to me and asked me if I wouldn't mind introducing him to Kasper and, naturally, I agreed to do so.

"Mick, this is our new Chairman, Paul Russell. Paul, this is Michael Kasprowicz."

They shook hands.

"Pleased to meet you, Mister Chairman," said Kasper.

"Good gracious me, you're tall" said Russell, then, after a short pause, added "though I suppose if I stood on my wallet, I'd probably be the same height as you."

So that went pretty much as expected then. The two other players who were with us in the group just looked down at their feet. Kasper's eyebrows went up for just a fraction of a second and then he was back into default nice-guy mode, asking Russell all about his background and his plans for Glamorgan. The conversation would have gone on for a while. Kasper wouldn't have been talking too much.

In the teams in 2002 and 2004, when Glamorgan won the then equivalent of the old Sunday League (it's had so many iterations I honestly forget what it was in either or both of those years – Norwich Union and Totesport respectively, I think), Kasper was a key figure. In the second, he was joined by the outstanding Matt Elliott, or, as we're using nicknames now, 'Herb' (after a famous Australian middle-distance runner). He had first come over in 2000 and he made an immediate impact, helping us to that elusive Lord's final and scoring a stack of runs. He was to return in 2004 and form a wonderful partnership with Kasper, though it was Kasper's replacement, Mick Lewis, who was to be present for the final knockings. In 2002 we'd won the title at Canterbury again (I can hear Chris Cowdrey's voice as I type, saying ever so politely, "Would you mind awfully not coming down to Kent to pick up your trophies? It's rather annoying.") Kasper had been involved in that game in 2002 but he'd been forced out of the final few matches in 2004, so we'd signed Mick Lewis, a state team mate of Herb's back in Australia. After Adrian Dale had hit the winning runs in the match against Lancashire at Colwyn Bay which sealed the title, I recall him pointing out to me that whilst he'd slaved through 15 years to get to today, Mick had just landed, taken the field, and picked up a winners' medal in his very first match.

In between Glamorgan stints Herb had appeared for Yorkshire in 2002, helping them to win a Lord's final. In the game immediately after that – a Totesport / Norwich Union / Sunday League / National League thingumabob) – Glamorgan were their opponents at Headingley. Most of our lot had drawn Elliott-imitation goatee beards onto yellow post-it notes and stuck them on their chins as he came out to bat, making sure that he saw them. He somehow grinned his way to 16 before David Harrison got him out. He probably smiled all the way back to the pavilion. We won. Handsomely. 2002 in that competition was our year.

Two years earlier he'd been involved in an incident with Mike Powell in Colwyn Bay. Herb had made 177 in the four-day game against Sussex, he and Steve James recording Glamorgan's highest ever opening partnership in first class cricket, 'Jamer' going on to make a club record 309 (probably 90% of them singles down to third man). A few of the players had been out for a quiet drink in Llandudno and were strolling back to the hotel when Mike and Herb had apparently had a contretemps outside a chip shop. Jamer came running up to Matt to tell him what had happened and to ask him what he was going to do about it. "Nothing," came the reply. I immediately questioned him in Sergeant Wilson style with a throwaway "Do you think that's wise?" "They're grown men," said Matt. "They'll sort it out." And they did. Something and nothing.

There must have been something about the North Wales air and 'Powelly' as two years later I drove into the car park at the ground in Colwyn Bay the afternoon before the start of our four-day game to be greeted by John Derrick telling me that Mike and Ian Thomas had been involved in a bust up during a pre-net game of touch rugby. 'Iron' Mike Powell had lamped Ian and promptly disappeared off in a huff. Ian, or 'Bolts' as he was rather cruelly christened after an operation which had inserted a couple of screws into his spine when he was younger, was shocked, but fine. It was hours before we heard from Mike, by which time we'd convened a disciplinary meeting with his close buddy Steve James, then skipper, having to inform him he'd been suspended for two matches. If you've ever had someone you've got a burning urge to sort out, go to North Wales, and take Mike Powell with you. Colwyn Bay seems to bring out the Joe Calzaghe in him. That propensity to 'get it on' evidenced itself with a fight between Mike and Welsh rugby international Peter Rogers (organized, this time) during Mike's benefit year, albeit this one was slightly less competitive. As one of my pals called it on the night, it was the boxing equivalent of a dull goalless draw.

I liked Herb. That slow Victorian drawl, with the emphasis always on the last word of each sentence, every final word a note or two higher and always accentuated with a questioning intonation (come on, I know you're doing it now, aren't you?). He was one of life's positive people and another who put the team first. He was amazed when he arrived in 2000, that the players didn't have a team song, to be sung after every win. Owen Parkin put all of his time as perpetual twelfth man (or so he always grumbled to me) to good use and came up with some lyrics and a tradition was formed right there. Herb was injured midway through the 2005 season and came back for the opening few matches in 2007 but it was in 2000 and 2004 that he really made his mark. How the hell he only played 21 Test matches – and just a single One-Day International – is completely beyond me. What a player.

Jimmy Maher was another whose company I enjoyed, at least until Matthew Maynard and I fell out with him in the mid-2000s. He'd first come over in 2001 and immediately made a positive impact with his performances, his energy and his rapier humour as the team won promotion in the Championship. Unfortunately, it didn't end well. After a second season in 2003, when he came over mid-summer as cover for Steve James, who had picked up the injury that eventually forced him to retire, we went back to Matt Elliott in 2004. But only after Jimmy, who had been our first choice, had told us he would be missing the first couple of matches of the season because he wanted to attend a friend's wedding. That didn't sit very comfortably with us and we didn't think it was unreasonable to be saying 'no.' Jimmy went on to play for Durham later that summer.

He eventually made a reappearance at Glamorgan in 2007. We'd originally decided we wouldn't be running with an overseas player that year. There were pressures on the finances with the ground being redeveloped and it was something we didn't feel we needed to do. However, there was a lot of pressure from the media and from members and eventually, largely through the promise of a donation from a wealthy supporter, James Hull, we felt that we had to act. Matt Elliott had been due to play for Yorkshire for the first month of that season instead of Younis Khan but Pakistan's early elimination from the World Cup meant that Younis would be available all summer. Herb approached us and offered to play for nothing, an act which, even if it was only for a month, was typically selfless. We had also that summer been expecting to bring in Jerome Taylor, the West Indian quick, via a sponsorship agreement with Digicel, for the last two months of the season, but he was injured and never made it over. It was like the set of *Carry On, Overseas Player*.

And so with Herb here for a month we looked at options beyond that. It seemed that Hull's offer of supporting an overseas player came with strings, though, those strings being that his donation was conditional upon the player having to be one James Patrick Maher. It wasn't nice to be boxed into a corner but we threw away any scruples we may have had and Jimmy signed a one-year contract for the remainder of the 2007 season. He wanted an agreement that brought him back in 2008 as well. I understood where he was coming from but felt that in the circumstances this was pushing things. We said that we would try to accommodate it but it would have to come with the proviso that he performed reasonably well for the rest of the season. We announced in July that Matt would be coming back to Glamorgan as Cricket Manager at the end of the 2007 season so we needed him to be on board with any contract extensions. Matt liked and rated Jimmy. But in the circumstances, with the only reason we had an overseas player at all being the fact that they were either offering to play for nothing or the supporters were funding one, we could hardly dive in with a two-year deal. I must admit I didn't think there was any confusion there. I thought we'd made ourselves very clear.

Anyway, what happened was that Jimmy bombed. His first-class scores were 1, 3, 4, 19, 19, 55, 16, 3, 4, 0, 4, 31, 29, 25 and 39: 252 runs at 16.80. In one-day cricket they were 20, 76, 22, 2, 5, 23,

14, 2, 5 and 26: 195 at 19.50. Hardly compelling numbers, especially for a high-profile overseas player. I didn't think we could possibly go ahead with a second year. Neither did Matt. We discussed it with our Operating Group, which Paul Russell chaired, but with continued financial pressures, not to mention the fact that Russell and Hugh Davies, as Chairman and Deputy Chairman both key players in any decision, had no time for Jimmy as either player or personality, there was no chance of it being agreed. I couldn't, and didn't, argue with that, though it was all about the stats for me, nothing else. I liked Jimmy very much and still do. However, he felt we'd reneged on a promise.

Being honest I was sick of the whole overseas player circus by 2007 anyway, irrespective of what was happening in this particular case. They were picking and choosing when suited them, moving from county to county in any given year, cutting stints short, pulling fast ones with injury, even moving arrival dates willy-nilly and more than occasionally for inventive and spurious reasons. There were seriously average cricketers earning a living, some of them not really giving a rat's arse if they made a contribution to their county, knowing someone else would offer them a gig the following year anyway. There were agents all over the place pushing ordinary players and asking the moon for them. And that was then. It's even worse nowadays. Players are coming in for a couple of matches here and there, often popping up for someone else the following year, or just whizzing around the globe going from Twenty20 tournament to Twenty20 tournament like some kind of willow-wielding circus act. Imran Tahir, for example, has played for no fewer than eight counties. I certainly don't envy the modern-day CEOs and Directors of Cricket. In the event Jimmy and I fell out over it, which is a shame because he was my type of bloke: he worked hard, he enjoyed himself, and he loved a laugh. And we had really got on. His two seasons in 2001 and 2003 were very happy ones even if it did end disappointingly. I didn't fall out with many players, but he'd be one who I'd jump at the opportunity to have a beer with again if that situation ever arose.

Towards the end of the second of those two earlier seasons Jimmy decided it would be fun to have a players' day out somewhere. In the end he settled on Worcester Races and sorted out a corporate facility via Steve Rhodes, then one of Worcestershire's senior players, eventually to become their Head Coach. Two limousines duly turned up at the ground to collect the party, which included Michael Kasprowicz, Ian Thomas, Mark Wallace, David Harrison, the physio Erjan Mustafa, myself and a few others. I hate racing. I really do. I find F1, boxing and, other than internationals, rugby union boring, but I positively loathe horse racing. However, the company would be good, the beers would be flowing and everyone was intent on having a good time. Kasper and I had nipped away from the box early on in the afternoon and bumped into Jeff Bird, one of Glamorgan's committee members. After the initial surprise (on both sides) we learned that Jeff and his wife owned a horse which was running in the fifth race: Parson's Pride, a 66-1 outsider. Jeff advised us to keep our hands in our pockets. It had only finished three races previously and had no form to speak of in the three it had finished. We duly relayed this back to the group. Now Jimmy loved a bet. He would quite literally bet on anything. He was even nipping out between races at Worcester to bet on races taking place elsewhere. After a successful bet on the first by the Gwent syndicate of Wallace, Thomas and Harrison (despite David putting the entire kitty on a horse to win the first, when he'd been asked to put a small portion of it as an each way bet) attention turned to Jimmy, who wasn't having the best of afternoons. He'd heeded Jeff's advice and was on the 13-8 favourite for the fifth race, the 4.05, a horse called Cherry Gold. So as the horses came galloping past, with Parson's Pride way out in front and Cherry Gold trailing in third, Jim's mood isn't too clever. As Kasper, coy enough to have ignored all logical advice and stick a modest quid on the winner, goes off to collect his £66, Jimmy storms off to the winner's enclosure. Thankfully, before he could launch into too extensive an abusive tirade, the team physio Erj Mustafa was able to pull him back, cursing and swearing ('Mahbo,' not Erj). How appropriate that the race was The Worcestershire Victim Support Novices' Handicap. Only one victim that day. As I said, I regret that things didn't work out with Jim. His own made-up race commentaries always made me cry with laughter. He was an engaging fellow and great company.

We made a number of short-term signings, including Damien Wright, Herschelle Gibbs and Brendon McCullum. McCullum was brilliant. His New Zealand team-mate James Franklin wasn't quite in the same league, though he was steady enough. He had a naturally casual air which was interpreted by some of our supporters as conveying the impression that he didn't really give a toss and would rather be doing something more interesting, like making origami giraffe figures or pressing wild flowers. I don't recall too many of his performances though I do recall him giving our Accountant one of his shirts at the end of the season – Franklin, as in Clive. McCullum had been recommended by John Derrick. But he'd had a job pushing it through as the Chairman assumed McCullum would be supplanting Mark Wallace as our 'keeper, whereas 'JD' just wanted him as a specialist batsman. Which both Russell and Hugh Davies didn't believe he was capable of being. He went on to be the world's leading one-day and T20 batsman.

We even had a brief flirtation with Sourav Ganguly in 2005. After Kasper had been picked for the Ashes tour that year we had wanted to bring in VVS Laxman but he couldn't commit and we were then approached by an agent offering us Mick Cleary for three months from the end of May. Another twist led to the home office refusing him a work permit as he hadn't played enough first-class cricket over the previous two years. We were then offered Ganguly for the same period (I did say the agents were everywhere). He was serving a six-match ban as Captain of an Indian side penalized for slow over rate and was on holiday in the UK and interested in 'keeping his eye in,' as the ban only applied to internationals. He played five matches and averaged 62, including a fine 142 in the game against Kent, but it came in a game in which we were thumped by ten wickets. He also played half a dozen Twenty20 matches, even though he'd never appeared in the format in competitive cricket before. I'm not sure how much he understood the concept of strike rate, either, as his 114 runs in those six matches couldn't have come at anything remotely approaching a run a ball. All in all, he joined a losing cause halfway through a season in which we'd started with Kasprowicz and Elliott, seen the former withdraw when selected for the Ashes tour, the latter injure his knee, and in which a callow, promoted team was being thumped week after week in the top division. I'm not sure Ganguly was ever really going to make much of an impact. The most exciting element to his signing had been the shenanigans over his work permit, in which our Chairman decided to become personally involved, with Ganguly having to travel to Brussels as part of the process of getting his paperwork sorted out. I think the phrase 'not worth the effort' best sums it up. Nice man, gargantuan ego, but in truth a bit of a pointless signing. Little wonder I was getting fed up with the whole overseas player thing by the time we encountered our issues with Jimmy Maher a couple of years later. I really don't envy the modern CEO and Director of Cricket with overseas players flying hither and thither, often staying for only the very briefest of tenures.

My own time finished with a good 'un, though. In my last season at the Club – 2008 – with Matt on board and starting to build a team, he wanted to go for Jason Gillespie as overseas player. He'd already signed Jamie Dalrymple, Matt Wood and Adam Shantry and would recruit Jim Allenby the following winter. He wanted 'Dizzy' to do the same job that Kasprowicz had done: lead the bowlers, influence the dressing room. He did that. A fantastic cricketer and a modest, engaging man. Nothing delighted me more than seeing him coach Yorkshire to the Championship title in 2014 and 2015.

I was never a fan of the short-term stint. Which is why I'd hate to be in the position of the modern-day CEO. It was so much easier when players committed for a season, or a good chunk of it at least. The most effective short-term stint I can recall for us came in 1999. That was a World Cup year and we had Duncan Fletcher back with us for a second summer after our Championship success eighteen months previously. Mind you 'Fletch' wasn't with us for long in one sense as it was announced early on that David Lloyd would not be having his contract as England coach renewed at the end of the tournament. It seemed that Fletch was the outsider of a trio of shortlisted candidates, behind Bob Woolmer and Dav Whatmore, but it was clear that he was interested. He came and spoke to me, decided to apply, and he was duly invited to an interview – a famous one where the ECB's Simon Pack greeted him with "Hello Dav" as Duncan walked into the room. He was eventually offered the job but he wanted to see the season out with Glamorgan, man of honour that he is. With hindsight, though, it might have been better for him to have gone straight away, though both Duncan and the Club thought we were doing the right thing at the time and the ECB was prepared to go along with it as well. We ploughed on. Back in the Winter, after Waqar's second season in 1998 had failed to live up to the highs of the Summer before, Duncan had suggested that we look for an all-rounder, the two leading candidates being Jacques Kallis and Lance Klusener. The former was a protégé of Duncan's and we knew he would relish the idea of linking up with him again over here.

Klusener was probably the bigger name at the time, mainly for his big-hitting exploits in one-day cricket for South Africa.

In the end we plumped for Jacques only for him to sustain a stomach injury in the second phase of the World Cup, which was being held in the UK in early Summer, necessitating his return to South Africa to have it sorted out. I had met Klusener's representative earlier in the year when we were mulling our options over. When we went for Kallis he wasn't best pleased but he suggested a further meeting, in a restaurant just behind Waterloo Station, to see if it might still be possible for him to change our minds. He cried off at the last minute but told me he would send someone who would be able to discuss options with me and who was authorized to throw around some figures. It turned out to be Donald Woods, a celebrated figure in South Africa, a journalist and close friend of Steve Biko who had stood up to the apartheid regime and whose story had been transferred to film in *Cry Freedom*. We didn't talk too much about Klusener, other than me finding out what he'd want and learning that Nottinghamshire and others were interested; most of the time I was happy just to listen to Woods talking politics. Not what I had anticipated at all.

We stuck with Kallis, who was available after the World Cup, stomach issue notwithstanding. He only spent two months at Glamorgan but those of us who were around at the time still talk fondly of them. From his first game, when he announced himself by smashing a Glamorgan record 155 in the Sunday League game against Surrey at Pontypridd, through to his last knock at Yorkshire (Mark Wallace's second Championship game) it was like having cricketing royalty in the side. He was with us from mid-July and travelled up to Blackpool for the four-day match against Lancashire (the week where Wayne Law played his two contrasting innings against Muralitharan, Andrew Flintoff thought I was Elvis and I ended up rugby tackling Richard Thomas). In those days the twelfth man would be charged with organizing a team meal during each away Championship match, the whole squad going out and socializing and the nominated 'dick of the week' being forced to sport the most garish Hawaiian shirt you could imagine for the duration of the evening. So there we are, one day into the game, Alun Evans trying to look conspicuous in his new multicoloured shirt, and the team event is to have a go on the Pepsi Max 'Big One' roller-coaster on the Pleasure

Beach with dinner afterwards. Everyone's in. Byron the scorer, Dean, Fletch, me, even Fred Raffle, our blind supporter. Three players opted not to do it and agreed to take a forfeit, to be nominated by our First XI Coach. When we were coming off the ride, past the display where they try to get you to buy a souvenir photo capturing your sheer horror at one of the plummeting drops, one image stood out. Ismail Dawood, our 'keeper, and Fred Raffle, with two players in front and two behind. Of the six, only Fred had his eyes closed. Later on, as we waited at the bar for the meal to be served, we noticed that the beer towels on the bar counter were all emblazoned with the word 'Scrumpy'. Scrumpy Jack. Scrumpy Jacques. A nickname was born. In Wales, to those of us who were around, he will always be known as Scrumpy Jacques Kallis. The forfeit for the three rebels, Cosker, Thomas and Watkin? As I walked into the ground I bumped into the Lancashire Chairman, Jack Simmons, and a little further on we were confronted by three of Glamorgan's professional cricketers, five minutes before the start of play, doing a three-way version of 'Pat-A-Cake' in front of a gaggle of confused Lancashire members in the pavilion. I've no idea what Jack made of it.

Kallis did come back, but not for the promised second season. I still have a copy of his contract, which was for two seasons, but we left the second one open, for both parties to agree. There was never an appropriate time for him, and I guess we never got around to it. However, in 2002 we invited him over for a couple of weeks to help us out. Duncan was by now established as England Coach and he wanted some proper warm-ups for his team prior to their triangular mid-season one-day tournament. We suggested to the ECB the idea of a Wales/England match and although a bit reluctant they went along with it, much to the fury of a few of the other counties, who saw it as a back door way of us hosting an international game. However, the ECB also rather patronisingly suggested we must field an overseas player, to stiffen the side up, as they weren't sure we would be able to provide a stern enough test otherwise. I knew this hadn't come from Duncan but we had pretty little option but to go along with it. Instead of Mick Kasprowicz, who was our designated overseas player in 2002, we invited Jacques to play. Kasper was keen but we preferred to give him a breather and we wanted it to look like a different side to the normal Glamorgan one. On the day Jacques arrived in the UK he watched at The Oval as Surrey smashed 438 against Glamorgan in a one-day game, Ali Brown making 268, only to see the visitors come within nine runs of matching them in what must be one of the gutsiest run chases in the history of the professional game. But on the day of the Wales/England game, which allowed me to witness the bizarre sight of Dean Conway – by now the England physio – rushing out of the visitors' dressing room and down the stairs to celebrate the fall of every England wicket, Wales won easily by eight wickets, Steve James carrying his bat. Kallis? He bowled ten overs and took 1 for 31, then came in to hit the winning runs.

I suppose my first "proper" overseas player (after Javed's non-arrival and the shared Moseley/Hickey relationship of 1986) was Ravi Shastri, who joined us in 1987. He originally came over as a left arm spinner who batted a bit. I say 'a bit', but that's a little patronizing, not to mention very misleading; he had scored seven Test centuries before he appeared in Wales and had become only the second cricketer to hit a full house of six sixes in an over in first class cricket a couple of years previously. He could bat alright. But the intention was that his left arm spin would complement Rodney Ontong's right arm off spin, with his batting being a bonus. As his time with us rolled by the opposite proved to be the case, but hey. His was a positive presence. He used to worry me during one-day matches, mind. He'd start slowly and build very carefully, aiming to explode – not literally, obviously – towards the end of the innings. That was a fine Plan A. But if he got out once set it caused almighty problems for those following him who would really have to force the pace as they scrambled to work out a Plan B.

Away from the cricket field Ravi was another one who was a pleasure to deal with. He settled on Dinas Powys as his location of choice. Quite why I'm not sure I ever really fathomed, but he went back to that area each year, with the Captain's Wife a frequent stop-off. No, he wasn't having an affair with Hugh Morris's wife. It's a pub. In Sully. Though he did enjoy playing up to his reputation as a bit of a playboy and he certainly wasn't shy in a bit of self-promotion – witness the occasions (long before he was married, I hasten to add) when one young lady was wined and dined chez Shastri before they settled down to watch a video. Of him batting against Australia. And making a call to one of the numbers in his little black book while in Leeds before turning, a couple of minutes into the conversation, to his room-mate and asking, innocently, "Matthew [more likely pronounced 'matt-hue'], what is maternity leave?" The boy exuded a princely air and was, appropriately, nicknamed 'Prince'. I've kept in touch with him periodically and caught up with him in 2014 when he had been brought in to manage the Indian side which Duncan Fletcher was coaching, and again after a T20 international in Cardiff in 2017. He hasn't changed. Still that mix of bonhomie and good humour laced with just a whiff of haughtiness. Lovely man.

In 1987 and 1988 we went for a lad by the name of Corrie Van Zyl or, to give you his full name, Cornelius Johannes Petrus Gerthardus Van Zyl. Remember that in those days you could sign two overseas players but you were only allowed to play one in any one game. Hugh Morris naturally looked around at all those other mean and nasty quick bowlers winning match after match for their counties and wanted some of the action for Glamorgan, so we brought in Van Zyl. It didn't work out, that one. He took 14 wickets in eight matches in 1987, and just three in four games the following year before citing homesickness and returning to South Africa. In 1989 we'd wanted Ravi and Viv together but Viv had to postpone, so we did some juggling with contracts, with Viv returning in 1990 before the West Indies came to the UK in 1991, Ravi standing down in 1990 because India were here, before filling in for Viv the following year, when counties were restricted to just one overseas player rather than the two we'd been allowed previously. So 1990 was the last Summer – for a while – when we could have two. We already had Viv. Who else should we go for? On Viv's recommendation – and presumably also because we had a long name tradition now to continue – we went for one Hamish Aubrey Gervase Anthony, a young Antiguan quick bowler who had caught Viv's eye back home. Of course, the intention now would be to play Viv in as many matches as possible so this was a bit more of a free-hit punt. It wasn't as though Hamish would be expected to play in more than a handful of matches and if he impressed, well, you never knew. He actually went on to play several first-class matches, but two of these were against the touring Indian and Sri Lankan sides and two against Oxford University (not sure quite why we played them twice that year but we did), with a fifth coming after Viv had returned home.

The contract negotiation wasn't a problem. Viv just told us to put something fair on the table and to tell him Viv said it was OK. Which we did. And that's exactly what happened. It would be a different story when he returned in 1995 as Ottis Gibson's locum. But in 1990 we were acquiring a quick bowler who wasn't so much a bit wet behind the ears in terms of his experiences of life as having ears that were submerged in a full barrel of water. Ian Smith was deputed to help him settle. Lord alone knows why I asked 'Smudge' – I think he was living the closest – but our first trip with him from his flat in Pontcanna and into town was a memorable one. Given the relatively short distance we opted to walk. It took an age. Every time we came to a crossroads Hamish would hesitate, smile, shake his head and say "nah, man." Even when there was no danger. And even when we came to a pelican crossing. "But it's the fookin' green man, mun," said Smudge at one point, clearly getting exasperated. "I don't care if it be de purple man, I is not movin'," came the Anthony rejoinder. Eventually, though, we made it into town. When asked what he wanted by way of provisions for the flat he had just two items on his list: beef and underpants. That was it. We managed a few other supplies (we thought it was probably wise to do so) and went back to his flat before leaving him to his own devices for the evening. The last thing we saw him do was attempt to put a frozen pizza into the tumble-dryer. And I worried myself sick for weeks about the fact that we'd found a car for him because of his reaction to traffic. If all of this sounds borderline racist, I can promise you it is told exactly how it unfolded. Hamish had never been out of his small village at home other than to play cricket. Travelling to the UK was way, way outside his comfort zone. 1995? He was obviously a lot more grown up then. But contract negotiations were far more of a test for me. In 1990 he did what his hero Viv – or 'Veev,' as Hamish referred to him – told him. But this time he was on his own. Negotiations were conducted on the phone over two consecutive evenings, me at home in Pontypridd, Hamish at home in Antigua. The following will give you a flavour. Bear in mind that the line's a bit on the ropey side, there's also a time delay, and imagine the consistent background noise of a bunch of hens clucking away.

"We've got an offer of £30k [figure is illustrative], with flights and accommodation. And a car."

Pause. "K."

"Does that sound reasonable?"

"K."

"Are you ok with £30,000? Sterling, obviously." Pause.

"Hamo?" Further pause. Chicken noises to the fore.

"What dis sterling?"

"It's our currency over here in the UK. You remember from a few years ago? You know, like you have US dollars or French Francs."

"I don't want no French Francs."

"No, we pay you in pounds. 30,000 of them. Does that sound about right? Obviously that's before tax and NI."

"What dis tax? I no pay no tax."

"You paid tax the last time you were here, Hamish. We all pay tax." Pause. Chickens cluck merrily away in the background.

"Hamish?"

"I don't pay no tax."

You get the picture. It took hours. And cost me a fortune on the phone. Fair play to him for not using an agent but for once in my life, parasitic breed though they can be at times, I really wished he did. I even contemplated ringing one, appointing him to speak to Hamish, and then letting him come back to me to do a deal, even if it cost me a few bob more. It was that tortuous. Lovely lad, though. Delightful. Always happy. Unlike me on the other end of the phone those two evenings.

We brought in another happy-go-lucky character towards the end of my time at the club: Mark Cosgrove. We thought we had 2006 sewn up but things can turn quickly, and they did. Matt Elliott was struggling following a knee operation and he withdrew on the advice of his surgeon; and in the same week Michael Kasprowicz pulled out of his contract to concentrate his energies on playing for Australia, for whom he'd recently been recalled. John Derrick turned to 'Cozzie' (yep, another nickname the boys were up all night thinking about) following Herb's recommendation of his then South Australia team mate, and after speaking to our old mate Terry Davies, who after retiring from cricket with Glamorgan and emigrating to Australia in the winter of 1986 was now based in Adelaide and working as Marketing Manager for the state side. Cozzie came with a bit of a health warning and when we saw him, we understood why. He was almost as big as me. There were a few mutterings around but when he hit the first ball he faced – kicking off an innings of 75 against Ireland at Sophia Gardens – over the stand and into the Taff, we all appreciated we had a lad here with a real attitude. He didn't seem to be upset by any jibes thrown at him; he just went out there with a smile on his face and hit the ball as hard as he could. I've known him for close to fifteen years now. He's not changed in all that time. He still enjoys everything that he does and he's generous and loyal to a fault.

I have said many times that it was a wonderful experience to come into contact with some of these men. A few of the stints were so brief that it was almost impossible to get to know the person anything other than superficially, but for those who were around for longer, even allowing for the working relationship required, it was wonderful to get to see behind the reputation or, in one or two cases, the legend. Kasper may have been – in my view – the best of the bunch in term of his all-round contribution, but one cannot argue with the contributions that Waqar Younis and Viv Richards made to the club. Glamorgan won four major trophies in my time with them and these three, with Matt Elliott, were the overseas players who led the charge to those trophies. Waqar's second season in 1998 was something of an anti-climax after his heroics in helping the team win the Championship the previous year. Injuries restricted his appearances and there was a somewhat embarrassing drink-drive incident as well, but he had already had a monumental impact. We did look at other pace bowling options for 1999 before eventually settling on Jacques Kallis for half of the season on Duncan Fletcher's recommendation.

The odd high-flier got away too. One player I would have loved to have seen at Glamorgan was Courtney Walsh. Matt Maynard and I had got as far as meeting with him at his home in Bristol after his manager had said he was unhappy at Gloucestershire and was keen to move across the Severn Bridge and play for Glamorgan. Walsh had had his contract offer withdrawn by Gloucestershire but despite being charming and courteous with us, he eventually settled his differences and re-signed with them. Pity. It would have been wonderful to see him in a Glamorgan sweater.

My favourite, though, has to be Viv. He was the first big name we brought in and I was still wet enough behind the ears to have been hopelessly starstruck at the news that he was going to be playing for us. The difference he made was stark too. Although we caught him when he'd mellowed and wasn't quite as good a player as he'd been in his pomp, he still brought a will to win attitude and a charisma that I've not seen in too many people. He managed to help the whole club understand what winning actually looked like and a handful of his team-mates went on to win a whole series of titles over the following decade or so. He didn't change that mindset on his own but boy did he play an important part. Even though people use the word 'legend' almost at the drop of a hat these days, no one could possibly argue that Viv Richards wasn't a proper legend of the game. To have seen him up close for three summers was nothing less than a privilege.

12   WALK OUT TO WINTER

'You may have the greatest bunch of individual stars in the world, but if they don't play together, the club won't be worth a dime.'
BABE RUTH

Every good team needs the water carrier, the player who knits the side together. We had our share of quality, particularly in those successful title-winning teams, but no Glamorgan squad was ever complete without the understated contribution of the many hardworking support players, a number of them characters in an era when characters could breathe, before the days of mobile phone cameras and a ubiquitous social media. This chapter shines a light on some of them.

While we're on the subject of genuine cricketing legends, I think it's probably safe to say that the word couldn't be applied too readily to some of the characters we're about to discuss. But although they may not have had the charisma or standing of a Richards or a Waqar many of them were – still are – good pals of mine and their contribution to Glamorgan was, in an overwhelming majority of cases, significant. I don't envy modern administrators. Not only is their every move scrutinized, criticized and instantly subjected to the rotten-tomatoes-in-public-stocks that is social media, it is also impossible to hide every mistake made by those within their employ, including cricketers. People bemoan the loss of real characters in sport. It's not a lack of characters; it's just that there aren't any hiding places any more. Most sportspeople rarely come out with anything too interesting these days. Indeed many don't come out of their shells at all. And who can blame them? I consider myself lucky to have been involved in professional sport in an era largely without camera phones or social media.

My first summer in cricket coincided with John Hopkins's Benefit. The whole benefit year thing was a completely new concept to me and it had to be explained. I eventually came to know all of the ins and outs, the original Reed-versus-Seymour court case in 1927 around which the principle has been based ever since, but back then the idea that cricketers could enjoy a year of tax-free fundraising seemed a strange one. John, or 'Ponty' as he was known to everyone, immediately roped me in to help out with all of the donations which came in to the office. I would keep a list, retain all the cash and cheques (and, bless their cotton socks, postal orders back then too), send out ties and brochures to all those who had asked, and arrange everything for John to see, bank the takings and take a list of names and addresses so that he could write back. I have no idea whether it's still the case but back then John replied to every single person who took the trouble to make a donation. And I mean everyone. It was helpful to me. I learned all about the rights and wrongs of how a benefit should be run and could attest to the fact that the individual at the centre, if he was doing everything by the book, as John was, would almost certainly be affected in terms of there being a likely dip in form. He scored just 738 first class runs that year, with one century, and that against the touring New Zealanders (albeit a quite magnificent knock with 16 fours and five sixes, thus absolutely earning the acclaim from the crowd as he walked back to the Swansea pavilion at his customary slower-then-a-snail-with-arthritis pace), meaning he made fewer than 600 Championship runs.

As I was learning the ropes in those early days two of the other more established players in the team were Alan Lewis Jones and Terry Davies, both of whom were extremely kind and supportive, and both of whom I have remained in touch with. The former had to pack the game in in 1987 after failing to recover from a shoulder injury and the latter emigrated to Australia six months before him, but my recent arrival and their almost immediate departures were genuinely coincidental, I assure you. There were some more fleeting relationships, such as with Simon Base, a South African pace bowler who had been born in Kent and who once, when a batsman played and missed, marched up to the stumps and proceeded to bend down, growl and then take a huge bite into one of the bails. He disappeared off to Derby in 1987 after being suspended for a fortnight for having been found to have been involved in an approach by Derbyshire, which was against the – then pretty Dickensian, it must be said – TCCB registration regulations.

That first-year team also contained one Geoff Holmes, who remained a very close friend right up to his untimely death in 2009. 'Holmesy' was a diamond of a man. By his own admission he was never the most talented of cricketers (though he was a lot better than he would have you believe) but he had an almost incalculable value as a team man. He was also, if memory serves, the stand-out player in Glamorgan's centenary season of 1988. Geoff was one of the most engaging, friendly, modest, sociable and supportive people it's ever been my privilege to meet. A modest drinker – three shandies and he was anyone's – he would invariably be the life and soul of any party. I remember one Lord's Taverners Christmas lunch in the early 2000s at the Marriott Hotel in Cardiff, when we were guests of Richard Jones's, following which we'd ended up around the corner in Flares, a '70s-themed nightclub. When we had to leave to get our taxi home (Geoff lived very near Matt Maynard in Pentyrch and they would be on my route back to Pontypridd) we literally had to drag Holmesy off the dance floor. "But it's Leo Sayer," he'd be shouting back at us in those inimitable Geordie tones, the disappointment etched on his face. "It's Leo, man," he'd be mumbling to complete strangers. "They took me away from Leo. How could you do that, man?" He'd have had his three shandies early in the day and here we were, hours later, with him dancing his heart out. As he said to me on one occasion, "This night's got my name all over it," meaning he'd be necking his three shandies early. But let's not kid ourselves that he needed those three liveners, either. He was one of life's natural enthusiasts. He'd finished playing in 1991 and gone to work for the Principality Building Society, rising to the post of Area Manager, but was tempted back into cricket when he became the Cricket Board of Wales's third Director after Peter Walker and Mark Frost, and in which role I worked very closely with him for several years. I was devastated when I heard that he'd died. As were so many others. As fit as a flea, non-smoking, not an ounce on him. He was sitting in a meeting with the CBW staff, had a massive brain haemorrhage and just collapsed. Although his close mate John Derrick organized an ambulance straight away there was nothing that could be done. I was one of the pall bearers at his funeral, along with John, Matt and Tom Maynard, and the turn-out was enormous. One of life's good guys.

John Derrick himself was another one of the good guys. A big, strapping bowling all-rounder from Aberdare, he was a good enough player to be capped, and although he left the club at the end of the 1991 season, going on to run the indoor cricket centre in Ebbw Vale, we brought him back in 1996 to look after the Second XI. And he proved to be a very good coach. In 1997 Duncan Fletcher leaned heavily on him and Alan Jones and although 'JD' didn't succeed Fletch immediately, he stepped up to the Head Coach role in 2002 and the team immediately won their second-ever one-day title. They would win a third in 2004, also reaching Twenty20 Finals Day the same year, and JD played a huge part in that success. He was very easy to work with. A man of tremendous integrity, although we had frequent debates and arguments in private – mainly about budgets, though often about football as well (he was a big Chelsea fan) – he would never break a confidence and always understood the importance of collective responsibility when pressed outside any meetings. I admired that. He was happy speaking his mind about players he thought should be pushed for places in the team or for a new contract and nor, as we have seen, was he shy in arguing with the committee if there were players he didn't think were good enough to be kept on.

It is one of my regrets that I didn't stand up to Paul Russell and the committee more when, after a disappointing couple of seasons in 2005 and 2006, they insisted on three coaches being whittled down to two, ostensibly for financial reasons, with the Director of Cricket post being abolished. I say 'ostensibly' because although there was a clear argument for that, the hand of Hugh Davies was all over that decision and, as we know, Hugh and JD did not see eye to eye. At all. This stemmed from John being pressured into having to express his opinion that Hugh's son Adam was not good enough to be awarded a full contract. JD, Steve Watkin and Adrian Shaw were invited to apply for the (now) two coaching positions being made available. John was the one to miss out, Adrian Shaw being offered the First XI Coach role. Relations between JD and I were strained for a little while after that, understandably. With hindsight I could have worked harder to oppose the decision to abolish his post. I'd probably have lost the argument anyway, but it remains a regret.

We patched things up, of course, and John went on to work with Cricket Wales as its performance director. I can't think of too many people better suited to that kind of role. He knew Welsh cricket inside out. Away from work he was another wonderful person, like his mate Holmesy. Wearing an almost perennial beaming smile, he was always there when you needed him, the kind of friend you'd want to be to others: supportive, loyal, pragmatic, positive, fun. He argued passionately but respected an alternative view. Having lost Holmesy so young, it was devastating to hear that John had been diagnosed with a brain tumour in 2016. We had worked to bring all of the 1997

County Championship-winning squad together for a reunion at St Fagans Cricket Club on one of the Tom Maynard Trust's annual fundraising days that August and the whole squad, including Adrian Dale all the way from New Zealand, were due. JD rang me a couple of days beforehand and said he was going to have to pull out. He'd been feeling unwell, his blood pressure was high and he'd been advised not to attend. Days later he was diagnosed. He remained positive throughout the next six months, despite an operation and subsequent chemotherapy. In December 2016 three of the players he coached – Mike Powell, Ian Thomas and Mark Wallace – organized a fundraiser at Sophia Gardens for him, raising £35,000 to help with his house conversion and other costs, but sadly he passed away the following March. His funeral in Aberdare was packed. He was an incredibly popular man. I confess I don't remember the detail of the day too well as my Mum had died that same morning and I was in my own world of shock. Even with all that was going on, JD's brother Tony took time during the day to check that I was OK and I appreciated that. I had an enormous fondness and respect for John. I think of him often.

In the late '80s a young lad by the name of Michael Cann was emerging through the ranks. He first played for Glamorgan in 1986 and hung around the first team for five years or so, someone who probably best defined that hackneyed old cliché 'fringe player'. Canny was a one-off. For a start he was a bright spark, with a Biochemistry degree, not exactly your predictable path into life as a professional cricketer. He was also a maverick, with a wicked sense of humour. He went on to work for a company called Accord Healthcare (and these are their words, not mine) "a multinational company which researches, develops, manufactures and markets generic and biosimilar pharmaceutical products," where he was vice-president of retail marketing. A bit different to life in the Glamorgan dressing room in the late 1980s, I would imagine. I loved 'Canny' (yes I know, yet another stunningly original nickname). We shared the same level of humour (intellectual but low brow, stupid, occasionally borderline toilet) and he never took himself too seriously. He was infuriatingly modest. He recognized that there were more talented players than him and although he worked hard and really wanted to get to the top of the tree he knew – like Gareth Rees twenty years later – that he had the intelligence to land comfortably whenever cricket chose to drop him. He was a bag of nerves on match days. On one morning in early 1988 before a zonal round match in the Benson and Hedges Cup I pulled into the car park early, as I always did, stopping to unlock the padlocked main gates as I did so. The fact that they had been padlocked indicated that I was indeed the first person in. But when I got out of the car and headed for the portacabin offices I quickly learned that I was, in fact, only second in that day: Canny was sat on his cricket coffin on the office steps puffing away on a cigarette.

"What the hell are you doing here at this time?" I asked.

"Couldn't sleep, mate," replied Canny, "so I thought I'd nip down and sample some of the early big match day atmosphere. I've come to one conclusion already."

"What's that?" I asked, unlocking the door to the office.

"The atmosphere at 7am is crap. Stick the kettle on, Mike, mun. I need to use your facilities."

I then realized he must have somehow thrown his cricket coffin over the top of the gates and climbed them to get in, barbed wire and all. Bonkers.

In the winter of 1989, we signed a seam bowler from Surrey by the name of Mark Frost (and for those of you by now playing the 'predict the nickname' game, go on, take a wild guess, add a Y. I guarantee you won't be too far wrong). In thirteen first-class matches for Surrey, he'd taken 25 wickets at an average of 40.20 so you could hardly call his arrival heralded, but it was a punt by Alan Butcher and he went on to do a more than decent job for Glamorgan as a seamer. In his first pre-season with the club, in 1990, our sponsors ASW had helped fund a tour to Trinidad. I don't know who was in charge of the rooming list (it wasn't me) but they paired Mark with Dean Conway, also making his first overseas tour with the club and relatively new to cricket having been with us for just the one season. On one of the early nights of the tour, 'Frosty' was tucked up in bed when Dean returned to their room in the wee small hours. With kit strewn across the floor and in an unfamiliar environment, Dean was conscious of the importance of trying to be a good roomie and not waking him up if he could possibly help it. The lights stayed off, he took a few minutes to get himself stripped down to his boxers, find the bathroom and manage to clean his teeth, only to trip heading back to his bed at the critical final moment and fall backwards into Frosty's cricket coffin. As the bedside light went on, an almost naked Dean looked up at Mark from among the pads and other cricket paraphernalia scattered around him, put his finger to his lips and uttered the classic, but in the circumstances rather futile, "Shhhhh!"

As a batsman Frosty was, well, shall we say, not very good. In one of the least effective tails in Glamorgan's history, in the early season Benson and Hedges Cup zonal matches in 1991, Colin Metson had to be dropped in favour of Martin Roberts because with a seam attack of Simon Dennis, Steve Watkin, Steve Barwick and Frosty, it would have meant him batting as high as seven. Which was probably three spots too high for him. And of those bowlers, Frosty was, by some distance, the obvious candidate for No.11. A first-class career batting average of 3.21 says it all. His fielding was also old school. During one game at Abergavenny he was fielding at long leg. Or, as it's known at Abergavenny, leg gully. Frosty kept wandering from his mark, much to Butch's exasperation. Tony Dilloway soon found a way to correct the problem. He nicked a marker from the nearby bowling green and planted it into the ground, with a label attached marked 'Frosty's Position'. It didn't do much good. Having lambasted his batting and fielding, and just in case his lawyers are looking in, let the record state that he was a very effective seam bowler. And a good man to work with, as I discovered when he spent five years running the Cricket Board of Wales from 1999. He and the likes of Graham Crimp and Roger Morris made it fun.

One of my favourite cricketers during my time as CEO was Darren Thomas. He burst through as a tearaway seventeen-year-old pace bowler in 1992, taking five wickets on his debut, and he went on to play a key part in the various titles in 1997, 2002 and 2004. One famous tale, oft-repeated, no doubt gathering apocryphal extras with every telling, centred around Darren as the organizer of the team meal which was routinely arranged on away trips in the second half of the 1990s. At said team meal the nominated 'dick of the week' would sport whatever garb the players had agreed for the season in question: their own Sunday League kit, Hawaiian shirts, whatever. As mentioned in the last chapter I recall Alun Evans sporting one of the loudest shirts I think I've ever seen at Blackpool in 1999. I'm not sure what his crime was. Anyway, on this occasion Darren had sought advice from the receptionist at the hotel the boys were staying at in Liverpool and announced to the rest of the boys that they were dining at the 'Maissez Vous'. Puzzled looks, especially as they normally headed for one of the restaurant chains – a Harvester, or a TGI Fridays. And those puzzled looks were reflected on the faces of the taxi drivers hovering around the marina in Liverpool without a clue which restaurant they were taking their passengers to. Eventually it emerged that it wasn't a bijou French brasserie called the Maissez Vous but, more earthily, a Beefeater. With a Mersey view.

Darren was also the subject of one of my favourite contract negotiations. To be fair to him, he never had an agent hovering in the background or anything. He backed himself. And because he was such an easy character to get on with, not to mention the fact that he was a consistent performer, it wasn't generally difficult to sort things out pretty quickly. I always found that the better the player, the easier the negotiation. Occasionally a player would genuinely be thinking of moving but more often than not it was the younger ones, those on the fringes or on the verge of breaking into the side, who tended to inflate their self-worth a little too much and drag things out. Or try to. Anyway, on this occasion Darren came in armed with a notebook, which he promptly flicked open. Interesting, I thought. He's thought this one through.

"I'd like you to consider a performance-related contract for me, Chief," was his opening gambit.

"Okay, shoot," I replied, and let him explain – at some length, I might add – what the Club should be paying him in the event of him taking X wickets, scoring Y runs and achieving Z landmarks. It was an impressive speech, very well thought through.

"What do you think, Chief? Good, isn't it? Got mileage, I think. What do you reckon?"

I admitted that it was a good effort and commended him on the trouble he'd gone to. However, I leaned forward and began a speech of my own along the lines that if he only took A wickets, scored B runs and failed to achieve C landmarks, across all cricket, then presumably the salary would have to drop commensurately. After all, performance-related contracts worked two ways. There was a long pause before Darren came out with, "Watty didn't tell me what to say next." I had to laugh at his honesty. And he was never anything but brutally honest, Darren. There was no side to him. And at that point we established that he was looking for a particular salary and a particular length of contract; we were happy with the contract length but wanted to offer a lower figure, and we agreed to meet exactly halfway. With a handshake, it was done. I really enjoyed players like that. Straightforward and a pleasure to deal with.

.   Most of the time that was also the case with another stalwart, Dean Cosker. He was selected very early in his career to go on a tour with England 'A.' He had asked the Professional Cricketers' Association (PCA) to represent him in contract discussions, something I encouraged ahead of the use of an agent, and David Graveney of the PCA opened up negotiations by pointing out the importance of that selection. Alan Jones, Glamorgan legend, coach and acknowledged lovely bloke, who knew Dean a lot better than I did and wanted to sit in on the discussions, jabbed a friendly finger back at 'Grav' saying, "Well we didn't pick him. What has that got to do with this? We're negotiating a contract for him at Glamorgan." I never thought I'd have to play peacemaker on account of Uncle Al! Dean was another who rarely bothered with agents but he did on one occasion, or rather he asked a family friend, Albert Francis, to meet me to discuss things. I knew Albert from way back as he'd been the head groundsman at Cardiff Athletic Club when I started and lived in the flat in the pavilion with his wife, Sybil. Many's the time we'd be sat in a meeting in our offices and hear her calling him in to the phone. "ALBEEEEEEEEERT!" she'd shriek out of the window. He could have been in Merthyr Tydfil and he'd still have heard her. As with Darren's performance-related proposal, Albert went through a whole host of scenarios about what would happen in the event of his client hitting certain targets. But it was all a bit over-engineered and I'm not sure Albert had really thought it all through. My natural sarcasm was just bubbling under, waiting for the right moment to be given an airing. "And if Dean scores a thousand first class runs," said Albert, now well into his stride, "he'll be looking for the county to pay him a bonus." I couldn't let that one go. "If Dean Cosker scores a thousand first class runs next season, Albert, or indeed in any season, I will get my arse out on market day on Pontypridd Town Hall steps." Wicket bonuses, yes, but bonuses for batting landmarks that would never be achieved? It was all a bit too contrived. Dean did his next contract negotiation himself. He didn't need others to do it for him, or certainly not when I was on the other side of the table. One of the good guys, 'Lurker,' and another who became a pal. He went on to be one of the ECB's Match Referees.

Player interaction with supporters only occasionally caused us problems during my tenure. But we did have the police calling us after a Twenty20 game in Taunton in the mid-2000s. One of our players, Andrew Davies, had apparently been reported for 'making gestures' at supporters in the crowd. I asked the officer what these gestures were and was told that they mimicked swimming strokes. It didn't sound much to me. However, it turned out that a group of Cardiff City fans had been giving him stick for his Swansea roots and he retorted with the mimed swimming gesture, which emanated from an incident after a South Wales derby in 1988 when Swansea City fans had supposedly chased some Cardiff fans into the sea. So it was nothing at all to do with Somerset, just a case of our own supporters and players riling each other.

'Diver' was another lad with whom I had, and continue to have, a really good relationship. By his own admission a more limited player than some of his team-mates, he was unlucky with injuries but maximized his talent and squeezed the very best out of himself such that he developed into a really useful one-day cricketer and picked up two one-day title winners' medals with Glamorgan. One of life's natural whingers, he's rarely too far from a negative comment. It figures that he supports Tottenham. Pessimism has obviously become a way of life for him. But on the basis that he now looks after my pension, such as it is, I suppose I'd be ill advised to be going on about that. Others complained that he complained too much (most completely failing to see the irony in that) but that was to take him too literally. He might grumble but he never fails to get on with things. He just likes everyone to know.

I took Diver to an Arsenal/Tottenham game at the Emirates Stadium in October 2009. I had left the club by then, but he was still playing. A couple of minutes before half time, with the score at 0-0, he said he would nip to the loo and grab a pint before the interval. We were a long way up at the back of the West stand so he had just about reached the exit point when Arsenal took the lead. I looked down to see him, hands on hips, giving it the full tea pot before disappearing from view. Within 40 seconds Arsenal had scored again through Cesc Fabregas, after Wilson Palacios had given away the ball straight from the kick-off. Out pops Diver again. Full tea pot on again. When they scored their third on the hour mark, he turned to me, shook my hand and said he'd see me soon, and promptly got up and left. We'd driven up so I wasn't sure how he was going to get home, but he subsequently got the tube to Kings Cross, changed for the Circle line to Paddington, and got the train back home to Bridgend. I was caught between thinking it was an incredibly rude thing to do to a mate who had taken the trouble to sort him out with a ticket, and being unbelievably proud of him for behaving like a true upset supporter. It never comes up in conversation…

One of my favourite crowd stories came at Tunbridge Wells in 1995. We'd signed the left arm spinner Neil Kendrick from Surrey and he was twelfth man for the game. As was normal for any Glamorgan side containing Roland Lefebvre and Robert Croft, the twelfth man would have been extremely busy ferrying items of clothing, sunglasses and drinks back and forth as the visitors went about their business in the field. Those two were always after something. After repeated stick from a gaggle of lads battling to hold their beer, his patience snapped. To the interminable chants of 'Sheep Shagger', he very politely put the tray of drinks down on the floor and turned back to the hecklers, responding, in full Kentish twang, "Sheepshagger?! I'm from f***ing Bromley!" After some consultation between the members of the group in the stands, presumably involving some element of research and confirmation of where this was, 'Kendo' had barely gone five yards with his tray before the chanting started again. Once you sign for Glamorgan you're labelled. Even by your own.

Coloured clothing for one-day matches came into county cricket after the 1992 World Cup and Glamorgan went on to win the Sunday League title in its first year with the new garb, the first time since its inception in 1969 that it had been played across 50 overs. The Club issued a very similar shirt to the 1993 version in 2013 and chose, somewhat cuttingly to those of us of an age, to refer to it as 'retro'. In the late '90s we saw the introduction of squad numbers, which caused some fun amongst the players. How would we divvy up the numbers? Some of the justifications were genius: Adrian Shaw was given the number 12 as he used to play in the centre for Neath; Steve James was allocated 15 as he had played full back; Robert Croft was number 10, presumably because in his own head he was a fly half (there was little evidence of that from any of the warm-ups I watched); Adrian Dale liked Jonah Lomu, so he was given 11; Steve Watkin fancied himself as a goalkeeper, so he naturally wore number

1; Matt Maynard originally went for number 9 as he saw himself as an Alan Shearer-like goalscorer (though he soon changed to 25, presumably as that was his shots-to-goals ratio); but the best was undoubtedly Wayne Law, who got number 4. Because it rhymed.

I mentioned him briefly a moment ago but one of the real characters of the side in the early '90s was a Dutchman by the name of Roland Lefebvre. A seam bowler with a miserly reputation (he yielded very little with ball in hand, and was just as careful with his wallet off the field), he was also an outstanding, if somewhat theatrically inclined, fielder in the deep. We only saw him for two and a half seasons before a serious groin injury forced him out of the county game but he made a wholehearted and significant contribution, helping us to that first one-day title in 1993. His new ball partnership with Steve Watkin was formidable and I doubt there was a better combination bowling at the death in county cricket than Roland and Steve Barwick. In a NatWest Trophy quarter-final against Worcestershire at Swansea we had left the opposition 280 to win in their 60 overs but because of a rain delay the match was going to spill into the reserve day allocated to such matches in those days so the opening spell by Watty and Roland was vital. Worcestershire were strangled so much that they could only manage 40 for 2 from 23 overs before the close. Roland ended up with figures of 2 for 13 from his eleven overs. I didn't share a dressing room with him but when I was in his company, I found him interested in everything the club was doing, in the people who were doing it and although I'm aware of the fact that he was opinionated (I haven't met too many Dutch people who weren't) you could debate with him and he'd always have a smile on his face. He was a very positive presence around the place.

There were few issues with players but one group who managed to wipe the smile from my face were the foursome who staged their own mutiny at the end of the 1996 season. It always used to frustrate me that the Cricket Committee, which in those days had to sanction any recommendations from the captain and coaches on contracts, more often than not had their end-of-season meeting while there was still cricket being played. We didn't learn lessons from 1991, when Michael Cann, Mark Davies, Simon Dennis, John Derrick, Geoff Holmes, Martin Roberts and Ian Smith were all told they were not being awarded new contracts with matches still to play (though Smith was about to sign for Durham anyway; Mark Davies subsequently moved to Gloucestershire). It even led to Canny walking out to the middle in the game immediately after the decisions had been taken and when the umpire, assuming he wanted a guard as he held his bat up in front of the stumps, asked him what he wanted he was surprised to hear the answer coming back: "a new two-year contract please." But in 1996 there was no such humour after Steve Barwick, Alistair Dalton, Neil Kendrick and James Williams were informed they weren't having their contracts renewed. On the basis that when there's bad news to impart it was important not to run away from it, I promised Alan Jones I would be at Barnt Green, where there was a Second XI match against Worcestershire taking place, to meet with him and the players to inform them. On arrival I was greeted by Alan in the car park telling me that, in his words, the players 'had mutinied.' Someone had passed the information on. Perhaps not surprisingly. And the players had reacted. Again, not surprisingly. Kendo had already packed his bags and headed back to London. As if that wasn't enough, the other three had originally said they wouldn't be taking any further part in the game either. Quite apart from the fact that they still had contracts – and were clearly breaching them – it wasn't exactly a great signal for the rest of the players. Williams actually did play on, to be fair to him (scoring a hundred, something he seemed to do almost every year around contract decision day), but Barwick and Dalton weren't budging. They were sat in the pavilion bar watching.

To be honest the whole thing was a shambles. The club could have held that contracts meeting at any time. It could also have ensured that it kept a lid on the news overnight (the committee leaked more than a faulty colander). But to refuse to play, whatever the reason and however bitter the disappointment, was so poor on the part of the players concerned and highlighted a real lack of professionalism. Not that the long-term damage was enormous. Let's chalk it down to experience. Williams was later appointed to the coaching staff and, in my view, did a decent job there. He now runs cricket at Clifton College in Bristol. Neil Kendrick went on to teach and coach at Whitgift School. Ali Dalton continued in club cricket and, with a lovely irony, was later elected to the Glamorgan committee. How would he have reacted had the same situation arisen then, I wonder? All three are still in touch. Baz was, well, just Baz. He argued that his long service deserved a better exit, which I get, and that his refusal to play was an inevitable consequence, which I certainly don't.

One of the more memorable characters was Owen Parkin. One of a handful of players spotted and pushed by Graham Reynolds, our schools' liaison officer, Owen was a useful seam bowler who carved out a decent career at the club. He also loved an argument. He was constantly chipping away about this selection or that to anyone who would listen as well as quite a few who wouldn't. It occasionally caused us a problem, such as the selection ahead of him of David Harrison by Maynard and Fletcher at the start of the 1999 season, and he was in Steve James's ear throughout his captaincy tenure about how his own stats meant he deserved a spot ahead of Darren Thomas: the classic methodology argument: quantitative (stats) against qualitative (hunches and match-winning potential), though the latter's stats were pretty decent too. A bright lad, we took 'Parky' on in the office for a couple of winters to help with our sales and marketing and he was brilliant. Always on the 'phone trying to make a sale. Never put off by the continued rejection. He had a positive attitude to work in the office. There was no doubt he would land very firmly on his feet in his life after cricket and, like Williams and Kendrick, he went into teaching. I liked him a lot but, like Andrew Davies, he didn't half love a moan. He did, though, write the lyrics to the Glamorgan team song. So he's forgiven much of the peripheral nonsense.

One of the more bizarre player tales concerned Mike Powell. He was taken into hospital in June 2007 when what had started out as a blood clot – serious enough – quickly escalated into something altogether more critical. He was taken down to a specialist hospital in Exeter and in one of the operations he had to have, one of his ribs had to be removed. It was genuinely touch and go for a while. After he'd been discharged and was back at home in Cardiff, I visited him and he asked me if he could have his rib buried under part of the outfield. I'd had requests for the scattering of ashes at Sophia Gardens before, of course, but never a request to have a body part buried. All very macabre. But I had no problem with it. 'Powelly' (yet another of those original nicknames) called it a legacy. I'm still not sure I saw that, but hey. The lad had had a seriously close shave. Why not, I thought?

I enjoyed helping Mike during his Benefit Year in 2011. I'd left Glamorgan by then but had been asked to work on Alex Wharf's committee in 2009 – something which brought me into contact with a good friend, Nick Evans, who was exasperatingly running around after 'Wharfy' [sic] and who I think welcomed someone with whom to share a moan about players, the club, benefits, anything. The following year it was Dean Cosker's turn, though his chairman, David Harris, a wonderful fellow and chairman at St Fagans, had most things under control. For Wharfy I think I was there to advise on benefit etiquette, dos and don'ts and just generally support, but for Powelly I was asked specifically to edit the benefit brochure. Despite having edited the Glamorgan Yearbook for donkeys' years I found that a lot tougher than I imagined it would be. First I managed to bribe an old mate Huw Owen into providing the design support (a bat given to me by Viv Richards did the trick there) and then it was a case of having to write and rewrite articles, chase promises of adverts (amazing how many say they'll support something and then seem to disappear off the face of the earth) and hope the whole thing holds together when it's handed over to the printers. In this case, 'the printers' consisted of Mike's brother Ben, an old Glamorgan staff colleague now working with Andrew Jones at Stephens & George in Merthyr, longstanding supporters of Glamorgan beneficiaries. I thought that that would be my last involvement with a beneficiary, other than propping up a bar at a function, obviously, but was asked to edit Michael Hogan's Testimonial brochure in 2020 and foolishly, having forgotten over the intervening nine years just what a slog it was, I agreed. We finished editing and proofing the day before the Coronavirus lockdown was enforced and Michael's Testimonial year was subsequently deferred for twelve months, and then another twelve. It could have been worse, though. Had we produced it to my original timetable, 'Hoges' would have had several dozen boxes of brochures in his garage gathering dust, all showing the wrong year.

I was very proud when Wharfy was picked for England. Glamorgan hadn't had too many England players in recent years – Greg Thomas, Matt Maynard, Steve Watkin, Hugh Morris, Steve James, Robert Croft, Simon Jones – but having worked with Matt to sign Wharfy in 1999 it was wonderful to see him get his opportunity in the one-day side. He'd been playing for Nottinghamshire in a game at Colwyn Bay when 'Watty' had reduced them to nine for six (they won the toss, by the way, before you start casting aspersions about the pitch quality) but Wharfy, coming in at eight, took the attack back to Glamorgan and hit a really fine 78. He could bat, as half a dozen first-class centuries would subsequently prove, but his bowling was what stood out in that game, or rather the effort that he put into it; unstinting, relentless, on a typically flat Colwyn Bay pitch. Matt had a bit of a battle with Hugh Davies over his signing. Wharfy wanted a three-year contract as he would be upping his family and moving to South Wales. Hugh insisted he was only worth two years and assumed Wharfy would agree. He didn't. Matt argued his case at committee, won, and Wharfy signed immediately. He went on to play 13 one-dayers for England, the first selection for which was preceded by a devastating six for five from five overs against Kent the week after Glamorgan had won their third one-day title. He was a great competitor. I wasn't at all sure what he'd end up doing after he finished playing. He seemed to butterfly around talking about dozens of different business ideas. He eventually settled on umpiring, which he proceeded to take seriously, and in which he has made fantastic progress and has developed into a highly respected and capable official. He has a real presence out in the middle. I wouldn't argue with him, put it that way.

It wasn't just our own players who stuck in the memory. Graeme Hick and Trevor Ward, for example, scored runs for fun against Glamorgan. Hick scored eight hundreds against us. Eight. Several of them doubles. He must have thought it was Christmas when he played us. Ward scored seven centuries. I know it will be a trick of the memory but there was a time in the late '80s and early '90s when it seemed that we were bowling at these two for half of the summer. I also recall Colwyn Bay as the venue where one of the umpires sent a player in to me to apologize for his behaviour. I was minding my own business in the office, which is closed off from everything and where you can barely hear anything at all, just as the lunch interval began, when there was a knock on the door. On opening it, I found Yorkshire quick bowler Steve Kirby stood in front of me, holding his cap in front of him in very apologetic pose. "I've been told by John Hampshire to come and find the ground authority and apologize for my bad language on the field this morning," he said. Lovely lad, 'Kirbs,' but he was a demon when he crossed the rope.

One of my favourite characters of all was our Scorer, Byron Denning. I've already related a couple of stories about 'Dasher' when he was announcing, but there are so many. In one game against Leicestershire in 1990 – Viv Richards's debut – he had forgotten to test the public address system before the game started so decided to give it a quick test as the umpires were coming out. "One two three four five," his voice came bellowing out of the speakers, "one two three four." Umpire Mervyn Kitchen acknowledged the announcement with a full teapot, both hands on hips, followed by him signalling 'one short.' Later that same summer Glamorgan played against the Sri Lankans at Ebbw Vale. We played both Sri Lanka and India that year and we needed to spread the matches around so the Sri Lankans had the distinction of being hosted up at the top of the Ebbw Valley, a stone's throw from Byron's own home. I knew that some of the surnames would be a challenge for 'Dasher' (Somerset batsman Peter Denning had been given that nickname, and Byron inherited it) so in the game prior we agreed that I'd write them out phonetically for him. Roshan Mahanama, Brendon Kuruppu, Sanath Jayasuriya, Aravinda Da Silva, Graeme Labrooy and Marvan Atapattu we could just about get our tongues around. But when it came to Kapila Wijegunewardene, Piyal Wijetunge, Hashan Tillekeratne, Champaka Ramanayeke and Asanka Gurusinha he was struggling a little. When he had to announce that Steve James had been caught by Ro-shan Ma-ha-na-ma bowled by Ka-pee-la Wee-je-goo-na-waard-e-naa I think he made his use of phonetics a little obvious. By the time he'd finished the announcement everyone was waiting for the match to restart, new batsman ready at the crease and all.

Dasher used to call each delivery by referring to it as a different town, the over running from East Wales to West Wales. All scorers had their own ways of cross-checking and counting properly and, as Byron explained to me when I first heard him doing it, Porthcawl was (his) valleys rhyming slang for 'fourth ball'. So he'd insist on doing this as his way of checking. In Welsh. Ball number one was Cas Newydd (Newport), followed, in turn, by Caerdydd, Pen-y-Bont, Porthcawl, Castell Nedd, Abertawe, and, if needed because of wides or no balls, Llanelli, Carmarthen and Haverfordwest. I remember being in the box with him and Clem Driver, the Essex scorer. Clem just turned to him halfway through the third over and said, "Byron, we all love you to bits, but I do wish you'd stop all this bollocks." To which Byron would continue, of course, smile on full beam. He told me he'd once had a ten-ball over to call, and after Haverfordwest for the ninth, the only town he could think of was Cork.

Against Lancashire at Colwyn Bay in 2001 I saw another example of Byron's waspish humour. As Neil Fairbrother and Glen Chapple were adding 104 for the eighth wicket for the visitors he decided to dabble with a prop. That year a red light had been installed in the scoreboard to indicate that the scorers had acknowledged the umpires' signals. As Fairbrother racked up the runs (he eventually made 158), one of George Sharp's boundary signals was met with a red flashing dot-dot-dot, dash-dash-dash, dot-dot-dot, the Morse code distress signal for S.O.S.. It was Byron's inimitably cheeky way of letting 'Sharpy' know that he'd had enough of the partnership.

It was tragic when Byron was admitted to hospital and died in November 2001. We had a good replacement scorer in Gordon Lewis, a fine man who used to get a fair bit of stick owing to the fact that he chose to combine his Second XI scoring with serving on the Glamorgan committee, but once he relinquished that role he proved a really supportive member of the management team and he too was taken too early when he died suddenly in April 2004, aged 73. After Byron died we wanted to mark his passing in some way and we came up with a new award in his name, to be voted on by the contracted players only, and given to the player who, in their view, best embodied the spirit of the game through his behaviour over the course of the season. The first winner the following September was Michael Kasprowicz, and I was delighted when Olwen, Byron's widow, was able to come along and present it. I must admit I didn't like it when the club opened it up so that backroom staff could win it. Nothing against the likes of Roger Skyrme or David Harrison, who have won it as non-players, but it was set up as an award for the players voted by the players. I'm probably just out of touch.

By then Glamorgan had an outstanding reputation for playing the game the right way. Steve James used to moan about the fact that he wanted his side to be associated with winning cricket, not as a collection of nice guys picking up the umpires' nomination for the MCC Spirit of Cricket award made to the county team deemed to be playing the game in the right spirit. We may as well have had that trophy on direct debit. Our lads won it in 2001, 2002, 2003, 2004 and again in 2008. I was proud of that, whatever 'Jamer' felt (though I'm sure that deep down, he was too). It proved the squad was full of good blokes. And with a promotion, a T20 Finals Day and two one-day titles in there, the 'nice guys can't be winners' line didn't wash.

13 ALWAYS THE SUN

'It is one of the blessings of old friends that you can afford to be stupid with them.'
RALPH WALDO EMERSON

In life we each come across thousands and thousands of people. Most we don't give a second thought to, nor they to us. We all have many people we would call acquaintances too, work colleagues, friends of friends. And if we're lucky we will enjoy a wide circle of friends. Close friends are rarer. And as for what I would call proper friends, I'd say you're fortunate if you've got more than a handful. Here are two of mine.

There are some relationships in our lives which just click. And so it is for me with Matthew Maynard and Dean Conway. One a dashing, blonde-permed-and-moustachioed 20-year-old boy racer from Anglesey with CSEs in woodwork and maths (qualifying him to count how many bats he had, presumably) who was just off the back of a century on first class debut. The other, three years later, a slightly-less-dashing, occasionally lightly moustachioed, 24-year-old Fiesta XR2 driver from deep in the Cynon Valley, freshly qualified in the dark arts of physiotherapy. Since then the pair of them have been integral elements of my life – often whether I liked it or not – and we have shared some memorable highs and some of the lowest depths it is possible to plumb.

I first came across Matt in late April 1986 as I was taking my tentative Bambi-like early steps as a Glamorgan administrator. As it was pre-season, I met the players almost on day one, my first experience of mixing with professional sportsmen. There I was, fresh-faced, naïve and innocent, mingling with real athletes: committed individuals, completely dedicated to the cause. At the other end of the bar (and where else would one have come across committed young professional athletes in those days?) sat this gravelly voiced (even then) blonde-haired bloke who was, so said the cognoscenti, the future of Glamorgan Cricket. "Blimey," I thought, "they must be in a spot of bother then." On first sight he looked more like a plumber's mate than a cricketer. I don't recall whether he was sporting the ear-ring that so used to annoy Ricky Needham; I think that came later.

I remember asking him, almost starstruck, about the hundred he'd scored on debut against Yorkshire the previous September. "Don't f***ing ask him that, you dozy t***", came the riposte from another corner of the bar from Ian Smith, a team-mate, in his broad Geordie accent. "We don't want to hear all that s*** again." Fair enough. So I didn't. Haven't to this day, in fact. To be honest if anyone nowadays starts to ask him about that hundred, or any other for that matter, my eyes will glaze over. The difference between what Ian Smith was saying then and what I would say now can probably be measured only in the accents in which the words would be delivered. That comes from getting to know someone really well. Matt has got so much to boast about with the career he's had. But at the same time we need to keep his feet on the ground. So if he starts, we just tell him he's boring. When him and Duncan Fletcher get going with their cricketing chat on the golf course, Conway and I just hurl abuse at them or go off in a different direction, sulking. Not difficult, if you saw the two of us play golf: we generally play the course completely differently to those two anyway.

Matt and I have shared a lot over the years (cricketing wise, we have 24,799 first class runs between us for a start). Some of it is even printable. He's become a very close friend, golfing partner (the two of us now have the Indian sign over Conway and Fletcher), drinking partner (yes, incredible though it might be to some of you, he has been known to put away the occasional glass over the years) and someone on whom – God help me – I've actually come to rely greatly as a confidante and good pal. I shan't forget the fact that they were the two who were there for me when I was going through my divorce from Carol. They made me realise that it wasn't the end of the world, that my daughters should always be my priority and that, if possible, falling out with Carol was something to be avoided. And we managed to do that.

Back in the day Matt was a bon viveur and lived his life at a Lewis Hamiltonesque pace. We enjoyed a holiday in the autumn of 1991 on the Norfolk Broads, a group of us and our wives. Matt and Sue gave me and Carol a lift there. Almost literally. Now Cardiff to Norwich isn't generally up there on the RAC's top ten easiest UK journeys. But when you're a passenger with M. P. Maynard, there is no such thing as a difficult journey: we made Membury services in half an hour, the M11 in around an hour and a quarter, and reached our destination – average journey time four hours – in two and a half hours. <u>And</u> it included a stop for lunch. The G-force was unbelievable. Berkshire was a blur as we raced through it, and we ended up around Heathrow racing aeroplanes. And beating them. OK, so I exaggerate just a smidgeon. It was in the days before speed cameras but he made Michael Schumacher's Benetton look like Steptoe's pony and cart and I'm convinced the cameras wouldn't have seen him anyway such was the speed at which he was travelling. Full ahead. Warp factor four.

Once in Norfolk the pace didn't let up and it was on with the marathon drinkathon. The only interruptions to the ale-quaffing were to repair to our respective barges and race them across the broads between pubs (and yes, he managed to do that quickly as well). Bedtime was a mere interlude between the drinking and the barge-racing. We mixed it up occasionally. He did spot a volleyball net outside one of the pubs we passed and attempted to show off his organizational skills by splitting the party into two teams: Wales and England. Only problem was that he then trotted off onto the Welsh team only to be recalled and reminded that he was born in Oldham. And I'm sure he threw the game as a result. To be fair, he may have been born in Lancashire but he's as Welsh as any Welshman I know.

When, a decade on, I was CEO and he was Captain we found ourselves, as we often did, chatting outside my office one day over a cigarette. He was in the process of sending a text message. Out of idle curiosity I asked to whom he was sending it. "Fred Raffle", said Matt (Fred, remember, is a committed and loyal Glamorgan supporter, who often stays with the Maynards when in Cardiff). "Would that be the same Fred Raffle who is blind, Matt?" "Yep", came the reply. It took a while to register, but Matt gradually realized that texting perhaps wasn't the cleverest way of communicating with a blind man. His jokes are delivered apace, too, and perhaps if he stopped to consider them he would occasionally get the punchline in in the right place. 'Naturally unfunny', as Dean refers to him.

If it weren't for the fact that there is a photograph in the book he wrote with Paul Rees in the early 2000s of him in one of the classic early-'70s Manchester City shirts (think Colin Bell, Mike Summerbee, Francis Lee) I'd have him down as a bandwagon hopper who leapt on board as the Abu Dhabi royal family were investing their squillions in the club and they had started to win things. Sadly, that photo means I have to believe he's supported them all this time, albeit from a bit of

241

a distance. We've been to watch our respective sides play a few times. The first was in October 2000. I picked Matt up in Pentyrch early on the Saturday to be greeted with the question, "Do you think I'll need a jacket?" "I've got mine in the back", I answered, the weather forecast for North London being a bit iffy. He didn't bother. And with glorious autumnal sunshine on the way up (me driving this time so we could appreciate the scenery it even if it did take a bit longer than it would have had he been in the chair), his confidence appeared justified. As Danny Tiatto was sent off on 38 minutes and Ashley Cole scored from the resultant free kick, it started to rain. Just then his mobile phone beeped. He was a subscriber to the (then) Orange football scores service and it was, rather helpfully, pointing out the obvious: "TIATTO S/O 38, COLE 40, ARSENAL 1 CITY 0". Presumably just in case he'd missed the roar of the crowd, the two main scoreboards flashing away excitedly, the action replays being shown over and over on the Jumbotron big screens and the PA announcer confirming the goalscorer. And all the while the rain was getting heavier.

The second half was a riot. Every time Arsenal came forward – kicking towards us – they scored. Or it seemed that way. And by now the rain was not only coming down heavily it was somehow adjusting around 20 feet from the ground and turning in at right angles so that it was coming right at us. And only one of us had a jacket. The rain was dripping off him. Just to round off a very pleasant afternoon (for me, anyway) his phone kept beeping to remind him of the score: Bergkamp 0-2, Wiltord 0-3, Henry 0-4, Henry 0-5…. True supporter that he is (or possibly because he was either daft enough not to think of it or didn't know how) he didn't switch it off. Sodden, humiliated, but somehow always smiling. Bit like City used to be before the money.

He bagged me for a visit in December 2019 (I went with a fellow Gooner, Neil Kendrick, instead) after having double-booked. Instead he fulfilled a commitment to lunch with one of our mates, Andrew Walker, a most un-football-fan-like thing to do. So our most recent Man City/Arsenal outing was to the government-gifted Etihad Stadium in December 2013. This trip wasn't quite so successful (for me) as City ran out winners by the small matter of six goals to three (it hurts to type in the actual numbers). And we were top at the time. But there was an obvious penalty for handball against Paolo 'David

Brown' Zabaleta and there were clear goals by Giroud and Bendtner which were ruled out. And one of their goals was offside too. Bitter? Me? Perish the thought.

But the most recent football match we went to together was in November 2014, for the Manchester derby at the Etihad. I have zero affection for their red neighbours and would support a Taliban XI against them, so I was very comfortable being a City man for the day. The previous day I had met the aforementioned David Brown, former Glamorgan all-rounder who Matt signed from Gloucestershire (and yes, he does look remarkably like Zabaleta) in London to watch Arsenal play Burnley, 'Browny' being a huge claret. I won't mention the result. Oh go on, then. 3-0. But the highlight for us was seeing the old desk sergeant from *The Bill*, Sergeant Cryer, played by Eric Richard, sat a few rows in front of us (no I'm not a 1990s soap aficionado, of course I had to look that up). We parted that evening knowing we would be meeting up for a beer the following night in Manchester, where Browny now lived, after Matt and I had been to the game and before we met the Professional Footballers' Association the following morning.

Matt had arranged his tickets through a contact at City whom he had met in the Caribbean when he was coaching the St Lucia Zouks in the Caribbean Premier League. And a decent contact it was, too. It turned out that on the day we were there the club was hosting a *League Of Their Own* penalty shoot-out, featuring James Corden taking penalties against Jack Whitehall, Josh Widdicombe and Andrew 'Freddie' Flintoff. Matt had arranged to meet Fred before the game, so there we were, hanging around the outdoor public stage, where they were due to conduct a question-and-answer session, waiting for them. He has often said that whereas he is just a supporter, I am a fan. I should explain that unlike the previous day, when I'd turned up at Arsenal with a replica shirt on and carted around a load of goodies purchased in the club shop, today I was just in normal casual garb and it was Matt who was dressed in his City replica shirt, with a carrier bag containing a 2015 desk diary and a garish blue Manchester City Christmas jumper. Every inch the stereotypical football fan.

As Whitehall, Widdicombe and Flintoff finished their fans' Q&A, Matt's ticket contact decided that because we were late we should be shepherded up to our seats via a short cut through the City admin staff offices. So, there was I, following this raft of celebrities, as we made our way upstairs. The main doors opened and we found ourselves in a very large, very tastefully lit room, full of very smartly dressed people. We'd passed a sign outside saying 'No Colours Beyond This Point' but we'd been whisked in without stopping to think where we were headed. It turns out we were headed into the private suite of Sheikh Mansour, the City owner. Sergeant Cryer was already a distant memory as we'd been introduced to Messrs. Widdecombe and Whitehall, and we were now in the company of footballing royalty. Alex Ferguson and Bobby Charlton were there, dining right in front of us; there was Roy Hodgson, the England manager; and there were former City legends all over the place – Tony Book and Francis Lee to name but two. Over in the corner were James Corden and Noel Gallagher. It was a celebrity-fest. And there was our Matt, resplendent in a shirt he wasn't supposed to be seen wearing and carrying a plastic bag, for all the world like he was a geeky football tourist who'd stumbled out of the back of a wardrobe and into another world. He did have the good grace to be embarrassed, though. And as Sheikh Mansour himself came past us in the queue to the bar and nearly tripped over his foot Matt just mumbled, "Come on Chief. I'm not happy here. Let's get out of here." And I'm the one who gets called the football hooligan.

I have been caught out in his company many times. When his son Tom was a nipper and barely crawling we enjoyed a convivial evening chez Maynard. Knowing his penchant for 'giving it a thrash' I decided to bring my own booze, arriving armed with a bottle of Vodka and a few bottles of Russchian mixers (yes, that is the correct spelling). I don't get drunk on Vodka, I reasoned. And I hadn't even tried Russchian (no, really, look it up), whatever that was. This way, I reasoned, I could avoid the risk of being served up a series of eye-catching and percentage-proof-defying home-made Maynard cocktails. As a strategy it was never likely to work, and indeed it didn't. Around midnight I staggered upstairs to the loo only to find myself spending what seemed like half an hour afterwards – and quite probably was – negotiating the anti-crawling child gate at the top of the stairs. Unbeknown to me, Matt, Sue, Carol and others were watching my efforts with increasing mirth from the bottom of the stairs. I was ashen-faced, mumbling to myself, and clearly pissed out of my brains. I've never touched Russchian (I'm telling you, it is) since.

244

Several years later, while Glamorgan were playing our annual home matches in Colwyn Bay, he managed to set me up in front of a load of other people. The one-day game against Lancashire was due to take place on the Sunday but every weather forecast we had seen was suggesting that we were more likely to see Armageddon than Akram the following day. Both sets of players, along with the umpires, journalists and the Glamorgan office and groundstaff contingent, could confidently play a rain card. Not everyone did, but a goodly-sized gathering was sat in the hotel bar well into the small hours, until eventually only the good grace of the night porter was able to keep us stocked with alcohol. We were a bit rowdy, tis true, and at one point singing (if you could call it that) broke out. Cue night porter, earnestly telling us to button it, which we did for a while. When it started up again the poor fellow had had enough. The bar was now officially closed, he said, and we should all disperse to our rooms. Matt, sat next to me, whispered, "Come on, Chief. We're not ready to go yet. Tell him." I rehearsed what I was going to say, something along the lines of never having been so shabbily treated, such that us and our opponents would be taking our business to an alternative institution the following year. The group waited expectedly. I opened my mouth. And I couldn't say 'bread.' In fact I was so pissed, I couldn't say anything. Not often that happened in front of the troops, but on this occasion, I was guilty as charged. I blamed Matt. And no, there was no play at all the following day, the game being called off shortly after breakfast, such was the deluge.

Back in the early 2000s we were talking to the University of Glamorgan (now the University of South Wales) about how we might work together to help Glamorgan players study for a degree or a diploma without them having either to take time out before becoming full-time professionals or waiting until their careers had finished in order to do so. This was before the greater flexibility in higher education that we see today. Matt expressed an interest (I think this was in his 'I'm gonna be in marketing when I grow up' phase). They had a few courses available online, meaning there would be no need to set foot on campus or attend lectures; basically, you could study at your own pace. We agreed to have a crack together. The University, to its credit, ignored the fact that Matt's academic record at school hadn't exactly been riddled with scholarly distinction, looking instead to credit the experience and knowledge he had gained from captaincy, for example, and happily offered him a place. Which, incidentally, I think is one of my proudest achievements in life: getting Maynard onto a degree course. Three weeks later, he'd bagged it. Claimed the technology wasn't working. So muggins had to go it alone. Thanks, mate. Not that it could have been that much of a hardship as I went on to do a Masters in the 2010s. But he's already caught me up. As he delights in pointing out, he has as many degrees as I do. Just that his are Honorary and I had to work for mine.

So what of 'Ollie' as a cricketer? He remains my favourite Glamorgan player. The early part of his career was a riot of cameo performances, but performances that demanded attention nonetheless. He emptied bars when he came to the crease (including, presumably, the one he was in himself at the time). He was compelling viewing. Although mightily frustrating. Alan Jones once told me, as we watched a Maynard innings, that he was the most natural talent he'd ever seen close up but one that constantly drove him to distraction. I remember at a former Glamorgan players' reunion in 2017, Matt describing Aneurin Donald, then on the club's books, as someone who needed to learn to convert good 30s and 40s into bigger innings and watching Alan Jones's expression. "Like someone I can recall, Matthew," came his knowing reply.

However, as he gained experience more and more of those cameo efforts started to be converted into match-winning performances. I could reel you off any number but his partnership with Tony Cottey in the penultimate Championship match of the 1997 season against Essex, when Glamorgan had slipped to 29 for three chasing a must-win 149, followed in the very next innings by a magnificent century at Taunton in the final game when, in the evening gloom, and with the lights on the scoreboard beaming out like searchlights in the fog, he and Hugh Morris carved the Somerset attack apart (Matt reaching his century without a single, interestingly). Very contrasting innings. Only the very best players can produce such different performances. And forget the rubbish about him not being able to perform under pressure. OK, so his international appearances should have been many, many more, and perhaps he didn't do himself justice at that level, but he could perform under pressure all right. Given the modern way of giving players a full series in which to bed in and make a mark he'd have kicked on, I'm sure. If a player is considered good enough to be selected only to be discarded a Test match or two later, then that is surely more a reflection on the people selecting him than on the player himself. Like so many others around that time – including the Welsh trio of Morris, Watkin and James – Matt was never really given a proper run.

Our close friendship hasn't got in the way of our professional relationship, or at least not often and not significantly. I've mentioned already my own take on his decision to join the rebel tour to South Africa in 1990. There were the occasional stand-offs during contract negotiations (though at no time did I ever believe he was actually going to leave); there was his drink-driving charge in the mid-'90s; there was also the time when he and Robert Croft had a bit of an altercation down at Southampton as his playing days were winding down. And although we would disagree in our roles as CEO and Captain, such as if he wanted a player and I didn't think we could afford it, these were always kept within the boundaries of politeness and professionalism. In his role as skipper Matt had a pretty open contempt for committees and the way they behaved and performed and he struggled to disguise that, even in meetings. I often felt that I had to be looking out for him. He'd listen to Tony Lewis, Ricky Needham and a couple of the others, including David Morgan, but I can't argue with the fact that our committee was lacking in real cricketing pedigree and credibility and his relationship with Hugh Davies was close to non-existent, so I shouldn't have been surprised. He improved considerably when he came back on the coaching side and I look at the coach he has gone on to become and marvel at how much he has grown up in that regard. He absolutely 'gets' the need to be politically savvy in that role.

It was wonderful to watch him grow as a leader. I remember having to ask Alan Butcher if he was serious when he first said he wanted Matt as his Vice Captain, but how right he was. He saw that Matt was an outstanding reader of the game. He grew into the captaincy and learned very quickly. Naturally instinctive in his decision-making, he was prepared to take risks in order to try to win matches, something he learned to temper when required, and he was comfortably the best captain I saw during my time at the club, a proper team man who put the team first at all times. When Glamorgan were bowled out for 31 against Middlesex in 1997 he, like Duncan Fletcher, didn't panic, and his declaration in the next game at Liverpool against Lancashire – setting the home side 273 in 60 overs – showed that his gambling instinct hadn't been dented, Waqar Younis and Steve Watkin blowing them away inside 14 overs.

When Glamorgan reached the Benson and Hedges Cup Final in 2000 – our first major showpiece Lord's occasion for 23 years – it was no surprise that Matt was at the forefront. He'd hit a century in the semi-final against Surrey and proceeded to do the same in the Final, picking up the Man of the Match award even though his pal Ian Harvey had essentially won the game for Gloucestershire with his five wickets. 'Harv' still chunters on about this occasionally when we see him. Matt's speech at the post-match wake in the hotel across the road from the ground wasn't his finest as it came a little late in the evening, after the beer and spirits had been flowing, though he did at least out-shine my efforts in Llandudno a couple of years earlier and manage to get some words out. But his disappointment was obvious. Bugger the fact that he'd made a hundred. That didn't matter. Glamorgan had lost.

There were so many qualities there that you just knew he would go on to make a very good coach. He was also learning all the time about the financial side of business and he has already demonstrated his ability to coach and lead a cricket team – Nashua Titans, St Lucia Zouks, Glamorgan and Somerset. He announced on his ECB Level 4 course, when asked why he was there, "Because my Chief told me to do it." Not altogether true, but my, how he embraced it. He's been like a sponge soaking up the theory, learning about personality profiling and psychology and all the rest. He's a very good communicator these days. I enjoyed the one summer we had working together as CEO and Director of Cricket before I was shown the door and I would love to have worked with him, and Jamie Dalrymple, for longer in building a newly competitive side. And I still cannot for the life of me understand the thought process that assumed Colin Metson would be better in the role than Matthew Maynard. It was a ridiculous notion then and it's even more ridiculous looking back now. He was driven out. Jamie too.

I could have a pop at him about a few things, just as you would with any mate, and he'd have plenty of things to come back at me with. 'That' dance to Kenny Loggins's *Footloose* whenever the blessed song comes on; the jokes; the attempts to dress like someone who is still in their early 20s; his thought process as he tries to solve cryptic crossword clues. He gets ribbed mercilessly, more often than not unfairly. I wrote in the 1991 Glamorgan Yearbook about his

248

penchant for reading *Postman Pat* books. Dean once said that the only book Matt had read was *Bingo Goes Up The Hill* (sound familiar?) but inside his head is one of the finest cricket brains there is. He also possesses a heart of gold. The earthy and friendly way in which he treated my mates Ty, 'Simmo' and 'Crow' on the rare occasions when they came down to watch Glamorgan, and in social situations since, may have been completely natural to him but it speaks volumes for the sort of bloke he is. Even when he didn't know Andy or Stef very well, he treated them like he'd known them for years. I'm very proud that he's a close friend, and that Sue and Pat have been part of my life for well over three decades. What happened to Tom a couple years after Matt and he had left Glamorgan, which I try to deal with in a later chapter, was absolutely tragic. No one deserves that. No one.

And so to the other half of the comedy partnership that has been a constant to the last 35 years of my life: one Dean Conway. There have already been a few stories about Dean dotted around this book and it's a good job: there are so many that it is impossible to fit them all conveniently into one chapter. And certainly not one that shares its billing with someone else. The man with the inveterately abysmal timekeeping, whose superficial unreliability belies a fierce underlying loyalty which is almost impossible to explain; the only Conservative voter in the Cynon Valley; the wisecracking people person. In short, the very best of men.

I've been on the end of that waspish sense of humour so many times it just washes over me nowadays. Just as Maynard's storytelling and dress sense gets it in the neck, it's my place to suffer jibes about football, music and socialism. It's part of the deal. The more he takes the piss out of you, the more you belong in his circle; it's a kind of acceptance. Even in the most sombre of life's moments, and there have been a few between us, Dean has the ability to turn seriousness into levity just with one off-the-cuff remark. And somehow it's always right, so he gets away with it. If anyone else had trotted out such a litany of inappropriate jokes and comments on the day I confided in him and Matt that Carol and I would be divorcing I'd have likely grabbed him by the scruff of the neck and given him a fearful lamping. But, as always, it fitted the mood. I don't know how he does it. And he is funny. Extremely funny. He is also the most brilliant people person I know. He manages to engage with everyone, to find their level and then deal with them at that level and in exactly the way that person would want to be dealt with. It's little wonder that he was so good at pulling disparate individuals and factions together to help create such a wonderful team spirit wherever he went. He really 'gets' people.

His stories are, genuinely, very funny, and he has a fantastic way of spinning them out, of hooking his audience and keeping them hanging on his every word – even if they become more apocryphal and distant from the truth with every telling. I enjoy hearing his tales of one of his England trips to South Africa, in 1999, specifically two lift stories. The first was when Sue and their two older children, Sophie and Josef, headed down to their Durban hotel lobby before going out for dinner, with Dean due to follow. He duly arrived a few minutes later to be greeted by a quizzical, eyebrow-raising look from his wife. "Forgotten anything?" Patting his pockets, Dean felt keys and wallet, and replied, "No, I don't think so, love." Turned out he'd left his younger son Adam, barely a month old, behind in the lift. And he nearly left him in his carrycot under a restaurant table a day or two later too. Later that same trip, he tells a wonderful story of him and Phil Tufnell in Port Elizabeth coming down from their rooms in the lift. They'd descended one floor when the doors opened and the Dalai Lama came in, along with two bodyguards. A few seconds later, Tufnell sniggered "It's the f***in' Dalai Lama, Deano," in what he imagined was a whispered voice, but in reality was loud enough for even His Holiness to understand the gist. One hopes he didn't understand the actual language but I'm sure 'Tuffers' would have been forgiven readily enough.

The philosophy Dean has when it comes to the game of cricket is one that both Matt and I share and buy into. That is to say, work as hard as you can, but don't forget to have fun along the way. So much of modern sport, especially as we've moved into the twenty-first century, is predicated on the myth that you have to be focused, to eat properly, to drink properly, never reveal your personality to the media, to train hard, and then train harder, to practice until you're blue in the face and to never (apologies for the split infinitive there but it suits the flow) ever show your emotion. In short, be serious at every turn. I don't buy that. And Dean certainly doesn't. It's about the team. You do your bit to ensure you've practised and prepared properly, proved that you've reached required fitness standards, demonstrated that you understand your role and the roles of everyone alongside you, contribute to team meetings and plans, act professionally when in a working environment, and then you go out and basically play with your friends. Not for Dean the obsession with stats and fitness, with weights and psychologists, with diet and over-analysis. They all have their place, of course, but it's about practicing your skills first and foremost, with all the other stuff there to support you. There are some people we've all come across who just want to show you their Level 4 coaching certificate and then proceed to suffocate the life out of you by just parroting a textbook. They have no imagination. No flexibility. Cricketers in particular have to learn how to stand on their own two feet when they're on the field, to adapt their game plans, not spend the minute at the end of every over looking up at a dressing room in the hope of constant nannying and guidance. Be yourselves, not a media-trained hologram. Anyway, where was I? Bit of a ramble there, sorry. Yes, Dean. Old school approach. And I applaud him for it. At the top level you shouldn't have to over-coach. It's about making players feel sufficiently relaxed, confident and comfortable that they will go out and express themselves. Sounds easy. It isn't. But what it should be is simple. Too many people over-complicate it.

Dean is one of those people who if you are out for a coffee or a pint with him, pretty much anywhere, will know a good number of people. He will also be on the phone for 75% of the time you are with him. I took to bringing a book with me whenever I was due to meet him one-to-one. Not only would he always be late (something he seems to avoid professionally but rarely socially) but he would also have a few calls during the meeting such that I could get on with whatever novel I was reading while he was sorting himself out. Rude? Nah. You get used to it. I, on the other hand, am berated for having a phone and ignoring his calls. Yeah, right, Deano. Whatever, butt.

Dean joined Glamorgan at the start of the 1989 season in place of Tudor Jones. We needed someone who was able to commit to match days, just home ones to start with, and Tudor had growing rugby commitments so wasn't able to do that. Dean came highly recommended (I can't remember by whom, but I mean to hunt him down and give him what's coming to him) and, at the age of 24 – just – and freshly-qualified, he brought with him a whole new energy and approach. He also brought with him a new level of expertise. Where Tudor relied on ultrasound for what seemed like almost everything Dean had much more in his locker. He was able to diagnose quickly (without that hardy perennial safety net of more recent incumbents, the obligatory referral for a scan), understood rehab, and picked up the vagaries of batsmen, bowlers and what different types of cricketer needed very quickly. In those days he had a flat in Roath and commuted to his room in the portacabin on the ground at Sophia Gardens in a rather swanky XR2. He must have made an impression because within a year or two he had moved, via another portacabin adjacent to the old pavilion, and thence to a suite of whitewashed-bricked rooms inside what had originally been the toilet block in the car park. Somehow, he seemed at home there.

Obviously on home match days he was with the team and he very quickly identified the needy ones and the ones who just cracked on regardless. He tells the story of treating Ian Smith after a day's play, whereby 'Smudger' just walked straight towards his physio bed, climbed onto it and issued the immortal instruction: "Just throw a towel over me head, Fizz, and treat the f***ing rest." We fell into a pretty settled routine, the two of us. He'd be in early and would come into the office expecting a coffee (him and Steve Barwick generally arriving at around the same time), then, when play was underway, I'd start my first lap of the ground by having a cigarette with Len Smith in his office underneath the pavilion and then have another coffee with Dean – and whoever the coach and twelfth man for the day were – in the dressing rooms. At one such early morning coffee gathering in my office in 1992, as Glamorgan were playing the Pakistani tourists, we were interrupted by a gaggle of enthusiastic young Asian lads banging on the window and yelling "Where's Pakistan!? Where's Pakistan!?" Given the stars in their team, they were obviously chasing autographs. (In fact this was the game when a dozen supporters all tried to get in with one Javed Miandad-issued complimentary ticket, which was flawed not only for the obvious reason, but because the said ticket was for the equivalent game in 1982, in Swansea. You had to applaud the creative ingenuity though.) Anyway, for once it wasn't Dean first in with the pithy riposte. Having endured the shouting for twenty seconds or so, I stood up, leant over to the open window and said, "Where's Pakistan? It's a country in South Asia formed out of the partition of India in 1947. Now sod off."

We followed that informal match day routine for nigh on a decade until England came calling for Dean in 1999. Then the relationship moved up a gear and into the world of texting. I think he

252

must have me filed in his phone under C for 'Clampy,' such is the frequency with which he addresses me with it in texts. 'Clampy' became his nickname of choice for me after I underwent a fistulectomy operation in early 1991 (nothing to see here, really; it's an operation on an ingrowing hair in your arse; go and look it up if you must), as Viv Richards had done a couple of years previously, preventing him from joining the club until the following season. Part of the surgical procedure (I'm aware I'll be losing readers here, but bear with me, it doesn't last much longer) is to insert a clamp inside the, ahem, bottom, in order to facilitate the operation. Hence 'Clampy'. Such an original boy, isn't he? And the fact that he too underwent something similar a few years later didn't prevent his continued widespread use of the nickname.

It's a bit like you and him being late. If you're just *slightly* behind the clock and he's on time for once, you get a pasting, but when he's late, it's just accepted. I have a real antipathy for unpunctual people. I'm almost always early. Part of that is a desire on my part to feel like I'm on the front foot. I like to be first, or among the first, in a room, so that I can believe that other people are coming into my space. However, that principle has to go out of the window where Dean is concerned. As Matt will confirm, if Dean says he's definitely attending something – a meeting, function, whatever – it means he might be there. If he says he *might* be, it means he has no intention whatsoever of turning up. If he says he *won't* be, you can be sure he's hurt and upset that you asked him in the first place and he would rather be spending the time jabbing rusty needles into his eyeballs.

He will never use the C word (use your imagination) in a text, preferring to call you a "K for…". As he says, 'we only have the K word up in the Mount'. But when you see the letter 'K' on its own it has nothing to do with that; it's generally because he couldn't be bothered to go to all the trouble of preceding it with an 'O.' But on one occasion, during England's tour of Sri Lanka in 2001, he went up another notch and decided to leave me a voicemail. "Clampy. Deano. Listen," which was followed by around ten seconds of barely discernible noise, though it was unclear exactly what it was. Back on he comes. "You hear that, butt? That's the sound of a warm sea. Bye, f***face." Such a charming boy. Another memorable voicemail message came during the opening ceremony of the 2003 World Cup in South Africa. And I really wish I'd kept this one. It was essentially a rant about having to march into the stadium in Cape Town. Not verbatim, but along the lines of "What the f*** am I doing marching behind the cross of bastard St George? It's the England and Wales f****ing Cricket Board so why isn't there some sort of f***ing recognition of the Welsh flag? Bloody ridiculous." And this from the man who, on his first visit to Lord's, asked why there were so many Spanish flags around the place, mistaking the red and yellow of Spain for the red and yellow of the MCC. Classic Conway.

You don't get close to someone without understanding the whole family. His wife Sue probably deals with Dean in the best way: by either ignoring him or just talking over him. The three Conway children – Sophie, Josef and Adam (aka 'The Bull') – are all very different, but all have some of their father's traits. I'll spare their blushes by suggesting what they might be in each case. The Bull is my Godson, Matt being a Godfather to Josef. Dean, in turn, is Godfather to my elder daughter Seanna, with Sue Godmother to Hannah, my younger. We like to keep all these things between us. And then there is the saga of Dave, the family Beagle. I am old enough to remember Stan, the Labrador, but Stan eventually moved up to the valleys with Dean's parents. Some years later along came Dave. Now if ever a pet mimicked its owner, it was here. Dave's a big unit. He hates walking (likewise, Dean would rather drive the 50 yards to the chippy than walk such a long way). Dave probably drinks wine by the gallon, owns ten widescreen televisions, which are all always on, and is an expert on the dark arts of the rugby union scrummage as well. He's probably always late too.

Dave was a focus for my favourite Conway story of all. In 2018 the Manic Street Preachers announced that they would be playing the Liberty Stadium in Swansea. My old mate Andy Tomlinson immediately got in touch and asked if I was thinking of going. I said I was, and I knew my daughter Seanna would be too. Andy duly booked tickets. A week before the gig Dean – also a fan of the Manics – said he wished he'd arranged tickets for himself. I knew he was on nodding terms with James Dean Bradfield, the lead singer and guitarist in the band, as he took his dog (Roger) walking across Pontcanna Fields in Cardiff, where he regularly came across Dean, walking Dave. I suggested he asked him if he saw him. Dean told me that the very next day he'd come across Bradfield on Dave's early morning walk and he'd waved away any inhibitions and gone up to him. "You won't know me," he said, "but I'm a huge fan. I just wondered if you know how I might be able to get tickets for the Swansea gig next weekend. I know it's sold out." To his surprise, Bradfield said that he knew who Dean was, and that he was a big cricket fan. He said he'd be delighted to put a couple of complimentary tickets on the door for him. Freebies. Of course they were. It's Dean we're dealing with here.

Come the evening of the gig I texted Dean to ask him where he was, with the intention of maybe meeting up somewhere in the venue for a beer. He was at home. He hadn't bothered coming down to Swansea as he wasn't sure if James Dean Bradfield would have remembered their conversation. He was probably inundated by such requests, he reckoned. I thought nothing more of it until the following time I saw him. He said he'd been out walking Dave the Monday following the gig, with Sue this time, when he'd seen Bradfield heading towards him, Roger in tow. By this time Dean and Sue were about to cross the road from the fields and head down Cathedral Road. He told me he was a bit too embarrassed to be bumping into him just a couple of days after the gig, and so he ducked back into a shop front hoping he'd not see him and walk past. A few seconds later up came the lead singer of the Manic Street Preachers, in full teapot mode, eyeballed our hero and asked him, "Where the f***ing hell were you?" Apparently, he'd put two VIP hospitality tickets on the gate for him only for Dean to be a no-show. For once he had wanted to go but he explained that he thought Bradfield would have forgotten. Silence. Before Dean said he'd make it up to him with a few Glamorgan Twenty20 tickets. I'm sure his very generous and much-sought-after offer received a bit of a strange look in return. The band were due to travel to Finland anyway. We did manage to make it to see the Manics together a couple of years later at Cardiff Castle having chosen the conventional route of buying him a ticket this time.

The Manics had featured in a Glamorgan story a couple of decades earlier. Back in 1997, a couple of weeks after Matt had led the team to the County Championship title, a huge hamper arrived, addressed to 'The Players.' And when I say 'huge' I mean it was enormous. Like one of those industrial laundry baskets with wheels on. It was choc-full of booze. There was just one card inside, which read: 'To the Glamorgan boys, from the Manics.' They were recording in France and being big cricket fans – they had penned a song called *Mr Carbohydrate* which included Matt in the lyrics, and Nicky Wire went on to be his Testimonial Patron in 2005 – they wanted to make a gesture. It went down very well too.

Carol and I spent a long weekend with Dean and Sue in Paris in 1990, staying with a friend of Carol's, Sue Lartigaut (Fitzsimons as was), who had lived in France since leaving Trent Poly in the mid-'80s. For once Dean's virtuosity at storytelling was to prove his downfall. Being 'lads on tour' we opted, as our drink du jour, for 'Une Formidable', a litre of lager in the one glass. As Dean was busy regaling everyone with his tales, I was quietly supping away at my 1.76 pints-worth of drink. As I got to the end, we ordered another one. By the time he'd even noticed, I had put away three of these things and we were all ready to move on. Leaving Dean having to drain two Formidables – four and a half pints – pretty much in one go. 'Pissed' doesn't cut it. We spent the next hour giggling, being scowled at by our respective other halves, and desperately searching for a loo. The trip hadn't started too well, either. Sat in the lounge at Cardiff Airport we looked out of the window to see an Air France plane, with Dean proudly announcing that he knew exactly what he was doing when he booked the flights. Just as he finished the sentence our designated plane taxied forwards and out of view, leaving behind it one of those dozen-seater propeller-driven Fokker Biplane lookalikes. When we boarded, the looks we got from the cabin crew suggested it may prove to be an interesting ride. Dean and I were very politely ushered to the back, and towards seats on either side of the aisleway. Ballast and balance.

In more recent times, since I moved back to Cardiff, we've established a routine of Friday night post-work beers with our good friends Nick Evans, Matthew Gough, Martyn Ryan and others. I must admit I rather live by Ogden Nash's definition of middle age: "when you're sitting at home on a Saturday night and the telephone rings and you hope it isn't for you." Invariably the call, or more accurately, the text, is from Dean, looking for someone to go out and play with. Dean is also a frequent golf opponent. Normally the partnership is Maynard and Fatkin against Conway and, well, whoever. It used to be Duncan Fletcher when he was about. In one of those fourballs, at the Vale of Glamorgan, Dean had driven his first shot on the sixth to a spot around fifty yards behind a large Oak tree. He proceeded to kick the ball twenty yards to the right, to looks of mild amusement from his partner and to the astonishment of his two opponents. "You can't do that, Deano," yelled Matt from his position a distance up ahead (he was always way ahead of us after the tee shots). "There's a tree in the way," replied Dean. "I know, butt, but you'll have to play sideways or find a way around it. That's the game," said Matt. "Not the way I play it," came the response as he proceeded to carry on as though nothing had happened. 'The Foot Wedge' duly entered folklore. He is the canniest of opponents: coughing, sneezing, burping, farting, treading on your line, playing around with shadows as you putt, every trick in the book. He even, on one memorable occasion, squashed my ball into the ground. We were in buggies and he had the hilarious (to him, anyway) thought that unbuckling my golf bag and watching as it fell off the buggy as I drove away was worth the laughs. When it happened for the third time – the third bloody time – I lost my temper and drove my buggy over to where he was standing by his ball, proceeding to drive right over it and squash it out of sight. Off I drove, sniggering. "I knew you'd do that, butt," he yelled after me. "That's yours. Mine's over there." Too clever by half.

Dean has a genuine love for the sport of rugby union. He absolutely adores the game. He played to a decent standard too. I can recall going up several times in the early '90s to the ground at Mountain Ash, where he played. Not that I had a clue what was going on. I think most people know I much prefer football. One of the more high-profile occasions was a Mountain Ash versus Llanelli Welsh Cup game, up on the top of the hill at their old ground. They might have lost 13-26 but it was a huge occasion, a sell-out, with the BBC Wales cameras there. On another occasion I trudged back to the clubhouse down in the town centre after the game and was ready to follow Dean's instructions that we were 'drinking with the seven'. This actually meant 'The Magnificent Seven' and they were so labelled for a reason, and it wasn't as Cynon Valley gunslingers. Seven valley commandos who could drink. Magnificently. It turned out they ordered jugs of bitter, draining them quickly before ordering more. I'm no shrinking violet when it comes to quaffing beer but at that time of my life, such a pace was a little out of my league so I politely told 'the seven' that I'd stick with lager. Before the minute was out a whole jug – seven pints – was placed on the table in front of me. And I was the only one on the lager. By the time Dean arrived I was completely sozzled. And by the time Carol and Sue were due to be with us – ostensibly for an evening out with their husbands – any colour had drained from my face and I was trying to muddle through on vodka and coke. When the girls did arrive we were hiding in shop front doors down the road. It was eight in the evening. We never did have that evening out. I was home by 9.30pm. Poor effort.

He recognizes that I'm not rugby union's most devoted follower (in fact, whisper it, but I much prefer rugby league) and pokes fun at football, about its supporters, its diving players, its vulgar glorification of money. One of the spin-offs of working closely with the Professional Footballers' Association in my later years supporting the Tom Maynard Trust led to an invitation from Paul Raven to the PFA Awards evening at the Grosvenor House Hotel in London in 2015. It was a very swanky do, with Jason Manford compering, the Charlatans providing the musical entertainment and Steve Gerrard and Frank Lampard winning the PFA's special Merit Award. Dean and I had a great time, though I somehow nearly tripped Gerrard up on the way in and managed to elbow Lampard out of the way in my rush to get to the urinals later in the evening. I blame the drink. Eden Hazard won the Players' Player of the Year award that year. I'm not generally a fan of individual awards in team sports (I'd be the opposite of Cristiano Ronaldo in that regard) but being in the presence of all those high-profile footballers was quite something, for me at least. I think Dean was a bit more grown-up about it.

Dean's more cosmopolitan side can be seen from the acquisition of a boat, moored originally on the Thames at Kew (though I think it may now have been relocated to somewhere down in Pembrokeshire). I recall a mid-'90s visit to the dressing room for coffee after the start of play during Glamorgan's annual pilgrimage to Colwyn Bay and spotting a copy of *Practical Boatkeeping* on Dean's medical bag. It took him another fifteen years but he did eventually get around to buying his own boat. Which Matt helped him – with some difficulty – transport down to London. The thinking (logical, actually, for Dean) was that if he stayed on the boat it would save him a lot of money in hotels as he was already spending a great deal of time developing two clinics in the London area. After an aborted effort to get the craft onto the Thames the two of them, along with Josef, spent the night asleep in the car and boat respectively before trying to launch HMS Valley Boy, or whatever it was called, the following morning. The fact that it eventually required the river police to rescue and assist them after he'd got caught at high tide says everything you need to know about Dean's salty dog seaworthiness. As Martyn Ryan christened him, he's a regular Captain Pugwash.

Having followed Fletch into the England set-up in 1999 Dean wasn't directly involved with Glamorgan for a good ten years, though he retained the main physio contract and employed the likes of Erjan Mustafa and the others who followed him. He also had a hand in bringing in some excellent people to the support team, including Rob Ahmun as Strength and Conditioning Coach. Rob, like Dean before him, went on to work with the senior England team, and as National Lead. He worked with Welsh Netball too. And, also like Dean, he owned a beagle. His was considerably smaller than Dave. Most are.

While with England, Dean played evening host to a few of my occasional forays up to London. One of these was to do some hosting at a Lord's Test match in the early 2000s. One of my guests was the Area Manager for the Club's bankers HSBC, Huw Morgan, also a friend of Dean's (he knows everyone, that ought to be pretty evident by now). At the end of the day's play Huw and I were in good spirits when we met up with Dean and a few of the England management team, including David Graveney, England's Chairman of Selectors, who was still talking to us after we'd penned our 'Disgusted of Danygraig' letter about Steve James a few years previously. After a couple of convivial liveners in St John's Wood, we grabbed a taxi and headed to the West End, where Dean had arranged to take us to a bar on Shaftesbury Avenue. Just before we went inside, though, he took a moment to give us a bit of a pep talk. Apparently the place we were about to enter had a reputation as a bit of a refuge for celebrities. It was important, he said, that we didn't draw any attention to ourselves and if we did happen to see anyone famous, even though he felt the chances of that were probably next to non-existent on a midweek evening, to leave them alone and not point or fuss or anything. OK, we all thought, that should be within our collective capabilities, and in we went. Just as the doorman closed the door behind us, someone halfway down the staircase in front of us slipped and tumbled over the last half a dozen steps, landing in a crumpled heap at our feet. Before we could say or do anything, up bounces a clearly-worse-for-wear Les Dennis, host and star of *Family Fortunes*, with thumbs outstretched and a cheery, 'Alright lads?!'

Dean was always willing to help me personally where he could too. When my daughter Seanna was looking for a school work experience placement some time in the mid-2000s, having expressed some tentative early thoughts about a possible career in physiotherapy, Dean kindly took her on for a short period. Not sure how much he was around – he always has several projects on the go – but when we asked Seanna how it had all gone, she expressed an interest in studying music technology instead.

When he did come back permanently from his England duties, he stood for Glamorgan committee after becoming frustrated with all of the shenanigans which had led to me leaving the club in 2008 and then Matt in late 2010, followed almost immediately by Jamie Dalrymple and Matt's son, Tom. Those of you who are able to recall earlier chapters of this publication will not have been left in too much doubt about the sort of rank amateur we used to have on the committee. One or two were still there when Dean was elected. Given his taste in music – old rocker, with the accent on Led Zeppelin – it wouldn't have been too much of a surprise were he to have regressed to dinosaur status, but he chose to relinquish his position after a few years. Now he just heckles from the sidelines like the rest of us.

If there had to be a moral to this particular chapter, apart from the fact that where Dean is concerned it's always your fault, it is that you should look out for the people who look out for you. It still amazes me that Dean made a nine-hour round trip to North Yorkshire to be at my Mum's funeral, someone he'd only met briefly a couple of times. But that's what close friends do. They support you. Despite my loathing for the football team he managed, I always call to mind a quote of Alex Ferguson, principled left winger and the most successful manager in English domestic football history. He defined a real friend as 'one who walks in through the door when the others are putting on their coats to leave.' That's what I think of my relationship with these two. I couldn't ask for two more loyal mates.

14 STEP INTO MY OFFICE, BABY

'Friendship is the only cement that will ever hold the world together.'
WOODROW WILSON

In county cricket the only area where we competed was on the field. Off it, we worked as collaboratively as we could for the good of the game. I learned such a lot from some of my fellow Chief Executives. Several had been around when I was taking my first tentative steps back in the mid-'80s and they became friends. Here are a few tales, including my favourite, someone I looked up to: Peter Anderson. And there's also a close call with Yorkshire.

Way back in the mists of time – well, the tail end of Chapter Three anyway – I described how I came to be working in the world of cricket administration. Having taken a career break (which in those days, unless it had been announced in advance, which was rare, amounted to being unemployed) I threw caution to the wind and wrote to the first-class counties offering to work for nothing in return for six months' experience. Among those who replied were the secretaries (this was still before the era of the Chief Executive) of Middlesex, Lancashire, Northamptonshire, Leicestershire and Worcestershire. Their names – Tim Lamb, Chris Hassell, Steve Coverdale, Mike Turner and Mike Vockins – would become very familiar indeed in the coming years and I would come to count them as friends as well as county colleagues. The fact that they bothered to reply at all said a lot. The county secretary – and Chief Executive, as we all seemed to morph into over time – was a solid, earthy citizen back in the mid-'80s. In a world before commercial pressures, before the counties began to be squeezed more and more by the TCCB, before we had any voracious social media, the county cricket club was a bastion of old-fashionedness; an organization which prized its role at the centre of the community and which put cricket very much at the forefront of everything it did, and the clubs were generally led by reliable and conscientious administrators whose first love was for the game of cricket. And having just re-read those last couple of sentences I can confirm that in addition to sounding like it could have come from a school Victorian social history project, it also happens to be true.

That picture changed slowly over the 1990s and early 2000s. From a committee-dominated institution employing what our Glamorgan committee members used to describe as "paid servants" as its handful of staff, the commercial realities bit ever deeper as time wound on. Television deals and the advent of the internet changed the whole financial picture: players started to demand more money, the 'centre' (TCCB first, ECB from the late '90s onwards) put more pressure on the counties to improve their facilities for players and umpires, and started to judge us against a set of measures, reducing the hitherto guaranteed core fee payment we all received in the process. Pitches were required to meet minimum standards and floodlights were essential as first satellite television and then the arrival of Twenty20 demanded evening cricket. Counties were asked to bid for international matches, beginning a cut-throat period which pitted county against county, each spending sums of money they could ill afford either to stay in the game in terms of staging major matches or, as in Glamorgan's case, to try to break into the old boys' club. Commercial arms had to be developed as counties were forced to look elsewhere for direct revenue. And venues were required to meet a more demanding spectator in terms of improving seating and other amenities, not to mention the need to meet the growing hunger of a prissy media corps, especially those precious snowflakes who worked for national newspapers. It was all a far cry from the county circuit I joined and the change in profile of the average secretary and CEO reflected that. It was a change I ended up having to make myself, one I struggled with.

In late 1988 I was introduced to a character called Peter Anderson, a high-ranking ex-Hong Kong policeman, newly installed as Chief Executive at Somerset. He would go on to run the club for sixteen years. To me, he was a breath of fresh air. He was the type of man who divided opinion. He spoke his mind, 'shoots from the hip' as the ECB's Chief Executive Tim Lamb put it, and that didn't always endear him to people. But to me, a relatively young Northern tyro in a world of men well over twice my age who tended toward the conservative and the bureaucratic, Peter was a revelation. It wasn't until I took over as Glamorgan Chief Executive in the mid-'90s that I saw him close up, as it was then that I joined in the various meetings of CEOs, of the TCCB and the counties. In 1997, as we won the County Championship title, I saw his generosity up close too. Even though we were about to win our first title in 28 years on his home patch at Taunton (and remembering that Somerset had yet to win the Championship at all) he went out of his way to sort out a facility for the players' wives, at no cost to Glamorgan. He also put a case of champagne in the away dressing room on the final day. Again, at no cost to Glamorgan. He waved it away as 'nothing'. But it wasn't. I remembered this when Surrey won the Sunday League title at Cardiff a couple of years later. Though perhaps I should have charged them, obviously: they were Surrey, after all. All Peter would say was, "If you're going to win trophies, Fatkin, make sure you do them well away from my bloody county in future," an instruction which, I'm pleased to say, I was able to observe. Nowhere near as politely as my old friend Chris Cowdrey would have put it.

Four years later, Somerset won the C&G Trophy, one of the (then) two knock-out cups available to the counties, breaking a sixteen-year-old trophy drought in the process. Having had to endure Glamorgan winning the Championship on his patch a few years earlier, Peter made sure he was in my ear for months afterwards reminding me that Somerset had won something. Sporting his 2001 C&G Trophy winners tie on all public occasions, he'd make eye contact with me when things were quiet in meetings and just wave it at me, or point to it and mouthing the word 'winners.' On one occasion he even passed a note around the table (we used to sit alphabetically) which, when it reached me, I found just contained the words 'SOMERSET – WINNERS' on it. He was insufferable.

The following year they reached the final again, though this time they were beaten by Yorkshire. A few days later I was minding my own business doing some routine work in the office when Joan Pockett, one of our administrative staff, knocked on the door. "I think this might be for you, Mike," she said, before handing me an opened envelope and retreating hastily. It was addressed to me, not marked 'confidential' or anything, and when I looked inside it became evident that it had once been a tie. It turned out to be Peter's 2001 C&G Trophy winners' tie, but it was cut up into around a dozen small pieces. There wasn't a letter with it, but there was a Somerset County Cricket Club compliments slip. It contained two words in capital letters in Peter's handwriting: "F*** IT." I had it framed.

The TCCB and ECB AGMs were always something of a trial for me. A trek all the way up to London to sit with a load of old men in suits (we were joined by the ranks of superannuated minor county and county board chairmen for this one) listening to a read-out state-of-the-nation address from whoever was chairman at the time. The 2003 version, though, was lit up by Anderson. We were all settled in a large conference room in the Warner Stand at Lord's, a small group of short-tie-and-mucky-knee equivalents of schoolboy rebels all at the back, giggling amongst ourselves, as David Morgan, at his first AGM since succeeding Ian MacLaurin as Chairman, was giving his address, and those of you who know 'FDM', great man though he is, will appreciate that he doesn't exactly have what can be described as an energizing oratorical delivery. A natural tubthumping speechmaker he is not. Anyway, he's around five minutes into his speech when the double doors to the room are almost taken off their hinges as one Peter W. Anderson bursts through them and strides purposefully into the meeting. Not unnaturally, David pauses, and the eyes of the room look across to the door, awaiting any apology for the latecomer's tardy appearance. "If any of you bastards so much as mention Scotland, I'll f***ing kill you," came the response, no hint of remorse manifesting itself, as, without so much as a breaking of his stride, he marched over to an empty seat in front of the lectern. Somerset had lost to Scotland in a Benson and Hedges Cup game a couple of days previously, I ought to explain. When Highland Spring was revealed as the bottled water on the tables during the lunch afterwards he made it clear that he thought it was further evidence of a deliberate anti-West country conspiracy.

In the early 2000s there had been a change in the way the county CEOs got together. We still had formal meetings with county chairmen and representatives of the ECB (the so-called 'First Class Forum') but after one of the biannual Chief Execs' meeting was done and dusted in an hour David Harker, Durham's CEO, expressed understandable frustration that we were being dragged into London (him further than anyone) for an agenda set by Tim Lamb and his senior executives, with the majority of items being for report rather than any kind of debate. From this we agreed that there was a place for some informal meetings which would allow us the time to select and get our teeth into a couple of topics of our choice, rather than being dictated to by ECB officials: catering rights, salary structures, safety certification, grant funding options – anything really, but stuff which affected us and which the eighteen county CEOs could discuss between ourselves, without the need for anyone from the ECB to be there regulating the discussion. We also agreed that it was important to spend some time mixing away from meetings and for this reason we threw in an overnight stop to the Autumn get together. Tim was suspicious of the idea, I felt, and wary of not being in control, but on the basis that there wasn't any covert plot or anything, we had no issue with him and/or Brian Havill, his Finance Director, attending the meetings. We also agreed that our meetings should be chaired by the senior CEO, who was already responsible for arranging the annual pre-Christmas 'bash' for current and former county CEOs. At the time that meant Steve Coverdale would chair the first, which was subsequently held at an RAF base in Northamptonshire.

The baton passed to Peter Anderson when Steve left Northamptonshire in 2004, Mike Vockins (Worcestershire until 2001) and Chris Hassell (Lancashire and Yorkshire, up to 2002), both long serving county CEOs, having retired by then. Again, I loved Peter's approach. He recognized that these meetings were for the county CEOs and not the ECB and he gave everyone their head. He was also, at the time, on the ECB's Management Board as one of two county-elected representatives, and his approach was to let everyone know what was being discussed and then to inform everyone afterwards of what had transpired. Obviously, there would have been certain confidentialities which he needed to be observing but his transparency wasn't to everyone's taste, and definitely not the ECB's. It was a time when counties were ceding more control and power to the ECB centrally. Not only were fee payments being more geared to performance but we were going through a period when players were being centrally contracted and often withdrawn from county cricket altogether, international cricket was being 'de-listed' and moving from terrestrial television to satellite, salary caps were being mooted, promotion and relegation was coming into the County Championship, and Twenty20 cricket was emerging. It was a time of real upheaval for the game and Anderson's view was that in a period of such change, he was there to represent those who'd elected him, whether others liked it or not.

I received a letter from him in May 2006, completely out of the blue as he'd retired from the Somerset job by then. With it he enclosed a 1952 FA Cup Final programme (Newcastle against Arsenal) and original match ticket, which his dad – recently passed away – had kept among his possessions. Probably worth a few bob but he knew that I was a massive Arsenal fan and thought I'd like to have them. I hesitate to use the word 'sensitive' to describe Peter, but despite the bluster and directness he always had a thoughtful side. He influenced me a lot. I thought the world of him.

Peter's final act as chair of our CEO group was to lead us at a two-day meeting in Guernsey before handing over to Jim Cumbes of Lancashire as the next most senior. On the second day the meeting broke up for the ceremonial firing of the island's noon day gun, with Peter the island's guest of honour given the privilege of actually firing it. The process involved him donning the appropriate clothing before doing so. For anyone who remembers the old Quality Street selection tins, there is a depiction of a soldier on those tins, dressed up in a red velvet jacket and black hat; tassels, epaulettes and brocade everywhere. That was pretty much what Peter had to wear. A fitting exit. He looked ridiculous.

Well, when I say exit... The second evening we were there had seen the kind of fog descend on the island which would have graced a *Hound of the Baskervilles* film set. And it caused chaos. Cumbes and Harker were able to escape early the following day but by 9.30am the island's airport had been closed. My flight back to Bristol was cancelled, and as I waited in the departure lounge the CEOs of Leicestershire, Nottinghamshire, Sussex, Derbyshire and Hampshire all saw their own respective flights cancelled. In the end we made a dash across the island and managed to get hold of the last remaining tickets for the ferry to Poole. And, from there, via train to Southampton and Bristol, then a taxi out to the airport. I eventually rocked up at home 15 hours later than planned.

I was in charge of writing the minutes of the meetings back then. For this one they were subtitled 'Escape From Guernsey' and loosely based on the plot of *The Great Escape*. Other titles included 'The Thoughts of Vincent Codrington, Aged 8 21/23,' based on the then Middlesex CEO's life and times, and on one occasion I even attempted a parody of a Shakespearian play. There were always separate notes and action points, before any of you get the impression that we were unprofessional and never did any work, but I discovered after I left cricket that deviating from standard minutes wasn't something every group enjoyed. The cricket CEOs loved it, and I still get references to those minutes years later, but at Sport Wales, after

I'd left Glamorgan and was working for Welsh Netball, there was a serious humour failure around the table when I delivered my first set of minutes after being volunteered for the task. They were nothing like the ones we'd got used to at the cricket CEOs' meetings but I did introduce what I thought was a balanced and reasonable measure of levity. After being unavailable for the next meeting I saw from the minutes that the CEO of Welsh Hockey had taken charge of recording the notes and actions as they 'needed to be set out in a more appropriate manner'. Talk about taking yourselves too seriously. But that was Sport Wales, and I hadn't read the room. Everything strictly by the book. No room for any deviation. Even the slightest attempt at humour to be sent firmly packing with a flea in its metaphorical ear. At least I never had to do the minutes again.

Those informal cricket meetings may have started at an RAF base, with an overnight stop on site, all nice and low key, but they quickly developed into a procession of demonstrations of one-upmanship as we all started to show off to each other. I was the third host in the series, in the Spring of 2002, and the group's visit to Wales coincided with a Wales/France Six Nations match, so I arranged for 20-odd VIP tickets to the game, with hospitality. The day before, half a dozen of the boys had played golf at the Celtic Manor resort. It was all great fun and the CEOs all had a really enjoyable time. But we had some very positive meetings as well. We were comfortable in one another's company and that definitely helped us relax and get some business done around the table.

My attempt paled into significance with the three that followed it. First, we had David East, of Essex, in late 2002. No, not the same one from Chapter 1. I get on with this one. You could rack your brains for an hour or more, and list a thousand potential venues, but you wouldn't come close. We all decamped to Reims, to the Veuve Clicquot Ponsardin chateau where Veuve Cliquot champagne was produced. Of course we did. 'Easty' used to work for Veuve, you see. So, we all headed over to France, a la *Monte Carlo Or Bust*, cars departing from all points. I hate wine. Always have. So as the 'sommelier supreme' (or whatever wine connoisseurs call the wine waiter at a specialist wine producers) trotted out his spiel about the champagne we were about to taste prior to each of the five courses of our meal at the Manoir de Verzy chateau, I just looked down at my feet and sipped quietly on my cidre. "Barbarian" and "Philistine" were two of the kinder insults hurled in my direction. And it wasn't unfair. David Morgan had tried very hard to get me interested. He had his own wine cellar at his home in Newport. But it was at a dinner near Tower Bridge for one of the domestic sponsors one pre-season, when he finally gave up trying. "I'd be interested in your view of this red, MJF," he'd said, continuing to refer to me by my initials, which he had done as long as we'd known each other (to me, he was 'FDM'). I tasted it, in what I thought was the correct manner – slowly, sipping, not gulping, taking time to look as though I was carefully considering its various merits. "It's very nice," I replied, hoping that might not elicit too much in the way of criticism by return. David tutted, shook his head and then said, "Wines are many things, MJF. 'Nice' is not one of them," before turning immediately to talk to the person on his other side. Conversation closed.

During the tour of the famous wine cellars at Veuve Cliquot, our French guide was pointing out to us all how the various vintages dated back to pre-Napoleonic times. The cellars comprised a series of connected caves with wines and champagnes racked into almost every nook, cranny and crevice. Given the nature of the subterranean surroundings, voices carried. The guide paused to invite questions. Tom Richardson, ex-army Lieutenant Colonel and then in charge of Gloucestershire, who has a whisper louder than a bank of Pete Townshend guitar amps turned up to 12, leaned over and, just to ensure he was heard, raised his voice to say, "How did they hide everything from the Nazis during the war?" All the rest of us got were the last three words as they echoed and reverberated around the caves. "During the war... war... war..." Not for nothing was Tom immediately christened Uncle Albert, after the *Only Fools and Horses* character. More of my very good friend the Colonel later...

After high end sports hospitality and champagne fine dining overseas, when it came to his turn to host, Jim Cumbes seemed somehow to find the right level. None of your one-upmanship for Jim. Like Peter Anderson, he gets straight to the point as well. As evidenced by some of the (occasionally non-PC) jokes he still emails us on a Friday afternoon. No need for rugby tickets or tours of continental champagne producers when it came to Lancashire hosting. He took us to see *Funny Girls* in Blackpool, by way of a mystery tour. We knew it was going to be something cheesy as we set off from Old Trafford, but none of us came close with our guesses even though it was soon apparent that we were headed to the coast. We were at the theatre early, around 9.30pm, after a pizza on the way, and our entrance didn't go unnoticed. There in front of us, stage left, was a bloke stupendously dolled-up and glamorously kitted-out as a member of the opposite sex, on the microphone. 20-odd middle-aged men coming into a drag show as a group, unaccompanied. It was as if we'd come in on cue. I was lagging a little behind in a trio at the back with Tom Richardson and Paul Millman, CEO of Kent, another good mate. "Ooh, 'ere they are. Tilly, Tom and Tiny," he said, as he spotted us, somehow singling the Colonel out by name (Paul was tinier than me, so I suppose I was Tilly), and proceeded to keep up a running commentary as we grabbed a drink from the bar and slinked off to hide in an alcove somewhere. Geoff Cope and Steve Coverdale were less fortunate. Geoff is a bit on the deaf side (as well as being short-sighted) and he was in the midst of explaining some sort of dismissal or other to Steve while the drag queen on the mic picked up on his hand movements and turned them into a commentary for the rest of the hall, which was rapidly filling up for the 10pm show. Steve could hear him and knew what was going on, so he had a bit of a smirk on his face as Geoff proceeded to describe – with accompanying demonstrations – the action involved in bowling an arm ball, and what happened to the ball as it spat off the pitch. Or something. It wasn't reported like that anyway. 'Copey' was completely oblivious.

There were some genuinely funny men in that group, and some outstanding people. There were a couple of arseholes too down the years but the law of averages gives you that, I guess, and they were sufficiently few and far between for the get togethers to be largely unaffected. In fact they tended to draw the ire and sarcasm of the rump, making for even more entertainment. Away from the arseholes, Hugh Griffiths (Sussex CEO), during a discussion about de-listing, the process of lobbying the government of the day to have Test cricket taken off the list of 'starred' events which had to be shown on terrestrial television, concluded a point about selling any move to Sky Sports with the question, "What about satellite dishes for members?" To which, sharp as a tack, came the reply from David Harker of Durham, "Is that a swap?" Harker was one of the great characters amongst our CEO group. He was part of the Durham backroom staff when they joined the first-class county ranks in 1992 and it was no surprise to see him ascend to the top job. Allied to an incredibly quick wit was an understated intelligence, a good business brain and a drive to make Durham the best they could be. He flirted with a career in wine at one point, learning French and swatting up on the subject (I think the idea came after Reims, though I can't be too sure of that) but Durham persuaded him not to leave until well into the 2010s. I don't blame them. They had become a real county success story and he must have been an integral element behind the scenes. From sharing a £15 beer (each) from the bottle in Claridges ("F*** it," he said, as our taxi had been going past en route to somewhere else, "we'll never get this chance again.") to watching us all lay up on the 275-yard, par four 10th at The Belfry's Brabazon course (a famous Ryder Cup hole which the bigger hitters can reach off the tee). In fact he used exactly the same language as he had with me as we were passing Claridges as he put his five iron back in the bag and brought out the driver, only then to mishit his drive embarrassingly and end up 20 yards behind the three of us, who had all laid up. We all struggled to keep a straight face as we walked down the fairway but he had the last laugh, chipping in with his second for an eagle. When I left Glamorgan David's was one of the more memorable messages on my voicemail. In amongst all the sincerity, concern and general disbelief there came a Geordie cry of "BIG ISSUE!" before he hung up. It raised a big smile at a real low point. I love that sort of humour.

It was a wonderful group. We had Vinny Codrington of Middlesex and his ropey hips and knees; based at Lord's but always either last to turn up at meetings there or the first to offer apologies for absence. And on match days he was a genial, but lethal, guide as we toured the various alcoholic outposts and corners of the home of cricket. There were the youngsters from Derbyshire – John Smedley, followed by Tom Sears – and it was with John's appointment that I started to feel my age as I was no longer the baby of the group. Paul Millman is one of my peer group I've remained in close contact with; we meet up in the Summer, generally at Cheltenham, hosted by Tom Richardson. Paul still refers to me as 'Wales', a longstanding habit, and in response to which I could only come up with 'Garden' (Kent being the Garden of England), email exchanges generally starting 'Hello Wales' and signing off with 'BW, Garden.' There was Dennis Amiss, Warwickshire's CEO, comfortably the best cricketer/CEO of my time; Stewart Regan, of Yorkshire, who led a discussion about hypothetical chanting of four-day Championship crowds when we were in a curry house in Copenhagen as part of Derbyshire's turn hosting the informal CEOs' group (tenuous link involving former Derbyshire bowler, Ole Mortensen, who hailed from Denmark: long story, best not ask), including the memorable "Sing When You're Knitting" – obviously that worked well as it subsequently saw him installed as CEO of the Scottish FA; Derek Brewer, of Nottinghamshire, then MCC, the mild-mannered Fulham fan; Gus Mackay, more CEO roles on his CV than I've had pints of cider; and Surrey's Paul Sheldon, affectionately known as The Queen Mother for the way he occasionally graced us with his presence – if he turned up at a meeting you sensed it was important, put it that way. There were so many good men. And they needed to be, because the ECB meetings we all attended with our chairmen that weren't fractious and divisive were, not to put too fine a point on it, interminably boring. The overwhelming majority passed by in an unmemorable fug of talking heads, clashing egos and, frankly, irrelevant posturing. Sure, there was the occasional genuine debate – central contracts for England players, two divisions, salary capping, Twenty20 (eventually, kicking and screaming) – but most of the time it was just a defensive and highly political ECB top table and a rabble of argumentative counties, usually split along Test Match or Non-Test Match Grounds party lines (obviously, highly originally, referred to as 'TMGs' and 'NTMGs').

The occasional one stays in the memory, though. In the early 2000s the question of internet online rights and the potential of emerging mobile technology was the County-versus-ECB battleground *du jour*. We had all been seduced into thinking that the advent of the internet would give counties untold riches in rights, provided we pooled those rights collectively. Crucially, we were advised that we needn't have to partner with ECB as a pre-requisite to being handed the keys to the golden vault. It was ECB, MCC and each of the counties as equal partners. Or so the flannel went. I admit to being taken in. To the extent that my CEO colleagues voted me onto a steering group looking at the subject. It was very quickly evident that I was just a pawn in a much bigger game being played out between ECB, MCC and the counties, along with the Professional Cricketers' Association. And I was so far out of my depth a lifeboat wouldn't have even contemplated coming out to try to rescue me. We had a series of meetings at Lord's, with presentations and promises galore but all I recall is the arguing. Eventually, having racked up a ludicrously large legal bill it ended up back with the ECB and we were all called to a First-Class Forum meeting at an hotel just outside Heathrow (probably to suit David Morgan's business schedule, he being Deputy Chairman of ECB and therefore Chairman of the Forum, and an inveterate business traveller) in May 2001. By way of an aside, the First-Class Forum was the group which met ostensibly to look after the first-class game, with the Recreational Forum covering the recreational game, both emerging out of the formation of the England and Wales Cricket Board in 1997 as successor to the old Test and County Cricket Board and National Cricket Association. Hopefully you're still with me. Anyway, the FCF (clearly abbreviated and never referred to by anyone other than by acronym) consisted of the eighteen counties and MCC, with meetings generally held biannually, normally attended by county chairmen and CEOs. With all of the ECB executives, this meant we were probably 50-strong around the table. Clearly conducive to punchy, sharp debate (he lied).

On this particular occasion the online rights stuff led off with a report by Robert Griffiths, a QC and MCC member, who chaired the steering group. His recommendation was that we all proceed to the next stage, whatever that was. ECB was lobbying against that, arguing that costs were spiralling and, understandably, they wanted to be more in control. Griffiths was in full flow, with most of us at least having the good manners to pretend as though we were interested as he rambled on, when Don Trangmar, the Chairman of Sussex, reached into his briefcase, pulled out a copy of that morning's *Daily Telegraph*, and very obviously flapped it loose and started reading it. A few moments later, Griffiths still reporting, Trangmar made a show of putting his paper down, turned towards the top table, and interrupted by saying, "Do you know, Mr Griffiths, the more you say, the less I believe you," before flapping loose his newspaper and starting to read again. It was a wonderful interruption. I don't remember the specific outcome of the discussions, other than the fact that the rights weren't really worth anything, certainly nothing like we'd been originally led to believe they might, but I do recall Trangmar's intervention, which was priceless.

I was quite glad when meetings took place away from Lord's. Nothing against the ground. I loved it then and I still do now.

I can't tell you the thrill it gave me when Duncan Fletcher invited me into the England dressing room during the opening Ashes Test match in 2005 (England were in the field so it was relatively unpopulated). I was entertaining in the Mound Stand but once I'd blagged my way past the pavilion stewards, who I swear were trained at Checkpoint Charlie on the Berlin Wall, that half hour over a coffee with 'Fletch' and Matt Maynard, who was one of his coaching assistants for the series, is one of my life highlights and I knew I was privileged to be there. But as far as meetings are concerned, whenever they were held at Lord's, we all used to stay in the Danubius Hotel (or whatever it's called now; it went through a name change every year, or so it seemed – the one across the road opposite the indoor cricket school, anyway). The hotel itself was fine. Usual London fare: getting on for £200 a night, with breakfast extra, £8 for a pint of watery lager... No, it was the fact that it prided itself, because of its location, as being a 'cricket hotel'. There was memorabilia all over the place, with seemingly every room named after a famous cricketer; Compton, Trueman, Graveney, Barrington, Hobbs, there was even a Wellington Suite, though I don't remember whether he batted or bowled. And on the wall right next to the gents by the main bar, there was a bat autographed by the Glamorgan and Middlesex teams from circa 1989. Except I knew that many of the signatures weren't those of the actual participants. I must confess to administering the odd forged scrawl of my own when the occasional player had been too lazy to sign or not readily available. Not as though we left hundreds of bats or shirts around but some players just couldn't be arsed. My Vivian Richards flourish was legendary. And I could replicate most of the Glamorgan players' signatures, so make sure any memorabilia you own from that era is genuine and not a Fatkin special. But on this particular bat it wasn't one of mine that concerned me. I was always confident that mine would pass muster. No, it was one of Tony Dilloway's efforts that concerned me. I'd obviously been through my repertoire with an attempt at a Tufnell or an Emburey and would have suggested it needed a different hand for a couple of the others. Tony's handwriting, already alluded to elsewhere in this tome, was heavy-handed, spiderish and very block-like. Much like the blunt "J.D.Carr" that appeared, literally carved half an inch into the bat. Most signatures fade with the passing years but I reckon this one will survive for thousands of years, so heavily did 'Dillers' hold his pen and almost drive it into the willow. I doubt whether John, who went on to head up professional cricket for the ECB after he'd finished playing, has ever signed his name with an un-Christian name-like "J.D.Carr" on a bat before or since, and certainly not in such an aggressive manner as to have it embedded deep into the bat itself. On one occasion in the hotel John and I ended up debating something into the wee small hours (probably domestic structure – it was normally domestic structure) and all I could see was this same bat behind his head, his child-like 'signature' and all. I dreaded him turning round.

All this was a far cry from my early dealings with 'The Centre,' as we all referred to TCCB and ECB. In the early 1990s, David Morgan, ever the career shepherd, felt I was ready to get more involved (deliberate use of the word 'get' in the same sentence as David is mentioned, for reasons he will understand and which will fly over the heads of everyone else) and suggested that I stand for election to one of the many TCCB committees that existed at the time. There were dozens. Alright, not dozens. But as well as meetings of captains, groundsmen, scorers, CEOs, marketing managers, coaches, physios, medical leads, FDs and heaven knows which other all-county groups, there were quite a few formal standing committees as well: Cricket; Registration; Finance; Marketing; Second XI; Selection; Pitches to name but a few. Selection (which meant picking the England team) was considered to be perhaps a step too far, but then having looked at the backgrounds of those involved in all of the other committees, I'm not sure there were very many which obviously lent themselves to a lad in his mid-20s who had never played the game, wasn't an FD, had no commercial experience and wouldn't know a pitch if he was asked to pick out the one straw coloured strip from a lime green square. Second XI, we decided. That's the one. David told me to go for it.

That committee was at the time chaired by Mike Vockins, Secretary of Worcestershire. The system in those days meant that the chairman of each committee could 'star' his favoured candidates, so that if those voting didn't really know a particular individual they could see that the chairman had identified him (occasionally her) as someone he preferred. There were pen pictures as well, but I'm not sure mine would have helped anyone. David reasoned – correctly – that there was unlikely to be a queue of people wanting to immerse themselves in a committee which spent its time focusing on non-first-class cricket, and he was right. David having secured Mike's endorsement I was surprised by the ease with which I was elected. The lead up to my first meeting at Lord's was a daunting experience. And, true to form, it was typically one of the very few occasions on which I was late. And I <u>hate</u> being late. Eventually stumbling in 25 minutes into the meeting I mumbled some weak joke about Great Western and skulked across to the one empty chair in the room. Mike I knew, and also Steve Coverdale, but they were the only ones. I remember the other names: Tim Tremlett (Cricket Secretary at Hampshire, then very recently retired as a player); Mick Newell (just finished at Nottinghamshire and about to start as Second XI Captain); Peter Robinson (Somerset's Second XI Coach); Neal Abberley (Warwickshire's Second XI Coach); Don Bennett (Middlesex Coach); Alan Hill (Derbyshire Second XI Coach); and Micky Stewart (then England's Cricket Manager). Alan Oakman, like Abberley from Warwickshire, was also on the committee for a while. From the off they all treated me as an equal, never once questioning either my lack of a playing career or my inexperience as an administrator. I learned so much from them. Micky, in particular, went out of his way to put me at my ease. It helped that he was a huge Arsenal supporter. I think we spent more time talking about football than about cricket. Tim Tremlett was polite, interested and encouraging. And Alan 'Bud' Hill, too: such a direct person, but never once patronizing, and never anything other than helpful and supportive.

I did my time on the Second XI Committee for a few years before being elected to the Registration Committee, later Registration and Contracts, which represented a step up. It was as part of that group that I came to know Jason Ratcliffe, of the Professional Cricketers' Association, and Janet Fisher, originally of the NCA (National Cricket Association), before moving to the TCCB, which morphed into the ECB, and finally moving employer to join the MCC. A walking advert for Lord's-based acronyms, in fact. As a committee we oversaw the redrafting of the standard players' contract and revised the regulations simplifying player movement between counties, both really important pieces of work. In addition to Online Rights I ended up on one of the many versions of the Domestic Structure Review Working Party, which was still in place years later. I used to joke to the ECB's Alan Fordham, who had to organize and facilitate all those meetings, that the Duke of Wellington was its first chairman, such has been the interminable ongoing dissatisfaction with the way the domestic cricket season has been structured down the years and the number of groups charged with coming up with a new one. Maybe that's why he has a room named after him at the Danubius (the Duke, not 'Forders.'). We've had the Murray Report, the Palmer Report, the Morgan Report – blueprints galore. I'm not sure that will ever change. The domestic season looks more than ever as though it has been designed by a five-year-old with a colour-by-numbers map of England and Wales and half a dozen crayons.

Our seats at FCF meetings were set out alphabetically, meaning that in addition to my own Chairman of the day I would be sat next to either someone from Essex or someone from Gloucestershire. In my early days Peter Edwards of Essex, a lovely man but a bit of a work obsessive, was the Secretary/General Manager, and Philip August was Gloucestershire Secretary. I enjoyed the company of both, though I preferred Phil as he was a fellow cynic and we shared a similar sense of humour. David East, of Reims champagne fame, succeeded Edwards and when Philip left Gloucestershire his replacement was an ex-RAF man, Colin Sexstone, a pleasant fellow but someone I didn't really get to know as well as some of the others but about whom I formed the impression that he did quite like the idea of talking about Colin Sexstone. Tom Richardson, he of the resonating voice in the caves in Reims, succeeded Colin. At Tom's first FCF meeting, chaired by David Morgan, the agenda was meandering along at its usual largely-irrelevant-but-of-vital-importance-to-a-few-in-the-room pace when Tom challenged me to a game: could I name the 50 States of America? Now many close to me will know where I unearthed this particular talent, because I can now reel all 50 off, in alphabetical order no less, but back then it was a new one to me. So, I started scribbling down some answers. I'd got to around 15 when I received a rather violent dig in my ribs, a pointing finger and – he thought it was a whisper, but as we know he can't whisper – the words "Baltimore's not a state!" Whoever was burbling on at the time stopped in full flow and David Morgan turned his attention to Tom. "Can we help you with something, Tom?" he asked, politely, but with the appropriate combination of disappointment and admonishment in his voice. "No, sorry, Chairman," replied Tom, coughing, as if the act of fabricating a cough sort of excused his outburst. Thirty seconds later, another – painful – poke in the ribs, and the words, "Baltimore's in Maryland, you fool." Righto, Thomas. Though as I hadn't had Maryland on the list, he actually helped me with the intervention.

Tom famously managed to lose his car in the car park at Taunton after one of our Chief Executives' meetings there. It's not that big a car park but he had me and Brian Havill, ECB's Finance Director, marching up and down looking for his Audi Estate for a good 20 minutes before he checked his pockets, seemingly for the tenth time, sheepishly producing a train ticket from his shirt pocket. Peter Anderson's retort was priceless: "How the f***ing hell did we win a bloody world war with people like you in charge?" And they were old mates from their days in Hong Kong, when Peter was in the police and Tom was based out there. Tom was one of a handful I used to talk to frequently when in the game and he remains a close friend. I left Glamorgan in 2008 and he retired from Gloucestershire in 2013. We're in touch regularly.

One of the other CEOs who I didn't really get to know was David Collier, either during his first incarnation on the circuit, with Essex and Gloucestershire, or his second, via Leicestershire, Nottinghamshire and then as Chief Executive at the ECB after Tim Lamb. I do know that he has the second limpest handshake I have ever encountered in any other human being, male or female. Rodney Berman, former Leader of Cardiff Council, remains out on his own in that regard. Even the Princess of Wales pressed a firmer handshake than those two. I don't think David ever took me seriously, being honest, which isn't a great thing when you think that in my last few years at Glamorgan he was one of the key people we had to convince to break a century of tradition and slip Cardiff in as a new Ashes Test venue. But then again, I don't think I ever took him seriously either. Certainly not as seriously as he took himself. I thought he was a bit too clever by half, overly Machiavellian as a politician, seeming openly to be running with both hare and hounds. I could be comfortable in the company of many of the other CEOs but with David I felt the need to be on my guard a wee bit more, The combination of David working with Giles Clarke as ECB Chairman didn't exactly inspire the remotest sense of professional trust or personal jollification in me, either. But by then I had Paul Russell alongside me, so it never really bothered me. He knew exactly how to play their game and was far better at it than I could ever be. Which was a good job. I found Giles Clarke insufferable. When he entered a room, I couldn't get out of that room fast enough. Not that it would have bothered him. He wouldn't have known who I was anyway.

Every meeting at Lord's would lead to one comedy routine that never varied. Even though you knew that Janet Fisher had sorted you out a car parking space, and that she had left instructions and your name with the steward on the appropriate gate, you had a ritual to go through. Up you'd pull to the main gate, barrier naturally down in front of you. Pause. Wait for at least 30 seconds while the steward inside the little hut, who knows you're there but is determined to take his time, eventually bothers to look up with an inquiring but utterly disinterested 'Yes?' You trot out details of who you are, where you're supposed to be, what meeting you have, and repeat the fact that your name will be on the list. Cue shaking of the head, perhaps interspersed with the occasional tutting. 'News to me, sir.' Further pause. Repeating your name is a waste of time. Even if you were the Queen of Sheba, riding in on a unicorn hand-carved in alabaster, with a giant sticker on its side saying "MCC: ACCESS ALL AREAS" it wouldn't make the tiniest jot of a difference. So, onto the phone he goes, while a queue starts forming behind you. He could have been ringing his bookie for all you know, but two minutes and a couple of occasional sneery looks up, and out he saunters with his clipboard. One more snooty look and the barrier slowly starts to come up, accompanied by a disdainful 'by the indoor school please, sir.' And off we go. Every sodding time. It never changed. You never seemed to have the same problems anywhere else, or that was certainly my experience. I went to every county ground during my 23 years in the county game, and many an outground and Second XI venue besides, and I don't recall any real issues at any of them. Obviously some venues you enjoy more than others – Trent Bridge was always a favourite of mine – but although incompetence hadn't been completely eradicated it only seemed to be at Lord's where the stewards seemed to have been specially trained to be such deliberately impersonal, awkward, obstructive, well, wankers.

One winter I was in full rant mode, taking every opportunity possible to moan to Tim Lamb – and anyone else within email-shot – that there was something of an anti-county game agenda on the part of the Board. I felt they weren't taking county cricket anything like seriously enough. The best players were being centrally contracted, we had performance-related fee payments squeezing us financially, two divisions... it brought to mind Kenneth Williams in *Carry on Cleo*: "Infamy, infamy, they've all got it in for me." Tim did a very clever thing. When the Spring came, he invited me to the official launch of the season at The Oval, where the TV cameras, radio microphones and journalists' pens would all be primed and ready, and suggested I make a speech praising the county game. I agreed. I didn't really have any option, to be honest, after all my bleating in the previous few months. And then thought about what that invitation actually meant. And then shat myself. I don't think I've ever been as nervous over anything. It was all I could do to go through with it. It went down OK, but it taught me a big lesson. Unless you're prepared to do something about the issue you're complaining of, keep your mouth shut in future. Lamb 1, Fatkin 0.

By the early 2000s I'd been around the block a bit even if I was still relatively young. We had achieved some success at Glamorgan on the field and we had even staged the occasional international match. I had established a bit of a foothold at the ECB, or at least was involved at a level I was comfortable with, respected by those who I felt counted. In the Spring of 2002, it was announced that Chris Hassell would be retiring as Chief Executive after twelve years at Yorkshire (having been 13 years at Lancashire before that). Knowing of my connections with the county, I was asked by more than one person, including some involved at Yorkshire, if I'd be interested in replacing him. I hadn't given moving any real thought, if I'm honest, but after a chat with our Chairman Gerard Elias, I decided to apply. I don't remember telling too many people. But it had a unique appeal to me and I felt I just had to go for it or I'd probably regret it for years to come. It was where I was brought up. I love the place. And even though Yorkshire folk can be cantankerous, argumentative, difficult, critical and downright bloody stubborn, in my view they are also the best people in the world. It was the only job in cricket I would have considered leaving Glamorgan for.

I knew there would be a strong field but perhaps I'd underestimated the respect I now had in the game and I was invited to a first interview. It took place on the day before England played Argentina at the football World Cup in Japan. I was nervous. About the interview as well as the football... Seriously, though, it was the first interview I'd had since Philip Carling had chatted to me about the Glamorgan job 16 years previously, and that was hardly a grilling, more him setting out what was required and what he would pay (or not), and me agreeing to everything there and then. I was shortlisted to come back for a final interview the following week and told there were only three of us being considered. Chris Hassell had told me I stood a very good chance but he also warned me that the county's finances weren't looking too clever. I didn't fully appreciate what he was saying to me and didn't really spot what was clearly a bit of a friendly warning.

But then I had to pull out anyway. I'd assumed Carol would welcome a move 'back' to Yorkshire – if it happened, which was far from guaranteed, of course. She was settled in Wales and Seanna and Hannah were both very happy at school. I felt that if we were ever going to move it was then, with them both at primary school, but I had been selfish enough to assume that everyone would welcome a move 'back home'. That she didn't want us to move rather set me back. I reflected, though, and of course, there was no way I could go through with it. So I rang the Yorkshire Chairman, Keith Moss, who tried hard to persuade me to change my mind again, even offering to speak to Carol himself, but there was no going back. I officially withdrew. A few weeks later it emerged that although the county had made an appointment – Alex Keay, who had a rugby union background – they were in such dire financial straits that the offer of the job to him had been withdrawn and the club had brought in Colin Graves, chair of the Costcutter supermarket chain, later Yorkshire Executive Chairman and then Chairman of ECB, as one of a so-called 'Gang of Four' to try to stabilize the situation. There but for the grace of God and all that. We had financial issues at Glamorgan, of course. Not many counties didn't. And we'd lived with them for as long as I could remember. But we'd also had some high spots in between, and 2002 saw the team go on and win its second Sunday League title (now sponsored by Norwich Union). I'd never had my head turned before so this was all new territory to me. The romantic in me still reflects on what might have been. But conversations with Colin a few years later made it abundantly clear that the same fate would have befallen me. And that the job at Yorkshire would have been vastly different to that which I had hitherto experienced at Glamorgan. Far more brutal. Far more commercial. Far beyond my comfort zone. As things turned out, I was in for a similarly bumpy ride at Glamorgan anyway.

15   APPETITE

'Somebody was trying to tell me that CDs are better than vinyl because they don't have any surface noise. I said, "Listen, mate, life has surface noise."'
JOHN PEEL

The landscape at Glamorgan was changing. We'd acquired the head lease, started to redevelop the ground and begun to stage international matches. These were the last knockings from what had been a great Glamorgan side during the 1990s and early 2000s. During this period we also generated the opportunity for Wales to take on – and beat – the full England one-day side. And we came within a whisker of recruiting Hansie Cronje as our Head Coach.

For much of my first dozen or so years at Glamorgan money hadn't really been a problem for the club. We lived the same hand-to-mouth existence as did the majority of the other non-Test match grounds. Turnover was modest, performance – bar a couple of exceptional seasons – was equally modest, and facilities were just about adequate. We focused primarily on the cricket, with a small but dedicated team of staff (complemented by a committee the size of the Halle Choir) servicing a couple of thousand loyal (but very chirpy) members. In the late 1990s all that began to change.

In the early part of the decade the decision had been taken that we needed to take control of our own ground. Ever since the club had moved to Sophia Gardens from Cardiff Arms Park before the 1967 season, we had been tenants at a venue controlled by Cardiff Athletic Club. We were only allowed to play there on four weekends each season, and with the (then) TCCB almost always having to allocate two or three home matches to each county in April, early May and September, when we traditionally struggled to take cricket to any other venue because they ground-shared with rugby or football (Swansea being one of them), Cardiff generally ended up with a very imbalanced fixture list, with little Championship cricket at the height of the summer months. We even had to ask permission for the players to be able to practice at Sophia Gardens. Until 1989 we didn't employ our own groundsman and we were, frankly, at the mercy of the Athletic Club. 'Amateur' doesn't even begin to describe it. So the club, and David Morgan in particular, drove through a proposal to purchase the site from the Athletic Club. In my view we ended up paying over the odds but if we wanted that control, we had to pay what was being asked. Thus, in 1995 we acquired the head lease. We could finally start to look at developing the venue and making potential improvements.

Since 1954 the players' pre-season had generally meant traipsing down to Neath, where the Club had built its own three-lane indoor cricket school. It wasn't exactly a cutting-edge facility. It was 40-odd years old for a start, the run-ups were too short for many of the quicker bowlers, the surface was in need of replacement and the changing facilities were primitive. OK, so it was ours, but that was pretty much all it had going for it. Having acquired the Cardiff lease we had to be pragmatic and focus on ground developments there, and particularly on those which would attract elements of grant aid funding. We were hardly going to be able to blag our way towards free money for a load of corporate facilities on their own; wider community use was going to be a key element if we were to be able to build any of the income-generating facilities we wanted. And we would have to justify the dreaded 'L word': legacy. An indoor cricket school was an obvious development as Cardiff didn't have one of any quality. What we had to do was to wrap that concept around other commercial facilities that we would need in order for us to be able to grow our income and, not before time, become more professional: corporate boxes were an obvious objective if we could weave them into any design, but a new scoreboard, medical rooms, a club shop and new outdoor nets were all on the shopping list too.

I had bugger all to do with the funding applications on this occasion other than acting as a sounding board and helping with the admin. Tony Dilloway led the charge, working hand in hand with Gerard Elias, then Deputy Chairman, to get all the plans drawn up, revised and submitted, and in approaching the Sports Council for Wales for potential lottery funding (the National Lottery had started in 1994 and in the mid-'90s was not unreceptive to substantial, seven figure applications). It consumed him. And I didn't fully appreciate just how much hassle he was having to contend with – on top of his day job as Commercial Director – until I went through something similar with the next phase of the ground redevelopment eight or nine years later. Tony saw us into the new facility, a £4.1 million development to the North West of the Sophia Gardens site in the

Spring of 1999 before surprisingly resigning the following year. Or it seemed surprising at the time. After I'd been through the whole process for the next phase I think I understood where he was coming from. It was draining. But he did a magnificent job, helping to cover much of the total cost in grants and driving through a planning application for that and for two further phases (and this in a very sensitive conservation area), but it had obviously taken a lot out of him. Not for the first – or last – time a Glamorgan Cricket business plan was a fly-by-the-seat-of-your-pants job, but it was a tremendous effort. Tony didn't receive the credit I felt he ought to have done.

The grant application process had been tortuous, culminating in a presentation by Peter Walker (of the nascent Cricket Board of Wales, which was now looking after junior development) and Paul Russell, wheeled in for his corporate expertise, and the reaction to their pitch to the 'Sportlot' panel hadn't been so enthusiastic as to suggest guaranteed success. One or two on the panel later commented that whereas Walker's speech had been very well-received, Russell's flowery trip down memory lane to the Rassau of his youth had put several of them off. But no matter. In October 1997 we were awarded a grant of £3.2 million – 78% of the total cost – and along with Cardiff Metropolitan University (UWIC as was), who were awarded £5.6 million towards the construction of an indoor athletics arena, we donned the metaphorical hard hats and cracked open the champagne. Hugh Morris, by now ECB Technical Director, opened the facility in May 1999 in time for the visit of the men's Australian squad who were to be based in Cardiff as part of their preparations for the Cricket World Cup (which they would go on and win). It was marked with a special lunch for 500 in the indoor school itself with the Aussies – Warne, Gilchrist, Waugh, Ponting & Co – as special guests. We felt like kings. And we drank like them that day, too, with one Duncan Fletcher probably as tipsy and playful as I think I'd ever seen him.

That World Cup was our first real toe in the water as far as staging international cricket was concerned. Swansea had hosted a One-Day International between England and New Zealand in July 1973 (the first official ODI had only taken place two years earlier, in January 1971, when, after the fifth Ashes Test at Melbourne had been washed out a 40-over match was hastily put together for the spectators in what was, at the time, viewed as a one-off. Even *Wisden* didn't carry a report. But 46,000 people turned up. My later CEO colleague Dennis Amiss scored exactly 100, Geoff Boycott blazing a T20 trail with 20 made from no fewer than 88 balls.) Swansea had also staged a 1983 World Cup pool game between Pakistan and Sri Lanka. That was it. Two ODIs in Wales across a quarter of a century. And for Cardiff, nothing. Nowt. Rien. Nada. Niente. Niets. Ничего. Zilch. Zip. In 1999, though, every county was allocated at least one match. Cardiff was awarded Australia against New Zealand. No extravagant ground capacity for this one. ECB wasn't insisting on minimum capacities at that stage. 6,500 people bought tickets to watch the Kiwis inflict on the Aussies their only defeat of the competition. We were on the map. A tiny dot stuck out in the corner, well off the beaten track perhaps, but on the map nonetheless. It gave us a start. We experienced an early taste of the sneering negativity that was to come over the next decade or so with *Wisden* snootily described the pitch as having 'lived down to expectations'. It marked the opening salvo in what was to develop into a remorseless barrage of patronizing jibes, insults and abuse from a London-based media that just couldn't accept the fact that venues outside the traditional six (Lord's, The Oval, Edgbaston, Headingley, Old Trafford and Trent Bridge) should have even the remotest claim to be staging international cricket, let alone a venue in Wales. It did nothing but spur us on.

Matthew Maynard had been a fine Captain of what had been a very competitive Glamorgan team, but he stood down at the end of the 2001 season. He had offered to do so the previous September, after leading the side to promotion following a draw against Middlesex in the final match of the Summer at Cardiff (two divisions had finally come in in time for the 2001 season, spawning Matthew Engel's famous quote in his *Wisden* Editor's notes in 1999: "The entire country was opposed to the introduction of two divisions in the County Championship. Unfortunately, the country concerned was Wales.") That Middlesex game took place in the middle of a nationwide blockade of fuel depots, leading to a severe shortage of petrol and diesel, but all I could focus on was keeping my fingers crossed that their skipper Justin Langer would insist on batting on, rather than opening the game up and declaring six down after they'd secured the batting point that meant they couldn't finish bottom – we would be promoted if we took nine wickets and went on to draw the match, but a declaration would mean we had to win the game and with time running out, the chances of that were rapidly disappearing. Matt was succeeded first by Steve James, and then by Robert Croft. Very different characters to Matt, and I can't pretend to have had the same relationship with either of them, but they were sound cricketing people and Glamorgan to the core. Ricky Needham had taken over as Cricket Committee Chairman following Hugh Davies's election as Gerard Elias's Deputy Chairman and I knew that with coaches such as Alan Jones and John Derrick, our cricket was in good hands.

'Fletch' left for the England job in 1999 and he had been succeeded by Jeff Hammond. We very nearly went down what would have been a very interesting road, having more than flirted with the idea of bringing in Hansie Cronje before going for Hammond. Both 'Fletch' and Jacques Kallis had suggested Cronje would be a really good fit as Head Coach, but at the time he was still playing. After an initial chat between him and Jacques I was asked to sound him out formally. He was keen. I was therefore asked to approach the United Cricket Board of South Africa through its Chief Executive, Ali Bacher. He told me that Cronje wanted to carry on playing. I explained that this wasn't what he'd just told me, literally an hour beforehand. Everything went quiet for a few days but in the end, Cronje committed to us. Somewhere in the archive at Glamorgan there will be a copy of the faxed contract we drew up and which Cronje signed. *Google* it. The story's out there. At which point it all kicked off. Bacher was furious, claiming that we'd gone behind his back. I pointed out that we'd actually gone straight to him to make our intentions clear only to be told that we must have got the wrong end of the stick from Cronje. Bacher told us we were wasting our time. When Cronje subsequently said he was retiring as a player there was nothing in our view which said we couldn't go ahead and bring him in as Coach. In the end, Bacher and Cronje met and found a solution, Cronje performing an about turn to say he had been persuaded to continue playing. I was thanked by Bacher for 'graciously' releasing him from his contract with us (not that I had a lot of option) and Ricky and I adjourned to the pub to agree with one another that we had just been royally shafted and publicly used by Cronje as a vehicle for manoeuvring Bacher and the UCB into whatever it was he was looking for. Still, consider what then happened: in April 2000 he was accused of match-fixing, tried, found guilty and banned from cricket for life. We would have been right in the middle of that. It was a proper *Sliding Doors* moment. Tragically, within two years, he had been killed in a plane crash.

We had looked at other coaches at this time too. I went to meet with Bob Simpson, the Australian Coach who had also had a stint at Leicestershire, and spent a fascinating day with him. We had got on well and he talked with enormous passion and knowledge about the game and his coaching philosophy. He went on to work with Lancashire for a couple of seasons instead. Neil Fairbrother was another name we considered. Matt Maynard and he had always got on very well and the two of us took time out one evening while Glamorgan were playing in Colwyn Bay to drive across to Cheshire to chat to him. He believed he was coming to the end of his playing career and we thought he'd be an ideal fit for us. In the end he opted to continue playing for three more seasons – two of them under Simpson, ironically – and then went into a successful career in sports management. We were also interested in Greg Chappell, but he wasn't comfortable that he could combine a job coaching Glamorgan with his existing commitments at South Australia. He at least took the trouble to phone me from Adelaide with his decision, a call Carol took at the crack of dawn one Sunday morning, rousing me from my slumber with a throwaway, "Phone for you. Someone called Greg Chappell," before getting back into bed and leaving me to it. Never knowingly starstruck or bothered by cricket reputations, our Carol.

Anyway, back at Glamorgan, and with Hammond on board and working with Matt, we still had Hugh Davies sticking his oar in at every opportunity, especially after his son Adam had been released at the end of the 2001 season. Even though he was only now loosely connected to the cricket decision making, Hugh just couldn't resist consistently interfering, especially as he didn't see eye to eye with the captain and coaches running the cricket, not to mention Ricky or me. Other areas of the club were operating well, albeit that we had only been in charge of our own venue for a few years and were still transitioning (I do hate that word, especially in a football punditry context, but promised myself I would use it at least once) from amateur to professional, with much to learn.

Commercially we were now in a much stronger position as an organization. Back in 1992 we had reviewed our membership offering, with stark results, but found a particularly enterprising way of dealing with the findings of the detailed study the club had

286

commissioned. Tony Dilloway and David Morgan had brought in Paul Russell, then of Andersen Consulting, to look at our membership, which was a bit of a mess, to see if we could find a way of boosting what was a pitifully low number – then around 2,900. It turned out that once you'd bundled all the various categories of membership together the average annual fee people were paying was just short of £19. Our full membership at the time was £45 but we had so many different options available, with lines drawn from Cardiff to allow for Country Inner, Country Outer, and then Country Exile; we also had Vice Presidents, students, juniors, executive members, affiliated clubs, all sorts of husband-and-wife options…. it was easier to decipher Mandarin. And there were dozens and dozens of cases of people listing the address of a relative or a friend in England to circumvent having to pay the going rate, and of others associated with a local league club paying a reduced affiliated club membership and then using the ticket for their own purposes. It desperately needed simplifying. Paul's solution was such a simple one it was perfect. If the average was £19, charge a standard rate of £15. Keep a couple of the premium categories (specifically VPs) but the price of the standard offering should be the sort of money that folk – even a something-for-nothing moaning Welshman – wouldn't blink twice about handing over.

Tony was sold on it. I was more sceptical. I thought it was very risky. But I was proved hopelessly wrong. We went from 2,900 members to over 14,000 after a concerted membership drive in the winter of 1992, led by Matt, whom we employed to organize a promotional campaign across Wales. The timing was perfect. We had a team on the field that was about to deliver Glamorgan's first trophy in 24 years – its first ever in one-day cricket – and we now had a significant following for the first time in aeons. Russell's argument was that the greater the crowd base the more people would spend inside the ground on food, drink, merchandise and the like. It was simple economics, but it took real balls to implement it. By then we were working closely with Huw John, a local photographer, and he captured probably the most memorable shot at the launch of the players' winter trek around Wales: a picture of then Wales rugby captain Ieuan Evans, Wales football manager Terry Yorath, BBC Wales presenter Sara Edwards and Matt's son, Tom, then three or four years old, together with a giant daffodil. We used it everywhere.

We were even trained in dealing with public questions about the scheme, with advice on using the word 'affordable,' rather than 'cheap' and such like. The whole place was buzzing as a group of players set off on a promotional tour around Wales. The media publicity was superb.

Fast forward six or seven years and we found ourselves in a position where we weren't really too sure what to do with that membership. £15 had moved to £20, then morphed into £25, and we had reached the stage where the sum wasn't the disposable donation it was once envisaged to be; we were caught betwixt a low-cost price and between what other counties were doing, which was placing a higher premium on membership and charging more than ever. They didn't like what we were doing and argued that it devalued the product. We'd lost our way a bit. Our commercial arm post-Dilloway had also lost its way a bit. Mari Thomas was given a brief go as chair of our Commercial Committee. I thought she was a breath of fresh air and exactly what we needed, but with ever-creeping financial constraints and Richard Weston, by now in post as Treasurer, bending Gerard's ear about appointing a friend of his, Tony Ball, as part-longer-term-fundraiser-part-commercial-director, she decided it wasn't really for her, and I couldn't blame her. Tony Ball was a decent bloke, someone with whom you could enjoy a pint and a laugh, and he had a few good ideas, but I don't think he fitted Mari's image of someone leading a first-class county's marketing and promotion, especially with the growing clamour for a shorter form version of the game to try to appeal to a younger audience.

By now we were all being squeezed financially, and staging international matches was looking like one of the few realistic options open to us in terms of raising significant new income streams. Under pressure from members of the committee we tried a club appeal year – grandly, but very cleverly, given our aspirations, entitled "*A Test For Wales*" – but although it did OK, led by a good man called Gareth Williams, it was never going to be the answer to our cash troubles. The committee's view appeared to be that the whole flag-days-and-whist-drives nature of a benefit year would raise hundreds of thousands of pounds, but club years rarely do. People prefer to give to individuals rather than organizations, which they consider ought to be above running appeal years, and although we put a chunk of money into the bank through various events, including a public vote and gala dinner to announce an all-time Glamorgan Hall of Fame XI, it was pretty obvious it would soon be swallowed up on signing players and other short term day-to-day pressures rather than being invested in longer term ground redevelopment. Our ambitions were still too modest. But it was becoming genuine hand-to-mouth stuff and there were a couple of Christmases in the early 2000s when I seriously thought we would struggle to meet major obligations, such as to HMRC. It was a tough period, not helpful if you're a glass-half-empty kind of person, as I am, and it was difficult to see how we were going to manage our way out of it. It took the arrival of Paul Russell, this time as Club Chairman, before there was any kind of plan for that.

In the meantime our ambitions, such as they were, were the subject of ongoing patronizing from the ECB. I don't think they took our *'Test For Wales'* very seriously and, frankly, I'm not sure I could blame them. What it meant in reality was a series of statements about how we were going to stage Test matches – without the infrastructure, without the ground, with 80% of the venue's capacity comprising temporary seats, and no money with which to undertake any further redevelopment. We'd put on ODIs between Australia and Pakistan in 2001 and South Africa and Zimbabwe in 2003 but the crowds were hardly clamouring to get in. The former was memorable for being the first occasion on which a speed gun clocked a bowler at a hundred miles an hour. In this case, Shoaib Akhtar, bowling to the Aussie captain, Ricky Ponting. And Ponting just rocked back on his heels and pulled him disdainfully for four. Let's just say I'm not too sure that the technology was yet at its optimum.

One example of the ECB's condescension manifested itself when we staged our first Wales against England one-dayer in 2002, something Duncan Fletcher had suggested we try and which I've mentioned in an earlier chapter. Terry Blake, the ECB's Marketing Director, when confirming the match, imposed the condition that we'd have to have at least one overseas player in the Wales side 'to try to make the contest more even'. For those who wonder why that statement is in inverted commas it is because I am quoting from his letter. They clearly thought it was going to be a right old mismatch. As I've referred to elsewhere, rather than impose an additional game on Michael Kasprowicz, our official overseas player, we brought over Jacques Kallis from South Africa, which 'Kasper' wasn't best pleased about. He really wanted to play. We'd asked Steffan Jones, then plying his trade in Somerset, and Tony Cottey, then at Sussex, to come back to Cardiff to play as well, but 'Cotts' was unfortunately injured and couldn't play. There was a fierce battle to be in the starting XI. This was something different for the Glamorgan lads: the chance to play against the old enemy wearing a special red and green kit with the Welsh dragon on it. I still have a signed shirt up on my wall at home. England made 189 for 9 in their allotted 50 overs (the comments about the quality of the pitch amongst the handful of national journos who'd bothered to come down for the game were already predictable) and we had a golden opportunity to stick one on the ECB. At one point England lost three wickets – Michael Vaughan, Graham Thorpe and Paul Collingwood – within the space of nine runs. Wales eventually won by eight wickets with almost ten overs of our 50 to spare. Kallis faced eight balls for his three not out. We had to complete an official match form for the Board. I couldn't resist adding a compliment's slip for Terry's attention to the effect that we were ever so grateful to have had that overseas player. Smug and childish, me? I'm not sorry. Terry took it in good heart.

We went on to stage two more such matches, in 2003 and 2004, before Russell's determination for us to be focusing on staging 'proper' international cricket took over. They were a fun diversion. For the record we lost by a handful of runs in 2003 (a game in which Kasper did at least get his opportunity and his official Welsh cap; and Cotts did finally take the field for Wales in that one, which was a good job as he would miss out in 2004 as well, when Wales were on the wrong end of a hammering). Russell felt that the Wales/England matches were a distraction. He was right. They probably were. And please don't start me on the 'Wales should break away to form our own ICC country' blind alley argument that comes up every World Cup as Welsh politicians clamber over one another to leap onto a temporary passing bandwagon.... I disagree. Strongly.

Balancing all of our commercial challenges with the cricket ones was difficult. In 2000 Glamorgan had – finally – reached a second Lord's Final, our only other appearance in a major showpiece occasion (I really hate that phrase, by the way) being the Gillette Cup Final of 1977. We'd had a few good cup runs in the '90s but not been able to get over the line (another sickeningly awful sporting cliché). In 2000, though, it came together. We hammered Hampshire in the quarter finals, bowling them out for just 69, and were drawn to face

Surrey at home in the semis where, in a rain-affected game that went into a reserve day, 109 from Matt Maynard saw us home by 32 runs. The picture of the Glamorgan lads celebrating in the dressing room after that game remains one of my favourites.

In the final we would meet Gloucestershire, the then acknowledged one-day kings, with one-day trophies galore: in 1999 (two titles), 2000 (three of them), 2003 and 2004. Just our luck to be facing them. Despite another Maynard century we were beaten, and well beaten too. Michael Henderson in the Telegraph described Matt in his wide brimmed sun hat as "a conquistador sniffing gold on some daring raid." David Morgan, with his ECB hat on, was presenting the Man of the Match award, and Duncan Fletcher, as England coach, adjudicating on who it should be awarded to. Fletch was clearly not sure which way to go, dragging me out of whatever bar I was in at the time to discuss it with me. He didn't want to be seen to be biased. Ian Harvey – now a mate, a very close pal of Matt's, and someone who has done an awful lot for the Tom Maynard Trust – had taken five for 34, two with the new ball and three as Gloucestershire kept us firmly in our place during the final 'death' overs. It's a source of mirth between the two of them now but the sight of Matt picking up his award from FDM, as nominated by Fletch, when we'd lost, did smack a little bit of incestuousness. There was nothing for it but to head across the road to the Danubius for what turned out to be more wake than celebration, and which passed most of us by in a blur. We'd probably exerted all of our energy into simply reaching a Final and when it came to the day of the game we perhaps subconsciously felt we'd done our jobs. Or that's how it felt. After we'd beaten Surrey I'd hunted Tony Dilloway out. We'd gone through much together and a Lord's Final was one of the shared ambitions that had continued to elude us. He was to leave the Club pretty much as soon as the Final had been played.

When Matt stood down, Steve James was appointed as his successor. By his own admission Steve wasn't a born county captain. He generally had enough on his plate just focusing on his own game and didn't have the sort of personality that was conducive to leading a disparate bunch of men, with their conflicting wants and needs, egos and personalities. Perhaps Adrian Dale may have been a better choice at the time, I don't know. Steve did lead the team (by now the 'Glamorgan Dragons' after ECB and Sky's insistence that we all had to have some epithet attached to our county names; only Sky's Bob Willis seemed actually to pay any attention to them, but that's by the by) to a triumph in the 2002 National League (I've lost track but I think the Sunday League was under a Norwich Union insurance banner at this point) but after sustaining a knee injury during a game at Bristol early in the 2001 season, it continued to dog him and despite a handful of operations he was forced to hand over the captaincy in 2003, and eventually forced out of the game the following year. (That's a long sentence, I know, and I also apologize for the proliferation of brackets.) From a Glamorgan perspective it was another experienced and talented cricketer falling by the wayside.

I enjoy Steve. He's a very likeable man and a very solid and reliable character; when you get past what some might interpret as a defensive veneer and get to know him (two 'gets' in one sentence – apologies, FDM) he is an engaging, if many would say opinionated, personality. He probably didn't have everything he would have wanted in terms of support when he was skipper. He and Jeff Hammond formed something of an uneasy partnership, though Jeff's departure at the end of the 2001 season and John Derrick's subsequent elevation to the Head Coach position gave us back some stability and Steve was far more comfortable with that relationship. Steve's knee injury hasn't stopped him becoming a middle-aged cycling bore, but we'll let that pass. He's carved out a really successful career as a journalist though I have to confess that I rarely read anything he writes. It's nothing personal. As I've mentioned elsewhere, much of his writing is on rugby union, which I have always found a bit boring (the rugby, not the writing), and his work appeared for many years in the *Telegraph*, which I wouldn't read if it was the only newspaper left on the planet, though he has since moved to the *Times*. The sudden death of his 21-year-old daughter Bethan early in 2020 hit him and his wife Jane very hard, as it would anyone. You wouldn't want that to happen to anyone, and especially not to such a lovely couple.

The baton passed, as it inevitably had to do eventually, to Robert Croft. 'Crofty' is an interesting character, at once charming and funny, yet at the same time with what some see as a tendency towards being a bit selfish and aloof. That said, I like him too. He is a strong character and argued passionately for what he wanted. Any disagreements we had were relatively rare, and always professional. And he, like Steve, enjoyed success in the role. In 2004 we won the

National League (by now sponsored by Totesport – I do hope you're all keeping up at the back) and we probably enjoyed our best-ever all-round season under his leadership. In addition to the trophy, we were promoted to the first division in the County Championship and also reached Twenty20 Finals' Day for the first time. Crofty led the charge, including scoring a century on the day we beat Lancashire at Colwyn Bay to win our third one-day trophy. Later that evening, back in the hotel, the boys were going around the room offering individual comments about what it meant to each of them. When it came to Mick Lewis, drafted in as a late season replacement for Michael Kasprowicz, who had left early after another recall by Australia, he just looked up, blinked, blinked again, and said: "Rock up and win a medal after one game. Can't f***in' fault it, mate."

Robert was a magnificent cricketer and a real Glamorgan man, one of the county's greatest ever players. He loved nothing better than to spend time chatting away about the game over a pint, in my view something much missed from the county circuit in recent times. He also had a wonderful cricket brain. He worked closely with John Derrick, who presided over two one-day triumphs, a couple of promotions and a finals day, but I felt that perhaps Robert dominated that relationship too much. I would like to have seen John force himself a little more. But that was just an observation. They obviously worked well together. John had been appointed in 2002. After Hammond left – and the respect he lost after falling asleep in the dressing room at Worcester during the very first four-day game he was in charge of in 2000 was something he'd found difficult to claw back from senior players, true Glamorgan pros like Maynard, James, Croft, Dale and Watkin – we didn't look overseas. We went straight for 'JD.'

But whatever Robert's style he immediately understood the importance of politics and he knew how to play the chairman and the committee. He was good to work with. He suffered, I felt, from the fact that we had allowed a good side to grow old together. I never accepted the argument that you just cull for the sake of it; these were all good cricketers, even if they were perhaps not what they were at their peak. You can't just go round firing people when you're unsure of the quality of the players coming in to take their places. It's a risk. But the price you pay for that is pretty obvious: they can all leave within a relatively short space of one another and leave a massive void. The second string of players coming through together in the mid-2000 just weren't anywhere near as good as Morris, Watkin, Dale, James or Maynard. We also had quieter senior players taking their place. The team of the '90s and early 2000s had some chopsy senior players, players who were prepared to speak their mind, call out team-mates if required. The squad Crofty was inheriting was running short of those types of characters. The lads stepping up to become senior players – Mark Wallace, David Harrison, Dean Cosker, Darren Thomas, Mike Powell, Alex Wharf – were much quieter, more inward-looking. Good lads and fine cricketers all, but there was a very different dressing room dynamic. It also didn't help that we were constantly scrambling around for money.

Twenty20 had been introduced in 2003, despite Glamorgan voting against it when the committee had previously agreed to support it. Long story. If you're dipping, it's over in chapter six. If you've forgotten, you clearly have memory retention issues but go back and have a re-read; I'll wait…

…Anyway, after a bit of a muted introduction the new format boomed. The early games were greeted with a healthy degree of scepticism, especially from the (largely elderly) county members. Players, too, viewed the new format with more than a touch of disdain, many describing it as just 'hit and giggle'. It took a while but Twenty20 (or T20 as it's more commonly referred to nowadays) is an established form of the game globally and it has revolutionised the longer one-day format of the game too. Many argue that it has impacted negatively on four-day and Test cricket as batsmen try to score too quickly and bowlers try too many variations, but anyone who saw Ben Stokes's breathtaking innings at Headingley in the 2019 Ashes Test series will want to argue with that. Some of the skills on show in T20 cricket nowadays are astounding, especially the fielding, much of which is breathtakingly good. As per usual we in the UK seemed to be slow off the mark and missing a trick, dithering over formats, whether to enter a champions league-style play-off tournament with the other countries, opting not to go down the franchise route, and as we stumbled around the likes of India and Australia got themselves organized and made a huge domestic hit out of the format. We were left having to invent a whole new format and competition: The Hundred.

Glamorgan reached Finals' Day in 2004, at Edgbaston, where, as had become traditional now for me at major games, I spent more time out on the concourses smoking and worrying about the result than enjoying the occasion and actually watching the game. Old habits and all that. And no, I don't mean the smoking (which I gave up in 2007). I hated the big occasion when Glamorgan were playing. Not that I didn't have any faith. I just wasn't a good spectator. Dig out all of the key moments in Glamorgan's history from 1986 through to 2008 and you will doubtless have found me in a car park or back office quietly smoking, chewing my nails and waiting nervously for the final outcome.

Although not there in person that was the state I was in in June 2002 when Glamorgan went to The Oval to play a second-round knock-out NatWest tie against Surrey. This was pre-T20 but the story of the day was runs, more runs, and then even more runs. Surrey went out and smashed it from ball one. Ian Ward and Ali Brown put on 286 for the first wicket with Brown going on to hit a remarkable 268. Darren Thomas went for 108 runs in nine overs, though in typical Thomas fashion he did pick up a few wickets as well. In all, Surrey made a staggering 438 for 5 in 50 overs. We needed 8.78 an over to win. From the off. I gave it up as a bad job and went to pick Seanna and Hannah up from their child-minder. No need for nerves today, I assumed. But by the time I got home with the girls it was a very different picture. Robert Croft and David Hemp had been smashing it around too and both went on to make centuries. We were flying. Adrian Dale and Darren Thomas kept that momentum going, but Darren ran out of partners and we ended up being bowled out for 429 with a ball to spare. Just ten runs away from what would have been an incredible win. It was a monumental effort. Jacques Kallis had flown in that morning in readiness for his stint as a Welshman in the forthcoming Wales/England game. John Derrick told me he just kept shaking his head in amazement.

By then we had a very settled admin team off the field. Vicky Snook had been with us since 1989, Caryl Watkin since 1994 and Joan Pockett since 1996. With Tony Dilloway and Phil Pullin (our accountant) that was pretty much it as far as the office went. We needed to expand a little as the indoor school development proceeded but for much of the time our back-office team was limited to half a dozen. Andrew Walker had been recruited by Tony in the mid-'90s to bring the catering operation back in-house and he employed his own team on match days, including Julie, Leigh, Cath, Phil Jones and the delightful Mr Greg. Len Smith was our Head Groundsman and we had John Derrick, Alan Jones and Graham Reynolds supporting the Head Coach before John's eventual promotion to the position in 2002. We weren't a big enough operation at that stage to justify greater numbers. And it worked extremely well.

Nowadays there are academies and performance pathways, with coaches and administrators looking after all sorts of age group squads – national and regional, boys and girls. In the 1990s it was basically Tom Cartwright – an excellent judge of a cricketer and a fine coach – managing the Wales Under-16s, the senior level that Cricket Wales looked after, before they were handed over to Glamorgan, who ran the Under-17s. There were Wales teams at Under-13 and Under-15, eventually Under-11s as well (though that's too young for a Wales national squad in my humble opinion). It all worked well. Glamorgan won trophies back then. Since the pathway has become more populous, more cluttered, we don't seem to be producing as many high-quality county players, but I'm sure that will change. It's not for the want of trying.

In the outground days we used to enjoy the overnighters to North Wales. Possibly the most enjoyable outground trip had been a visit to Aberystwyth in 1989. Staged in the middle of a Championship match at Swansea, we all – players, match day staff, journalists and committee – hit the A486 and weaved our way in and out of the bank holiday traffic from Swansea. The players were staying in an hotel on the sea front; the staff billeted in halls of residence up at the University. We all just dumped our bags and headed out. None of this nipping down to the venue to have a look at the pitch or ground layout, there was beer to be drunk. The evening ended with Tony climbing up flagpoles on Aberystwyth sea front for a dare – and they were tall, these flagpoles, mark you – and six of us in the club car (which just happened to be a Mini Metro) being stopped by the police and Pauline McCarthy, one of our office staff at the time, who was driving, being breathalysed. She hadn't had very much to drink at all and also swore by an old wives' tale about swallowing a few ice cubes as a means of sobering up. Either way she comfortably passed the breathalyser test as me, Len, Tony, Dean Conway and Tom Oldknow, our Cricketcall commentator, who was supposed to have been driving but was in a worse state than the rest of us put together, all looked on, Tom through very glazed and rheumy eyes. Very unprofessional. But happy days.

When I look back, there were an awful lot of people who worked at Glamorgan over the years. In the early years – what I refer to as our 'portacabin period' – there was Sue Wood, assistant to Phil Carling, though she left less than a year after I'd arrived, which opened up all the cricket and match day admin for me to take on; and then, at various points, Sian Thomas, Shelley Williams, Jane John, Jan Herbert, Diane Parker, Freddie Wraight, another Sian Thomas, Pauline McCarthy, Caroline Rowlands, and finally the period when Vicky, Caryl and Joan gave us that settled look for a few years before we kicked on with new staff in readiness for the second phase of the ground redevelopment in the 2000s.

There were some sad moments as well, though. In the early '90s our accountant Keith Little, who had taken over from Mostyn Stacey not long previously, was found dead in an hotel in Cardiff in what were described at the time as 'bizarre circumstances'. Something to do with auto-erotic asphyxiation, we were told, but we didn't know how much truth there might have been in that. Much further down the line Andrew Jenkins, who had started in 1993 as a casual helper in what was a busy summer following the relaunched membership and the NatWest Trophy run, was to die at the tragically young age of 50 in 2008. 'Jenks' (yes, even we in the office were guilty of under-elaborate nicknames) then took over the match day running of the shop before moving onto a more permanent position supporting Phil Pullin and then Clive Franklin in accounts. He wasn't especially tolerant of fools, Andrew, and when running the shop, which was a tiny walk-in-walk-out unit in the car park opposite our portacabin offices, he would once a season sneak in a portable television so that he could watch the Open Golf on the BBC, he being a huge fan of golf. The kids would be given close to zero tolerance if they got in the way of the TV or, heaven help them, dislodged the aerial he'd spent an age correctly tuning in. He was also a passionate rugby man and a knowledgeable historian and many's the fag break we spent chewing over the politics of the day and reminiscing about political figures from days gone by. He was a highly intelligent man.

I have never seen a creature more driven by habit, though. Andrew would arrive at work at 8.44am, one minute before the allotted start time, before immediately marching into the kitchen and starting the process of making himself a cup of tea. Tea bag safely stewing in boiled water, he'd open up the patio doors of the room he was working in and light up the first of what must have been 40 of his day's cigarettes (and that's not a judgmental comment – I wouldn't have been far off him around that time myself). Fag over, he'd grab the Telegraph and off he'd go for his early morning – ahem – dump. Only <u>then</u> was the tea, by that time brewing for around a quarter of an hour, deemed ready to be drunk. Mid-morning he'd march off down nearby Cathedral Road to the nearby garage, buying more cigarettes, and a sandwich for lunch. After slaughtering his sandwich (he was a particularly noisy and aggressive eater), he'd be off for a walk through the park and into the city centre, generally leaving between 12.50pm and 12.55pm and returning somewhere in the approximate region of 1.48pm. In the evening, he'd be out of the door like a shot at 5pm and head straight to the Discovery pub in Cyncoed for four and a half pints (always 4½) before wandering back to dinner on the table at his mum and dad's around 8pm. Every day. And I mean Every. Single. Day. Dean Conway and I once met him up at the Discovery and attempted to hijack his routine with an extra drink, me at the bar while Dean held him back to stop him leaving. He almost had a fit.

As part of his job looking after the shop Andrew would join us for our annual week up in Colwyn Bay where, substitute the King's Arms in Llandudno for the Discovery, he pretty much kept up his usual Cardiff office routine. During our 1999 week on the North Wales coast, Duncan Fletcher came down to breakfast one morning complaining bitterly about the person in the hotel room next to his, whose noise had kept him awake all night. It turned out to be Jenks or, as Fletch continued to refer to him, 'the storeman', who needed the TV turned up to a ridiculously high volume just so that he could hear it. And who had then proceeded to fall asleep. But we all loved Jenks and we tolerated his many eccentricities as a result. He left Glamorgan in July 2007, the first of many Paul Russell decided would have to leave as the Club geared up for the Ashes Test it had by then been awarded. It threw him completely, however, and despite the constant support and encouragement of his close friend Andrew Walker, he quickly descended into depression and started drinking very heavily, passing away the following January. I sat back and essentially gave my approval to the decision to let him go. I don't have too many regrets in my time at Glamorgan, but that is one of the biggest. I should have seen what was likely to happen. And I should have behaved much more as Andrew Walker had.

The early 2000s weren't all bad. Despite sharing the pain of defeat at the first FA Cup Final staged in Cardiff with Adrian Dale, in the midst of a load of Liverpool fans to boot, I was privileged to be able to see Arsenal win at the Millennium Stadium in 2002 (when Adrian and I sat either side of John Derrick as we beat JD's beloved Chelsea), 2003 (with my great mate and Southampton fanatic Ty Minett) and 2005 (when we thrashed Manchester United 0-0 and then sneaked the trophy on penalties). But in my professional life things were very definitely changing. Our itinerant days had gone: the days of 'Dillers' enjoying a small bet at the mobile betting stall that turned up on those outgrounds; the girls sneaking an ice cream; of us doing the PA announcements between us; undergoing laps of the ground, enjoying the banter with members and press; it had all slowly disappeared. We were about to enter an era when the team barely seemed to matter; where all that counted was international ambition, ground redevelopment and greater commercial clout. In the early 2000s Glamorgan was a much bigger beast, with much greater pressures, and we had a Chairman coming in who was determined to make it bigger and brasher still, and hang the consequences. We would become much more corporate and, dare I say it, more professional. But for many of us, me included, things would never be quite the same again.

16   THE PERFECT COUPLE

'Sometimes, you have to step outside of the person you've been and remember the person you were meant to be. The person you want to be. The person you are.'
H. G. WELLS (The Time Machine)

Around this time my role changed and I moved well out of my comfort zone. The new chairman had lofty ambitions for the club. Together we implemented an ambitious plan to stage Ashes Test match cricket, necessitating a multi-million-pound ground redevelopment. It was exhilarating, challenging and utterly exhausting. It meant I had to change the way I did my job and I didn't like the person I was being asked to be. The last act before the axe was wielded.

Three wavy green squiggly lines and a yellow dot on a piece of paper. Our new logo, apparently. When I first clapped eyes on it, that's when I knew for certain that the Glamorgan I had grown up with and come to love was on its way out. For as long as anyone could remember our logo had been a daffodil, and it was readily identifiable as the Glamorgan logo at that. It had been modernized in time for the Club's centenary in 1988 and altered in the mid-2000s, when for commercial reasons it had been changed to a daffodil inside a cricket ball, apparently so as to make it clear we were a cricket club. As far as I was concerned, we already had a perfectly solid brand and a widely recognizable logo. But compared to what was to come a logo with a daffodil inside a cricket ball was what one might consider 'a result.'

When Paul Russell had come in as Chairman, he had set up something called an Operating Group, which comprised Chairman, Deputy Chairman, CEO and the respective department heads, including the Captain, meeting every fortnight to push the club's day to day business on. Far better than being governed by a large committee, he promised. And indeed it was. In 2007, after being allocated an Ashes Test match, we'd started to look at rebranding and when we came to start discussing the logo for once I wished it was actually the more cautious and traditional committee making the decision. It was clear that the Chairman thought our image and logo needed a complete refresh and after looking at some examples he'd asked a contact of his to knock up, he sought views from around the table about his preferred choice, the marketing drivel accompanying the proposed new design 'hinting at a contemporary fusion.' It had been his initiative to incorporate the daffodil into a cricket ball a couple of years previously, something I felt was totally unnecessary, but as it only applied to the commercial arm of the club it wasn't something I chose to go to the stake over, though I firmly believed the daffodil stood on its own without the need for any embellishment. By comparison with this new preferred design of his, though, well…

I spoke first. I loathed it. And I said so. Matt Maynard, back as Cricket Manager since the end of the previous season, agreed. Caryl Watkin, recently installed as Operations Director, also agreed. Alan Hamer, the Finance & Commercial Director, sat on the fence, as he often did when it came to any issue of potential conflict, at least until he knew what Russell's intentions were, but he expressed some reservations. Had his predecessor, Clive Franklin, been sat in the room, I know he would have been very vocal in saying he too disliked it; Clive was never shy in offering an opinion, irrespective of who his audience was. I was also sure the same opinion would have been ventured by Arthur Turner, until the previous year our Commercial Director. And on this occasion Hugh Davies, thorn in so many of our sides so often over the previous fifteen years, also agreed with us. He hated it too. I don't recall David Hemp, by then the captain, being at the meeting, but I'd have been surprised if he'd not disliked it too.

The decision? Russell told us we were all too emotionally attached to a failed past, whatever on earth that meant, and said he intended to recommend a change to the committee anyway. I have the notes from the meeting and I'm still unclear how such opposition could have resulted in such an outcome. A Trump-like disdain for process ten years before Trump. Less Operating Group than absolute autocracy. It went through the committee. Of course it did. I'm convinced they didn't want it either but they adopted their customary invertebrate position when faced with something the Chairman wanted to do. And so it was changed. And almost universally reviled until it was changed back again a few years later. It was something of a metaphor for the changing times. Other than Russell I never met anyone who was prepared to admit they liked it. It couldn't have looked less like a daffodil; it looked more like a fish drawn vertically in green crayon by a hyperactive three-year-old.

Up to my 40th birthday, life had been very good to me. I loved my job, I felt that I was good at it, I loved the people I worked with, and I had a very happy and settled personal life. But the four or five years that followed it were a real slog. Much of that was down to a complete change in the way I had to approach my job. The business was growing rapidly. In 2006 we had been allocated the Ashes Test, much to the disgust of the establishment and the London-based media, and we had a new Chairman. The two events were not unconnected. Paul Russell had taken over from Gerard Elias at the end of May 2003. Almost immediately the atmosphere around the place changed. Gerard had, as I have mentioned on a number of occasions previously, been something of an absentee chairman owing to his commitments as a barrister. And they were high profile commitments. But we enjoyed a very good relationship. He felt that it was the right time to stand down, and Russell came in with the added sweetener of providing sufficient financial clout to be able to keep the financial wolf from the door in the immediate term, so I'm sure he was right.

In his parting statement, Gerard said: "I could not leave office without a special "thank you" to our most splendid and devoted permanent staff, in the office and on the ground, so ably led by Chief Executive, Mike Fatkin. They epitomise the "family" that is Glamorgan." Nice words. Family indeed. Within five years Russell would respond to my own departure by telling the *Western Mail*: "Fans tell me the family feeling's gone. I can only say 'good'. It was a pretty dysfunctional family." Well, it wasn't when you took over, sunshine. It was a very happy place, with a winning team. Russell may have brought his own brand of professionalism. But it would come at a cost.

Straight away there was a swagger to him. What he saw was clearly not to his liking. Nothing we did was going to be good enough. I probably ought to have appreciated it might be a bumpy ride when someone told me that one of his children, sat in the committee room watching us get thumped by Derbyshire in a 50-over knock-out game not long after Russell had taken over, had been overheard saying it was 'daddy's club now.' Paul said all the right things to me but then he needed to keep me onside for a while as I would be the one to bring others into line for him. It was also obvious that we were very different beasts, leading eventually to a somewhat fractious working relationship. I'd first come across him back in the early '90s when he was one of our new Premier Club members and, of course, through his work – quite brilliant work, it has to be said – in repackaging the membership prior to the 1993 season. I hadn't taken to him back then. All bombast and narcissism. And nothing had changed when he came back in as Chairman. I couldn't take to him. And I was sure I wasn't his cup of tea either. We were from opposite sides of the personality tracks. Our work habits were very different too. I was in at the crack of dawn but liked to leave at tea-time; he would roll in late morning and work through until very late. He loved office protocol, revelling in the formality, the hierarchy, the profile; I wasn't into all that. He enjoyed the authority and status of being chairman, of people *calling* him 'chairman' – even his own son, reputedly, but quite possibly apocryphally, on one occasion – whereas I, whilst very proud of being CEO, refused to treat my title with anything more than a functional nod. Matt and I used to refer to him privately as 'TC' which he always proudly assumed came from the kids' cartoon character, *Top Cat*, whereas it was actually short for something altogether different – 'That' was the first of the two words. I'll leave the other one to your imagination.

He used to proffer advice on how to dress, how to speak in public, how to behave in certain situations, how to negotiate; pretty much anything that he believed a *real* Chief Executive should be like. I didn't mind the odd piece of advice. I'm not a bad self-reflector and he had a lot of high-level experience, after all. He was trying to be helpful, I'm sure. But the advice always seemed to arrive accompanied by a lengthy allegory, tales I grew sick of as I heard them repeated time after time after time. The cannon on the deck; the pet food conference and the sales salaries; Harold MacMillan's tailor; the pioneer with arrows in his chest as well as his back…. He even managed to tell one story twice in the same meeting. Everything was 'granulated' or 'iconic,' sentences were punctuated with management bollocks such as 'shifting the paradigm.' Members were to become 'customers', games 'match day experiences.'

If it meant compromising the way I behaved, well hey, I was all for the easy life initially and I went along with it all for a while. But the more he tried to change my role the more I began to resent it. It was clear to both of us that I just wasn't going to conform to his idea of what a CEO should be, though I didn't for one moment doubt the sincerity with which he meant some of it. Our chalk-and-cheese relationship worked for a while. And despite our issues we did achieve a lot together. But it was always an uneasy partnership. In the end, my stubbornness would cost me.

I couldn't get over the fact that so many people fawned over him so much. And how much he revelled in them doing so. Some of the General Committee members were so unctuous they may as well have had fully furnished individual apartments up his backside. He could have spouted any manner of rubbish at meetings and they'd have applauded and nodded any recommendations through. The way they behaved towards him must have made him feel positively omniscient. But the senior staff saw an altogether different side of him: impatient; intolerant; dictatorial. His ego was gargantuan. In complete contrast to his brother Marcus, incidentally. Marcus, who managed the band Oasis, amongst others, was a kind, gentle personality. I'm sure he had his moments when pushed but the difference between the two brothers seemed stark to us.

Sharing an office with Paul was quite the experience. It got to the stage when I dreaded coming in, knowing he would be driving down that day from his lord-of-the-manor-style estate in Warwickshire. Rarely dressed in anything other than navy blazer and beige slacks (I reckon at night he forewent pyjamas in favour of a blazer), one of his nuggets of advice was that I should always look in a mirror before going out to address an audience. OK, I said, I would. And I did. I saw an early middle-aged, overweight, scruffily dressed character with a squashed nose, overly hirsute eyebrows, who always seemed in critical need of a haircut. No manner of tarting up or blazer-wearing was going to change that, I thought. Russell would spend all morning regaling me with tales of his sundry accomplishments in the world of business. Whatever I did, he'd done it. Only faster, more efficiently, more dramatically, and always better. He told me he wasn't a boss who interfered. And promptly gatecrashed meetings he should have been nowhere near, taking them over, whatever the subject – often when he had no knowledge at all *of* the subject. He couldn't bear to be on the periphery of any conversation. It had to have him foursquare at the centre of it. If he wasn't, he'd engineer it so that he was. Whatever I was working on he sought to change, just because he could, or so it felt to me. On one occasion when we were considering the structure of a contract for Simon Jones, then centrally contracted by England, he instructed me to offer him over £100,000 a year. I couldn't understand why, as Simon had told me he was

305

willing to sign for quite a bit less. But no, I was instructed. I didn't see the point. It was his way of being able to boast to others that he would have been the first person to pay a player at that level. He wanted everyone to know who was in charge. Constantly. Had I at any stage contested who was in charge I might have comprehended. But I had no desire to do so, and I never did. As Chairman, he was my boss, just as Tony Lewis, David Morgan and Gerard Elias had been before him. I couldn't understand the persistent insecurity that demanded this be reinforced at every opportunity. I was never any competition.

In an effort to mould me into something like the Chief Executive he expected to have working for him he had arranged for me to undergo a leadership development course at Cranfield Management School. He said it would change my style, which he claimed was too 'folksy', which he didn't like (although he never defined it, one of the definitions of the word is 'unpretentious and informal', which I'm actually rather proud of). As things transpired, I'm not quite sure what he expected it would turn me *into*. It would have cost around £15,000 in today's money so it wasn't a throwaway investment either.

It started quite surreally. There were around 25 of us, coming together initially for a nine-day residential stay. On the first day – a Saturday – we were split into groups and told to go to certain rooms. Our group of five decamped to a room on the first floor and I gravitated towards a spot in the corner of the room by a table with a computer on it. After hearing what our team task was (something to do with Formula 1, I recall), I was deputed to do research. Mainly, I think, because I happened to be sat next to the computer. I was told in the feedback session at the end of the weekend that they'd earmarked me as a details man from that very moment. If the truth be told, for the two hours between 3 o'clock and 5 o'clock in the afternoon I was actually far more interested in how Arsenal were getting on. We'd had to hand over our mobile phones for the daytime sessions so I had sat by the computer as I reasoned it would be the only way to follow the football. True to form, I can therefore date it to 5th November 2005. We beat Sunderland 3-1, Thierry Henry bagging what is known in the game as 'a brace.' When I told them this had been the reason, I think I flummoxed them. They didn't really know what to say. I don't I was what they would have termed a textbook student, though I managed to pass straightforwardly enough at the end of the year.

It was a really interesting course, though. The group enjoyed a diverse range of characters and backgrounds and I learned an awful lot having been taken out of an environment I'd known and become comfortable with for 20 years, but in addition to showing me all sorts of different leadership traits it also taught me a lot about styles of leadership that had gone out of fashion. Autocratic, dominant, egotistical.... coincidentally all traits that many of us saw in Paul Russell as a leader. The course lasted just over a year. And it was a valuable experience. However, at the end of it the one thing I was very clear of in my mind was that I would be far truer to myself with my own personality and style of leadership, for all its faults and weaknesses, rather than trying to turn tail and leap out of character in my 40s just because the bloke I was working with didn't like some of the detail of how I went about my job. I couldn't do that. One leadership commodity I have always valued is that of authenticity and I wasn't going to put on a sustained performance, for anyone. Cranfield actually reinforced this, which probably wasn't what the Chairman had had in mind when he'd originally enrolled me.

I never felt that Paul was really in tune with the cricket. He talked a wonderful game, of course, and many people listening to him positively encouraged him to do so, plenty of them laughing sycophantically at his observations and his stories. But however erudite he was and whatever the quality of his tales I saw no evidence of any real affinity or empathy with the players or the coaches, the umpires or the groundstaff. He kept saying in meetings that he wouldn't dream of interfering in selection but the hints were always there. When the decision was taken – two years after I'd left – to sign Alviro Petersen as overseas player and captain, thus supplanting Jamie Dalrymple as skipper and going over the head of Matt Maynard, a highly respected coach who he'd personally wanted brought in, as well as being someone he claimed as a close friend of his, it was perhaps proof that deep down he wanted to be involved in cricketing decisions after all. That episode was all a bit ridiculous and the Petersen appointment heralded the beginning of a period where Glamorgan went backwards on the field at a rate of knots.

Having been Chairman in 2004, his first full season, meant the bar was set high as he came in. That was a decent Glamorgan side, one which won promotion to the first division of the County Championship, reached Twenty20 Finals Day and won the Totesport National (aka Sunday) League for a third time. But the likes of Maynard, Croft, Dale, Kasprowicz, Wallace, Thomas (Ian and Darren), Elliott, Wharf, Davies, Cosker, Harrison and Powell were hardly newbies. The side had been a while in the making. What we saw over the next few years was very ordinary by comparison. Partly this was how it was heading anyway, with the younger players coming through not being of the same high quality as the players they were replacing, but partly it was because the focus was taken away from the cricket and put very firmly onto the ground redevelopment. In Russell's eight years as Chairman, Glamorgan on the field were, not to put too fine a point on it, dreadful. He wouldn't have liked the correlation. In fairness, there was more than an element of coincidence, with the spine of what had been a really good team having to be replaced. Not easy. But the cricket was certainly nothing to write home about on his watch. It seemed to get progressively worse every year he was there, and when it did start to show signs of improving, Maynard and Dalrymple ended up leaving.

Gradually, Paul stamped his personality on the club, with all that entailed – good and bad. And there were certainly areas where it was needed. He was more than just hands-on; he was an out-and-out micro-managing executive chairman. That made for a pretty uncomfortable relationship with me as his chief executive. He didn't like me in an open plan office with the other staff, so he arranged to have the whole space partitioned, first installing me in my own office across the corridor, which I vacated on busier match days when it was sold as a hospitality box, before deciding that we should share office space, with Carys Rees, recently redeployed as his PA, also sharing the same area. So, we had me in at 7am, before he appeared late morning; me wanting to be away tea time and him expecting to work on until late. Sharing meant there was little chance of any confidentiality. My important meetings had to be held elsewhere, otherwise he'd just take them over. And when phone calls were fielded, or someone came in with a question, or looking for support for a decision, he'd be quick to disagree and try to change what had been agreed if he didn't like it. All I got back in return was the fact that he had more business experience than me. In some respects, that's difficult to argue with. But in terms of running the club, dealing with the staff, he may have *thought* he knew better, but he didn't. I was the one with the track record. I was the one with the relationships.

In late 2005 the ECB ripped up the rule book and completely changed the way that international cricket in the UK was allocated. Gone were the days of decisions taken behind closed doors, of matches being awarded based on historical precedent, of the old boy network at its mutual back-scratching worst. Instead, it promised longer term staging agreements with venues, introducing a balanced scorecard based on a range of facilities and services, such as ticket prices, crowd capacity, media accommodation, playing surface, practice pitches, transport infrastructure, team hotels, security and floodlighting. Essentially there was now an exam paper for venues to sit. Crucially for us at Glamorgan, 50% of the first such scorecard was based on the size of the financial guarantee on the table. As soon as Russell saw that, he knew that there was now a way in for Glamorgan, a way that hadn't previously existed. It would require a complete turnaround in thinking, some serious political lobbying, and the small matter of knocking down much of the ground and building a venue fit for regular international cricket, but the opportunity was now there. The door had been opened.

I remember him and I, alone in my office, one day in January 2006 as he threw out the possibility of Cardiff staging an Ashes Test match in 2009. I recall laughing. Loudly. And then realising that he was deadly serious. We'd spent the thick end of two years between us working out how best to get out of a cycle of losses by developing the venue. We'd had proposals based on on-site hotels, ice rinks and offices, all of them fraught with potential pitfalls, all of them at the mercy of a local authority planning department which had long shown a marked reluctance to allow any commercial development on the existing Sophia Gardens site: all of them ideas designed to shift the emphasis so that we wouldn't be so hopelessly reliant on domestic cricket for our income. We both knew we needed to develop an alternative income base.

As he got up from his chair, lit a cigarette and started prowling the room – always a sure sign of serious intent – he argued that the balanced scorecard gave us our most obvious exit strategy. 'Why not?' was his question. A bit like the 'What have the Romans ever done for us?' segment in the Monty Python film *Life Of* Brian, I pointed out that there were a series of pretty stark and obvious caveats and issues: we'd have to rebuild the ground, meaning we'd have to go and find the funding, this for an organization not renowned for delivering regular profits of any size, let alone significant ones; we'd have to overcome or circumvent any planning restrictions (and there were many); we'd have to find the money with which to outbid at least three of the traditional Test match-staging grounds; we'd have to persuade a membership and supporter base that investment in the team, at least for the time being, would have to go on the back-burner; hell, we may even have to start building before the ECB made any kind of decision. Oh, and we had just a month in which to submit a compelling formal bid.

But he was right. With the weight of cricket history against us, we set about trying to deal with some of those challenges. This was where Paul Russell, whatever any reservations I or anyone else had about his personality, was simply unbeatable. He divvied up the various tasks and off we went. Most of the conversations went the same way. Yes, we were serious. No, really. Yes, we did believe that this represented a fabulous opportunity. And no, we didn't think we were wasting our time. One of my jobs was to go to the Welsh Assembly Government (as it was then) and ask for financial support for the bid. I explained that if we were to even get past first base we had to blow any other bidding venue out of the water financially. It was a no-lose situation for them, I explained: if our bid was turned down it would cost them nothing; and if the ECB supported us, it would mean Cardiff would become the first new Ashes venue in the UK since Bramall Lane in Sheffield in 1902, with all the publicity and the enormous economic benefit that would bring for Wales. They warmed to the idea and agreed to our proposals.

In the meantime, Paul was working on the local authority, much the tougher sell. The same advantages would be open to them as the potential staging city but they were also being asked to support the longer-term ground redevelopment with public money and they would be under unimaginable pressure when it came to planning because of the sensitive conditions and covenants on the site. Paul also had to persuade our bankers – new bankers; we had moved from HSBC to Allied Irish – to support us. He even put a chunk of his own money in. Without the venue redevelopment Cardiff could not be awarded 'Category A' status by the ECB's major match inspection team, and without that status Test matches would continue to be a pipe dream. Only Category A venues could stage Test cricket. So the redevelopment had to come before anything else. The Council went along with it, though it was made very clear to us that planning was an independent process and they could make no promises. The risk was all with us.

We had previously drawn up plans to redevelop the venue based on the potential siting of a new ice rink at the North end of the ground, bordering Pontcanna Fields, but this had already met with any number of objections and problems. There was also a longer-term planning permission in place from Tony Dilloway and Gerard Elias's original indoor school development in 1998, on which project they had worked closely with Geoff Hunt of Arup, so there was something to work with. That permission had been granted for any future redevelopment, based on plans that had been submitted at the time. Neil Macomish of HLN Architects, who had done all the work on those plans, was asked to go against all of his creative and artistic instincts and produce a more functional design which would satisfy both the local authority planners and the ECB's criteria on capacity, covered seating, sightlines, playing and media facilities. Much of that went wholly against his own aesthetic principles. More challenging, perhaps, was the budget. Paul Edwards of Davis Langdon was tasked with putting together a design team capable of delivering all of these facilities for a bargain basement price of £9.2 million, that being the very outer limit of what we felt we could afford. It took some negotiation but he eventually got the price down from £17m to £9.2m.

Somehow the bid was pulled together and submitted within the month timescale. And it was a really professional job. The Major Match Group's (MMG's) scorecard was used as an exam paper, with us answering each question in as much detail as we could. For example, although there were only five percentage points available for hotel accommodation in bidding cities, we met with the Park Plaza and the St David's hotels in Cardiff and agreed to underwrite the discounted costs they offered us. It might only seem a small point, but it would mean we would have to be awarded five marks. No one else would have thought to do that. We made sure we would meet the minimum criteria for the press, for the players, for the capacity; we submitted innovative ticket pricing which guaranteed that youngsters would have access to the cheapest possible tickets on each day; we demonstrated how the local authority would promote and get behind the bid. And we played our main trump card in the form of a financial guarantee that we were absolutely certain none of the other non-London venues would be able to get anywhere near. We then turned to the MMG's follow up visit, rehearsing key questions and answers over and over. The Leader and Chief Executive of Cardiff Council came along on the day to demonstrate their commitment. We presented to them as 'Team Wales' on the basis of trying to leave them with no questions left unanswered. It was us at our very best. There was a lot of carping in the media and across the game afterwards, an awful lot, but the reality was that we had simply interpreted the questions and answered them in turn. We had effectively given the major match group team no option but to award us Category A status and, having decided only to bid for a single Test match for the period in question – 2009 to 2011 – and no other games, we had ensured that they had no get out or fall-back position of offering us a lesser game. It was an Ashes game or nothing. I thought that might be a risk too far but Russell argued that it would be more likely to lead to us being awarded the game. Shit or bust indeed. Again, he would be proved right.

I can recall the day the decision was made to award us an Ashes Test match in 2009. It was chaos. It was 21st April 2006, coincidentally 20 years to the day since I had walked through the rickety old gates and into the prefab Glamorgan offices to have my introductory meeting with Philip Carling. And here we were, with a Test match ground that hadn't been built yet, indeed for which we didn't even know if would get full planning permission for, but with an England/Australia Test match allocated to a venue outside England for the first time, the first new venue in the UK in over a century. It was one hell of a coup.

However, over on the other side of the Severn Bridge the news was received ever-so-slightly less enthusiastically. Paul deputed me to deal with all of the media enquiries and there were dozens and dozens of them, very few of them in any way friendly. The first question I was asked, by Radio 4's *Today* programme, was how a ground that wasn't built could stage a Test match? Listening back, I don't think I did too good a job of keeping the sarcasm out of my voice when replying that the game was three years away and if we didn't build it, we obviously wouldn't be staging it. But it was a sign of the hostility out there towards us. There were accusations of a supposed Welsh influence at ECB, with the Hampshire Chairman Rod Bransgrove reflecting on 'the silent W in ECB.' Cardiff had – still has – a deserved reputation for staging major international sporting events; the ground was a five-minute walk from the city centre; traffic management plans were spot on; the planning application had been submitted (and was approved a fortnight or so later); we had met every single element of the facilities staging criteria; the local authority and the Welsh government were 100% behind us. What it boiled down to was this: the rules were changed, we played the game according to those new rules, and we were awarded a match as a result. Others may have carped. I say that others were complacent. Why should we be apologizing? But that day I felt like the proverbial punch bag. Everyone, it seemed, was against the decision. And the media rounded on Glamorgan and Cardiff as would a hundred guns on a grouse on the glorious twelfth. It was in turn both exhilarating and exhausting.

In the space of just over a hundred days we had gone from scratching our heads over finding a way to develop the venue to help us generate new income streams to being allocated an England/Australia Test match. Even as I type those words, I find it astonishing that we did that. All in a hundred days. To determine the extent of the ambition, interpret the various elements of the balanced scorecard, persuade the politicians, arrange the planning, find the funding to support the build and for the bid, to pull it together and submit it, meet the major match group team, deliver Category A status, and then deal with the media. Incredible. And, for the record, whereas the delivery of a lot of that, and of the subsequent ground redevelopment, was down to me, there is only one person who deserves to be identified as the catalyst: Paul Russell. He had the perspicacity to see it as a viable goal and the balls of steel to go out and make it happen. I heartily commend him for that. He was outstanding. We were outstanding. Team Wales was outstanding. But without his drive the idea wouldn't have got past the starting gate.

Once the euphoria had died down the realisation dawned that we now had to go out and deliver everything. I also understood that it would almost inevitably cause enormous internal disharmony. There was no way we could squeeze the pips financially by delivering everything required in connection with staging the Test match as well as investing in the Glamorgan team. It was almost a given that the playing operation would end up suffering. And that would bring future tensions that I would have to wrestle with. Paul would argue that it was a greater risk to stay as we were but the fact was that doing all of this was an enormous risk in itself. We actually started looking at carrying out some of the demolition before we'd been given formal planning permission, a decision which, looking back, was crazy and could have blown up spectacularly in our faces. But with the world watching us after the announcement, I knew that we had to deliver. As Russell kept reminding us, the eyes of the world were on Cardiff.

The design team was set up and I was asked to work with them all on every aspect of the redevelopment project. Paul Edwards led it, with Neil Macomish and Steve Quin as the architects. The other key players were Robin Williams of Boyer Planning (as they were then, they're now Asbri); Matthew Evans of Arup as mechanical engineers; and Paul Hinam of Gallese as electrical engineers. Working with them were the appointed contractors, Carillion, through Gareth Davies, Justin Moore, Mike Baynham and Gary Smith. Others dropped in and out but these ten were the constants. Mike Baynham was my key link as site manager. Every day for as long as the project was live I spent talking to or meeting with Mike on one facet or another. Change requests were something I'd never heard of up to 2006. For thirty months they dominated my life. Any deviation from the original plan would lead to the issuing of a change request detailing the reasons for that deviation, the cost implications and the timescales. Mike did a superb job and supported me throughout.

Alongside the design team we had to develop a key relationship with the local authority, and that meant my old friend Graham Bond. He led the Council's safety advisory group and was the primary go-to on all matters relating to the safety certificate, which I had to rewrite completely, and in interpreting everything we were doing in relation to the Safety Of Sports Grounds Act. Ah, the old Green Guide. I remember it well. He and David Bond, his brother, were familiar figures as the buildings went up, along with Gareth Owen, the police match liaison officer. Gareth became a good pal and continued in a consultative role with the Club on major match days following his retirement from the force. Both he and Graham were hugely supportive of everything we did.

All the while we had a raft of people willing us to fail. Or 'the whole of England,' as we termed it. The sniping from some of the other counties, Lancashire in particular, was vitriolic, and that animosity manifested itself almost every time the Sky television cameras visited Cardiff. The Manchester commentary 'mafia' of Mike Atherton, Paul Allott and David Lloyd couldn't resist making cheap pops and generally moaning about the unfairness of it all, Atherton in particular. Not once did they pause to consider whether Lancashire hadn't themselves been a bit complacent about the whole thing or that the ECB's major match group had been the ones making the award, not Glamorgan. Others, such as David Gower and Ian Botham, supported the Hampshire bid and put us down in comparison to the work being done at the new ground down in Southampton. The likes of Charles Colville, Bob Willis and Nasser Hussain just had a pop regardless. It didn't help that on so many occasions when the cameras were there Glamorgan performed badly. It gave us something of an inferiority complex. But it also made us more determined. For the whole of the 2007 season the ground was, quite literally, a building site. We took matches across Wales, only using Sophia Gardens to bookend the season when other venues traditionally struggled to host games. In addition to more cricket at Swansea and Colwyn Bay, we returned to Abergavenny and Ebbw Vale, and there was a one-day game against Surrey at Cresselly, in Pembrokeshire, a step back in time for those of us who could remember the seasons in the late '80s when we took in venues such as Llanelli, Merthyr Tydfil, Aberystwyth and Neath.

The rebuilding work at Cardiff caused us a few pitch headaches too. Whilst it was great to be out and about again it meant we had to put our faith in more outgrounds to deliver four-day quality pitches. In May we played Middlesex at Swansea, the first of, with the benefit of hindsight, a rather ambitious programme of three Championship matches there in the space of three weeks. For any non-HQ ground this was always going to be a challenge but alternatives weren't exactly thick on the ground. 21 wickets fell on the first day, with Glamorgan bundled out for just 60 after losing the toss. The game was over inside two days and it was inevitable that the designated ECB Pitch Liaison Officer, Jack Birkenshaw, would report it, meaning, for the first and only time in my tenure as Chief Executive, an official ECB pitch panel investigation, with the potential of us losing County Championship points. The panel was chaired by former England opening batsman Chris Broad, who acted throughout as though he was annoyed at having been dragged away from the golf course and couldn't wait to get back to it. Both coaches and captains were interviewed, as well as the umpires, Jeff Evans and Trevor Jesty. Ed Smith, later Chairman of the England selectors, was Middlesex skipper. The first stock question to all of them was 'what in your opinion was a reasonable score batting first on that surface?' Smith reckoned it was around 40, and proceeded to shower congratulations on Glamorgan for beating that by a cool 50%. His patronizing tone continued as he told the panel that he didn't want Glamorgan to be docked any points. He always looked forward to his 'jaunts to the Principality', he said, adding that he'd enjoyed family holidays in West Wales as a child. Apparently he 'loved the Taffs.' Jack Birkenshaw was just managing to keep himself from laughing as he observed my own emotions going down a slightly different route. I don't often lose my temper in any context, and especially in those sorts of situations, but I was staggered by his insouciant pomposity. I started challenging him and questioning his own attitude, which just made Jack smirk even more. Broad just wanted to get home, though, so it was never going to drag on. In the end we were told we were guilty of producing a pitch with excessive turn and docked eight points. I thought that was a bit harsh as Glamorgan hadn't had a pitch reported for 20 years, but we decided not to appeal. My primary concern was the fact that we were due back at the venue the following week for another four-dayer. And another one the week after that. But thankfully both of those games passed off without any further pitch issues. My impression of the Middlesex captain, though, was of a condescending, arrogant young man, not someone I would have wanted captaining any club I was involved in, however talented he might have been as a player. The eight points were never going to make any real difference. Glamorgan finished way off the pace at the bottom of the second division anyway.

But although the adrenaline was pumping with all the outground cricket as well as everything that was going on with the ground redevelopment and the prospect of England playing Australia at Sophia Gardens a couple of years further down the line, the fault lines were beginning to appear in my relationship with Russell. He could do no wrong in the eyes of the committee, who fawned on him at every opportunity. And I could no longer fight that. It was his vision that was delivering an Ashes Test match venue. And with a large personal investment on the table, he was in as powerful a position as he ever would be.

In November 2005, Russell had decided that Arthur Turner should be offered the opportunity to take over day-to-day responsibility for cricket, moving me into a far more strategic role. Arthur had been with us for around eighteen months in a commercial role and he was a super character, a real lover of cricket, and a very honest person. I nodded my assent and vowed to make the new structure work but in truth, I disliked the idea. I could see the logic, especially as within weeks we would be bidding for a Test match, with all the high-level shenanigans that would entail, but being involved in the cricket, albeit now only from the perspective of negotiating and finalizing contracts rather than anything more detailed, was what I loved. The stadium redevelopment and the whole Ashes-to-Cardiff saga would take over my life for the final few years I was in post, but to be squeezed out like that wasn't something I wanted. It smacked of Hugh Davies trying – yet again – to get his oar in. In the end Arthur decided it wasn't for him and he chose to return home to South Africa a month before we were awarded the Test match. For me, it was a clear signal that there were moves to remove some of my responsibilities. I should have had the foresight to see what else might be coming.

Which brings us back to that daffodil logo. I was by now full-on with all things ground redevelopment. Matt Maynard was back to run the cricket, a move I welcomed, but our way of working wasn't what Russell or Davies had in mind (Hugh would have had to be persuaded long and hard before agreeing to Matt's return, I know that) and I expected there would be moves to take more of the cricket admin away from me and give it to Matt even though the pair of us had a perfectly sound idea of how to divvy everything up. But although I give Paul Russell all of the credit for spotting and exploiting the opportunity to pursue a new strategy around the change in the allocation of major matches in early 2006 and for driving everything towards our Ashes goal, including me, it was also clearly the perfect vehicle in which to drive his personality through the club. When the logo was changed Matt successfully fought to have the traditional daffodil kept on the players' clothing – blazer, sweater, shirts, caps and the like – and I applauded him for doing so. I also kept the three daffodils which we'd worked into the seating design in the main Grandstand of the Ashes redevelopment. So there were pockets of resistance. But despite almost unanimous opposition from the management team, the logo was introduced and Russell had all the non-cricket staff uniforms changed to include it. As far as he was concerned, he was demonstrating that things were changing and that he was driving those changes. The new sheriff was very firmly in town. It was the beginning of the end of 'our' Glamorgan, the first of a series of significant steps which, to my mind, ripped the very heart out of the organization.

I mention in Chapter 1 that I only subsequently came across Russell twice after he'd drummed me out of the club, both occasions in 2009. I sometimes wish I had exited in the manner of my erstwhile colleague Len Smith, our Head Groundsman. Len was a guest of John Moore's at Pentyrch Cricket Club's end-of-season dinner that same year, which was being held in the new pavilion at Sophia Gardens. As is his wont, Len was grabbing a quick cigarette before going back in to the dinner, with various people coming down the steps and out of the building past where he was stood. He was happy to shake hands with Mike Powell when Russell emerged and offered his own hand to Len, who was still chatting to Mike. When he realised who was shaking his hand he withdrew it with a flourish, saying, "Whoah! I'm not shaking hands with you, you ****." When I heard that, I thought, 'Perhaps that's how to do it, Michael.'

By the time that ridiculous squiggly line logo was ditched prior to the 2013 season, to be replaced with the traditional Glamorgan daffodil (a change that as far as I could tell was completely unmourned by anyone), I had long gone, as had virtually everyone else I had worked with at the club. Including Russell.

17 WHIRRING

'If you aren't fired with enthusiasm, you will be fired with enthusiasm.'
VINCE LOMBARDI

Talking of operating outside of one's comfort zone, my next job after leaving Glamorgan was with Welsh Netball. I knew little about the sport but quickly came to respect the people who played and ran it. This section looks at some of the challenges we had in building a team off the field, trying to help the senior team qualify again for the Commonwealth Games, and how chasing those ambitions brought me into conflict with a few of the bureaucrats at Sport Wales.

I can't say that the six months after I was shown the door by Glamorgan were particularly productive. Other than acting as a dummy run for the Coronavirus pandemic a dozen or so years down the line, they amounted to very little. After working for the same employer for 20-odd years you pick up the ebb and flow of the place, the seasonality, the personality even, and finding myself at a loose end, with no routine to speak of, was something I found incredibly difficult to adjust to. Everyone else – and bear in mind most of the people I was close to were still at the place I'd been catapulted out of – was, of course, continuing with their own daily lives, their own routines, dealing with their own issues. The mobile was hot for a few weeks – with hundreds of calls, texts and messages – but after a while it inevitably settled down. People move on.

So how to fill the time? Carol was working, so doing the school run each day became part of the new routine. I spent time sorting out the CV, looking for jobs (not with any great sense of urgency to begin with as the settlement had been sufficient for us not to be worrying too much financially in the immediate term), dusting down the contacts book, sorting out a new email address and arranging some kind of office set up. I tried to establish a routine as best I could. I imagined that would help. Out for a coffee somewhere, book in hand; go for a walk; go for a swim; pick the girls up....

One amusing story emerged just a week after I'd left the club when David Hemp held a Benefit Year function at Sophia Gardens. David Harris, the St Fagans Chairman, was conducting the auction and made a remark about there being an additional lot for the dagger that had been used to knife Mike Fatkin and Len Smith in the back with. I was told that Paul Russell got up and walked out. Presumably in disgust, as he knew the real thing was locked in a drawer in his office down the corridor.

The 2008 cricket season having been meandering to its conclusion when I left the club, Matt, Dean and many of the people working at Glamorgan had a bit more free time, so I was able to improve the golf handicap. Well, no, strike that, it's quite obviously a lie. I didn't improve the handicap at all. What I did was what I *always* do when I play golf: hacked around with some mates, hitting the occasional good shot; talked about that good shot far too much; relied most of the time on my playing partner; questioned why the f*** I bother playing such a stupid game (normally around the 12th); and then tired alarmingly around the 14th fairway before ambling back to the clubhouse and throwing back a couple of ciders. Fun, though. And it kept my mind from wandering. As did the books. It was around this time that I started reading voraciously. I'd always had a book on the go, generally a few pages before going off to sleep (often, given how tired I sometimes was, the same pages over and over again), but at this point I started *really* reading. Reading, along with music and football, is one of my three genuine passions in life.

I tried to keep myself positive, not easy for someone whose life glass has traditionally been half empty. I saw that the England and Wales Cricket Board was looking to recruit someone to work with the major international venues on operational matters, a role I thought I could bring a huge amount to, so I spoke about it to Gordon Hollins, later Somerset's CEO but at that time the primary link between the counties and the ECB, and went to meet him at a game at Edgbaston to discuss it. I never heard anything back. He wasn't interested. He barely gave me the time of day. I also went for the Chief Executive's job at Sussex, vacated after Gus Mackay had left. Their chairman, Jim May, had been very encouraging, as had Ian Gould, one of the UK's leading umpires who was still close to Sussex, one of his former counties, and I chatted to them both on several occasions. I applied, was shortlisted, and was invited for interview. It was the worst interview in the history of interviews. I was terrible. Absolutely shocking. Even had Jim been minded to offer me the position beforehand there was no way he could possibly do so after that interview. A waxwork would have performed better. I was very nervous. I tried to give the panel answers I thought they wanted to hear, rather than just relying on my track record at Glamorgan and being myself. It was a car crash of an interview, useful only as an instructional 'How Not To' film. I also knew deep down that even if I were offered the position the likelihood was that I would have ended up turning it down anyway. Despite the fact that Carol and I were finalizing our divorce I wasn't ready to up sticks and move from South Wales to Brighton. The realization dawned that if I wanted to remain in cricket, I would almost certainly have to relocate, something I didn't really want to do. I'd have to consider doing something completely different.

I went through the experience of signing on. My elder daughter Seanna was in the throes of applying for education maintenance allowance and was likely to be in receipt of a healthier sum if her father was registered as a jobseeker. So I made an appointment at Pontypridd Job Centre. During the mandatory interview I was asked if I had any qualifications. "Yes," I replied. Log pause. "Would you like to know what they are?" I asked. The clerk on the other side of the counter nearly fell off her chair. "Oh, yes, if you want to tell me, of course," she stammered, quickly turning back to the appropriate section of the form. I was reminded of the UB40 song 'One In Ten.' A number on a list indeed. It was demeaning.

In the middle of all this came the welcome distraction of a lads' week in Florida. There is a six-a-side tournament held in Sarasota every November around Thanksgiving and Dean Conway had arranged for 14 of us to spend the week out there. We had four current Glamorgan cricketers in our party – David Harrison, Michael Powell, Alex Wharf and Dean Cosker – as well as Matt Maynard. With one of Jon Rees, Huw 'Googie' Withers, Matthew Gough and Ian Williams making up a six, we'd entered a team, with a select group of squad hangers-on also making the trip. But the boys drank so much booze that the cricket became too much of a distraction. Our team of two full England internationals, three England 'A' players and one clubbie was knocked out before the semi-final stage by a team of Cayman Island exiles playing under the banner of Houston. We had a great week, though. One of those weeks that spawns a thousand stories, very few of them printable. I'm not sure I was too engaging a travelling companion, though. I was still very much in bitter-and-twisted mode, veering from angry to sulky to anxious about the future in rapid order. I'm delighted to say the bulk of the group made a return trip in 2015 and I was on much better form.

In truth, employment options were limited but in any event I wasn't ready just to dive in to the first one. The Sussex experience had confirmed for me that not only was I highly unlikely to move away from Wales but I couldn't take for granted any likelihood I would be able to find a role within cricket. That ship, as the saying goes, had probably sailed. As the weeks went by, I began to appreciate that actually my next job probably shouldn't be anything to do with cricket at all anyway. Alex Wharf had asked me to be involved in his Benefit Year, which gave me a vehicle for staying in touch – I would subsequently help out with Dean Cosker's in 2010 and Mike Powell's in 2011 as well – and I realised that this was what I wanted from cricket now: to keep my hand in peripherally, enjoying the game from the fringes, rather than being at the centre, as a career. I needed to find something different. But cricket was all I knew. I couldn't realistically pretend that the commercial, financial and selling elements of the business had been strengths of mine either; my fortes were the cricket, the operations, the people. And the county game was no longer on the lookout for people with those sorts of strengths. It was now seeking individuals with more sales and commercial nous than I possessed.

I had 20 years of working life ahead of me. What did I want to do with that time? In addition to the Cranfield leadership programme, I'd done a postgraduate diploma in Business Enterprise in 2001 at the then Glamorgan University (now the University of South Wales) and quite enjoyed the distance learning process. Matt Maynard and I had originally both enrolled on it. Elisabeth Elias, wife of former Glamorgan Chairman Gerard Elias, was involved at the university and she said there was a push to try to attract 'non-academic types' by crediting their life skills instead of obsessing about their formal qualifications, or the lack of them. Matt sounded keen to put his woodwork and maths 'O' levels to good use (a cheap jibe, I know, but he'll be smiling at it), so we went through the whole enrolment process together. They were delighted to take someone with his profile. But as I've related in an earlier passage, when push came to shove he felt it wasn't for him (even though, for the record, he would have passed without any major difficulty). I had my determined hat on and having argued hard for Matt to be given a place

I didn't want to let anyone down any further by withdrawing myself, so I ploughed on and completed it. The discipline was tough; balancing your work and home life with some studying was a challenge, but I found a method and it was only for eighteen months after all.

I began to think about some sort of qualification which might help me retrain and do something different, something away from sport. In the end I alighted on Human Resources. I had always enjoyed working with people (well, most people) but I hadn't received any formal training in it. I wasn't even sure if institutions would look particularly kindly on recruiting middle-aged men, especially an application for an advanced HR course from someone with no HR background at all. But, encouraged by my old CEO colleague Tom Richardson, I plucked up the courage to apply for a place on Glamorgan University's three-year Human Resource Management Masters course and was accepted. There was an on-site attendance requirement once a week so it made sense to stay close to home. I hadn't gone for the full-time option as it wasn't practical and I would need to get back to full employment at some stage very soon anyway. It wasn't cheap, even part time, but I looked upon it as a sound investment. And it was a Master of *Science* too: if all went well, finally I could join my scientist parents and siblings with a formal 'Sc' qualification next to my name.

In the meantime, another vacancy had come to my attention. Welsh Netball was looking for a Chief Executive to replace the outgoing Sue Holvey. A few people mentioned it to me, though they will have known that my knowledge of netball was, not to put too fine a point on it, minuscule. I hunted out Mark Frost, who having played for Glamorgan in the early 1990s and gone on to run the Cricket Board of Wales from 1999 to 2005 was by now working with Sport Wales. I had a lot of time for Mark and I valued his advice. It sounded an interesting job and it would certainly be challenging to be involved in a sport I knew little about, working on improving its profile, with a bunch of people I'd never met. On the basis that my employment options weren't exactly manifold, I decided to have a go. It had piqued my interest. I'd had a couple of interviews for other positions away from sport but on both occasions I'd been told that as a recent Chief Executive I was over-qualified for the roles I was going for. It begged the question of why on earth they were bothering interviewing me if that was the case but I kept that thought to myself. I've never understood the whole 'we think you're over-qualified' line: if your intentions are honourable and you fit the job criteria, why do people assume they know better? Do they conclude that you would become bored too easily or something? I don't get the argument. Anyway, a few folk suggested it was a step down but I didn't agree. Welsh Netball may have been a smaller organization than Glamorgan but it was facing some serious challenges, and I wouldn't have applied if I hadn't been genuinely interested. I was invited to go and talk to them and having somehow blagged my way through an interview, I was offered the job.

It was an eye-opener. I'm not sure they could have hired more of a polar opposite to the person they were replacing. Perhaps that was the attraction, I don't know. The premises comprised a second-floor suite of offices on Cathedral Road in Cardiff and the two members of staff I met on day one were, as they say, 'it'. Lyanne Fairclough (as she was then) looked after membership services and Louise Carter looked after what amounted to pretty much everything else. They'd just got rid of their performance director, there was no coach in place, no coach education lead, no community or development lead, a small and disaffected development officer team out in the field, covering some, but not all, of Wales; membership numbers were sliding; and they had just failed to qualify for the Delhi Commonwealth Games. It all looked a bit of a mess. As a non-Olympic sport, the Commonwealth Games was the peak for netballers to aim for, alongside the World Championships, so there were a lot of furrowed brows on the part of the funding providers, Sport Wales, when they'd missed out.

On the upside, they had good financial reserves. Sue had run a very tight financial ship. By the time I left four years later Wales were qualifying for Commonwealth Games and World Cups, had a performance and coaching lead, an education lead and a team of good development officers covering the whole of Wales, but all of that had come at a cost, and I ended up presiding over a significant drain to the reserves. In the world of public-funded sport, as championed by the quango that is Sport Wales, that's a huge no-no and it would result in me leaving. But at the time I started, they wanted improved performance and a better connection with members. So that's what I focused on.

I enjoyed working with Louise. She had a bit of a fiery temper if you got on the wrong side of her but we got on extremely well and I very rarely saw that side of her. Like Caryl Watkin at Glamorgan, I found her to be incredibly well organized and efficient, hardworking, full of drive and initiative, and hugely passionate about her job. She had exactingly high standards and woe betide you if you fell short of them. She certainly wasn't shy of calling a spade a spade. I liked her and she had my back throughout my time there.

I spent the first eighteen months on the road. Or it felt like that. I did close to 30,000 miles, getting to know every single nook, corner and cranny of the Welsh highway network as I rocked up at junior taster sessions, league meetings, regional AGMs, festivals and, in one case, two Women's Institute meetings in one evening. They may have run a tight financial ship, but it was soon clear why. There had been a massive disconnect between many of the members and the main office back in Cardiff, with something of a marked reluctance for people to get out and about and engage with the rank and file. By way of example, one of the development officers had gone through a full recruitment process and been in post for close to a year without once meeting anyone from the main Welsh Netball office. That might be normal in a pandemic, with all the lockdowns we ended up experiencing, but in normal times? No excuse, surely. I felt I had no choice but to nose the old VW Jetta out onto the road and pretty much stay there for a year and a half. It seemed to be the only chance we had of reeling any of these people back in. They needed some TLC. They needed someone to be listening to them. It didn't help that I knew absolutely bugger all about the sport. There was a lot of world class blagging. A hell of a lot. But I'm nothing if not a quick learner. After a year I even somehow found my way onto the management group looking after the England Netball-run Superleague competition.

The Celtic Dragons, the Welsh franchise in that competition, was struggling as well as the national side, so we agreed the priority should be for us to recruit a coach to look after the interests of both of our senior shop window squads. Developing qualified people was an issue too, so we recruited a Coach Education lead. Over the course of the first eighteen months or so we managed to put in place development officers covering each of the eight regions in which Welsh Netball operated. Performances improved, membership started to increase and we set up a series of regional forums (or should that be *fora*? – as the reader may recall from Chapter Three, I failed Latin 'O' Level twice) to bring different stakeholders together in each area. The first couple of years in the job were really exciting and highly enjoyable and I felt we were making good progress. It was a bit of a blank canvas and the job required me to try to pull people together around a plan, something I enjoyed doing.

There was one element that I found really difficult, however, and that was the procedural and bureaucratic world I seemed to have landed myself in. Nothing to do with Welsh Netball itself, though. It had its own board, comprising a group of netball stalwarts from across Wales, and I'd expected everything to be very process-driven, but it wasn't. Or at least not in the sense of being an encumbrance. The Board behaved in a far more businesslike manner than had its equivalent committee at Glamorgan Cricket. There were rules, regulations, bye laws and all sorts of other constitutional procedures, of course, and they were sticklers for following them all, but Stephanie Hazlehurst, the chair, and her fellow directors were very professional and I couldn't grumble. They largely allowed me to get on with things. We didn't have the level of funding or the commercial backing for us to be able to do everything we wanted to, but the Board was always very supportive. And the directors knew the sport far better than I did anyway. No, it was the part Sport Wales played that frustrated me. I thought they were slaves to paperwork and process. From day one I was told that netball in Wales was under scrutiny for under-performance, with the added threat that our funding would be cut further if we didn't sort it all out (and by 'it all' I refer mainly to the national team's performances and the lack of any real plan for community or regional development). It felt like we spent the whole of the first couple of years living under that threat.

The forms you had to complete when applying for your annual funding were, to me at any rate, close to unfathomable. There were more numbers than you'd find in a Shanghai telephone directory, and a host of requests for what I thought was largely irrelevant data. I also questioned whether anything was actually being *done* with this data. In year one I spent ages completing the application and was delighted to receive a grant for the following financial year only for one of our Board members to point out that it matched exactly the sum we had been told two years previously that we would be receiving. So, the following year I did the administrative equivalent of bugger all by way of homework and preparation, just adding a few numbers where required and updating a few results and player and coach names. And lo and behold, we received, to the penny, exactly the same sum of money. It didn't look particularly scientific or well thought through to me. What it looked like was a complete waste of management time. I felt that Sport Wales as an organization suffered from corporate inertia and ruled through suffocation by red tape. I fully acknowledge that it was accountable for the distribution of public money but there seemed to be very little creativity or original thought. It felt like we were being invited and encouraged to train for a 100m race only to find when we got down on our blocks that someone was busy putting out high hurdles for us to jump. And then someone else was setting them alight for us as well. There was a decent sprinkling of outstanding people across Sport Wales, of course, some of them very good at what they did and many of whom became friends, but I am afraid I didn't find it a particularly supportive environment at all. Some of their staff spoke more management jargon than I've come across anywhere else, before or since; there were so many acronyms and corporate clichés it was exhausting trying to keep up and understand what everything meant. It was as though there were a directive from on high mandating them to avoid speaking in plain English at all costs.

It was a balancing act I struggled with throughout the four years I was at Welsh Netball. I learned I had to play ball with the rules and processes that were in place. To improve, we needed to invest in personnel and programmes but it was incredibly difficult raising third party commercial income because of the low media profile of the sport. It took working right at the very heart of an overwhelmingly female-dominated sport to appreciate just how pathetic the coverage of women's sport actually was at that time. Plenty of participants and loads of interest but that translated into negligible coverage. Barely even tokenism. It's been wonderful in subsequent years to have seen the growth in coverage of women's sport in general, and to see netball enjoying far greater exposure. Not before time too. But without that coverage we were almost exclusively reliant on Sport Wales for all of our funding. And that meant dancing to their tune. I didn't like it, and the two women who chaired the organization while I was there –

Steph Hazlehurst and Catherine Lewis – had to remind me to grit my teeth and get on with it.

At one point we were asked to set ourselves some participation targets, the objective clearly being that Sport Wales wanted us to be really bullish and to try to stretch ourselves. Perfectly laudable to have some ambitious targets to go for. We had, at the time, something of the order of 8,000 paying members in one guise or another. After a full session with the staff, development team and some of the Board members, we came up with what we thought was a reasonable target of 25,000, a threefold increase, a number that would stretch us but which, with the right mix of creative ideas, energy and resources we thought we could hit over time. It would also have provided a significant uplift to our income. We felt confident that there was at least some element of science behind it too. We were told it wasn't anything like ambitious enough. We had to listen to a facilitator wheeled in by Sport Wales for an additional day's 'collaboration,' the figure he arrived at being a cool, not to mention somewhat fanciful, 500,000, representing an ever-so-slightly-more-modest-than-ours increase of 6,150%. He called it a big, hairy, audacious goal. I just called it plain bloody ridiculous. His logic was that we had seven years over which to do it (so that was OK then: insert your own sarcastic face emoji here). The science behind his reasoning, such as it was, appeared to be that there were just over three million people in Wales, half of whom were women, with half of those being, in his eyes, 'target market': either girls at school or university or adults wanting to find a means of keeping fit. That probably amounted to three quarters of a million or thereabouts, so he was presumably doing us a favour by discounting it by a further 33%. 8,000 to half a million. Yeah, right. Piece of cake. And all to be achieved with a similar spending outlay as before. Bearing in mind that whatever figure we finally settled upon we were going to be measured against for a chunk of our funding, I just felt that was bonkers. Meaningless finger-in-the-air stuff. We would be setting ourselves up to fail. Spectacularly. Sport Wales originally seemed happy to go along with it. Eventually even they accepted it was probably a bit ambitious.

At the outset the imperative was for Wales's senior team to qualify for the Commonwealth Games, having missed out on Delhi in 2010. It wasn't going to be possible to fund the recruitment of both a replacement Performance Director and a separate post of National Coach, so I pushed for the latter. I wanted someone capable of coming in and shaking the place up, someone I could then leave to manage the ins and outs of the performance side of the business, with their focus being on court and not tied to a desk in an office. We recruited Melissa Hyndman, a New Zealander who had just left her post as Fiji's coach under something of a cloud, albeit not one of her making. She came over to Cardiff with her partner, her two older children, a new born baby and a teenage stepson. Quite an entourage. But she immediately demonstrated a determination to sort the performances out. She knew her stuff and although not everyone took to her, I felt she was just the type of person to knock the top end of the game into shape. She also demonstrated something else in the first few months: she was going to be a bit of a handful.

The Celtic Dragons had been part of the Netball Superleague for several years but by and large had just made up the numbers. Results were very poor, with wins very thin on the ground, and questions were consistently being asked about whether they merited a continued place in the competition. Sport Wales made it very clear that the Dragons' continued place in Superleague was a key priority for them. Melissa's brief was to run that squad as well as the national senior squad, not as daunting as it might sound as there was a substantial player overlap between the two, and she showed over the first couple of years that as a coach she really knew what she was doing. League rules permitted the recruitment of overseas players in Superleague, so we brought a couple in (Lattysha 'Timmy' Cato from Grenada was a real hit with supporters as a goal shooter) and they started to have an effect. In 2012, Melissa's third year, the team went as far as the Superleague Grand Final and although they lost to a strong Bath side the progress in just over two years, going from what amounted to wooden spoon to silver medal, had been incredible. We sent the Wales team out to the Cook Islands on tour the same year, and they rewarded us at the end of the year with a (then) highest-ever world ranking of eighth. They'd already performed well in the World Cup in Singapore in 2011 and qualified for the Commonwealth Games in Manchester in 2014. Wales's age group squads were also back where they should be – beating Northern Ireland and Scotland consistently: the best of the rest behind England. Thanks in no small part to Melissa's coaching, we'd got ourselves back on track.

The senior players in the national squads were an integral part of that upward trajectory. They were wonderful ambassadors for sport, and for netball in particular. I have come across few, if any, sportspeople who are better role models in Welsh sport than Suzy Drane, who went on to captain the Celtic Dragons and earn over a hundred caps for the Wales senior team. She had an outstanding attitude and I continue to use her as an example of how an elite athlete should behave. Working full-time (in Suzy's case she started as one of our regional development officers before going into lecturing at Cardiff Metropolitan University), these girls trained on their own before going off to their work, or places of study, often coming together again for team sessions in the evening, with all of the matches and the travelling eating into their weekend free time or taken out of their annual leave allocation. Nia Jones was another. There were some really shining examples. Professional in everything but wage. Never a request for money. Rarely a grumble. When people talked about netball becoming a fully professional sport, which they did frequently, part of me wondered whether, if that's a road they ever went down fully, the gains would outweigh the losses. All of the players at senior Wales level make incredible sacrifices to play the sport they love. Our professional cricketers could certainly learn a few lessons from them. And let's not even begin to mention all of the financially-bloated *prima donna* male footballers out there.

All of this focus on improving elite performance was coming at a cost, however. We were spending more and more in the chase to improve standards and rankings and bring on board more members. Not only that, but towards the end of my time I felt that Melissa's rather controlling nature had begun to cast a bit of a shadow over the organization. Her and Louise, both incredibly strong personalities, didn't see eye to eye and we ended up with an office that was effectively split down the middle. That such an atmosphere was allowed to linger was my fault. We'd achieved much of what we were asked to do performance-wise. I'd worked hard on my Masters degree through that period and was mulling over what to do with that, and I took my eye off the ball at precisely the wrong time and was too slow to deal with the issues. It didn't help, either, that Melissa, whose understanding of budgets was, shall we say, more abstract than scientific, behaved as though money was no object, operating as though we were some kind of financial bottomless pit. She was clearly a heck of a good coach, but I think I allowed her too much rein when it came to some of the admin. Despite Louise's best efforts in badgering me, I didn't act on that until it was too late. Everything came to a head in the summer of 2013 when Sport Wales, unhappy about the continued erosion of our reserves, decided that perhaps my tenure might have run its course. Being honest, it probably had. My heart was no longer in it. The politics had ground me down and I was no longer as effective as I had been. It was time for a change.

I came across some passionate people while I was working in netball. Jean Foster on the board, for example, was a real force, working full time but coaching, educating and committing to netball for much of her free time; Wendy White, the President, who sadly passed away in 2017, had devoted her whole life to the sport; the development team, who were all mad about netball and wanted to make a difference – Lyn, Sarah, Anneka, Claire, Caroline and co.; Kate Peckham (then Donnelly) as our early Coach Education lead; and Catherine Lewis, who took over as chair from Steph Hazlehurst. Catherine was great company: very focused, very grounded, very direct, and very funny too. I thought both did a terrific job. Steph eased me into the role when I knew very little about anything to do with netball. Catherine also had to pick up the pieces with Sport Wales after I'd gone, when the organization would have been put back into the same special measures it had been in when I arrived. Performance levels were now in an acceptable place but we'd eaten up our reserves to get there: it was the exact opposite to when I'd come in four years previously, when we had been very solid financially but very poor on court and disengaged with our membership. However, I maintain that we couldn't deliver everything we were being expected to without a significantly increased sum of money, and that was never going to be forthcoming because the Sport Wales pot was finite and there were dozens of other competing sporting mouths to feed. We were constantly being challenged to achieve far more with less money. It was like running around a stage spinning a load of plates while people in the wings were hurling oil onto the floor you were scrambling around on.

I didn't begrudge anyone at Welsh Netball anything. They were, on the whole, good people, totally committed to the improvement of their sport, and they probably deserved better than they got from me in my last six months. I was disappointed with the

331

way it ended, though. I had flagged up for some time the fact that the business was weak when it came to financial management, something Sport Wales was aware of as one of their team attended all of our board meetings. I had also mentioned it in conversation with several of their senior managers. We didn't have a finance director or a financial strategist, either in the office or on the Board, someone who would have been able to spot and deal with the issues, though we were in the process of addressing that weakness when I went. We had an accountant who came in every month to ensure the numbers were all present and correct but he hadn't raised any concerns. In the end I thought it was typical of Sport Wales to prefer to adopt a blame-shifting, finger-pointing stance, rather than offering to work with me to sort the issues out, but I shouldn't have been too surprised. I guess I was an obvious scapegoat and we agreed it was the right time to part company. That's what the textbook said, and as they played everything by the textbook, that was always going to be the outcome.

I know when I'm at my best – motivated, engaged, energetic – and I know when I'm at my worst – isolated, detached, confrontation-avoiding – and in the final few months at Welsh Netball I was definitely closer to the latter than to the former. The summer of 2013 had been spent attempting to put together a new strategy, working with an external consultant appointed by Sport Wales, someone with whom I can't say I always saw eye to eye but who knew how to dance to the Sport Wales fiddle. I started by challenging but grew weary of all the politicking. I was also becoming a bit irritated with Melissa's 'I'm always right' approach and our relationship had become increasingly more fractious and superficial. When I start feeling a bit overwhelmed it's as though some internal switch is flicked and I start to lose interest and withdraw. I should have grabbed the initiative and gone in and sorted the bickering out and then sorted the reserves issue. That I didn't is no one's fault but mine.

When I left that September, it was a delight knowing I wouldn't have to deal any more with a few of the characters at Sport Wales (though the word 'characters' probably implies personality, which I thought one or two of them seemed successfully to have hidden well away from view). I've never come across a more bureaucratic, controlling and dogmatic organization. They seemed to have the corporate equivalent of control freakery. To thrive in that sort of environment you have to be possessed of a particular character.

I didn't fit the bill. I was better off out of it. I enjoyed my time in netball and I remain grateful to have had the opportunity and the experiences. But it was time for me, and them, to move on.

Having battled through the Masters while trying to juggle the various challenges at Welsh Netball, I was already thinking of where I wanted to go with that shiny new MSc, and those thoughts may have contributed to me switching off a bit towards the end of my time with them. I'd performed really well on the course and surprised myself by achieving a Distinction even while everything was going on in the day job. Within a couple of weeks of leaving Welsh Netball I had set up my own company – Highbury Management (for those of you who know your football, and my allegiances, it doesn't take a genius to determine the origins) – and started work as a self-employed organization and HR consultant.

One of the people I began working with was a fellow called Richard Green, someone I'd spent some time with over the previous year, including a week in South Africa where we were visiting Matt, who was coaching the Nashua Titans in Pretoria after his own falling out with Russell and parting company with Glamorgan in 2010. Rich is a larger-than-life character. He established his company – Abbey Glass – when he was in his early 20s, and it was growing rapidly when he asked me to become involved. They made one move from Pontyclun to Llantrisant just as I was starting with them, and they made another one, this time to Porth, just after I left. I've had a few very interesting years working with Rich, Angela Worgan, Helen Smallman and the team at Abbey. It was my first foray into the manufacturing sector and I found it a real eye-opener. But ultimately it came down to people. It doesn't really matter what industry you come across, people can make or break a business. Abbey Glass is no different.

As well as South Africa, Rich and I went out to St Lucia in 2014, where Matt had been invited to coach the St Lucia Zouks franchise in the Caribbean Premier League, and he was in our group when we returned to Sarasota in 2015. When we were in South Africa a couple of years previously, he'd acquired the nickname 'The Stork' when, having been discussing nicknames around the pool one evening, he confessed to never having had one. He sounded genuinely upset that he'd missed out. Matt was on his iPad as quick as a flash and came up with a photo of a stork, turning it round to show Rich and telling him, "You've got one now, butt." Long, gangly, red, radio-aerial-thin legs, beneath a largely white, occasionally pink-tinted body above. Rich is a bit of a sun warrior and his skin resembled an Arsenal kit on occasions: red raw, with occasional flashes of white. 'The Stork' had taken wing. That was our second trip to South Africa. I'd visited with friends Matthew Gough and Andrew Walker the previous year. Well, if one of your mates ends up coaching in South Africa or the Caribbean, why wouldn't you make the effort to visit him?

By now Carol and I had split up and I had bought a place in Cardiff. We drifted apart and although it was a tough time for us both – packing my stuff up and moving away from the two girls was one of the most heartbreaking days of my life – we ensured that we didn't fall out and we remain very good friends and see a lot of each other. I still blame myself for not trying harder at the time to make it work, but work was so frantic, and perhaps it wouldn't have made any difference. These things happen. My work routine changed too. I was now supporting different companies and individuals, choosing those I worked with, when, and for how long. The pace slowed a touch, the everyday pressure becoming that little bit easier to deal with as I was in control of the work I was taking on.

After my initial stint working with Rich Green ended, I enjoyed building up an equally good relationship with Richard Gambling and his management team (Michaela, Tim and James) at GRM Windows, where he is Owner and Managing Director. Richard is a lovely bloke, a fanatical cyclist (despite a couple of horrific riding accidents, he has yet to be put off), and although it was demanding working our way through a number of complex and different strategic and personnel challenges, he managed to retain his sense of humour throughout and I still help the company out, albeit now at more of a distance. I enjoy those kinds of relationships, where I am able to do some mentoring and coaching as well as looking at the practical elements of helping put a business plan and management team in place before stepping back. I struggle with the cycling chat though. Not a topic I'm too well-versed in. Or too interested in, for that matter.

I've also done quite a bit of performance management work, one of my favourite clients being Jon Rees and his team at Carston Accountants, who have offices in Cardiff and London. I really like that sort of work. I enjoy seeing how people can be opened up,

334

challenged and developed. Not everyone is responsive, of course, but it's great to come across those who are, those who want to learn, improve and push themselves. It's rewarding to see them progressing and to see those managing them developing their own people skills as part of the same process. I look back at the people who have supported and helped me with my own career – you'll have met them all at various stages in this publication – and I try to apply practical examples to the conversations I have with the individuals I work with, both good and bad. I like being able to explain that making mistakes is normal, illustrating this with the many and varied mistakes of my own. One of the most important lessons I try to pass on is that we should all take ownership: of decisions; of projects or jobs; of our careers; of our mistakes. Authenticity is important to me, as I have mentioned elsewhere. I prize humility, loyalty and integrity too. I also believe that you can get more from people if you are able occasionally to glimpse their vulnerable side and they yours. I'm not a believer that you should never show vulnerability to people. Be yourself, however your emotions are aligning. If you're struggling, or need help, or want to know something, say so. Ask. If you feel you can't, it may say more about the environment you're operating in than it does about you.

The Masters degree taught me such a lot. As well as employment law and all the technical HR stuff there were some real game-changers, one of which was opening a window onto the wide world of psychometric testing. But I learned so much about myself as I went through the process. Working full-time I had to fit in the dozen or so assignments, all the cramming for exams and the lengthy research project around my job. I was also doing it while going through a divorce and moving out to live on my own, which taken together added up to a particularly challenging time. But I'm sure that helped me channel all of my energy into studying. I resolved that I would throw myself into the first assignment and whatever mark I was awarded for that would be my benchmark for the three years. I duly scored 72%, which was in Distinction territory. And I'm proud of the fact that in the other 11 assignments I managed ten 70%+ marks, including for my exam results and for the research project, in which I focused on performance appraisals in professional sport. Fascinating reading, that project, by the way – I still have several copies available should anyone be interested. Recommended for insomniacs everywhere. Don't all rush at once.

335

Revisiting the whole examination process was a huge culture shock. Filing into the sports hall up at Glamorgan University for the first time at the end of year one brought back many memories, none of them positive. I was allocated seat A2, right at the front, just one desk away from the main entrance. It all came flooding back: the coughing and spluttering around the hall; the invigilators wandering up and down the aisles; the requests for more paper, or to go to the loo, or to get something from a bag or rucksack at the front of the hall (if you could find yours – there were hundreds of them); and something I'd forgotten – after the half an hour minimum, the mini-exodus from all those who didn't want to be there or were struggling. I froze for a little while. It wasn't the subject matter or any lack of preparation, it was the process, the rekindling of the whole nervous experience. It was 30 years since I'd been through it, after all, and being a mere two yards away from the main entrance and exit hardly aided the powers of concentration. Unlike at school, though, I had revised hard and once I got going, I knew I was going to be fine. How I wish I'd worked as hard back at school and at Trent Poly as I did for that Masters degree. Though as I told my Mum, who'd been so disappointed that I hadn't attacked 'O' Levels and 'A' Levels with the same vigour, you're only as good as your last performance.

My decision to go back to university provided me with the perfect kick up the backside just when I needed it. It fired up my enthusiasm and confidence just as it was beginning to wane and my drive and motivation had started flagging, and it opened a door to a new career I couldn't possibly have envisaged in the summer of 2008 just before Paul Russell decided he'd had enough of me. Without that degree, I'm not sure where I would have ended up. Still scrambling around trying to find a job somewhere on the edge of sport, probably. The degree brought with it full membership of the Chartered Institute of Personnel and Development (CIPD), which badge of accreditation enables me to practice the work that I now do. By the winter of 2013 I'd moved completely away from sporting governing bodies, away from full-time sport, and away from full-time permanent employment. Life within my own personal bubble had changed irrevocably too.

336

18 ABSENT FRIENDS

'Watson. Come at once if convenient. If inconvenient, come all the same.'
ARTHUR CONAN DOYLE (Adventure of the Creeping Man)

One minute you're strolling through life, enjoying the variety of colours and sounds, and the next minute you're brought to a shuddering standstill, everything around you suddenly transformed into black and white. That's how it felt the day Tom Maynard was tragically killed. This chapter tells of how that tragedy brought the best out of me in what were ridiculously trying times for his family. It also relates how the Tom Maynard Trust emerged in its wake as a force for good.

At this point the narrative, such as it is, stumbles a little. We were probably heading in the general direction of 'a bit more serious than before' in the last couple of chapters but we're definitely looking at a different style for this one, as will become clear. I'm far more at home writing in a jocular style, taking the mickey out of people – especially myself – but as several bosses and contemporaries of mine over the years are only too aware, that somewhat nervy, crack-a-joke-to-relieve-the-tension approach just doesn't work in certain circumstances. Something I've learned to my cost. And here is one of those situations. Serious head on.

It's 18th June 2012. A fairly typical Monday morning in the Welsh Netball offices in Sophia Gardens. Louise Carter, our Office Manager is, as always, first into the office after the weekend and, kettle boiled and a strong black coffee at the ready, I'm in the process of firing up the computer to check emails and see what the day and the week has in store. Before I'd had the opportunity to get my teeth into any work, though, the phone rang, Dean Conway's number coming up on the screen.

"Morning Mike," I heard him say, not picking up immediately on the fact that instead of 'Clampy,' 'butt,' or, better still, 'f***face,' Dean has used my actual name to address me. "Are you sitting down?" he asked, somewhat cryptically, and with an unusually serious tone to his voice.

"Why?" I replied, obviously with no inkling of anything other than the anticipated standard piss-take about to come my way.

He got straight to the point.

"Not sure if you've heard but Tom Maynard's been involved an accident up in London. We're not a hundred per cent sure exactly what's happened. The police aren't saying very much. But from what we can gather, he's dead."

Although I can't remember exactly what I said in reply, I do know that at this point I did sit down. We exchanged a few more words, more in mutual disbelief than anything, but what Dean knew was pretty sketchy. He was at that point doing some physio work with Surrey so he would have the ear of those who would be in the know. But apart from the fact that the family had been contacted he didn't know a lot else. And, of course, in a situation like this it isn't at all clear how you are supposed to behave. We agreed to talk later that morning.

Fifteen minutes later I rang him back. We couldn't just sit there and do nothing, I argued, we needed at least to offer to help. Dean had come to the same conclusion. He came round to our offices in Sophia Gardens an hour or so later and we headed for Matt and Sue's up in Pentyrch. I don't really know what I expected we would be able to achieve. I'm not too sure Dean did either. We weren't even sure they'd welcome any visitors. I don't know if I would have done. If I'm honest I don't recall too much more about the specifics of that day, other than a vivid recall of the scene greeting us: family members predictably in complete shock and in floods of tears, the news on the TV on in the background with the lead story about Tom. It was all so surreal.

Instinct took over, I guess. We offered to do what we could. Anything. We weren't sure at that point what that might end up looking like but we knew there would be plenty of ways we could take some of the pressure off Matt and Sue. In the first couple of days there wasn't a lot. It was just a question of being around, comforting them, letting them vent or running the odd errand. We were also able to act as vehicles through which others could make contact, the pair of us filtering requests and dealing with those that we didn't think the family should be bothered with. I think the two of us were up there every day until the funeral, which took place in Llandaff Cathedral well over a fortnight later. Each day we tried to take away some of the more petty, non-family logistical jobs to save Matt or Sue having to deal with them. Many of these centred around dealing with Surrey and Glamorgan, the two counties Tom had played for, and we positioned ourselves as a pair of buffers (that's with a b, not a d...) for the family so they could use us to shield them from calls and emails from journalists and others. I appreciate that the media has a job to do but it was during those dark days in the second half of that June I began to realise just what a highly intrusive and impersonal profession journalism can actually be. Those cricket writers who knew Matt were very respectful, but some of the sensationalistic nonsense some of the news journalists were coming up with was highly personal and much of it insensitive and offensive. I well remember a row with one writer (I use the word 'writer' here advisedly – guttersnipe would have been more appropriate) who was arguing about it 'being in the public interest.' If he'd have been within range, I'd have punched his lights out. Some of the stuff that appeared in the days following was just lurid sensationalism. And very little of it anywhere close to being in the public interest. As if grieving for the loss of one of your children wasn't enough to have to contend with. I hoped the family wasn't looking. I suspect they probably couldn't help themselves. And knowing that upset me more.

In short, Dean and I just tried to take away some of the crap. It's what mates do. Our friend Andrew Walker was also very prominent and supportive, as was John Derrick on the day of the funeral. We didn't have a textbook we could readily pull off the shelf and follow. We just did what we thought was right, what we were asked, and what we thought the family would want us to do. Clearly, they had far more challenging issues to deal with in simply coming to terms with what had happened. Even now, years on, I cannot imagine the pain they must have been going through. I'd grumbled to anyone who had been prepared to listen (and many who weren't) about being booted out of Glamorgan, or about the pain and hassle of a divorce. But these were meaningless issues when compared with the trauma the Maynard family was having to contend with. It actually doesn't matter what the circumstances are: no parent should expect to see his or her child predecease them. History somehow contrived to repeat itself in February 2020, when Steve and Jane James's daughter Bethan was taken ill and died suddenly at the age of just 21. That those friends of his and the wider Glamorgan family had experienced something like this before didn't lessen the grief. If anything it probably made it worse. Because we knew exactly what the family would be going through. Such tragedies are a terrible reminder of the fragility of life. My heart went out to Steve and Jane and to their son Rhys.

Tom was a lovely lad. Oh, I'm sure he could be a bit of a rogue at times, but isn't that true of so many young men? I know I could be a bit of a tearaway when I was in my teens and early 20s. I remember him from the days when he'd come down to the ground at Sophia Gardens with Matt, hitting balls on the edge of the field from a very early age. And you had to beware: once you were roped in to offering throwdowns for him, you would struggle to get away. He loved it. We often watched knowingly as unsuspecting folk were lured into playing cricket with him on the outfield. We shook our heads and smiled wryly, aware that they were going to be there for a very, very long time indeed. Tom developed into an impressive young man, and an extremely talented sportsman in his own right. Who knows how far he might have gone in the game? His personality was infectious and he had a very wide circle of friends. I was incredibly proud of him for the way he handled himself after Matt had effectively been driven out of the Director of Cricket role at Glamorgan a couple of years earlier. Tom made it very obvious to Paul Russell and Alan Hamer that he couldn't be expected to continue working under a regime that had undermined his father in such a public way and he argued for and then negotiated a move, eventually choosing to join Surrey, where he was making a real mark at the time of his death. He didn't take any crap from them, making it abundantly clear that he expected to be allowed to move on without opposition.

On the day of the funeral itself our aim was simply for the family to get through the day with as little fuss as possible. They were on autopilot anyway, as would anyone had they been unfortunate enough to have found themselves in their shoes. There were over a thousand people at Llandaff Cathedral on the day. Both Glamorgan and Surrey were well-represented and there were people coming in from all over the place to pay their respects. We had the odd awkward run-in. The ECB Chief Executive arrived late and asked where he was expected to sit. John Derrick had to pull me away as I started to point out – probably a bit too forcefully – that it was a family funeral, not a corporate business lunch with a seating plan for ego-driven executives. I shouldn't have been so snappy but it was pretty stressful for us as well and it was probably just in there waiting to come out. I sought him out later and apologized. Hugh Morris spoke on the day about Tom's cricket. Mark Wallace, an old team-mate of Tom's, also spoke. Both were superb. I stood up at my Mum's funeral a few years later and said a few words on behalf of my sister and brother. Or at least I tried to. What actually happened was that I completely went to pieces and it took me an absolute age to finish. I had practiced, but it's different when you're being asked to read a eulogy with your Mum's coffin only a few feet away. In a parallel universe I'm probably still there, burbling away. Hugh and Mark held it together really well. You can't underestimate how tough that would have been for them.

The wake took place at Pentyrch Rugby & Cricket Club just down the road from the Maynard family home. The place was absolutely heaving. I hope it showed the family what Tom meant to people. Afterwards, when the public fuss had started to die down a little, I continued to pop in every day. Dean was a frequent visitor too. To us it was a gesture, something automatic you just do. I was working in Llantrisant much of the time around then and Pentyrch wasn't too far out of the way. But I know that Matt and Sue appreciated it and I'm pretty certain they would have done exactly the same for me. It was an horrific time for them. An impossibly difficult time. How do you start to move on when you have no idea where you're supposed to go?

A month or so later, Martyn Ryan, a mutual friend of ours, suggested that establishing a charity in Tom's memory might be a good way to help the family channel their energies, keep his name alive and to try to raise some funds in the process. We did some research and settled on some objects that would involve supporting young cricketers between the ages of 16 and 24, an age when the tiniest bit of support can help them live their dreams, as Matt had always said that Tom was doing. I particularly liked the fact that the striking Trust logo was designed by his sister Ceri.

These aims eventually expanded, as we were told they inevitably would, into other areas. We decided that in addition to awarding individual grants we would extend our remit to support education and career transition programmes in cricket, and to widen that to other sports. Over the next few years, we agreed to sponsor the Professional Cricketers' Association's Rookie Camp, where first year contracted professionals across the 18 counties are invited to a special day with presentations and discussions on every topic – from agents and contracts to finance and pensions, from anti-corruption to social media. That concept was replicated by the Rugby Players' Association in England, with their Academy Induction Day, which we have supported for a number of years too. And we have helped with career and personal development programmes run by the Welsh Rugby Players' Association, Rugby Players Ireland, the Professional Footballers' Association in both England and Scotland, the Rugby League Players' Association, the Ladies European Tour Golf, the Netball Players' Association and horse racing's Jockeys' Education and Training Scheme. There has also been support for the Professional Players' Federation, the umbrella body for players' associations across all of the different sports by sponsoring the Mental Health Charter for Sport, another area we saw as natural territory for us, and more recently their annual Careers Transition Week.

All of this good work helps to educate young sportspeople, who are at an age where they consider themselves to be a bit bombproof; in a place where they feel nothing bad could possibly happen to them. The Tom Maynard Trust helps to make them aware that careers do unfortunately get cut short for a whole host of reasons and that some planning is always prudent. These youngsters are living very firmly in a bubble in which all they want to do is enjoy life, play sport and work hard to get to the top, but the pathway they're following is littered with potential pitfalls nonetheless. Important issues such as financial mapping, personal branding or post-sport career development understandably tend to be put on the backburner. At their age they're just playing their sport with their mates. They're not thinking about mental health awareness, pensions, gambling responsibly or any of these other challenges. Our support helps the different associations to point all these trip-wires out, to help the young men and women negotiate and navigate their way over them and to be there in terms of offering ongoing support. They all do a cracking job for their members and we (I am one of five Trustees and do much of the administrative work) are all privileged to be able to help them.

Our original plan was for the Trust to operate for 55 months (55 being Tom's squad number at Surrey) or when we had managed to raise £250,000, whichever came sooner. We smashed that figure a few years in so we kept it going. In its first nine years it had given out well over twice that amount and in addition to the grants and the education projects we also ran five annual Tom Maynard Academy cohorts in Spain. Supported by a charity close to Jamie Dalrymple, Matt's captain at Glamorgan when he was Director of Cricket, 50-odd young professional and aspiring professional cricketers enjoyed the benefit of warm weather training and practice in Spain working with Matt, Ian Harvey and the likes of Mark Wallace, Paul Nixon and Mark Garaway. I've gone along, largely in a management 'I've got the cheque book' capacity, and enjoyed their company as well, as has Dean, all of us supported by our local, Tottenham-supporting 'man on the ground', Andy House. I'm not sure I added too much to the enterprise but it was fun, and it was good to see the best of the charity in action. Some seriously good cricketers have come through that programme, 45 of them current or future county players, including a trio of full England international cricketers in Tom Curran, Ben Duckett and Lewis Gregory. They were informative but fun weeks and I learned a lot about Matt's coaching philosophy by watching him at work close up. He had clearly picked up a heck of a lot on his own coaching journey and he puts it across well. I can imagine responding positively to his coaching and management style as one of the youngsters on those programmes. But (he says with a smile on his face) as I'm in my 50s and have known him for 35 years, I don't have to listen to him these days if I don't want to.

In August 2012 we held our opening Trust 'fundraising event,' a two-day bike ride from Sophia Gardens in Cardiff to the Kia Oval in London, linking the two counties Tom played for. Many of Tom's former team-mates took part, as did Matt himself, along with the likes of Andrew Flintoff, the group's arrival at the Oval being timed to coincide with the scheduled start of a televised one-day match between Surrey and Glamorgan. The England and Wales Cricket Board had given a special one-off dispensation for all of the Glamorgan team members to wear shirts with 'MAYNARD 33' on them, with the home players wearing shirts with 'TLM 55' on the back. It was all very poignant and emotional. (As I was when I was given my Glamorgan life membership and discovered that my official membership number was 3355.)

As the cyclists came into the ground just before the start of the game, the big screen on the ground showcased a short video of Tom, accompanied by the Stereophonics' *Dakota*. Heaven knows what emotions would have been going through the heads of Sue, Pat and Ceri and especially Matt, who was on the outfield and had Sky's TV cameras trained on him and his face up on the Oval big screen. I was in bits up in the corporate box we were in. Everyone who mattered was there. Except one. As the French writer and politician Alphonse de Lamartine once said, "Sometimes, when one person is missing, the whole world seems depopulated."

The following day the Maynards departed for South Africa, where Matt was in his second season coaching the Nashua Titans in Centurion. I had mixed emotions about the family going away for six months. Part of me thought that the three of them would be in the best place they could be, miles away from home and therefore unlikely to be pestered by journalists or anyone else. But another part felt that the isolation couldn't possibly do them any good; that they'd be left alone for far too long with their thoughts, with no one in their close circle to offload to. That really worried me. Coaching-wise, Matt would have something to channel his emotions into and, predictably, the players there loved him. But Sue and Ceri were on their tod without that distraction. It was upsetting thinking about them alone out there. Andrew Walker, Matthew Gough and I had visited them for a week earlier in the year and had a great time, and Rich Green and I decided we'd do the same the following February. Those two trips were equally memorable but my they were seriously contrasting ones. The first was a hoot; second one, with Rich, was filled with a lot of laughter but understandably punctuated by plenty of tears too. But it was good to be able to offer them our support, even briefly.

I know I'm ridiculously biased. Matt is one of my closest friends. The Maynards, or the 'Farmyards' as a few of us affectionately refer to them, are a wonderful family. I think the world of them. They've always been so open and accommodating, friendly and welcoming, and I don't know anyone who has ever said anything different. Sue is lovely, one of the warmest people you could ever wish to meet, a constant and fierce supporter of all those in her close circle, and possessed of an endless bank of goodwill and integrity and tolerance. Ceri has had to shoulder her own burden as Tom's sister and although people immediately think of Matt and Sue when they recall their terrible loss, it's easy to forget the fact that Ceri has suffered and struggled just as much. She's outwardly a tough nut but it doesn't matter what your external demeanour is, you don't take something like losing a sibling without facing your own personal demons and I know there have been many dark days for her too. I'm proud of the way she has carried herself and worked hard in recent years to develop her career. She's a good 'un. She has definitely inherited her father's loyalty, stubbornness and determination. For the Trust, she's done a mountain trek in Borneo (with Ed Jackson, one of Tom's close pals at Millfield, who later became paralysed after a swimming accident but who has fought back from it so determinedly). She has also done a 'Tough Mudder' with a dozen of her friends – one of those madcap endurance obstacle courses with everything human nature can throw at you, all of it grimy and grubby. And in 2017 she joined Matt on the third 'Big Bike Ride,' which the Trust organized in conjunction with the Professional Cricketers' Association. The first two of these were from Durham to Lord's (via Leeds, Manchester and Nottingham) in 2013 and then from Truro to The Oval (this time via Instow, Taunton, Southampton and Brighton) in 2015. On this third occasion, which we agreed would be the last one, we wanted to link Edgbaston, where the PCA had been founded 50 years previously, with Cardiff, where the Tom Maynard Trust was based. To make it 'go the distance' we needed more miles than the 108 separating the two cities so we plotted a route that headed north to Sheffield and took in Nantwich, Worcester and Monmouth along the way. It was fitting that the penultimate stop, where everyone gathered so that they could ride the final few miles together, was St Fagans Cricket Club, where Matt and Tom played so much of their formative cricket. The Club, led by Dave Harris and Jane and Rob John, continue to organize fundraisers for the Trust each year, with speakers and an auction, the day hosted originally by the incomparable Richard Adler, a really good friend to both Matt and me, and, more recently, by Mark Wallace. Ceri showed the Maynard family grit and spirit by completing the whole thing. Never in doubt. She subsequently joined her dad on a joint Three Peaks walking challenge in 2019, again working alongside the PCA for their Professional Cricketers' Trust charity, and nailed that too.

I really enjoyed helping with the ride organization, though it didn't always feel quite like enjoyment at the time. Partnering with the indefatigable Ali Prosser of the PCA (along with Caryl Watkin, Louise Carter and two of the ECB's finest – Medha Laud, the England Team Administrator, and Janet Fisher, the Administration Manager –

one of the five genuine organizational wonders it's been my pleasure to work with) we attacked everything on the second and third rides – from hotel accommodation, kit provision, publicity, test routes, support vehicles, mechanics, and arranging to stop at small local cricket clubs for tea and lunch breaks along the way. All bar one of them did so for free too. And not 'attacked' literally, obviously. There was a real sense of achievement seeing the money come in and between us, before costs, the two charities raised well over a third of a million pounds on those three rides. The camaraderie along the way was fantastic. I think the riders were all nuts choosing to ride 400+ miles up hill and down dale ostensibly for pleasure purposes, but they seemed to love it and, especially, to enjoy moaning about it. There is a steely masochism to cyclists, I find, where the rule appears to be that the more they moan, the more they enjoyed it. Though I do manage to switch off when the talk turns to cleats, Garmins and lycra, something I also have to pull Richard Gambling at GRM, another cycling obsessive, up on. Apropos of nothing, why do people post maps of their rides all over social media? I really don't get that. By all means be proud of what you've done, and feel free to keep a record of it. But the rest of us are really not interested. You must know that, surely. I took to posting occasional hand-drawn 'Saturday Strava' maps – me going to the shops to buy a Guardian or a pie and a loaf of bread, me heading to the pub, that sort of thing – showing distance walked, calories in and out, and other nonsense. I know Jim Allenby loved them. No, I can't say cycling talk grabs me. And it never will.

The original plan was that the Trust would occupy me for one day a week. It's always been more. But that was never going to be a problem. It really is a privilege to do it, to be able to help the family and to keep Tom's name alive as well as supporting so many young sportspeople as they try to live their own dreams. It has also kept me in contact with cricket and elite cricketers. For example, the Academy we ran from 2014 to 2018 enabled me to get to know the likes of Paul Nixon, Gary Metcalfe and Mark Garaway, as well as getting to know Mark Wallace better and in a more informal and collaborative capacity than just cricketer-to-CEO from back in our Glamorgan days. Prior to the Academy concept I'd only heard of Ian Harvey by playing reputation – and as the poor sod who was overlooked for the Man of the Match award in the 2000 Benson & Hedges Cup Final despite taking five wickets and ending up on the winning side. I love 'Harv.' Before meeting him my idea of a typical Aussie was pretty much an identikit of Jimmy Maher: brash; outgoing; funny; enjoys a beer, a smoke and a bet. Harv is most of these too. Clearly a hugely talented cricketer and, by then, coach too, he is also one of the most generous and loyal people I've ever come across. A diamond. He loves Matt and shares his philosophy on the game. It was a perfect fit. And we had the perfect management team for those Academy weeks. We said we would run the project for five years, and that is what we did. Ten days in Southern Spain where a dozen young, aspiring pro cricketers from different counties and backgrounds come together – most never having met any of the others – to work on their individual skills and to practice together before a couple of T20 matches against a Spanish select team. Each year I loved watching the group dynamic develop, from a series of nervous and reticent preliminary encounters at Birmingham airport through to the last night's group Karaoke singsong at La Manga as they forged bonds for life. It's great to know that in its own small way the Trust set up in young Tom's name has helped 50-odd young cricketers to develop as players and as human beings. I was sad when we decided to call a halt to it in 2018 but it had a shelf life and it was the right decision.

There has been a lot written and said about the circumstances of how Tom died. That's not really any of my business and I certainly wouldn't be wanting to elaborate here on what happened even if it was. I don't know what sort of environment there was at Surrey back in 2012. I'm way too removed from that. I also don't know what sort of impact moving from Cardiff up to London may have had on Tom's own behaviour. One can only speculate, and that's often dangerous. But I do find it difficult to fathom, if some of the allegations that were floating around at the time were to be believed, how no one in that dressing room had any notion that the culture wasn't quite what it ought to be, or how no one seemed prepared to speak up if they did. I don't know about you, but I've always been reasonably aware of the culture of the workplace I'm operating in. I'd say most people are. Certainly, in a professional sport such as cricket, where individuals are living in each other's pockets pretty much day-to-day for weeks and months on a stretch, they ought to be. Yet somewhat conveniently everyone seemed to agree that they hadn't had any inkling of anything at all being out of the ordinary. I can remember following the inquest into Tom's death in the news the following February and being shocked at some of the things that were being said, at some claims being made. I'll be honest: I thought a couple of Tom's supposedly close friends hung his reputation out to dry with some of their denials, but then I wasn't there and I can't possibly know everything that went on, and anyway, to me it said more about them than it did about Tom. Yes, he made some bad choices. Most young men do. But I can scarcely believe he was making those choices all on his own, unbeknownst to anyone in his immediate circle. I know my friends well enough to appreciate that if I'm out of line or misbehaving, I'll be pulled up for it. That's what friends do, especially those purporting to be close to you. If those pals of Tom's can look themselves in the mirror and say categorically that they didn't let him down with some of their comments, then they're better men than I am.

The manner of Tom's death certainly doesn't define him. It's hard for me to look back and remember him with anything but a smile. I can't imagine how I would react if anything similar befell Seanna or Hannah. You just don't expect it, and so you can't possibly plan for it. Those days immediately after it happened are a blur. At the time it probably seemed to Matt, Sue and Ceri that they would never be able to escape what is the worst kind of nightmare. I know how I reacted when I took that call from Dean – try multiplying that a million times and you still probably won't come remotely close. I don't suppose that even now, years later, they can go even a short period of time without Tom being somewhere in their thoughts. The pain of him not being there with them will always be present, either overtly or subconsciously following the tiniest and most tenuous of triggers. It will be exactly the same for Steve and Jane James with Bethan, just that they're earlier on in the grieving process. But with the passage of time, I hope the memories have begun to feel that little bit warmer and that time is enabling them perhaps just to deal with the emotion of it all that little bit better. Matt and Sue have learned to live with it, even if they can never forget it, and if the Trust has helped them channel some of their inner feelings – be it the challenge of fundraising or knowing that the work being done in his name is making a difference to so many people who were of a similar age and aspiring to a similar dream to Tom – then it will have fulfilled its purpose.

My work with the Trust, allied to regular contract work I've undertaken for a variety of other friends and businesses – Abbey Glass, GRM Windows, Glamorgan Cricket (yep, again, this time a short-term contract personality profiling each of the players, which was fascinating), SBL Carston Accountants and the Professional Players' Federation have been the main clients) – has been really good for me and, I hope, for them too. I also look after the admin for the Glamorgan Former Players' Association, which keeps me in touch with all of them and is a joy to do. I can do a full five-day week if I want to or if a project demands but probably average out between three and four days a week. It allows me to pick and choose work based on what interests me, which at my – ahem – advancing years is important. And although it means I have to be pretty dextrous and responsive, and it puts a lot of pressure on my time management and the discipline of working in my own office, I don't worry or figuratively take that work home with me on anything like the scale that I used to. 'Taking work home' in my case only means moving from one room of the flat to another, so it's a futile energy and I'm glad it doesn't apply. Inwardly I have always been a bit of a worrier and my glass is generally more half empty than half full. You'd think it might have the opposite effect but being my own boss has in fact helped to reduce my anxiety. I don't sit on the sofa of an evening worrying about work, sweating the small stuff. It's enabled me to compartmentalize so much better. I wish I'd made the move sooner.

It's only in relatively recent times that the issue of mental health has moved up the agenda in terms of the importance we attach to it, and rightly so. I'm not talking about the ordinary pressures, strains and stresses of life, the ups and downs we all experience, which are often used as a surrogate for genuine mental health problems. We all face those. No, I mean real mental health problems that affect the way we go about our everyday lives. I've known several people who have been seriously affected by anxiety and depression and I appreciate the difference between those problems and the everyday bumps in the road we have to navigate. I'm fortunate that I've never suffered from serious issues but I do experience occasional lows and there were periods during the Coronavirus pandemic and the various lockdowns when, living on my own and separated from my family and friends, I had to keep cajoling myself to shuffle through from day to day, week to week. It was tough going for many people. I'm lucky that I can now recognize the triggers and can clearly identify the signs that herald a downward swing. I touched on this in the last chapter but when I go into denial about something, when I'm withdrawn or detach myself, when I battle with motivation, or do anything I possibly can to avoid confrontation, indeed often do whatever it takes to avoid even conversation – then I know I need to shake myself up, do something different, try to be more positive. There have only been three times in my life when I've felt at a low ebb, two of them probably brought on by the pressures and stresses of work, one of them personal – and if you've got this far in the story you probably don't need to have an Einsteinian intellect to be able to work out when these were – but I have a wonderful network of friends and they, together with my family, kept me going, kept me positive. If you're struggling, ask for help. It sounds simple advice, but so many people don't follow it.

Who knows what's around the corner? I'd like to think how I work now will be how I work until I eventually decide to pack it all in, whenever that may be. Not for a while, for sure. As long as I enjoy what I do and I'm stimulated and motivated to do it, I'd like to keep working. But I do like the idea of reducing the days and hours. I've heard plenty of stories of people who retired from work only to fall ill or even die just a few weeks or months later. Work isn't everything. And doing it for someone else on a permanent basis is not for me, not any more. The thought of immersing myself again in the whole corporate environment, with all the political shenanigans and hassles that that brings, is not one I would want to dwell on for very long. Life is good. I'm a Grandpa now and having seen what happened to Tom, and either side of that to Geoff Holmes and to John Derrick, both barely into their 50s, makes me realise more and more what's really important. It's not, as Benjamin Disraeli put it, climbing the greasy pole; or chaining yourself to your desk 24/7. Been there, done that. And not doing it again. As my much-missed old friend and colleague Peter Walker once told me over half a pizza and a glass of something cold, 'no one ever says on their death bed, "I wish I'd spent more time in the office."' Too true, 'Hookey,' too true.

And so to the tricky bit. How best to wrap all this nonsense up? In simple terms, as far as the story itself goes, that's pretty much it. Just a few personal indulgences and irritations to come in one final wrap-up chapter. Fasten your seat belts, folks. We're nearly there.

19 THE MASSES AGAINST THE CLASSES

'Writing a book is a horrible, exhausting struggle, like a long bout with some painful illness.'
GEORGE ORWELL

There were three reasons for this final chapter. The first was that I didn't want the book to end on what I felt was the low of Tom's passing and the subsequent fall-out. The second was that I wanted to write more generally and to have a good old grumble in the process. It's in part football, in part political, in part 'Room 101 meets Grumpy Old Men.' Hopefully it tidies things up to a conclusion. The third reason is mine alone. And no, I'm not telling.

Had this been what you might call a 'proper' sportsperson's autobiography, the final chapter would probably feature the author's 'All Time Best XI' or 'The Best Players I Played Against.' But it isn't. So it's good news. You're going to be spared that kind of thing. However, the bad news is that I quite fancy using the space to ramble on about other stuff and on the basis that I'm in control of the process, I get to do so. If you don't like it, you're more than welcome to put the book away and go and put the kettle on. Black, no sugar, please.

Of all the many books I've read, and my home is littered with them, *Fever Pitch* is the one I really wish I'd written. It's a wonderful piece of work. The fact that it was about someone supporting the same football team as I do is immaterial. Its author Nick Hornby was speaking for every football fan out there, irrespective of which team they follow. It was about the experience of *being* a fan. The whole thing resonated so much. As I outlined in the early chapters of this book, I have had a proper passion for football for the whole of my life. It's cooled a little in recent years, a combination of television's ridiculous hype (particularly Sky, who seem to persist with the stance that football only began in 1992, when they started covering it); as well as the scripted angry phone-ins; the banks of anodyne, uninsightful, occasionally exaggerated shock-jock pundits; VAR; the play-acting and the diving; the ludicrous kick-off times; and the whole greedy, grubby, money-obsessed Premier League circus generally. But I still care deeply about the sport. I go up to London at least a dozen times a year to watch Arsenal (or at least I did before the Coronavirus pandemic) and, win, lose or draw, it's a rite of passage I don't think I'll ever tire of. The routine, the tube delays, the overpriced tat, the pantomime booing, the whingeing, the hope, the despair: much as I've gone off watching games on TV, I still enjoy the live experience. I still obsess about results. And I retain an element of hero worship for (just about) anyone who dons the red and white (or yellow and blue, off white, lime green, aquamarine, drake's neck, flame-of-burnt-brandy, incarnadine (no, really, these are actual colours) or whatever other ridiculous colour name the club chooses to assign to that season's oh-so-essential fifth change kit).

Whatever people remember of me, which, let's be honest, may not amount to too much, I'm convinced a majority who came across me more than fleetingly will likely remember me as much for the fact that I had an unbreakable, delusional bond with football, and with Arsenal Football Club in particular, than for anything else. Whenever they win anything (or, far more likely these days, when they exit a cup to lower league no-rankers (the list is endless, but try Walsall, Rotherham United, Wrexham and York City for starters)), I guess my name may creep into the thoughts of some of the folk I've known down the years.

As Matt Maynard once said to me, 'I'm just a supporter; you're a fan.' By which I have always assumed he means that I buy the shirts every year, arrange my life around match days and kick-off times, know the most trivial of trivial information about players, such as those which players' Christian and surnames start with the same letter, for example. Yes, that's me. A fan. Many would say an obsessive. But one man's football bore is another man's expert. And for obvious reasons I much prefer the latter label. Many's the conversation where I have had to listen to someone telling me all about their love of Thierry Henry or Dennis Bergkamp after they've discovered my football allegiance. I haven't the heart to tell them that unless they can give me their thoughts about Gervinho falling over when one-on-one with the goalkeeper; or on Nelson Vivas, out of position at full back, being skinned by some spotty teenage debutant Scandinavian winger; or Shkodran Mustafi, pointing wildly at anyone he can find before gesticulating imploringly for a non-existent offside after ushering through yet another striker into a perfect goalscoring position; or the likes of Glenn Helder or Marouane Chamakh missing yet another gift-wrapped open goal, then they don't come close to my level on the obsession-ometer. (And I'm aware that even in a book littered with long sentences, that one may have been the longest of the lot.) Paul Rees and I used to test one another's knowledge as we drove up to matches at Highbury. Name as many black players who have played for Arsenal. Or, more niche, perhaps naming as many players as we could whose Christian names start with the same letter as their surnames end. (For the record, I can give you 13, including a fiendishly unexpected Bob McNab. I won't list them all here but if anyone's sad enough to want to find out, you know where I am.) Hours of fun. For the two of us, anyway, as we headed to his seats in the North Bank stand, two rows behind Matt Lucas of *Little Britain* fame. Beyond obsessive, you say? Guilty, m'lud.

Ever since I was taken to watch those two Inter Milan games back in the 1971-72 Serie A season and saw the great Ajax side of the early '70s on TV, I've been completely hooked. I was taken to my first game in England by Pat Rawnsley's dad. Pat was a pal from Brontë House School. Mum and Dad were still in Italy when an early leave day came around so my brother Duncan and I were invited to lunch with Pat and his family at their home in Guiseley and, later that afternoon, his dad took us all to watch Leeds United play Coventry City at Elland Road. Leeds won 3-0. And with the benefit of *Google* I can tell you it was on 17th November 1973, during a season Leeds went unbeaten in the opening 29 matches and won the First Division title. Though of course from Sky Sports's perspective it was still 19 years BPL (before Premier League) so technically football hadn't yet been invented and the game probably doesn't count. Nor, presumably, did Leeds's title. I still like the fact that I was part of Leeds's unbeaten run. Just as I enjoy knowing I was at Highbury for the first and last games of Arsenal's 49-game unbeaten run between May 2003 (6-1 v Southampton) and October 2004 (3-1 v Aston Villa). And I didn't even have to look those two up. That Coventry game was my brother's first experience of watching Leeds and despite living most of his life in Australia and the United States, he tries to get over and see them live at least once a year. He's probably even more one-eyed and delusional about Leeds than I am about Arsenal.

Being a proper football fan is as much about being passionate as it is about being partisan. It's my contention that true football fans should be able to take sides whoever is playing and come up with a reason for doing so, however spurious. If, say, Coventry

353

City are playing Carlisle United, I would choose Coventry, as they played in the first game I saw in the UK. If it's Plymouth Argyle against Exeter City, I'd go for Plymouth on the basis of the fact that I'm a sucker for a rare green kit. If Gillingham/Peterborough, it'd be Gillingham because my sister once lived there. If Ipswich are playing Stoke, well, it has to be Ipswich because I positively loathe Stoke City. And so on it goes. There is no such thing as being neutral as far as I am concerned. The result of any game bothers me at least to some extent, whoever is playing, and especially if anyone is playing against Manchester United. I'd support a Margaret Thatcher-managed Conservative Party Select XI against that lot.

I don't enjoy watching Arsenal as much as I used to. I have to watch, of course I do, but I can't say that I enjoy it. I am at my most nervous and animated when we're clinging on to an undeserved one goal lead in the fifth minute of stoppage time and the opposition are streaming forward like ants across a discarded raspberry jam sandwich at a picnic. I just want to fast forward to the end of the game and, if we've won, I can then decide that it's worth watching. Many's the time I've gone onto my phone whilst having a post-match beer or coffee at the Emirates and cancelled a recording of *Match of the Day* on the basis that some little upstart substitute winger from Central America has squeezed in an equalizing goal for Hull or Middlesbrough or whoever in the dying seconds. Had it been our equalizer, perhaps. But theirs? Nah. Delete. Rather watch another repeat of *Bargain Hunt* instead.

When the so-called 'big six' clubs in England announced in 2021 that they were going to be founder members of the new European Super League, with no promotion or relegation, I was disgusted. Not surprised, especially, but disgusted. The fuss only lasted 48 hours but it showed just how greed has completely taken over the game. Quite how Arsenal – then 11th in the league and as far away from European competition as Bourton Studley Academicals Fifth XI – had the brass neck to do that is only exceeded by the fact that Tottenham, just a couple of weeks away from the Diamond Jubilee anniversary of their last (black and white Pathé-newsreel heralded) league title in 1961, were in the mix as well. It made Arsenal's presence seem logical by comparison. Within 24 hours I had signed up to join a club called Dial Square FC. Dial Square was the name Arsenal were founded under back in 1886, when a gaggle of workers from the Woolwich Arsenal armaments factory decided to form a football team, which they called Dial Square as a reference to the sundial on top of the entrance to the factory. The new club was formed by disillusioned Arsenal fans, originally playing in Guildford but with the aim of locating to Woolwich when the opportunity arises, the main objective being for the fans who own it to be involved in taking the key decisions affecting it. I look forward to following their progress as a founder member and if things ever go pear-shaped over in Islington, that's where my loyalties will be transferred.

One Arsenal match I hated watching was the 2006 Champions League final, their first and, to date, only final appearance in the competition's finale. The year before I had, through work contacts, been able to sort out four tickets for the Liverpool/West Ham FA Cup Final in Cardiff for one of my Liverpool-supporting buddies, Jason Simms, and three of his friends. I went into town with them and watched the game in a nearby pub with two of my other football-watching mates – Ty Minett and Mike Bedford. Liverpool rescued a draw in the last minute of extra time and took the game to a penalty shoot-out, which they went on to win. As the boys were due back in 15 minutes, I ordered a couple of bottles of champagne at the bar and had their drinks ready for them when they returned. Within half an hour we had Johnny Vegas at our table regaling us with showbiz stories. Heaven knows how that happened, but it was certainly one of the good days. Anyway, the following week 'Simmo' was away working as Arsenal took on Barcelona in that Champions League final in Paris, with me watching in our local, the Otley Arms in Treforest. I'd tried desperately to get hold of tickets, umpire Ian Gould even ringing Liam Brady, with whom he'd been on the Arsenal academy back in the '70s, for me but to no avail. (And if you are struggling to work out who Liam Brady is, you really have no place reading this book, frankly.) Arsenal took the lead, despite us having had our goalkeeper sent off, but conceded two late goals and lost 2-1. That was bad enough but it was made worse by the fact that five minutes after the final whistle one of the lads Simmo had taken to the FA Cup Final, 'Toggish' (I still don't know his real name) came over and presented me with a bottle of champagne. I didn't know what to say. What would he have done if we'd actually *won*, I wonder?

There's nothing better in my eyes than finding someone who is as passionate about the game as I am. I find football to be a real icebreaker with people I don't know. I'm far more introvert than extrovert by nature, which may surprise a few people who don't know me very well, and mixing is not something that comes naturally. I've learned more about this having acquired a knowledge of psychometric testing in recent years through my HR work, specifically how your personality fits in with those of others operating in a team around you. I understand that not everyone is comfortable initiating a conversation. Social occasions drain me. I can enjoy them, of course, but I like nothing better than when I've managed to make my escape home and I can close my front door behind me and lock the rest of the world out. My Mum was the opposite. She would strike up a conversation with anyone, anywhere, any time, and on any subject. And frequently did. I can do that, but I really have to force it, which she didn't. It doesn't come naturally to me like it comes naturally to my sister and brother. So if I can find a subject where there's some common ground, that helps. Sport does that. And football more than most. I've been in situations in places as diverse as Zimbabwe, Morocco and Singapore and managed to strike up conversations with complete strangers about football. It's a common language. And I come alive when I find someone who has the same passion for the game that I do.

It wasn't always easy being a football fan. Attending a match in the 1980s rarely passed off without some kind of trouble. We all stood to watch back then – or at least most of us great unwashed who couldn't afford seats – and the era wasn't just punctuated by acts of hooliganism, the football actually appeared to be getting in the way of the fighting. Other than sometimes running to avoid the frequent battles at Elland Road or the occasional spats at the City Ground I never found myself involved, but you had to be a pretty hardy soul to attend live matches regularly in those days. In February 1984 I recall having to walk the mile and a half from West Bridgford to Nottingham station in order to walk all the way back up to the City Ground (barely a stone's throw from West Bridgford) so I could take my place with the Arsenal supporters for the game. We were accompanied by hundreds of police officers who made it very clear that football fans, especially those from London, were only one rung above pond life on the evolutionary scale, all the while having dogs' abuse (along with some other interesting physical detritus, including 'dogs' abuse') hurled at us by Forest fans on the other side of the (not

356

so) thin blue line. I hope it was all worth it, my Mum said, when we next spoke on the phone. Of course it was. Paul Mariner nicked the only goal of the game for us in injury time. After being penned in for an unnecessary hour after the game, walking back to the station with the Gooners was a joy. Though when I thought back to the realization that I then had to walk all the way back home, alone, with an Arsenal shirt on, and with Forest fans everywhere, I rather saw her point.

In 1985 Liverpool fans rioted and caused the deaths of 39 Juventus supporters at the European Cup final in the Heysel Stadium in Brussels. Earlier that month 56 Bradford City supporters had died when a fire broke out in a dilapidated old stand at Valley Parade. Four years later 96 Liverpool fans were killed at the FA Cup semi-final against Nottingham Forest at Hillsborough in Sheffield. These were grim times to be proclaiming you were an avid football supporter. Fans were treated like dirt. Contrast that with today. Largely a TV sport, though match-going fans are still treated with contempt. And the shameless opportunism of your Johnsons and Patels during the Euros was just embarrassing. They probably think Declan Rice is a Donegal takeaway and Mason Mount is a headstone manufacturer.

That said, I loved the whole terrace culture back then – at Elland Road, when we'd bunk off the last Saturday lesson at school in order to be able to make it to the ground in time for the game; to alternating between Forest and County while at Trent Poly; all woven in between my much-anticipated visits to Highbury. But the modern game, for all its many, many faults and its obsession with chasing the money, has delivered proper stadia, and although fans are exploited mercilessly and milked for every last pound in their pockets, at least we're safe. A far cry from being treated like social pariahs back in the 1970s and '80s, fenced in, browbeaten and treated with scorn by society's moral high-grounders, stewarded by untrained halfwits who would no more understand how to implement a ground regulation than they would calculate Pi to a thousand decimal points. The modern supporter doesn't know they're born!

I loved Highbury. No ground comes close. Especially the evening games. My last evening match there was in February 2005 when we played Crystal Palace. As I drove up to Osterley tube station I heard a bang and having managed to pull up in the bus stop waiting area outside I got out and saw that my driver's side front tyre had been shredded. I was meeting Brian Havill, the ECB's Finance Director and a Palace supporter, at Highbury and was already running late, so I hurriedly scribbled a note and stuck it in the windscreen. After the game, and after Brian had got off the tube at King's Cross, it dawned on me that I could have been clamped or, worse, the car could have been towed away. After all it was in a no waiting zone. Having got back to Osterley around 11pm I was relieved to see the car still there, though I had a ticket, inevitably. I couldn't get the tyre off as it had become welded to the wheel so had to call – and join – the AA. They arrived two hours later, put a trainer tyre on and warned me against driving more than 50 miles an hour for safety reasons. I got home at 4.30. Before dashing to work after a couple of hours' sleep Mum, who was staying with us, asked (again) if it was worth it. Again, yes Mum. Bergkamp was on fire. We won 5-1. Carol just rolled her eyes. She'd seen it all before. Though it has to be said that I only very rarely go to evening games these days. I'm obviously not a proper supporter.

There was a time when I was younger when cricket wasn't too far behind football in the pecking order. I followed every Test match ball by ball, right up to when I started working at Glamorgan. But as I became more and more wrapped up in professional cricket it undeniably started to feel more like a job than an interest. I would be introduced to people with a brief explanation of what I did for a living and I began to resent the fact that they would only want to talk to me about cricket: had I met so-and-so, what did I think of such-and-such a player, why didn't Wales have its own cricket team, blah blah. I appreciate they were only trying to be polite and friendly but it used to grate with me. Since I've left Glamorgan that has changed, I'm pleased to say. I really enjoy going back to Sophia Gardens and watching without any feeling of anxiety about the result, following the game as a Glamorgan supporter and a lover of cricket and nothing else. For me, Glamorgan winning used to be incredibly important because it affected how members or sponsors or the committee reacted, and how we were being judged in the media. Nowadays, whilst I want them to win every time they take the field, if they don't it's no longer the end of the world. I can appreciate good cricket and good players, whoever they're playing for. And I enjoy chatting to people about the game more than ever.

Music is another passion. Tastes have certainly changed over the years but it's been a constant throughout my life. From the 1970s, with Radio 1 as an accompaniment throughout the school holidays, to Trent Poly and a narrowing of those tastes, and along into my fifties with a growing love of classical music; we've gone from Queen as a youngster on to Squeeze and new wave, post-punk and bands like The Smiths and The The, right on through to Dvořák, Mendelssohn, Schubert and Beethoven. Not opera. I don't think I'll ever get into opera. All that warbling wrecks the music. My favourite artist remains Elvis Costello. I've seen him so many times I've lost count. I refer to him as the greatest living Englishman.

We'd be here forever listing every singer or band that I like. I'm an inveterate gig-goer even now and music is almost always on in my house. There are some clues to my main musical leanings in the chapter headings. If I had to categorize it, it would be Indie music, 'Indie' in the true sense of the word, not the media fabrication, which seems to assume that anything slightly off the Radio 2 norm is Indie. Give me Radio 6 Music any day of the week, though the rap and hip-hop stuff I can happily leave behind. I enjoy hearing new bands for the first time and then exploring. I am also a sucker for a female voice. Lulu was probably my earliest girl singer crush and I moved quickly from Debbie Harry to Chrissie Hynde to Clare Grogan in my late teens. These days I have a soft spot for Ritzy Bryan and The Joy Formidable. But there's an eclectic mix to my music collection. My i-Tunes catalogue amounts to over 20,000 songs. Laid end to end, so to speak, assuming eight hours' sleep a day, it'd take more than three months to listen to everything just once. Music > TV every time.

I have lived in Wales for over 35 years now. It's my home. My daughters and my granddaughter Willow were all born here. But for some strange reason I still call Yorkshire 'home' even after all that time. I was brought up there, went to school there. When Mum was alive I used to make the journey North with a real sense of anticipation that I was indeed going back home. She moved to North Yorkshire in the early 1990s and I grew to love Harrogate but I am at heart a Keighley lad. West Yorkshire: the county where people chuck away the letter T just as soon as they can. Where the word 'aye' can, depending on the situation and intonation, mean 'I agree with you,' 'I am happy with the world and my place within it,' or 'I could tell you a thing or two, but maybe we'll save that for another time.' Where 'summat' and 'nowt' are used almost as liberally as are 'literally' and 'like' by the millennial generation. Where when you ask for two portions of fish and chips, you simply have to say 'twice, open.' In short, Yorkshire is the finest county in Her Majesty's Britannic Kingdom of Great Britain, Northern Ireland and dominions. Home to the grumpiest, but perversely the most contented, people in the world. And West Yorkshire is its beating heart.

The Welsh are similar people. They too have a long heritage of being largely downtrodden, then ignored and marginalized by the powers-that-be at Westminster. They also share a sense of humour. England is, well, what is England? The North is completely different to the South. Devon and Cornwall nothing like much of the rest of the country. When the word 'England' is mentioned, I'm convinced that it's basically an image of the barbour-jacketed, Range Rover-driving commuter-belted South East that most people conjure up in their minds; certainly the London media often ignores the fact that there is an England beyond the M25 and a UK that – shock, horror – comprises other actual countries. I enjoy visiting London but I don't think I could ever live there. When I first moved down to Cardiff back in the mid-'80s, I would root passionately for England whenever they played Wales, at anything. As the years have trundled by, I find that I have largely turned tail and now enjoy seeing England beaten. Not at football, not yet at least, and not at cricket, where Welsh players still represent England (don't let's start that one here: it's complicated, and we're doing so well), but in every other case I'm quite happy to see Wales coming out on top. The underdog giving its long-time oppressor a bloody nose. After all, as my old friend Geoff Lister had it, England is just that strip of land which connects Yorkshire to Wales.

Do you remember a programme on TV called *Grumpy Old Men* in the early 2000s? A group of men (and later women in their own show) who moaned away to camera about every topic under the sun? A kind of scripted *Room 101* with a wider cast. I've always had a pretty solid streak of grumpiness in me but there is no doubt that I have grown even more and more intolerant as I've snaked my way through middle age (Hi, Mr Marchbank: *waves*). Among the topics I could drone on about here – but won't, you'll be delighted to hear – are: people who say they've been too busy [code for 'disorganized']; 'influencers'; the Conservative Party; lemon curd; societal inequality; false sincerity; Piers Morgan; hypocrites; car bores; vacuous so-called 'celebrities'; middle lane motorway drivers; the Daily Mail; flag-shaggers and little Englander xenophobia; people who proudly tell you that they don't read; Hallowe'en; arrogance; gym zealots; Nigel Farage; money worshippers; barbeque obsessionals; vacuous football punditry; snow; bigotry; people who can't spell or who don't understand basic grammar; hip hop; untidiness; Donald Trump; management speak; opera; fireworks; journalistic self-importance; the honours list; *BBC Sports Personality of the Year* [a staple of my childhood, now reduced to two hours of showbiz dirge]; most politicians; fashion; tabloids; banks; serial complainers; ketchup; in-your-face tattoos; self-important people; reality TV; people who don't vote; incomprehensible perfume adverts [which is all of them]; forced fun; privatization; groups with no musical instrument in sight labelled as 'bands'; Boris Johnson; vox pops with thick people; tea; misplaced apostrophes; Piers Morgan again; people who are late (hello, Dean); garlic; the squeak of trainers on the floor of a basketball court; the *X Factor*; divisive right wing hacks like Rod Liddle and Julia Hartley-Brewer; and supposedly secret ingredients in hair products (Ceramide R, anyone?). There are loads more. It's both an extensive and eclectic list. But I am by now extensively grumpy. I add to it all the time.

Another love of mine is political history, but politics still manages to drive me barmy. I've always been interested in current affairs and I have been a Labour Party member since I was 19. Unsurprising, therefore, that I have never warmed to the Conservative Party. I know plenty of people, some of them very close friends, who are passionate Tory supporters, my old pal Andrew Walker springing immediately to mind. Of course, in itself that doesn't make any of them bad people (which sounds very patronizing, but is not intended to be). The nineteenth century philosopher and politician John Stuart Mill once said, "Although it is not true that all Conservatives are stupid people, it is true that most stupid people are Conservative." Mum was a vociferous Conservative and had no truck with anything left wing. And to her, even David Cameron was left wing. I had no problem with that. Nor did I have any issue with her being a passionate Brexiteer, though it was a view which none of her three children felt able to share. I enjoyed the Brexit debates we had before she died suddenly, ironically on the day Theresa May triggered Article 50, meaning the UK was signalling two years' notice of its formal departure from the EU. I actually prefer someone with an opinion to someone who doesn't bother voting at all. That's much the greater evil in my book. But I can't say I have ever been attracted by

361

any policy that sets out, whether cravenly or by stealth, to exclude the worse off in society. We all vote with a combination of our wallets and our consciences. How will a government affect the pound in my own pocket? An important question, obviously. But I am likely to be far more swayed by any argument which demonstrates the extent to which the poorer in society are either being supported or excluded by a particular policy. There are a number of obscenely wealthy people in the world. Sadly, they are massively outnumbered by those who are just muddling along or who are struggling. I'm afraid I can't find it in myself to support any political party that is comfortable exacerbating the divide between the two. Under Johnson, the country is moving ever closer to being a kleptocracy.

I first became interested in politics at university in Nottingham. The miners' strike of 1984/1985 was the catalyst but because left-leaning folk in county cricket were as rare as kneecaps on a snake my professional world was largely inhabited either by middle class conservatives or by those who had no interest in politics at all. That actually hardened my beliefs. I'm certainly not what anyone would call an activist. I don't go out campaigning during elections, knocking on doors and canvassing or anything. But I do express my opinions on Twitter, for example, often a bit too caustically, as people have pointed out to me on many occasions. I won't stop doing that. People have every right to disagree, or to unfollow. I am not someone who believes that my view is the only view in the world. I enjoy a debate and I recognize that others will disagree with what I have to say, often fundamentally. By way of illustration, I acknowledge that the Miners' Strike in the mid-1980s was always going to be flawed because the National Union of Mineworkers never held an official ballot of its members. I never understood why they didn't. Had they done so, they'd have achieved an overwhelming majority in favour of strike action. That they didn't made it almost impossible for Neil Kinnock and the Labour Party to defend them. Any show of support would always be challenged by the Thatcher government on the grounds that the strike wasn't in any way legitimate. And whilst I could not abide Thatcher, that still doesn't prevent me from understanding and sympathizing with the economic arguments behind the pit closures. It was the way they were implemented that bothered me. With a callous disregard for the fact that communities were being destroyed in the process.

The same can be said for the arguments over Britain exiting the European Union. I don't know many people who were absolutely, firmly 100% in one camp or another. Most people I spoke to about it (before it became *vetiti subiecti*) had at least some reservations about the way they were intending to vote, or had voted. Mum spoke often of the fact that when we joined the EEC, as it was, in the early 1970s, we were joining a Common Market, a trade bloc. That it morphed into a federal state is something I couldn't disagree with her about. I do see other folks' arguments, even if I don't always agree with them. And I much prefer debates about policy than about people. The credibility of a party leader is important, of course, but I don't support Arsenal because someone is their manager or their captain and the same is true for my political choices. I vote for the policies. For me, the leader should be a 'nice to have,' not the determining factor.

That said, I could never vote for a mendacious clown like Boris Johnson. Or an automaton such as Theresa May. Or such a cravenly ambitious careerist like David Cameron. That's not to say that voting for their opponents has always been a given. Michael Foot, principled though he was, was never going to win a general election. Tony Blair's latter years were in stark contrast to the wave of popularity that brought him to power in 1997 and which saw him carrying out such a reforming agenda in the first of his three terms. And as for Jeremy Corbyn, well, what can I say? An exercise in sixth form socialism; an ideological experiment that deprived the country of a properly functioning opposition for half a decade during which the Tory government was taking a scythe to public spending and hitting the poorest people as hard as it is possible to hit them. What a waste to have an opposition that couldn't win an election against a party of Minions led by a human Teletubby. Corbyn was probably the only opposition leader Johnson would have been able to beat. Labour may as well have put the result in a filing tray somewhere in Conservative Party central office and posted a sign above it that read: 'General Election Victories: Please Take One.'

I may hold many politicians in contempt but I also have a high regard for some of them, mainly from days gone by, though there are a few around these days if you look very carefully, even a sprinkling of Tories. My Grandpa's hero, Aneurin Bevan, is someone I've read widely about. He polarized opinion, as did one of my own political heroes, Tony Benn. A hero not so much for his left-wing views as for his principles. I like early Tony Blair, and Gordon Brown and Alan Johnson, too, and despite there being plenty of people who criticize him, I have a lot of time for Alastair Campbell. Many dismissed Neil Kinnock as a bit of a windbag but I always loved listening to him in full flow and having met him during my time with Glamorgan I thought he was a good man. He generously used to send us a cheque every year despite not being required to pay after having been made an Honorary Life Vice President of the Club. But arguably the politician whose views, principles and philosophy were most closely attuned to my own would have been John Smith, who succeeded Kinnock as leader of the Labour Party, and who died suddenly at the very young age of 55 in May 1994. I liked his quiet, understated and principled leadership. Set alongside Arsene Wenger, Duncan Fletcher and Mike Brearley from the world of sport, Smith, Benn and Alan Johnson were the three politicians I admired the most.

But I digress. Quite possibly for the last time, you'll be relieved to hear. There is a lot in the world to like. Unfortunately, in this age of ubiquitous social media we tend to hear either only from those who want to criticize, to personalize and vilify, or those who are merely echoing our opinions, mainly because we choose to lock out anyone who dares to disagree with them. I never expected I would be a devotee of social media. I'm not particularly 'with it'; I'm the only person in the world, it seems, never to have had a Facebook account, for example. Or been in a Nando's, or watched *Game of Thrones*, or seen any of the 6,441 *Star Wars* films, sequels, prequels and pre-prequels, come to that. But that's by the by. I am on Instagram but use it solely for keeping up with what my granddaughter is up to. Not for me following the narcissistic so-called celebrities and 'influencers' (what is that all about?) giving us Instagram glimpses into their fascinatingly interesting lives. But Twitter. Now Twitter is my kind of thing. I appreciate it houses all sorts of trolls and that there is an awful lot of rubbish (much of it mine) and plenty of hate too. But it's a licence to be sarcastic, cynical and acerbic in public and I for one thoroughly enjoy the opportunity of taking advantage of that.

Regrets? As the incomparable Frank Sinatra would have said, 'Aye, I've had a couple.' (Well, he would have done had he been to school in Bradford.) Professionally, hardly any. I do wonder very occasionally about that Yorkshire job but it doesn't really constitute a regret as such. Carol didn't want to move and she was spot on, and of course there were no guarantees I'd be the one they'd have gone for. Either way, even though my Glamorgan exit half a dozen years or so further down the line was all a bit messy, there were still plenty of happy times between pulling out of the Yorkshire process and me exiting Glamorgan. There was also a rebutted approach around the same time from a firm of London headhunters trying to find a CEO for a Premier League football club. Same reasons, same outcome. And as it wasn't Arsenal, it couldn't possibly constitute a regret of any kind anyway. Personally? Well, I've said elsewhere that perhaps I could have worked harder to try to prevent splitting up with Carol, but it's pointless reflecting too much on that, years on. I was overwhelmed with work at the time and I buried my head in the sand. But, as so many people seem to conclude these days, 'it is what it is.' Things have worked out OK for us both. My one real personal regret is that I never made things up with my Dad before he died. When he and Mum divorced in the early 1990s, the circumstances were such that I didn't speak to him for several years. There was one rather awkward meeting at a golf club down in Sussex around the time of his 60th birthday in 1995 but that was the extent of our contact until I was told he was seriously ill over in Majorca, where he lived, early in 2005. By the time I'd decided I had to fly over and see him, he'd passed away. Every time I hear Mike and the Mechanics' *The Living Years*, especially the third verse, I struggle to keep it together. Life, as they say, is too short. Whatever the circumstances, I could – and should – have done something about that far sooner. My bad, as the youth would put it. I have to live with that stubbornness.

And so, folks, there you have it. A process that feels as if it was started in the last century but was only finally completed during the Coronavirus lockdowns (during which I also walked miles, read copiously and taught myself to play a few tunes on the keyboard), is done. What kind of a life has it been (so far, he adds, hastily)? A life which began with dreams of emulating Alan Knott until I realised that being six feet tall, having the catching hands of a Dr No/Captain Hook hybrid and possessing all the suppleness of a breeze block would make that quite difficult. A life which moved on to thoughts of imitating David Gower until it dawned on me that as a batsman, I was more flares than flair; and I'm not even left-handed anyway. A life in which I longed wistfully to be able to replicate the famous (Johan) Cruyff Turn on the highest stage of them all, a move I once tried in my kitchen at home only to come close to ending up in A&E with a dislocated kneecap. It was also a life which a late 1970s school careers day had indicated I might be suited to spend in a career as a police officer. I later discovered that several of my friends were told that very same day that they too would make good police officers. That we went on to be, respectively, a builder, a teacher, a sales manager and a sports administrator simply confirms the fact that our assessment on the day was carried out by probably the laziest schools' careers adviser in Christendom.

For someone who turned down a potential career in journalism (and I emphasize the word 'potential' as there would have been no guarantees, especially with this flowery prose style: I'd have been a sub-editor's wet dream) because he was fascinated by the idea of working in professional sport, even at a struggling county cricket club in South Wales, an unpaid position that was originally given a shelf life of just six months but which developed into a labour of love for a quarter of a century, it was far from being the worst choice I could have made (another spectacularly long sentence). It may have positioned me firmly on the periphery of sport but not many folk have had the opportunities I have had, met the people I've met, and it is sport, and cricket in particular, that has given me those opportunities.

Being a sports administrator was what I *did*. It was not who I *am*. Life's twists and turns and bumps in the road teach us lessons, from which we all hope to learn and mature as a natural evolutionary process, but I hope that anyone who knew me way back in the day who happened to meet me again now would still be able to recognize the same person they knew. I've never had much of an ego. I've certainly never considered that the world should revolve around me. And I've never been particularly interested in money, power or empty fame. I leave all that nonsense to others. Where I can I've always tried to be kind, empathetic, consistent, authentic and loyal, never lost my thirst for learning, and whatever else I may have done, I've never taken myself too seriously.

I guess it could have been a whole lot worse. I have many incredible friends; a decent education that's lasted throughout my life; two wonderful daughters; and a lifetime of amazing experiences. Who knows? I might have ended up as a tone deaf, book-burning, Manchester United-supporting, Conservative-leaning police officer who hated cricket. And that just wouldn't have done at all.

366

I KNOW IT'S OVER:
SOME THANK YOUS

'Goodbye? Oh no, please. Can't we go back to page one and do it all over again?'
WINNIE THE POOH

Here we go then. The equivalent of an awardless acceptance speech…

I wouldn't have got anywhere in this world without the love and backing of my Mum. She supported me in absolutely everything that I did; the good, occasionally the bad, and more frequently the very iffy. I miss her every day. And to Dad, I'm sorry. We were probably never destined to be especially close, but I should have tried harder.

Despite all the blether in this book, no achievement in my life comes close to the pride and joy I take in being Dad to Seanna and Hannah, still comfortably the best things to have happened to me. Beautiful and bright, the pair of them. David and Lewis: make sure you look after the two of them. And now Grandpa to Willow too. I'm blessed.

And to their mum, Carol, the loveliest ex-wife in the world, someone who tolerated me for such a long time and who put in the real hard yards in bringing up our two lovely daughters. There's so much I should have said in the past. But you know how utterly hopeless I was – still am – at expressing my feelings.

To t'big sister and t'little brother, Catherine and Duncan. Thanks for being there. And for occasionally allowing me to get a word in edgeways. And a belated 'hello' to Matthew, Evie, Anne, Thomas and Sarah.

To lifelong friends Andy Tomlinson, Stefan Cockerill and Steve Burnhill, along with John Haigh, Greg Marchbank, Andrew North, Tony Walker, Mark Hammes and Tony Hope, with whom contact has been re-established more recently. We've tolerated one another off and on for the thick end of half a century now. Strong bonds. They must have been good times. And, in a different 'Grove Boys' thread, to Dave Tillotson: the music still binds us.

I learned something from every person who worked at or served on a committee for Glamorgan Cricket, even the ones I didn't particularly like or respect. To the players, just about every single one of them, thanks for all the smiles, the highs, the friendship and, of course, the hassle and the moaning, all of which kept me honest. And love and respect to 'Holmesy' and 'JD', both so sorely missed.

To all of the Glamorgan staff, far too many to mention individually here (though honourable nods are due to Tony Dilloway, Caryl Watkin and Andrew Walker in particular), thank you. Up to the last dog days, it was an absolute pleasure. So many friends for life.

I picked up so much from the three Glamorgan chairmen I worked under during the happier years – Tony Lewis, David Morgan and Gerard Elias. A big thank you to them for the advice, encouragement and, of course, the bollockings, and also to the likes of Ricky Needham for making the committee bureaucracy feel almost like fun.

To the South Wales Chuckle Brothers – Matt Maynard and Dean Conway – and families: much love and here's to many more beers and G&Ts to come. Thank you for always being around, for the incalculable number of laughs, and the occasional tears, some of them so gut-wrenchingly difficult to deal with. Diamonds, both.

And, of course, to Philip Carling for giving me a chance way back when. I know he took a big risk and he never failed to give me genuine opportunities to learn during my first four years working at the Club. I can't thank him enough for opening that first professional door.

I'm grateful to ('Don't Call Me Professor') Steve Rollnick, with whom I share regular chats over a coffee (that frequently turn into psychological counselling sessions), for wading through the proof and offering advice on where to chisel, change or chop. I can't believe he actually read all of it, but he's adamant he did so I'll just have to take his word for it.

Thanks too to Alan Ball, Liam Brady, Charlie Nicholas, David Rocastle, Tony Adams, Ian Wright, Dennis Bergkamp, Patrick

Vieira, Thierry Henry, Aaron Ramsey and all the others; to George Graham and Arsene Wenger. Up The Arsenal. To Johan Cruyff as well. It's his fault I'm obsessed.

There are two sets of lyrics on the dedication page. The first is from a song called *Somewhere in My Heart*, by Aztec Camera, from 1988, written by Roddy Frame. The second is taken from a song called *Let Them All Talk*, written by Elvis Costello, from the 1983 Elvis Costello & the Attractions album *Punch the Clock*. Every effort has been made to seek permission to reproduce both sets of lyrics.

If the Latin for 'without which nothing' on page three is wrong, I'm more than happy to put any complainant in direct touch with Steve James.

It would have been easy to have gone with Costello song titles for all of the chapter headings, but I'll play that game in my own head and in my own time. I opted instead for a bit of variety. The quotes preceding each chapter are, well, just random. They seemed to fit.

The chapter headings are from songs by: Introduction – Super Furry Animals; 1 British Sea Power; 2 Gang of Four; 3 The The; 4 Talk Talk; 5 Killing Joke; 6 Squeeze; 7 Half Man Half Biscuit; 8 Bauhaus; 9 KT Tunstall; 10 Lightning Seeds; 11 David Bowie; 12 Aztec Camera; 13 The Stranglers; 14 Belle and Sebastian; 15 Prefab Sprout; 16 Paul Heaton; 17 The Joy Formidable; 18 The Divine Comedy; 19 Manic Street Preachers; Thank Yous – The Smiths.

Oh, and if you're searching for a more detailed index, stop being so lazy. It took me ages just sorting out all the names. What more do you want? A list of topics and sub-headings, all handwritten in my own blood? You'll be complaining about the price next…

Right then. That's your lot. Bingo's done. Over and out.

INDEX

371

373

374

Printed in Great Britain
by Amazon

81986898R00214